PUFFIN CLASSICS

THE COMPLETE ADVENTURES OF THE TREASURE SEEKERS

Also in Puffin Classics By E. Nesbit

THE COMPLETE ADVENTURES OF
THE TREASURE SEEKERS

E. Nesbit

with illustrations by
Cecil Lesley

PUFFIN BOOKS

PUFFIN BOOKS

Published by the Penguin Group
Penguin Books Ltd, 27 Wrights Lane, London W8 5TZ, England
Penguin Books USA Inc., 375 Hudson Street, New York, New York 10014, USA
Penguin Books Australia Ltd, Ringwood, Victoria, Australia
Penguin Books Canada Ltd, 10 Alcorn Avenue, Toronto, Ontario, Canada M4V 3B2
Penguin Books (NZ) Ltd, 182–190 Wairau Road, Auckland 10, New Zealand

Penguin Books Ltd, Registered Offices: Harmondsworth, Middlesex, England

The Story of the Treasure Seekers first published 1899
Published in Puffin Books 1958
The Wouldbegoods first published 1901
Published in Puffin Books 1958
New Treasure Seekers first published 1904
Published in Puffin Books 1982
Published in one volume in Puffin Books 1992
1 3 5 7 9 10 8 6 4 2

All rights reserved

Printed in England by Clays Ltd, St Ives plc
Filmset in Plantin

CONTENTS

THE STORY OF THE TREASURE SEEKERS

CONTENTS

INTRODUCTION

E. NESBIT AND THE BASTABLES

EDITH NESBIT was born on 19 August, 1858, and died in 1924. She was nearing forty when she began to write about the Bastables. She had been married for seventeen years, and had two sons, a daughter, and an adopted daughter, all between twelve and sixteen. She had been scribbling magazine stories and verse for a year or two before her marriage, for her mother's income seemed suddenly to peter out, and money had to be earned. There was not much she could do, but she tried writing verse and stories for newspapers and magazines, and discovered she could turn out very easily the slight, sentimental stuff they could use.

She married Hubert Bland, one of the founders of the Fabian Society, when she was twenty – and found it still necessary to earn money, for he caught small-pox just after their first child was born, his partner absconded, and his business failed. After that he devoted most of his time to the Society.

Bernard Shaw, Sidney Webb, and other early Socialists soon joined the Fabians and started hammering out a new way of life for this country, but they never quite accepted Bland. He was an excellent debater who could safely be put on at difficult meetings, and he became a good journalist with a special appeal to the young. ('Remember the respect due to youth,' he used to say.) But as a person there was something theatrical and unreal about him.

Nesbit went to most of their meetings, public and private. She listened, argued, and learned, thrilled to be in at the birth of a new epoch. She became the modern woman of her time, cut her hair short, threw away her corsets, revelled in physical fitness, walked a great deal and leaped over gates when she had a mind to. She wore Liberty dresses and refused to adopt fashions that were uncomfortable. She smoked a great deal, carrying about an old cardboard corset box with a roller, tobacco, and papers so that she could make her own cigarettes.

The Blands lived first at Lewisham, and remained in that neighbourhood for the rest of their lives. Lewisham, Blackheath, and Eltham are mainly the scene of the Bastable stories. Their home was a regular meeting place on Saturday evenings for the young and the famous. The famous grumbled about the journey and the slow trains, but they went, and talked for all who cared to listen. There were wonderful discussions and stirring conversations which changed whole lives and outlooks. Sometimes there was music and all had to be ready to take part. Nesbit would not have onlookers. Or again, the floor might be cleared for dancing, with Nesbit at the piano, playing tirelessly for as long as they wanted her to go on. She had been known to go into a corner, when a story was overdue, and finish it there, amid all the babel of talk. The Blands could not afford to provide conventional meals for so many, but a cauldron of soup with plenty of bread, or a mountain of sausages sufficed. Whatever was provided was always served with an air, on clean linen with an abundance of flowers.

Then, in 1896, her thoughts were suddenly turned inwards by a request from the Editor of the *Girls' Own Paper* for a series of articles on her schooldays. School had not been a very vital part of her childhood but she accepted and in the first described her first school. It was interesting, but did not strike gold. The second, however, began to glow, and after that she abandoned the literal title of the series and simply rummaged joyfully through her early experiences, recovering memories of sunny days in gardens sweet with lilac and laburnum, or jasmine, roses, and lilies. She remembered tall hollyhocks against various red brick walls, and hedges hung with convolvulus, white and deepcupped. She thought of green lawns and of meadows golden with buttercups. The colours, scents, and feeling of those days still rise vividly from the pages.

Hers was a happy childhood, with more freedom than

was usual at that date, and a sense of security which was even rarer. She lived in an atmosphere of affection and confidence. Her mother was always ready to listen, and Edith never afraid to try to explain when things went wrong. Strong guiding ropes of right and wrong were evident through all the love and devotion.

Her earliest memories were of the Agricultural College, with its small experimental farm in Lower Kennington Lane, where she was born. It was run by her father, who was famous in his own field as one of the first agricultural chemists. He died young, when Edith was four. Three years later his widow gave up trying to manage the place when her second daughter, Mary, was ordered to Brighton for her health. There were two boys between Mary and Edith.

One day, when Edith was three, the younger brother 'planted' her in a hole he found prepared for a gooseberry bush. They were both going unwillingly to a party. Tucking her frock neatly round her knees, he shovelled in the earth and stamped it down. 'Now you'll grow, like a gooseberry bush,' he told her, quite kindly, 'and if you howl, they'll make you go to the party.' Thus, she knew what it felt like when, in *The Story of the Treasure Seekers*, she described how Albert-next-door got buried up to his neck when he fell through the tunnel the Bastables had been digging.

The boys went to boarding school as a matter of course, but Edith's going seems generally to have been connected with Mary's health. When she was sent to Brighton, a boarding school for Edith was found nearby, so that she could come home at the week-ends. It was a sad experience though, for the children proved ill-natured and the discipline severe. However, measles brought her a glorious release and an extra holiday among the beechwoods of Buckinghamshire. She did not go back there, but after an interval another school was found for her at Stamford in Lincs. On the whole that was better, and the E. Nesbit of 1896 could recall with a chuckle its three major miseries – hair, hands, and arithmetic. Her hair could not be made smooth. It was crisp and curly. Her hands would not come clean in the drop of cold water she was given with a scrap of mottled soap. As to arithmetic, she arrived in the middle of long division and it was never adequately explained to her.

The punishment for all three was solitude and meals missed. But the Headmistress's mother used to lie in wait, beckoning her silently into the store cupboard where, behind locked doors and with only a taper to light the place, she fed her on cake or bread and jam, while she sniffed out the many good food smells. Kissed and comforted, she was let out, holding her hands stiffly before her in case tell-tale stains were found on her pinafore.

In the middle of the third term, Mrs Nesbit arrived to tell her that Mary had to be taken abroad. She would rather have left Edith at school, for Mary wanted to see Rouen, and her mother did not want to miss Paris. At not quite nine, Edith would not have enjoyed sightseeing. But after three 'delicious' days, Mrs Nesbit saw that she could not go so far away, leaving her there.

The next two or three years, spent in France, were rich in memories of enchanting places and strange experiences. She saw a ghost, and drove by moonlight through the Auvergne Mountains, expecting to be murdered before daylight came. She remembered a town built on and around many swiftly tumbling mountain streams. She saw a shepherdess spinning out on the hillside as she watched her sheep. She had a French doll with two wigs, one brown the other flaxen. Finally, there was a house so perfect that it set the pattern for the rest of her life of what a family home should be. That was at Dinan, a square, whitewashed place with rich, overgrown gardens and orchards, with haylofts to play in, goats to milk, ponies to ride, and a cider press to watch day by day through all the processes of cider-making.

There lay the seeds of many of the Bastable adventures, with exactly the same, easy family feeling. Her brothers came there too, and the three children played together going on expeditions of discovery, tracing a stream to its source, digging a cave out of a wet clay bank with ludicrous results, to the ruin of their clothes. They purloined food from the larder and packed it into a horse's nosebag, which proved so heavy it had to be abandoned and was left in a ditch.

From France, she went to school in Germany and was caught there by the Franco-Prussian war of 1870. Mary must have been getting steadily worse, for she died of consumption in the following year; but there is no reference to the fact in any of her sister's recollections, though it must have torn a great hole in her life and affections. When she came to the last chapter for the *G.O.P.*, she sighed over so much to tell, so little space, but chose to leap clean over Mary's death, to the last home of her childhood, an English one, at Halstead in Kent. It was after the beloved Dinan pattern, and she spent her adolescent years there, reading voraciously, tucked away in the garden or in a secret nook on the roof. She was scribbling too, and full of hope that – if not a Shakespeare, she might yet be another Christina Rossetti.

Almost as soon as these articles were finished, in 1897, she began to write the stories which became *The Story of the Treasure Seekers*. There is no need to praise them; they are here to speak for themselves, but that they grew out of that year of casting back into her own childhood, there can be no doubt, specially when they are compared with what she had been writing immediately before then. There were *Doggy and Pussy Tales*, and little fairy tales, equally trivial. It must be said that they still had something of her breezy style, and the good detail that comes from personal observation, but they neither expected, nor encouraged any intelligent response from the listener. In the Bastable stories, Nesbit showed herself clearly aware of the reader at the receiving end of her tale-telling, and showed just that good respect for the young which her husband had so often recommended.

As soon as *The Story of the Treasure Seekers* was published, the Blands moved again, and to the best-loved of all their homes, Well Hall, Eltham. That was the Moat House of *The Would-be-goods*, and is described there, though inaccurately as standing *within* the moat. It stood outside it, in fact, along one bank, looking over the water to the square lawn which it surrounded. The site was an ancient one, and the grass covered the foundations of houses going back at least to a Norman manor house. There are still a group of Tudor out-buildings along the moat-side at right angles to where Nesbit's house stood, and a fifteenth-century bridge connects the small island with the mainland. When Nesbit lived there, her back door opened right on to the bridge. To-day, her lawn is a flagged bandstand. Nothing at all remains of the house she loved but if you go there you can still pick out a great many things she must have known. There are great lovely beech trees standing along the lawn edge, and a spreading cedar tree to which she certainly attached one end of a hammock in summer. There are ducks instead of swans on the waters of the moat, where so many Bastable adventures took place. Nesbit used to float round it in an old punt on sunny days, writing. Children skated on it in winter, bathed in it in summer, and played all manner of games in it at all times. Laburnums used to dip down into the water, amid a riot of red may and lilacs. It was a romantic, 'magical' place, people who knew it then say. Many of the most famous men and women of the day went there – and quite a remarkable number of young people who have since become famous. For twenty-three years Nesbit lived there and Hubert died there. It is alive with eloquent ghosts, many of whom left their own impression of the life that went on, and the things that happened there – foremost among them Bernard Shaw and H. G. Wells.

ELEANOR GRAHAM

THE COUNCIL OF WAYS
AND MEANS

THIS is the story of the different ways we looked for treasure, and I think when you have read it you will see that we were not lazy about the looking.

There are some things I must tell before I begin to tell about the treasure-seeking, because I have read books myself, and I know how beastly it is when a story begins, ' "Alas!" said Hildegarde with a deep sigh, " we must look our last on this ancestral home" ' – and then some one else says something – and you don't know for pages and pages where the home is, or who Hildegarde is, or anything about it. Our ancestral home is in the Lewisham Road. It is semi-detached and has a garden, not a large one. We are the Bastables. There are six of us besides Father. Our Mother is dead, and if you think we don't care because I don't tell you much about her you only show that you do not understand people at all. Dora is the eldest. Then Oswald – and then Dicky. Oswald won the Latin prize at his preparatory school – and Dicky is good at sums. Alice and Noël are twins: they are ten, and Horace Octavius is my youngest brother. It is one of us that tells this story – but I shall not tell you which: only at the very end perhaps I will. While the story is going on you may be trying to guess, only I bet you don't.

It was Oswald who first thought of looking for

treasure. Oswald often thinks of very interesting things. And directly he thought of it he did not keep it to himself, as some boys would have done, but he told the others, and said –

'I'll tell you what, we must go and seek for treasure: it is always what you do to restore the fallen fortunes of your House.'

Dora said it was all very well. She often says that. She was trying to mend a large hole in one of Noël's stockings. He tore it on a nail when we were playing shipwrecked mariners on top of the chicken-house the day H. O. fell off and cut his chin: he has the scar still. Dora is the only one of us who ever tries to mend anything. Alice tries to make things sometimes. Once she knitted a red scarf for Noël because his chest is delicate, but it was much wider at one end than the other, and he wouldn't wear it. So we used it as a pennon, and it did very well, because most of our things are black or grey since Mother died; and scarlet was a nice change. Father does not like you to ask for new things. That was one way we had of knowing that the fortunes of the ancient House of Bastable were really fallen. Another way was that there was no more pocket-money – except a penny now and then to the little ones, and people did not come to dinner any more, like they used to, with pretty dresses, driving up in cabs – and the carpets got holes in them – and when the legs came off things they were not sent to be mended, and we gave up having the gardener except for the front garden, and not that very often. And the silver in the big oak plate-chest that is lined with green baize all went away to the shop to have the dents and scratches taken out of it, and it never came back. We think Father hadn't enough money to pay the silver man for taking out the dents and scratches. The new spoons and forks were yellowy-white, and not so heavy as the old ones, and they never shone after the first day or two.

Father was very ill after Mother died; and while he was ill his business-partner went to Spain – and there was never much money afterwards. I don't know why. Then the servants left and there was only one, a General. A great deal of your comfort and happiness depends on having a good General. The last but one was nice: she used to make jolly good currant puddings for us, and let us have the dish on the floor and pretend it was a wild boar we were killing with our forks. But the General we have now nearly always makes sago puddings, and they are the watery kind, and you cannot pretend anything with them, not even islands, like you do with porridge.

Then we left off going to school, and Father said we should go to a good school as soon as he could manage it. He said a holiday would do us all good. We thought he was right, but we wished he had told us he couldn't afford it. For of course we knew.

Then a great many people used to come to the door with envelopes with no stamps on them, and sometimes they got very angry, and said they were calling for the last time before putting it in other hands. I asked Eliza what that meant, and she kindly explained to me, and I was so sorry for Father.

And once a long, blue paper came; a policeman brought it, and we were so frightened. But Father said it was all right, only when he went up to kiss the girls after they were in bed they said he had been crying, though I'm sure that's not true. Because only cowards and snivellers cry, and my Father is the bravest man in the world.

So you see it was time we looked for treasure; and Oswald said so, and Dora said it was all very well. But

Once a long blue paper came, a policeman brought it

the others agreed with Oswald. So we held a council. Dora was in the chair – the big dining-room chair, that we let the fireworks off from, the Fifth of November when we had the measles and couldn't do it in the garden. The hole has never been mended, so now we have that chair in the nursery, and I think it was cheap at the blowing-up we boys got when the hole was burnt.

'We must do something,' said Alice, 'because the exchequer is empty.' She rattled the money-box as she spoke, and it really did rattle because we always keep the bad sixpence in it for luck.

'Yes – but what shall we do?' said Dicky. 'It's so jolly easy to say let's do *something*.' Dicky always wants everything settled exactly. Father calls him the Definite Article.

'Let's read all the books again. We shall get lots of ideas out of them.' It was Noël who suggested this, but we made him shut up, because we knew well enough he only wanted to get back to his old books. Noël is a poet. He sold some of his poetry once – and it was printed, but that does not come in this part of the story.

Then Dicky said, 'Look here. We'll be quite quiet for ten minutes by the clock – and each think of some way to find treasure. And when we've thought we'll try all the ways one after the other, beginning with the eldest.'

'I shan't be able to think in ten minutes, make it half an hour,' said H. O. His real name is Horace Octavius, but we call him H. O. because of the advertisement, and it's not so very long ago he was afraid to pass the hoarding where it says 'Eat H. O.' in big letters. He says it was when he was a little boy, but I remember last Christmas but one, he woke in the middle of the night crying and howling, and they said it was the pudding. But he told me afterwards he had been dreaming that they really *had* come to eat H. O., and it couldn't have been the pudding, when you come to think of it, because it was so very plain.

Well, we made it half an hour – and we all sat quiet, and thought and thought. And I made up my mind before two minutes were over, and I saw the others had, all but Dora, who is always an awful time over everything. I got pins and needles in my leg from sitting still so long, and when it was seven minutes H. O. cried out –

'Oh, it must be more than half an hour!'

H. O. is eight years old, but he cannot tell the clock yet. Oswald could tell the clock when he was six.

We all stretched ourselves and began to speak at once, but Dora put up her hands to her ears and said –

'One at a time, please. We aren't playing Babel.' (It is a very good game. Did you ever play it?)

So Dora made us all sit in a row on the floor, in ages, and then she pointed at us with the finger that had the brass thimble on. Her silver one got lost when the last General but two went away. We think she must have forgotten it was Dora's and put it in her box by mistake. She was a very forgetful girl. She used to forget what she had spent money on, so that the change was never quite right.

Oswald spoke first. 'I think we might stop people on Blackheath – with crape masks and horse-pistols – and say "Your money or your life! Resistance is useless, we are armed to the teeth"– like Dick Turpin and Claude Duval. It wouldn't matter about not having horses, because coaches have gone out too.'

Dora screwed up her nose the way she always does when she is going to talk like the good elder sister in books, and said, 'That would be very wrong: it's like pickpocketing or taking pennies out of Father's greatcoat when it's hanging in the hall.'

I must say I don't think she need have said that, especially before the little ones – for it was when I was only four.

But Oswald was not going to let her see he cared, so he said –

'Oh, very well. I can think of lots of other ways. We could rescue an old gentleman from deadly Highwaymen.'

'There aren't any,' said Dora.

'Oh, well, it's all the same – from deadly peril, then. There's plenty of that. Then he would turn out to be the Prince of Wales, and he would say, "My noble, my cherished preserver! Here is a million pounds a year. Rise up, Sir Oswald Bastable." '

But the others did not seem to think so, and it was Alice's turn to say.

She said, 'I think we might try the divining-rod. I'm sure I could do it. I've often read about it. You hold a stick in your hands, and when you come to where there is gold underneath the stick kicks about. So you know. And you dig.'

'Oh,' said Dora suddenly, 'I have an idea. But I'll say last. I hope the divining-rod isn't wrong. I believe it's wrong in the Bible.'

'So is eating pork and ducks,' said Dicky. 'You can't go by that.'

'Anyhow, we'll try the other ways first,' said Dora. 'Now, H. O.'

'Let's be Bandits,' said H. O. 'I dare say it's wrong but it would be fun pretending.'

'I'm sure it's wrong,' said Dora.

And Dicky said she thought everything wrong. She said she didn't, and Dicky was very disagreeable. So Oswald had to make peace, and he said –

'Dora needn't play if she doesn't want to. Nobody

asked her. And, Dicky, don't be an idiot: do dry up and let's hear what Noël's idea is.'

Dora and Dicky did not look pleased, but I kicked Noël under the table to make him hurry up, and then he said he didn't think he wanted to play any more. That's the worst of it. The others are so jolly ready to quarrel. I told Noël to be a man and not a snivelling pig, and at last he said he had not made up his mind whether he would print his poetry in a book and sell it, or find a princess and marry her.

'Whichever it is,' he added, 'none of you shall want for anything, though Oswald did kick me, and say I was a snivelling pig.'

'I didn't,' said Oswald, 'I told you not to be.' And Alice explained to him that that was quite the opposite of what he thought. So he agreed to drop it.

Then Dicky spoke.

'You must all of you have noticed the advertisements in the papers, telling you that ladies and gentlemen can easily earn two pounds a week in their spare time, and to send two shillings for sample and instructions, carefully packed free from observation. Now that we don't go to school all our time is spare time. So I should think we could easily earn twenty pounds a week each. That would do us very well. We'll try some of the other things first, and directly we have any money we'll send for the sample and instructions. And I have another idea, but I must think about it before I say.'

We all said, 'Out with it – what's the other idea?'

But Dicky said, 'No.' That is Dicky all over. He never will show you anything he's making till it's quite finished, and the same with his inmost thoughts. But he is pleased if you seem to want to know, so Oswald said –

'Keep your silly old secret, then. Now, Dora, drive ahead. We've all said except you.'

Then Dora jumped up and dropped the stocking and the thimble (it rolled away, and we did not find it for days), and said –

'Let's try my way *now*. Besides, I'm the eldest, so it's only fair. Let's dig for treasure. Not any tiresome divining-rod – but just plain digging. People who dig for treasure always find it. And then we shall be rich and we needn't try your ways at all. Some of them are rather difficult: and I'm certain some of them are wrong – and we must always remember that wrong things –'

But we told her to shut up and come on, and she did.

I couldn't help wondering as we went down to the garden, why Father had never thought of digging there for treasure instead of going to his beastly office every day.

DIGGING FOR TREASURE

I AM afraid the last chapter was rather dull. It is always dull in books when people talk and talk, and don't do anything, but I was obliged to put it in, or else you wouldn't have understood all the rest. The best part of books is when things are happening. That is the best part of real things too. This is why I shall not tell you in this story about all the days when nothing happened. You will not catch me saying, 'thus the sad days passed slowly by' – or 'the years rolled on their weary course' – or 'time went on' – because it is silly; of course time goes on – whether you say so or not. So I shall just tell you the nice, interesting parts – and in between you will understand that we had our meals and got up and went to bed, and dull things like that. It would be sickening to write all that down, though of course it happens. I said so to Albert-next-door's uncle, who writes books, and he said, 'Quite right, that's what we call selection, a necessity of true art.' And he is very clever indeed. So you see.

I have often thought that if the people who write books for children knew a little more it would be better. I shall not tell you anything about us except what I should like to know about if I was reading the story and you were writing it. Albert's uncle says I ought to have put this in the preface, but I never read prefaces, and it is not much good writing things just for people to skip. I wonder other authors have never thought of this.

Well, when we had agreed to dig for treasure we all went down into the cellar and lighted the gas. Oswald would have liked to dig there, but it is stone flags. We looked among the old boxes and broken chairs and fenders and empty bottles and things, and at last we found the spades we had to dig in the sand with when we went to the seaside three years ago. They are not silly, babyish, wooden spades, that split if you look at them, but good iron, with a blue mark across the top of the iron part, and yellow wooden handles. We wasted a little time getting them dusted, because the girls wouldn't dig with spades that had cobwebs on them. Girls would never do for African explorers or anything like that, they are too beastly particular.

It was no use doing the thing by halves. We marked out a sort of square in the mouldy part of the garden, about three yards across, and began to dig. But we found nothing except worms and stones – and the ground was very hard.

So we thought we'd try another part of the garden, and we found a place in the big round flower bed, where the ground was much softer. We thought we'd make a smaller hole to begin with, and it was much better. We dug and dug and dug, and it was jolly hard work! We got very hot digging, but we found nothing.

Presently Albert-next-door looked over the wall. We do not like him very much, but we let him play with us sometimes, because his father is dead, and you must not be unkind to orphans, even if their mothers are alive. Albert is always very tidy. He wears frilly collars and velvet knickerbockers. I can't think how he can bear to.

So we said, 'Hallo!'

And he said, 'What are you up to?'

'We're digging for treasure,' said Alice; 'an ancient

Albert-next-door sniggered and said, 'What silly nonsense!'

parchment revealed to us the place of concealment.
Come over and help us. When we have dug deep
enough we shall find a great pot of red clay, full of gold
and precious jewels.'

Albert-next-door only sniggered and said, 'What
silly nonsense!' He cannot play properly at all. It is
very strange, because he has a very nice uncle. You see,

Albert-next-door doesn't care for reading, and he has not read nearly so many books as we have, so he is very foolish and ignorant, but it cannot be helped, and you just have to put up with it when you want him to do anything. Besides, it is wrong to be angry with people for not being so clever as you are yourself. It is not always their faults.

So Oswald said, 'Come and dig! Then you shall share the treasure when we've found it.'

But he said, 'I shan't – I don't like digging – and I'm just going in to my tea.'

'Come along and dig, there's a good boy,' Alice said. 'You can use my spade. It's much the best –'

So he came along and dug, and when once he was over the wall we kept him at it, and we worked as well, of course, and the hole got deep. Pincher worked too – he is our dog and he is very good at digging. He digs for rats in the dustbin sometimes, and gets very dirty. But we love our dog, even when his face wants washing.

'I expect we shall have to make a tunnel,' Oswald said, 'to reach the rich treasure.' So he jumped into the hole and began to dig at one side. After that we took it in turns to dig at the tunnel, and Pincher was most useful in scraping the earth out of the tunnel – he does it with his back feet when you say 'Rats!' and he digs with his front ones, and burrows with his nose as well.

At last the tunnel was nearly a yard long, and big enough to creep along to find the treasure, if only it had been a bit longer. Now it was Albert's turn to go in and dig, but he funked it.

'Take your turn like a man,' said Oswald – nobody can say that Oswald doesn't take his turn like a man. But Albert wouldn't. So we had to make him, because it was only fair.

'It's quite easy,' Alice said. 'You just crawl in and

dig with your hands. Then when you come out we can scrape out what you've done, with the spades. Come – be a man. You won't notice it being dark in the tunnel if you shut your eyes tight. We've all been in except Dora – and she doesn't like worms.'

'I don't like worms neither,' Albert-next-door said this; but we remembered how he had picked a fat red and black worm up in his fingers and thrown it at Dora only the day before.

So we put him in.

But he would not go in head first, the proper way, and dig with his hands as we had done, and though Oswald was angry at the time, for he hates snivellers, yet afterwards he owned that perhaps it was just as well. You should never be afraid to own that perhaps you were mistaken – but it is cowardly to do it unless you are quite sure you are in the wrong.

'Let me go in feet first,' said Albert-next-door. 'I'll dig with my boots – I will truly, honour bright.'

So we let him get in feet first – and he did it very slowly and at last he was in, and only his head sticking out into the hole; and all the rest of him in the tunnel.

'Now dig with your boots,' said Oswald; 'and, Alice, do catch hold of Pincher, he'll be digging again in another minute, and perhaps it would be uncomfortable for Albert if Pincher threw the mould into his eyes.'

You should always try to think of these little things. Thinking of other people's comfort makes them like you. Alice held Pincher, and we all shouted, 'Kick! dig with your feet, for all you're worth!'

So Albert-next-door began to dig with his feet, and we stood on the ground over him, waiting – and all in a minute the ground gave way, and we tumbled together in a heap: and when we got up there was a little shallow hollow where we had been standing, and Albert-next-door was underneath, stuck quite fast, because the roof of the tunnel had tumbled in on him. He is a horribly unlucky boy to have anything to do with.

It was dreadful the way he cried and screamed, though he had to own it didn't hurt, only it was rather heavy and he couldn't move his legs. We would have dug him out all right enough, in time, but he screamed so we were afraid the police would come, so Dicky climbed over the wall, to tell the cook there to tell Albert-next-door's uncle he had been buried by mistake, and to come and help dig him out.

Dicky was a long time gone. We wondered what had become of him, and all the while the screaming went on and on, for we had taken the loose earth off Albert's face so that he could scream quite easily and comfortably.

Presently Dicky came back and Albert-next-door's uncle came with him. He has very long legs, and his hair is light and his face is brown. He has been to sea, but now he writes books. I like him.

He told his nephew to stow it, so Albert did, and then he asked him if he was hurt – and Albert had to say he wasn't, for though he is a coward, and very unlucky, he is not a liar like some boys are.

'This promises to be a protracted if agreeable task,' said Albert-next-door's uncle, rubbing his hands and looking at the hole with Albert's head in it. 'I will get another spade,' so he fetched the big spade out of the next-door garden tool-shed, and began to dig his nephew out.

'Mind you keep very still,' he said, 'or I might chunk a bit out of you with the spade.' Then after a while he said –

'I confess that I am not absolutely insensible to the dramatic interest of the situation. My curiosity is excited. I own that I should like to know how my nephew happened to be buried. But don't tell me if you'd rather not. I suppose no force was used?'

Albert-next-door's uncle asked him if he was hurt

'Only moral force,' said Alice. They used to talk a lot about moral force at the High School where she went, and in case you don't know what it means I'll tell you that it is making people do what they don't want to, just by slanging them, or laughing at them, or promising them things if they're good.

'Only moral force, eh?' said Albert-next-door's uncle. 'Well?'

'Well,' Dora said, 'I'm very sorry it happened to

Albert – I'd rather it had been one of us. It would have been my turn to go into the tunnel, only I don't like worms, so they let me off. You see we were digging for treasure.'

'Yes,' said Alice, 'and I think we were just coming to the underground passage that leads to the secret hoard, when the tunnel fell in on Albert. He *is* so unlucky,' and she sighed.

Then Albert-next-door began to scream again, and his uncle wiped his face – his own face, not Albert's – with his silk handkerchief, and then he put it in his trousers pocket. It seems a strange place to put a handkerchief, but he had his coat and waistcoat off and I suppose he wanted the handkerchief handy. Digging is warm work.

He told Albert-next-door to drop it, or he wouldn't proceed further in the matter, so Albert stopped screaming, and presently his uncle finished digging him out. Albert did look so funny, with his hair all dusty and his velvet suit covered with mould and his face muddy with earth and crying.

We all said how sorry we were, but he wouldn't say a word back to us. He was most awfully sick to think he'd been the one buried, when it might just as well have been one of us. I felt myself that it was hard lines.

'So you were digging for treasure,' said Albert-next-door's uncle, wiping his face again with his handkerchief. 'Well, I fear that your chances of success are small. I have made a careful study of the whole subject. What I don't know about buried treasure is not worth knowing. And I never knew more than one coin buried in any one garden – and that is generally – Hullo – what's that?'

He pointed to something shining in the hole he had just dragged Albert out of. Oswald picked it up. It was a half-crown. We looked at each other, speechless with surprise and delight, like in books.

'Well, that's lucky, at all events,' said Albert-next-door's uncle. 'Let's see, that's fivepence each for you.'

'It's fourpence – something; I can't do fractions,' said Dicky, 'there are seven of us, you see.'

'Oh, you count Albert as one of yourselves on this occasion, eh?'

'Of course,' said Alice; 'and I say, he was buried after all. Why shouldn't we let him have the odd some-things, and we'll have fourpence each.'

We all agreed to do this, and told Albert-next-door we would bring his share as soon as we could get the half-crown changed. He cheered up a little at that, and his uncle wiped his face again – he did look hot – and began to put on his coat and waistcoat.

When he had done it he stooped and picked up some-thing. He held it up, and you will hardly believe it, but it is quite true – it was another half-crown!

'To think that there should be two!' he said; 'in all my experience of buried treasure I never heard of such a thing!'

I wish Albert-next-door's uncle would come treasure-seeking with us regularly; he must have very sharp eyes: for Dora says she was looking just the minute before at the very place where the second half-crown was picked up from, and *she* never saw it.

BEING DETECTIVES

The next thing that happened to us was very interesting. It was as real as the half-crowns – not just pretending. I shall try to write it as like a real book as I can. Of course we have read Mr Sherlock Holmes, as well as the yellow-covered books with pictures outside that are so badly printed; and you get them for fourpence-halfpenny at the bookstall when the corners of them are beginning to curl up and get dirty, with people looking to see how the story ends when they are waiting for trains. I think this is most unfair to the boy at the bookstall. The books are written by a gentleman named Gaboriau, and Albert's uncle says they are the worst translations in the world – and written in vile English. Of course they're not like Kipling, but they're jolly good stories. And we had just been reading a book by Dick Diddlington – that's not his right name, but I know all about libel actions, so I shall not say what his name is really, because his books are rot. Only they put it into our heads to do what I am going to narrate.

It was in September, and we were not to go to the seaside because it is so expensive, even if you go to Sheerness, where it is all tin cans and old boots and no sand at all. But every one else went, even the people next door – not Albert's side, but the other. Their servant told Eliza they were all going to Scarborough, and next day sure enough all the blinds were down and the shutters up, and the milk was not left any more. There is a big horse-chestnut tree between their garden and ours, very useful for getting conkers out of and for making stuff to rub on your chilblains. This prevented our seeing whether the blinds were down at the back as well, but Dicky climbed to the top of the tree and looked, and they were.

It was jolly hot weather, and very stuffy indoors – we used to play a good deal in the garden. We made a tent out of the kitchen clothes-horse and some blankets off our beds, and though it was quite as hot in the tent as in the house it was a very different sort of hotness. Albert's uncle called it the Turkish Bath. It is not nice to be kept from the seaside, but we know that we have much to be thankful for. We might be poor little children living in a crowded alley where even at summer noon hardly a ray of sunlight penetrates; clothed in rags and with bare feet – though I do not mind holes in my clothes myself, and bare feet would not be at all bad in this sort of weather. Indeed we do, sometimes, when we are playing at things which require it. It was shipwrecked mariners that day, I remember, and we were all in the blanket tent. We had just finished eating the things we had saved, at the peril of our lives, from the fast-sinking vessel. They were rather nice things. Two-pennyworth of coconut candy – it was got in Greenwich, where it is four ounces a penny – three apples, some macaroni – the straight sort that is so useful to suck things through – some raw rice, and a large piece of cold suet pudding that Alice nicked from the larder when she went to get the rice and macaroni. And when we had finished some one said –

'I should like to be a detective.'

I wish to be quite fair, but I cannot remember exactly who said it. Oswald thinks he said it, and Dora says it was Dicky, but Oswald is too much of a man to quarrel about a little thing like that.

'I should like to be a detective,' said – perhaps it was Dicky, but I think not – 'and find out strange and hidden crimes.'

'You have to be much cleverer than you are,' said H. O.

'Not so very,' Alice said, 'because when you've read the books you know what the things mean: the red hair on the handle of the knife, or the grains of white powder on the velvet collar of the villain's overcoat. I believe we could do it.'

'I shouldn't like to have anything to do with murders,' said Dora; 'somehow it doesn't seem safe –'

'And it always ends in the poor murderer being hanged,' said Alice.

We explained to her why murderers have to be hanged, but she only said, 'I don't care. I'm sure no one would ever do murdering *twice*. Think of the blood and things, and what you would see when you woke up in the night! I shouldn't mind being a detective to lie in wait for a gang of coiners, now, and spring upon them unawares, and secure them – single-handed, you know, or with only my faithful bloodhound.'

She stroked Pincher's ears, but he had gone to sleep because he knew well enough that all the suet pudding was finished. He is a very sensible dog.

'You always get hold of the wrong end of the stick,' Oswald said. 'You can't choose what crimes you'll be a detective about. You just have to get a suspicious circumstance, and then you look for a clue and follow it up. Whether it turns out a murder or a missing will is just a fluke.'

'That's one way,' Dicky said. 'Another is to get a paper and find two advertisements or bits of news that fit. Like this: "Young Lady Missing," and then it tells about all the clothes she had on, and the gold locket she wore, and the colour of her hair, and all that; and then in another piece of the paper you see, "Gold locket found," and then it all comes out.'

We sent H. O. for the paper at once, but we could not make any of the things fit in. The two best were about how some burglars broke into a place in Holloway where they made preserved tongues and invalid delicacies, and carried off a lot of them. And on another page there was, 'Mysterious deaths in Holloway.'

Oswald thought there was something in it, and so did Albert's uncle when we asked him, but the others thought not, so Oswald agreed to drop it. Besides, Holloway is a long way off. All the time we were talking about the paper Alice seemed to be thinking about something else, and when we had done she said –

'I believe we might be detectives ourselves, but I should not like to get anybody into trouble.'

'Not murderers or robbers?' Dicky asked.

'It wouldn't be murderers,' she said; 'but I *have* noticed something strange. Only I feel a little frightened. Let's ask Albert's uncle first.'

Alice is a jolly sight too fond of asking grown-up people things. And we all said it was tommy-rot, and she was to tell us.

'Well, promise you won't do anything without me,' Alice said, and we promised. Then she said –

'This is a dark secret, and any one who thinks it is better not to be involved in a career of crime-discovery had better go away ere yet it be too late.'

So Dora said she had had enough of tents, and she was going to look at the shops. H. O. went with her because he had twopence to spend. They thought it was only a game of Alice's but Oswald knew by the way she spoke. He can nearly always tell. And when people are not telling the truth Oswald generally knows by the way they look with their eyes. Oswald is not proud of being able to do this. He knows it is through no merit of his own that he is much cleverer than some people.

When they had gone, the rest of us got closer together and said –

'Now then.'

'Well,' Alice said, 'you know the house next door? The people have gone to Scarborough. And the house is shut up. But last night *I saw a light in the windows.*'

We asked her how and when, because her room is in the front, and she couldn't possibly have seen. And then she said –

'I'll tell you if you boys will promise not ever to go fishing again without me.'

So we had to promise.

Then she said –

'It was last night. I had forgotten to feed my rabbits and I woke up and remembered it. And I was afraid I should find them dead in the morning, like Oswald did.'

'It wasn't my fault,' Oswald said; 'there was something the matter with the beasts. I fed them right enough.'

Alice said she didn't mean that, and she went on –

'I came down into the garden, and I saw a light in the house, and dark figures moving about. I thought perhaps it was burglars, but Father hadn't come home, and Eliza had gone to bed, so I couldn't do anything. Only I thought perhaps I would tell the rest of you.'

'Why didn't you tell us this morning?' Noël asked. And Alice explained that she did not want to get any one into trouble, even burglars. 'But we might watch to-night,' she said, 'and see if we see the light again.'

'They might have been burglars,' Noël said. He was sucking the last bit of his macaroni. 'You know the people next door are very grand. They won't know us – and they go out in a real private carriage sometimes. And they have an "At Home" day, and people come in cabs. I daresay they have piles of plate and jewellery and rich brocades, and furs of price and things like that. Let us keep watch to-night.'

'It's no use watching to-night,' Dicky said; 'if it's only burglars they won't come again. But there are other things besides burglars that are discovered in empty houses where lights are seen moving.'

'You mean coiners,' said Oswald at once. 'I wonder what the reward is for setting the police on their track?'

Dicky thought it ought to be something fat, because coiners are always a desperate gang; and the machinery they make the coins with is so heavy and handy for knocking down detectives.

Then it was tea-time, and we went in; and Dora and H. O. had clubbed their money together and bought a melon; quite a big one, and only a little bit squashy at one end. It was very good, and then we washed the seeds and made things with them and with pins and cotton. And nobody said any more about watching the house next door.

Only when we went to bed Dicky took off his coat and waistcoat, but he stopped at his braces, and said –

'What about the coiners?'

Oswald had taken off his collar and tie, and he was just going to say the same, so he said, 'Of course I meant to watch, only my collar's rather tight, so I thought I'd take it off first.'

Dicky said he did not think the girls ought to be in it, because there might be danger, but Oswald reminded him that they had promised Alice, and that a promise is a sacred thing, even when you'd much rather not. So Oswald got Alice alone under pretence of showing her a caterpillar – Dora does not like them, and she screamed and ran away when Oswald offered to show it her. Then Oswald explained, and Alice agreed to come and watch if she could. This made us later than we ought to have been, because Alice had to wait till Dora was quiet and then creep out very slowly, for fear of the boards creaking. The girls sleep with their room-door open for fear of burglars. Alice had kept on her clothes under her nightgown when Dora wasn't look-ing, and presently we got down, creeping past Father's study, and out at the glass door that leads on to the veranda and the iron steps into the garden. And we went down very quietly, and got into the chestnut-tree, and then I felt that we had only been playing what Albert's uncle calls our favourite instrument – I mean the Fool. For the house next door was as dark as dark. Then suddenly we heard a sound – it came from the gate at the end of the garden. All the gardens have gates; they lead into a kind of lane that runs behind them. It is a sort of back way, very convenient when you don't want to say exactly where you are going. We heard the gate at the end of the next garden click, and Dicky nudged Alice so that she would have fallen out of the tree if it had not been for Oswald's extraordinary presence of mind. Oswald squeezed Alice's arm tight, and we all looked; and the others were rather frightened because really we had not exactly expected anything to happen except perhaps a light. But now a muffled figure, shrouded in a dark cloak, came swiftly up the path of the next-door garden. And we could see that under its cloak the figure carried a mysterious burden. The figure was dressed to look like a woman in a sailor hat.

We held our breath as it passed under the tree where we were, and then it tapped very gently on the back door and was let in, and then a light appeared in the window of the downstairs back breakfast-room. But the shutters were up.

Dicky said, 'My eye!' and wouldn't the others be sick to think they hadn't been in this! But Alice didn't half like it – and as she is a girl I do not blame her. Indeed, I thought myself at first that perhaps it would be better to retire for the present, and return later with a strongly armed force.

'It's not burglars,' Alice whispered; 'the mysterious stranger was bringing things in, not taking them out. They must be coiners – and oh, Oswald! – don't let's! The things they coin with must hurt very much. Do let's go to bed!'

But Dicky said he was going to see; if there was a reward for finding out things like this he would like to have the reward.

'They locked the back door,' he whispered, 'I heard it go. And I could look in quite well through the holes in the shutters and be back over the wall long before they'd got the door open, even if they started to do it at once.'

There were holes at the top of the shutters the shape of hearts, and the yellow light came out through them as well as through the chinks of the shutters.

Oswald said if Dicky went he should, because he was the eldest; and Alice said, 'If any one goes it ought to be me, because I thought of it.'

So Oswald said, 'Well, go then'; and she said, 'Not for anything!' And she begged us not to, and we talked about it in the tree till we were all quite hoarse with whispering.

At last we decided on a plan of action.

Alice was to stay in the tree, and scream 'Murder!' if anything happened. Dicky and I were to get down into the next garden and take it in turns to peep.

So we got down as quietly as we could, but the tree made much more noise than it does in the day, and several times we paused, fearing that all was discovered. But nothing happened.

There was a pile of red flower-pots under the window and one very large one was on the window-ledge. It seemed as if it was the hand of Destiny had placed it there, and the geranium in it was dead, and there was nothing to stop your standing on it – so Oswald did. He went first because he is the eldest, and though Dicky tried to stop him because he thought of it first it could not be, on account of not being able to say anything.

So Oswald stood on the flower-pot and tried to look through one of the holes. He did not really expect to see the coiners at their fell work, though he had pretended to when we were talking in the tree. But if he had seen them pouring the base molten metal into tin moulds the shape of half-crowns he would not have been half so astonished as he was at the spectacle now revealed.

At first he could see little, because the hole had unfortunately been made a little too high, so that the eye of the detective could only see the Prodigal Son in a shiny frame on the opposite wall. But Oswald held on to the window-frame and stood on tiptoe and then he *saw*.

There was no furnace, and no base metal, no bearded men in leathern aprons with tongs and things,

but just a table with a table-cloth on it for supper, and
a tin of salmon and a lettuce and some bottled beer.
And there on a chair was the cloak and the hat of the
mysterious stranger, and the two people sitting at the
table were the two youngest grown-up daughters of the
lady next door, and one of them was saying –

'So I got the salmon three-halfpence cheaper, and
the lettuces are only six a penny in the Broadway, just
fancy! We must save as much as ever we can on our
housekeeping money if we want to go away decent
next year.'

And the other said, 'I wish we could *all* go *every* year,
or else – Really, I almost wish –'

And all the time Oswald was looking Dicky was
pulling at his jacket to make him get down and let
Dicky have a squint. And just as she said 'I almost,'
Dicky pulled too hard and Oswald felt himself toppling
on the giddy verge of the big flower-pot. Putting forth
all his strength our hero strove to recover his equi-
what's-its-name, but it was now lost beyond recall.

'You've done it this time!' he said, then he fell
heavily among the flower-pots piled below. He heard
them crash and rattle and crack, and then his head
struck against an iron pillar used for holding up the
next-door veranda. His eyes closed and he knew no
more.

Now you will perhaps expect that at this moment
Alice would have cried 'Murder!' If you think so you
little know what girls are. Directly she was left alone in
that tree she made a bolt to tell Albert's uncle all about
it and bring him to our rescue in case the coiner's gang
was a very desperate one. And just when I fell, Albert's
uncle was getting over the wall. Alice never screamed
at all when Oswald fell, but Dicky thinks he heard
Albert's uncle say, 'Confound those kids!' which would

Dicky pulled too hard, and Oswald felt himself toppling

not have been kind or polite, so I hope he did not say it.

The people next door did not come out to see what the row was. Albert's uncle did not wait for them to come out. He picked up Oswald and carried the insensible body of the gallant young detective to the wall, laid it on the top, and then climbed over and bore his lifeless burden into our house and put it on the sofa in Father's study. Father was out, so we needn't have *crept* so when we were getting into the garden. Then Oswald was restored to consciousness, and his head tied up, and sent to bed, and next day there was a lump on his young brow as big as a turkey's egg, and very uncomfortable.

Albert's uncle came in next day and talked to each of us separately. To Oswald he said many unpleasant things about ungentlemanly to spy on ladies, and about minding your own business; and when I began to tell him what I had heard he told me to shut up, and altogether he made me more uncomfortable than the bump did.

Oswald did not say anything to any one, but next day, as the shadows of eve were falling, he crept away, and wrote on a piece of paper, 'I want to speak to you,' and shoved it through the hole like a heart in the top of the next-door shutters.

And the youngest young lady put an eye to the heart-shaped hole, and then opened the shutter and said 'Well?' very crossly.

Then Oswald said –

'I am very sorry, and I beg your pardon. We wanted to be detectives, and we thought a gang of coiners infested your house, so we looked through your window last night. I saw the lettuce, and I heard what you said about the salmon being three-halfpence cheaper, and I know it is very dishonourable to pry into other people's secrets, especially ladies', and I never will again if you will forgive me this once.'

Then the lady frowned and then she laughed, and then she said –

'So it was *you* tumbling into the flower-pots last night? We thought it was burglars. It frightened us horribly. Why, what a bump on your poor head!'

And then she talked to me a bit, and presently she said she and her sister had not wished people to know they were at home, because – And then she stopped short and grew very red, and I said, 'I thought you were all at Scarborough; your servant told Eliza so. Why didn't you want people to know you were at home?'

The lady got redder still, and then she laughed and said –

'Never mind the reason why. I hope your head doesn't hurt much. Thank you for your nice, manly little speech. *You've* nothing to be ashamed of, at any rate.' Then she kissed me, and I did not mind. And then she said, 'Run away now, dear. I'm going to – I'm going to pull up the blinds and open the shutters, and I want to do it *at once*, before it gets dark, so that every one can see we're at home, and not at Scarborough.'

WHEN we had got that four shillings by digging for treasure we ought, by rights, to have tried Dicky's idea of answering the advertisement about ladies and gentlemen and spare time and two pounds a week, but there were several things we rather wanted.

Dora wanted a new pair of scissors, and she said she was going to get them with her eightpence. But Alice said –

'You ought to get her those, Oswald, because you know you broke the points off hers getting the marble out of the brass thimble.'

It was quite true, though I had almost forgotten it, but then it was H. O. who jammed the marble into the thimble first of all. So I said –

'It's H. O.'s fault as much as mine, anyhow. Why shouldn't he pay?'

Oswald didn't so much mind paying for the beastly scissors, but he hates injustice of every kind.

'He's such a little kid,' said Dicky, and of course H. O. said he wasn't a little kid, and it very nearly came to being a row between them. But Oswald knows when to be generous; so he said –

'Look here! I'll pay sixpence of the scissors, and H. O. shall pay the rest, to teach him to be careful.'

H. O. agreed: he is not at all a mean kid, but I found out afterwards that Alice paid his share out of her own money.

Then we wanted some new paints, and Noël wanted a pencil and a halfpenny account-book to write poetry with, and it does seem hard never to have any apples. So, somehow or other nearly all the money got spent, and we agreed that we must let the advertisement run loose a little longer.

'I only hope,' Alice said, 'that they won't have got all the ladies and gentlemen they want before we have got the money to write for the sample and instructions.'

And I was a little afraid myself, because it seemed such a splendid chance; but we looked in the paper every day, and the advertisement was always there, so we thought it was all right.

Then we had the detective try-on – and it proved no go; and then, when all the money was gone, except a halfpenny of mine and twopence of Noël's and three-pence of Dicky's and a few pennies that the girls had left, we held another council.

Dora was sewing the buttons on H. O.'s Sunday things. He got himself a knife with his money, and he cut every single one of his best buttons off. You've no idea how many buttons there are on a suit. Dora counted them. There are twenty-four, counting the little ones on the sleeves that don't undo.

Alice was trying to teach Pincher to beg; but he has too much sense when he knows you've got nothing in your hands, and the rest of us were roasting potatoes under the fire. We had made a fire on purpose, though it was rather warm. They are very good if you cut away the burnt parts – but you ought to wash them first, or you are a dirty boy.

'Well, what can we do?' said Dicky. 'You are so fond of saying "Let's do something!" and never saying what.'

'We can't try the advertisement yet. Shall we try rescuing some one?' said Oswald. It was his own idea, but he didn't insist on doing it, though he is next to the eldest, for he knows it is bad manners to make people do what you want, when they would rather not.

'What was Noël's plan?' Alice asked.

'A Princess or a poetry book,' said Noël sleepily. He was lying on his back on the sofa, kicking his legs. 'Only I shall look for the Princess all by myself. But I'll let you see her when we're married.'

'Have you got enough poetry to make a book?' Dicky asked that, and it was rather sensible of him, because when Noël came to look there were only seven of his poems that any of us could understand. There was the 'Wreck of the *Malabar*', and the poem he wrote when Eliza took us to hear the Reviving Preacher, and everybody cried, and Father said it must have been the Preacher's Eloquence.

So Noël wrote:

> *O Eloquence and what art thou?*
> *Ay what art thou? because we cried*
> *And everybody cried inside*
> *When they came out their eyes were red –*
> *And it was your doing Father said.*

But Noël told Alice he got the first line and a half from a book a boy at school was going to write when he had time. Besides this there were the 'Lines on a Dead Black Beetle that was poisoned':

> *O Beetle how I weep to see*
> *Thee lying on thy poor back!*
> *It is so very sad indeed.*
> *You were so shiny and black.*
> *I wish you were alive again*
> *But Eliza says wishing it is nonsense and a shame.*

It was very good beetle poison, and there were hundreds of them lying dead – but Noël only wrote a piece of poetry for one of them. He said he hadn't time to do them all, and the worst of it was he didn't know which one he'd written it to – so Alice couldn't bury the beetle and put the lines on its grave, though she wanted to very much.

Well, it was quite plain that there wasn't enough poetry for a book.

'We might wait a year or two,' said Noël. 'I shall be sure to make some more some time. I thought of a piece about a fly this morning that knew condensed milk was sticky.'

'But we want the money *now*,' said Dicky, 'and you can go on writing just the same. It will come in some time or other.'

'There's poetry in newspapers,' said Alice. 'Down, Pincher! you'll never be a clever dog, so it's no good trying.'

'Do they pay for it?' Dicky thought of that; he often thinks of things that are really important, even if they are a little dull.

'I don't know. But I shouldn't think any one would let them print their poetry without. I wouldn't I know.' That was Dora; but Noël said he wouldn't mind if he didn't get paid, so long as he saw his poetry printed and his name at the end.

'We might try, anyway,' said Oswald. He is always willing to give other people's ideas a fair trial.

So we copied out 'The Wreck of the *Malabar*' and the other six poems on drawing-paper – Dora did it, she writes best – and Oswald drew a picture of the *Malabar* going down with all hands. It was a full-rigged schooner, and all the ropes and sails were correct; because my cousin is in the Navy, and he showed me.

We thought a long time whether we'd write a letter and send it by post with the poetry – and Dora thought it would be best. But Noël said he couldn't bear not to know at once if the paper would print the poetry, so we decided to take it.

I went with Noël, because I am the eldest, and he is

H.O. called 'Good Hunting!' as the train started

not old enough to go to London by himself. Dicky said poetry was rot – and he was glad he hadn't got to make a fool of himself: that was because there was not enough money for him to go with us. H. O. couldn't come either, but he came to the station to see us off, and waved his cap and called out 'Good hunting!' as the train started.

There was a lady in spectacles in the corner. She was writing with a pencil on the edges of long strips of paper that had print all down them.

When the train started she asked –

'What was that he said?'

So Oswald answered –

'It was "Good hunting" – it's out of the Jungle book!'

'That's very pleasant to hear,' the lady said; 'I am very pleased to meet people who know their Jungle book. And where are you off to – the Zoological Gardens to look for Bagheera?'

We were pleased, too, to meet some one who knew the Jungle book.

So Oswald said –

'We are going to restore the fallen fortunes of the House of Bastable – and we have all thought of different ways – and we're going to try them all. Noël's way is poetry. I suppose great poets get paid?'

The lady laughed – she was awfully jolly – and said she was a sort of poet, too, and the long strips of paper were the proofs of her new book of stories. Because before a book is made into a real book with pages and a cover, they sometimes print it all on strips of paper, and the writer make marks on it with a pencil to show the printers what idiots they are not to understand what a writer means to have printed.

We told her all about digging for treasure, and what we meant to do. Then she asked to see Noël's poetry – and he said he didn't like – so she said, 'Look here – if you'll show me yours I'll show you some of mine.' So he agreed.

The jolly lady read Noël's poetry, and she said she liked it very much. And she thought a great deal of the picture of the *Malabar*. And then she said, 'I write

serious poetry like yours myself, too, but I have a piece
here that I think you will like because it's about a boy.'
She gave it to us – and so I can copy it down, and I will,
for it shows that some grown-up ladies are not so silly as
others. I like it better than Noël's poetry, though I told
him I did not, because he looked as if he was going to

She asked to see Noël's poetry

cry. This was very wrong, for you should always speak
the truth, however unhappy it makes people. And I
generally do. But I did not want him crying in the
railway carriage.

The lady's piece of poetry:

> *Oh when I wake up in my bed*
> *And see the sun all fat and red,*
> *I'm glad to have another day*
> *For all my different kinds of play.*

54

GOOD HUNTING

There are so many things to do –
The things that make a man of you,
If grown-ups did not get so vexed
And wonder what you will do next.

I often wonder whether they
Ever made up our kinds of play –
If they were always good as gold
And only did what they were told.

They like you best to play with tops
And toys in boxes, bought in shops;
They do not even know the names
Of really interesting games.

They will not let you play with fire
Or trip your sisters up with wire,
They grudge the tea-tray for a drum,
Or booby-traps when callers come.

They don't like fishing, and it's true
You sometimes soak a suit or two:
They look on fireworks, though they're dry,
With quite a disapproving eye.

They do not understand the way
To get the most out of your day:
They do not know how hunger feels
Nor what you need between your meals.

And when you're sent to bed at night
They're happy, but they're not polite,
For through the door you hear them say:
'He's done his mischief for the day!'

She told us a lot of other pieces but I cannot remember them, and she talked to us all the way up, and when we got nearly to Cannon Street she said –

'I've got two new shillings here! Do you think they would help to smooth the path to Fame?'

Noël said, 'Thank you,' and was going to take the shilling. But Oswald, who always remembers what he is told, said –

'Thank you very much, but Father told us we ought never to take anything from strangers.'

'That's a nasty one,' said the lady – she didn't talk a bit like a real lady, but more like a jolly sort of grown-up boy in a dress and hat – 'a very nasty one! But don't you think as Noël and I are both poets I might be considered a sort of relation? You've heard of brother poets, haven't you? Don't you think Noël and I are aunt and nephew poets, or some relationship of that kind?'

I didn't know what to say, and she went on –

'It's awfully straight of you to stick to what your Father tells you, but look here, you take the shillings, and here's my card. When you get home tell your Father all about it, and if he says No, you can just bring the shillings back to me.'

So we took the shillings, and she shook hands with us and said, 'Good-bye, and good hunting!'

We did tell Father about it, and he said it was all right, and when he looked at the card he told us we were highly honoured, for the lady wrote better poetry than any other lady alive now. We had never heard of her, and she seemed much too jolly for a poet. Good old Kipling! We owe him those two shillings, as well as the Jungle books!

THE POET AND THE EDITOR

IT was not bad sport – being in London entirely on our own hook. We asked the way to Fleet Street, where Father says all the newspaper offices are. They said straight on down Ludgate Hill – but it turned out to be quite another way. At least *we* didn't go straight on.

We got to St Paul's. Noël would go in, and we saw where Gordon was buried – at least the monument. It is very flat, considering what a man he was.

When we came out we walked a long way, and when we asked a policeman he said we'd better go back through Smithfield. So we did. They don't burn people any more there now, so it was rather dull, besides being a long way, and Noël got very tired. He's a peaky little chap; it comes of being a poet, I think. We had a bun or two at different shops – out of the shillings – and it was quite late in the afternoon when we got to Fleet Street. The gas was lighted and the electric lights. There is a jolly Bovril sign that comes off and on in different coloured lamps. We went to the *Daily Recorder* office, and asked to see the Editor. It is a big office, very bright, with brass and mahogany and electric lights.

They told us the Editor wasn't there, but at another office. So we went down a dirty street, to a very dull-looking place. There was a man there inside, in a glass case, as if he was a museum, and he told us to write down our names and our business. So Oswald wrote –

OSWALD BASTABLE.
NOËL BASTABLE.
Business very private indeed.

Then we waited on the stone stairs; it was very draughty. And the man in the glass case looked at us as if we were the museum instead of him. We waited a long time, and then a boy came down and said –

'The Editor can't see you. Will you please write your business?' And he laughed. I wanted to punch his head.

But Noël said, 'Yes, I'll write it if you'll give me a pen and ink, and a sheet of paper and an envelope.'

The boy said he'd better write by post. But Noël is a bit pig-headed; it's his worst fault. So he said –

'No, I'll write it *now*.' So I backed him up by saying –

'Look at the price penny stamps are since the coal strike!'

So the boy grinned, and the man in the glass case gave us pen and paper, and Noël wrote. Oswald writes better than he does; but Noël would do it; and it took a very long time, and then it was inky.

DEAR MR EDITOR, I want you to print my poetry and pay for it, and I am a friend of Mrs Leslie's; she is a poet too.

Your affectionate friend,
NOËL BASTABLE.

He licked the envelope a good deal, so that that boy shouldn't read it going upstairs; and he wrote 'Very private' outside, and gave the letter to the boy. I thought it wasn't any good; but in a minute the grinning boy came back, and he was quite respectful, and said –

'The Editor says, please will you step up?'

We stepped up. There were a lot of stairs and passages, and a queer sort of humming, hammering sound and a very funny smell. The boy was now very polite, and said it was the ink we smelt, and the noise was the printing machines.

After going through a lot of cold passages we came to a door; the boy opened it, and let us go in. There was a large room, with a big, soft, blue-and-red carpet, and a roaring fire, though it was only October; and a large table with drawers, and littered with papers, just like the one in Father's study. A gentleman was sitting at one side of the table; he had a light moustache and light eyes, and he looked very young to be an editor – not nearly so old as Father. He looked very tired and sleepy, as if he had got up very early in the morning; but he was kind, and we liked him. Oswald thought he looked clever. Oswald is considered a judge of faces.

'Well,' said he, 'so you are Mrs Leslie's friends?'

'I think so,' said Noël; 'at least she gave us each a shilling, and she wished us "good hunting!" '

'Good hunting, eh? Well, what about this poetry of yours? Which is the poet?'

I can't think how he could have asked! Oswald is said to be a very manly-looking boy for his age. However, I thought it would look duffing to be offended, so I said –

'This is my brother Noël. He is the poet.'

Noël had turned quite pale. He is disgustingly like a girl in some ways. The Editor told us to sit down, and he took the poems from Noël, and began to read them. Noël got paler and paler; I really thought he was going to faint, like he did when I held his hand under the cold-water tap, after I had accidentally cut him with my chisel. When the Editor had read the first poem – it was the one about the beetle – he got up and

When the Editor had read the first poem, he got up and stood with his back to us

stood with his back to us. It was not manners; but Noël thinks he did it 'to conceal his emotion,' as they do in books.

He read all the poems, and then he said –

'I like your poetry very much, young man. I'll give you – let me see; how much shall I give you for it?'

'As much as ever you can,' said Noël. 'You see I want a good deal of money to restore the fallen fortunes of the house of Bastable.'

The gentleman put on some eye-glasses and looked hard at us. Then he sat down.

'That's a good idea,' said he. 'Tell me how you came to think of it. And, I say, have you had any tea? They've just sent out for mine.'

He rang a tingly bell, and the boy brought in a tray with a teapot and a thick cup and saucer and things, and he had to fetch another tray for us, when he was told to; and we had tea with the Editor of the *Daily Recorder*. I suppose it was a very proud moment for Noël, though I did not think of that till afterwards. The Editor asked us a lot of questions, and we told him a good deal, though of course I did not tell a stranger all our reasons for thinking that the family fortunes wanted restoring. We stayed about half an hour, and when we were going away he said again –

'I shall print all your poems, my poet; and now what do you think they're worth?'

'I don't know,' Noël said. 'You see I didn't write them to sell.'

'Why did you write them then?' he asked.

Noël said he didn't know; he supposed because he wanted to.

'Art for Art's sake, eh?' said the Editor, and he seemed quite delighted, as though Noël had said something clever.

'Well, would a guinea meet your views?' he asked.

I have read of people being at a loss for words, and dumb with emotion, and I've read of people being turned to stone with astonishment, or joy, or something, but I never knew how silly it looked till I saw Noël standing staring at the Editor with his mouth open. He went red and he went white, and then he got crimson, as if you were rubbing more and more crimson lake on a palette. But he didn't say a word, so Oswald had to say –

'I should jolly well think so.'

So the Editor gave Noël a sovereign and a shilling, and he shook hands with us both, but he thumped Noël on the back and said –

'Buck up, old man! It's your first guinea, but it won't be your last. Now go along home, and in about ten years you can bring me some more poetry. Not before – see? I'm just taking this poetry of yours because I like it very much; but we don't put poetry in this paper at all. I shall have to put it in another paper I know of.'

'What *do* you put in your paper?' I asked, for Father always takes the *Daily Chronicle*, and I didn't know what the *Recorder* was like. We chose it because it has such a glorious office, and a clock outside lighted up.

'Oh, news,' said he, 'and dull articles, and things about Celebrities. If you know any Celebrities, now?'

Noël asked him what Celebrities were.

'Oh, the Queen and the Princes, and people with titles, and people who write, or sing, or act – or do something clever or wicked.'

'I don't know anybody wicked,' said Oswald, wishing he had known Dick Turpin, or Claude Duval, so as to be able to tell the Editor things about them. 'But I know some one with a title – Lord Tottenham.'

'The mad old Protectionist, eh? How did you come to know him?'

'We don't know him to speak to. But he goes over the Heath every day at three, and he strides along like

62

a giant – with a black cloak like Lord Tennyson's flying behind him, and he talks to himself like one o'clock.'

'What does he say?' The Editor had sat down again, and he was fiddling with a blue pencil.

'We only heard him once, close enough to understand, and then he said, "The curse of the country, sir – ruin and desolation!" And then he went striding along again, hitting at the furze-bushes as if they were the heads of his enemies.'

'Excellent descriptive touch,' said the Editor. 'Well, go on.'

'That's all I know about him, except that he stops in the middle of the Heath every day, and he looks all round to see if there's any one about, and if there isn't, he takes his collar off.'

The Editor interrupted – which is considered rude – and said –

'You're not romancing?'

'I beg your pardon?' said Oswald.

'Drawing the long bow, I mean,' said the Editor.

Oswald drew himself up, and said he wasn't a liar.

The Editor only laughed, and said romancing and lying were not at all the same; only it was important to know what you were playing at. So Oswald accepted his apology, and went on.

'We were hiding among the furze-bushes one day, and we saw him do it. He took off his collar, and he put on a clean one, and he threw the other among the furze-bushes. We picked it up afterwards, and it was a beastly paper one!'

'Thank you,' said the Editor, and he got up and put his hand in his pocket. 'That's well worth five shillings, and there they are. Would you like to see round the printing offices before you go home?'

I pocketed my five bob, and thanked him, and I said

we should like it very much. He called another gentleman and said something we couldn't hear. Then he
said good-bye again; and all this time Noël hadn't said
a word. But now he said, 'I've made a poem about you.
It is called "Lines to a Noble Editor." Shall I write it
down?'

The Editor gave him the blue pencil, and he sat
down at the Editor's table and wrote. It was this, he
told me afterwards as well as he could remember –

> *May Life's choicest blessings be your lot*
> *I think you ought to be very blest*
> *For you are going to print my poems –*
> *And you may have this one as well as the rest.*

'Thank you,' said the Editor. 'I don't think I ever had
a poem addressed to me before. I shall treasure it, I
assure you.'

Then the other gentleman said something about
Maecenas, and we went off to see the printing office
with at least one pound seven in our pockets.

It *was* good hunting, and no mistake!

But he never put Noël's poetry in the *Daily Recorder*.
It was quite a long time afterwards we saw a sort of
story thing in a magazine, on the station bookstall, and
that kind, sleepy-looking Editor had written it, I suppose. It was not at all amusing. It said a lot about
Noël and me, describing us all wrong, and saying how
we had tea with the Editor; and all Noël's poems were
in the story thing. I think myself the Editor seemed to
make game of them, but Noël was quite pleased to see
them printed – so that's all right.

It wasn't my poetry anyhow, I am glad to say.

NOËL'S PRINCESS

SHE happened quite accidentally. We were not looking for a Princess at all just then; but Noël had said he was going to find a Princess all by himself, and marry her – and he really did. Which was rather odd, because when people say things are going to befall, very often they don't. It was different, of course, with the prophets of old.

We did not get any treasure by it, except twelve chocolate drops; but we might have done, and it was an adventure, anyhow.

Greenwich Park is a jolly good place to play in, especially the parts that aren't near Greenwich. The parts near the Heath are first-rate. I often wish the Park was nearer our house; but I suppose a Park is a difficult thing to move.

Sometimes we get Eliza to put lunch in a basket, and we go up to the Park. She likes that – it saves cooking dinner for us; and sometimes she says of her own accord, 'I've made some pasties for you, and you might as well go into the Park as not. It's a lovely day.'

She always tells us to rinse out the cup at the drinking-fountain, and the girls do; but I always put my head under the tap and drink. Then you are an intrepid hunter at a mountain stream – and besides, you're sure it's clean. Dicky does the same, and so does H. O. But Noël always drinks out of the cup. He says it is a golden goblet, wrought by enchanted gnomes.

The day the Princess happened was a fine, hot day, last October, and we were quite tired with the walk up to the Park.

We always go in by the little gate at the top of Croom's Hill. It is the postern gate that things always happen at in stories. It was dusty walking, but when we got in the Park it was ripping, so we rested a bit, and lay on our backs, and looked up at the trees, and wished we could play monkeys. I have done it before now, but the Park-keeper makes a row if he catches you.

When we'd rested a little, Alice said –

'It was a long way to the enchanted wood, but it is very nice now we are there. I wonder what we shall find in it?'

'We shall find deer,' said Dicky, 'if we go to look; but they go on the other side of the Park because of the people with buns.'

Saying buns made us think of lunch, so we had it; and when we had done we scratched a hole under a tree and buried the papers, because we know it spoils pretty places to leave beastly, greasy papers lying about. I remember Mother teaching me and Dora that, when we were quite little. I wish everybody's parents would teach them this useful lesson, and the same about orange peel.

When we'd eaten everything there was, Alice whispered –

'I see the white witch bear yonder among the trees! Let's track it and slay it in its lair.'

'I am the bear,' said Noël; so he crept away, and we followed him among the trees. Often the witch bear was out of sight, and then you didn't know where it would jump out from; but sometimes we saw it, and just followed.

'When we catch it there'll be a great fight,' said Oswald; 'and I shall be Count Folko of Mont Faucon.'

'I'll be Gabrielle,' said Dora. She is the only one of us who likes doing girl's parts.

'I'll be Sintram,' said Alice; 'and H. O. can be the Little Master.'

'What about Dicky?'

'Oh, I can be the Pilgrim with the bones.'

'Hist!' whispered Alice. 'See his white fairy fur gleaming amid yonder covert!'

And I saw a bit of white too. It was Noël's collar, and it had come undone at the back.

We hunted the bear in and out of the trees, and then we lost him altogether; and suddenly we found the wall of the Park – in a place where I'm sure there wasn't a wall before. Noël wasn't anywhere about, and there was a door in the wall. And it was open; so we went through.

'The bear has hidden himself in these mountain fastnesses,' Oswald said. 'I will draw my good sword and after him.'

So I drew the umbrella, which Dora always will bring in case it rains, because Noël gets a cold on the chest at the least thing – and we went on.

The other side of the wall it was a stable yard, all cobble-stones. There was nobody about – but we could hear a man rubbing down a horse and hissing in the stable; so we crept very quietly past, and Alice whispered –

''Tis the lair of the Monster Serpent; I hear his deadly hiss! Beware! Courage and despatch!'

We went over the stones on tiptoe, and we found another wall with another door in it on the other side. We went through that too, on tiptoe. It really was an adventure. And there we were in a shrubbery, and we saw something white through the trees. Dora said it was the white bear. That is so like Dora. She always begins to take part in a play just when the rest of us are getting tired of it. I don't mean this unkindly, because I am very fond of Dora. I cannot forget how kind she was when I had bronchitis; and ingratitude is a dreadful vice. But it is quite true.

'It is not a bear,' said Oswald; and we all went on, still on tiptoe, round a twisty path and on to a lawn, and there was Noël. His collar had come undone, as I said, and he had an inky mark on his face that he made just before we left the house, and he wouldn't let Dora wash it off, and one of his bootlaces was coming down. He was standing looking at a little girl; she was the funniest little girl you ever saw.

She was like a china doll – the sixpenny kind; she had a white face, and long yellow hair, done up very tight in two pigtails; her forehead was very big and lumpy, and her cheeks came high up, like little shelves under her eyes. Her eyes were small and blue. She had on a funny black frock, with curly braid on it, and button boots that went almost up to her knees. Her legs were very thin. She was sitting in a hammock chair nursing a blue kitten – not a sky-blue one, of course, but the colour of a new slate pencil. As we came up we heard her say to Noël –

'Who are you?'

Noël had forgotten about the bear, and he was taking his favourite part, so he said –

'I'm Prince Camaralzaman.'

The funny little girl looked pleased.

'I thought at first you were a common boy,' she said. Then she saw the rest of us and said –

'Are you all Princesses and Princes too?'

Of course we said 'Yes,' and she said –

We heard her say to Noël, 'Who are you?'

'I am a Princess also.' She said it very well too, exactly as if it were true. We were very glad, because it is so seldom you meet any children who can begin to play right off without having everything explained to them. And even then they will say they are going to

69

'pretend to be' a lion, or a witch, or a king. Now this little girl just said 'I *am* a Princess.' Then she looked at Oswald and said, 'I fancy I've seen you at Baden.'

Of course Oswald said, 'Very likely.'

The little girl had a funny voice, and all her words were quite plain, each word by itself; she didn't talk at all like we do.

H. O. asked her what the cat's name was, and she said 'Katinka.' Then Dicky said –

'Let's get away from the windows; if you play near windows some one inside generally knocks at them and says "Don't ".'

The Princess put down the cat very carefully and said –

'I am forbidden to walk off the grass.'

'That's a pity,' said Dora.

'But I will if you like,' said the Princess.

'You mustn't do things you are forbidden to do,' Dora said; but Dicky showed us that there was some more grass beyond the shrubs with only a gravel path between. So I lifted the Princess over the gravel, so that she should be able to say she hadn't walked off the grass. When we got to the other grass we all sat down, and the Princess asked us if we liked 'dragées' (I know that's how you spell it, for I asked Albert-next-door's uncle).

We said we thought not, but she pulled a real silver box out of her pocket and showed us; they were just flat, round chocolates. We had two each. Then we asked her her name, and she began, and when she began she went on, and on, and on, till I thought she was never going to stop. H. O. said she had fifty names, but Dicky is very good at figures, and he says there were only eighteen. The first were Pauline, Alexandra, Alice, and Mary was one, and Victoria, for we all heard that, and it ended up with Hildegarde Cunigonde something or other, Princess of something else.

When she'd done, H. O. said, 'That's jolly good! Say it again!' and she did, but even then we couldn't remember it. We told her our names, but she thought they were too short, so when it was Noël's turn he said he was Prince Noël Camaralzaman Ivan Constantine Charlemagne James John Edward Biggs Maximilian Bastable Prince of Lewisham, but when she asked him to say it again of course he could only get the first two names right, because he'd made it up as he went on.

So the Princess said, 'You are quite old enough to know your own name.' She was very grave and serious.

She told us that she was the fifth cousin of Queen Victoria. We asked who the other cousins were, but she did not seem to understand. She went on and said she was seven times removed. She couldn't tell us what that meant either, but Oswald thinks it means that the Queen's cousins are so fond of her that they will keep coming bothering, so the Queen's servants have orders to remove them. This little girl must have been very fond of the Queen to try so often to see her, and to have been seven times removed. We could see that it is considered something to be proud of, but we thought it was hard on the Queen that her cousins wouldn't let her alone.

Presently the little girl asked us where our maids and governesses were.

We told her we hadn't any just now. And she said –
'How pleasant! And did you come here alone?'

'Yes,' said Dora; 'we came across the Heath.'

'You are very fortunate,' said the little girl. She sat very upright on the grass, with her fat little hands in her lap. 'I should like to go on the Heath. There are

71

donkeys there, with white saddle covers. I should like to ride them, but my governess will not permit it.'

'I'm glad we haven't a governess,' H. O. said. 'We ride the donkeys whenever we have any pennies, and once I gave the man another penny to make it gallop.'

'You are indeed fortunate!' said the Princess again, and when she looked sad the shelves on her cheeks showed more than ever. You could have laid a sixpence on them quite safely if you had had one.

'Never mind,' said Noël; 'I've got a lot of money. Come out and have a ride now.' But the little girl shook her head and said she was afraid it would not be correct.

Dora said she was quite right; then all of a sudden came one of those uncomfortable times when nobody can think of anything to say, so we sat and looked at each other. But at last Alice said we ought to be going.

'Do not go yet,' the little girl said. 'At what time did they order your carriage?'

'Our carriage is a fairy one, drawn by griffins, and it comes when we wish for it,' said Noël.

The little girl looked at him very queerly, and said, 'That is out of a picture-book.'

Then Noël said he thought it was about time he was married if we were to be home in time for tea. The little girl was rather stupid over it, but she did what we told her, and we married them with Dora's pocket-hand-kerchief for a veil, and the ring off the back of one of the buttons on H. O.'s blouse just went on her little finger.

Then we showed her how to play cross-touch, and puss in the corner, and tag. It was funny, she didn't know any games but battledore and shuttlecock and *les graces*. But she really began to laugh at last and not to look quite so like a doll.

She was Puss and was running after Dicky when

suddenly she stopped short and looked as if she was going to cry. And we looked too, and there were two prim ladies with little mouths and tight hair. One of them said in quite an awful voice, 'Pauline, who are these children?' and her voice was gruff, with very curly R's.

The little girl said we were Princes and Princesses – which was silly, to a grown-up person that is not a great friend of yours.

The gruff lady gave a short, horrid laugh, like a husky bark, and said –

'Princes, indeed! They're only common children!'

Dora turned very red and began to speak, but the little girl cried out 'Common children! Oh, I am so glad! When I am grown up I'll always play with common children.'

And she ran at us, and began to kiss us one by one, beginning with Alice; she had got to H. O. when the horrid lady said –

'Your Highness – go indoors at once!'

The little girl answered, 'I won't!' Then the prim lady said –

'Wilson, carry her Highness indoors.'

And the little girl was carried away screaming, and kicking with her little thin legs and her buttoned boots, and between her screams she shrieked: 'Common children! I am glad, glad, glad! Common children! Common children!'

The nasty lady then remarked –

'Go at once, or I will send for the police!'

So we went. H. O. made a face at her and so did Alice, but Oswald took off his cap and said he was sorry if she was annoyed about anything; for Oswald has always been taught to be polite to ladies, however nasty. Dicky took his off, too, when he saw me do it; he says he did it first, but that is a mistake. If I were really a common boy I should say it was a lie.

Then we all came away, and when we got outside Dora said, 'So she was really a Princess. Fancy a Princess living *there!*'

'Even Princesses have to live somewhere,' said Dicky.

'And I thought it was play. And it was real. I wish I'd known! I should have liked to ask her lots of things,' said Alice.

H. O. said he would have liked to ask her what she had for dinner and whether she had a crown.

I felt, myself, we had lost a chance of finding out a great deal about kings and queens. I might have known such a stupid-looking little girl would never have been able to pretend, as well as that.

So we all went home across the Heath, and made dripping toast for tea.

When we were eating it Noël said, 'I wish I could give *her* some! It is very good.'

He sighed as he said it, and his mouth was very full, so we knew he was thinking of his Princess. He says now that she was as beautiful as the day, but we remember her quite well, and she was nothing of the kind.

BEING BANDITS

NOËL was quite tiresome for ever so long after we found the Princess. He would keep on wanting to go to the Park when the rest of us didn't, and though we went several times to please him, we never found that door open again, and all of us except him knew from the first that it would be no go.

So now we thought it was time to do something to rouse him from the stupor of despair, which is always done to heroes when anything baffling has occurred. Besides, we were getting very short of money again – the fortunes of your house cannot be restored (not so that they will last, that is), even by the one pound eight we got when we had the 'good hunting.' We spent a good deal of that on presents for Father's birthday. We got him a paper-weight, like a glass bun, with a picture of Lewisham Church at the bottom; and a blotting-pad, and a box of preserved fruits, and an ivory penholder with a view of Greenwich Park in the little hole where you look through at the top. He was most awfully pleased and surprised, and when he heard how Noël and Oswald had earned the money to buy the things he was more surprised still. Nearly all the rest of our money went to get fireworks for the Fifth of November. We got six Catherine wheels and four rockets; two hand-lights, one red and one green; a sixpenny maroon; two Roman-candles – they cost a shilling; some Italian streamers, a fairy fountain, and a tourbillon that cost eighteen-pence and was very nearly worth it.

But I think crackers and squibs are a mistake. It's true you get a lot of them for the money, and they are not bad fun for the first two or three dozen, but you get jolly sick of them before you've let off your sixpenn'orth. And the only amusing way is not allowed: it is putting them in the fire.

It always seems a long time till the evening when you have got fireworks in the house, and I think as it was a rather foggy day we should have decided to let them off directly after breakfast, only Father had said he would help us to let them off at eight o'clock after he had had his dinner, and you ought never to disappoint your father if you can help it.

You see we had three good reasons for trying H. O.'s idea of restoring the fallen fortunes of our house by becoming bandits on the Fifth of November. We had a fourth reason as well, and that was the best reason of the lot. You remember Dora thought it would be wrong to be bandits. And the Fifth of November came while Dora was away at Stroud staying with her godmother. Stroud is in Gloucestershire. We were determined to do it while she was out of the way, because we did not think it wrong, and besides we meant to do it anyhow.

We held a Council, of course, and laid our plans very carefully. We let H. O. be Captain, because it was his idea. Oswald was Lieutenant. Oswald was quite fair, because he let H. O. call himself Captain; but Oswald is the eldest next to Dora, after all.

Our plan was this. We were all to go up on to the Heath. Our house is in the Lewisham Road, but it's quite close to the Heath if you cut up the short way opposite the confectioner's, past the nursery gardens and the cottage hospital, and turn to the left again and afterwards to the right. You come out then at the top of the hill, where the big guns are with the iron fence round them, and where the bands play on Thursday evenings in the summer.

We were to lurk in ambush there, and waylay an unwary traveller. We were to call upon him to surrender his arms, and then bring him home and put him in the deepest dungeon below the castle moat; then we were to load him with chains and send to his friends for ransom. You may think we had no chains, but you are wrong, because we used to keep two other dogs once, besides Pincher, before the fall of the fortunes of the ancient House of Bastable. And they were quite big dogs.

It was latish in the afternoon before we started. We thought we could lurk better if it was nearly dark. It was rather foggy, and we waited a good while beside the railings, but all the belated travellers were either grown up or else they were Board School children. We weren't going to get into a row with grown-up people – especially strangers – and no true bandit would ever stoop to ask a ransom from the relations of the poor and needy. So we thought it better to wait.

As I said, it was Guy Fawkes Day, and if it had not been we should never have been able to be bandits at all, for the unwary traveller we did catch had been forbidden to go out because he had a cold in his head. But he would run out to follow a guy, without even putting on a coat or a comforter, and it was a very damp, foggy afternoon and nearly dark, so you see it was his own fault entirely, and served him jolly well right.

We saw him coming over the Heath just as we were deciding to go home to tea. He had followed that guy right across to the village (we call Blackheath the village; I don't know why), and he was coming back dragging his feet and sniffing.

'Hist, an unwary traveller approaches!' whispered Oswald.

'Muffle your horses' heads and see to the priming of your pistols,' muttered Alice. She always will play boys' parts, and she makes Ellis cut her hair short on purpose. Ellis is a very obliging hairdresser.

'Steal softly upon him,' said Noël; 'for lo! 'tis dusk, and no human eyes can mark our deeds.'

So we ran out and surrounded the unwary traveller. It turned out to be Albert-next-door, and he was very frightened indeed until he saw who we were.

'Surrender!' hissed Oswald, in a desperate-sounding voice, as he caught the arm of the Unwary. And Albert-next-door said, 'All right! I'm surrendering as hard as I can. You needn't pull my arm off.'

We explained to him that resistance was useless, and I think he saw that from the first. We held him tight by both arms, and we marched him home down the hill in a hollow square of five.

He wanted to tell us about the guy, but we made him see that it was not proper for prisoners to talk to the guard, especially about guys that the prisoner had been told not to go after because of his cold.

When we got to where we live he said, 'All right, I don't want to tell you. You'll wish I had afterwards. You never saw such a guy.'

'I can see *you!*' said H. O. It was very rude, and Oswald told him so at once, because it is his duty as an elder brother. But H. O. is very young and does not know better yet, and besides it wasn't bad for H. O.

Albert-next-door said, 'You haven't any manners, and I want to go in to my tea. Let go of me!'

But Alice told him, quite kindly, that he was not going in to his tea, but coming with us.

'I'm not,' said Albert-next-door; 'I'm going home. Leave go! I've got a bad cold. You're making it worse.' Then he tried to cough, which was very silly, because we'd seen him in the morning, and he'd told us where the cold was that he wasn't to go out with. When he had tried to cough, he said, 'Leave go of me! You see my cold's getting worse.'

'You should have thought of that before,' said Dicky; 'you're coming in with us.'

'Don't be a silly,' said Noël; 'you know we told you at the very beginning that resistance was useless. There is no disgrace in yielding. We are five to your one.'

By this time Eliza had opened the door, and we thought it best to take him in without any more parleying. To parley with a prisoner is not done by bandits.

Directly we got him safe into the nursery, H. O. began to jump about and say, 'Now you're a prisoner really and truly!'

And Albert-next-door began to cry. He always does. I wonder he didn't begin long before – but Alice fetched him one of the dried fruits we gave Father for his birthday. It was a green walnut. I have noticed the walnuts and the plums always get left till the last in the box; the apricots go first, and then the figs and pears; and the cherries, if there are any.

So he ate it and shut up. Then we explained his position to him, so that there should be no mistake, and he couldn't say afterwards that he had not understood.

'There will be no violence,' said Oswald – he was now Captain of the Bandits, because we all know H. O. likes to be Chaplain when we play prisoners – 'no violence. But you will be confined in a dark, subterranean dungeon where toads and snakes crawl, and but little of the light of day filters through the heavily mullioned windows. You will be loaded with chains. Now don't begin again, Baby, there's nothing to cry about; straw will be your pallet; beside you the gaoler will set a ewer – a ewer is only a jug, stupid; it won't eat you – a ewer with water; and a mouldering crust will be your food.'

But Albert-next-door never enters into the spirit of a thing. He mumbled something about tea-time.

Now Oswald, though stern, is always just, and besides we were all rather hungry, and tea was ready. So we had it at once, Albert-next-door and all – and we gave him what was left of the four-pound jar of apricot jam we got with the money Noël got for his poetry. And we saved our crusts for the prisoner.

Albert-next-door was very tiresome. Nobody could have had a nicer prison than he had. We fenced him into a corner with the old wire nursery fender and all the chairs, instead of putting him in the coal-cellar as we had first intended. And when he said the dog-chains were cold the girls were kind enough to warm his fetters thoroughly at the fire before we put them on him.

We got the straw cases of some bottles of wine some-one sent Father one Christmas – it is some years ago, but the cases are quite good. We unpicked them very carefully and pulled them to pieces and scattered the straw about. It made a lovely straw pallet, and took ever so long to make – but Albert-next-door has yet to learn what gratitude really is. We got the bread trencher for the wooden platter where the prisoner's crusts were put – they were not mouldy, but we could not wait till they got so, and for the ewer we got the toilet jug out of the spare-room where nobody ever

Albert-next-door never enters into the spirit of a thing!

sleeps. And even then Albert-next-door couldn't be happy like the rest of us. He howled and cried and tried to get out, and he knocked the ewer over and stamped on the mouldering crusts. Luckily there was no water in the ewer because we had forgotten it, only dust and spiders. So we tied him up with the clothes-line from the back kitchen, and we had to hurry up, which was a pity for him. We might have had him rescued by a devoted page if he hadn't been so tiresome. In fact Noël was actually dressing up for the page when Albert-next-door kicked over the prison ewer.

We got a sheet of paper out of an old exercise-book, and we made H. O. prick his own thumb, because he is our little brother and it is our duty to teach him to be brave. We none of us mind pricking ourselves; we've done it heaps of times. H. O. didn't like it, but he agreed to do it, and I helped him a little because he was so slow, and when he saw the red bead of blood getting fatter and bigger as I squeezed his thumb he was very pleased, just as I had told him he would be.

This is what we wrote with H. O.'s blood, only the blood gave out when we got to 'Restored', and we had to write the rest with crimson lake, which is not the same colour, though I always use it, myself, for painting wounds.

While Oswald was writing it he heard Alice whispering to the prisoner that it would soon be over, and it was only play. The prisoner left off howling, so I pretended not to hear what she said. A Bandit Captain has to overlook things sometimes. This was the letter –

'Albert Morrison is held a prisoner by Bandits. On payment of three thousand pounds he will be restored to his sorrowing relatives, and all will be forgotten and forgiven.'

I was not sure about the last part, but Dicky was certain he had seen it in the paper, so I suppose it must have been all right.

We let H. O. take the letter; it was only fair, as it was his blood it was written with, and told him to leave it next door for Mrs Morrison.

H. O. came back quite quickly, and Albert-next-door's uncle came with him.

'What is all this, Albert?' he cried. 'Alas, alas, my nephew! Do I find you the prisoner of a desperate band of brigands?'

'Bandits,' said H. O., 'you know it says bandits.'

'I beg your pardon, gentlemen,' said Albert-next-door's uncle, 'bandits it is, of course. This, Albert, is the direct result of the pursuit of the guy on an occasion when your doting mother had expressly warned you to forgo the pleasures of the chase.'

Albert said it wasn't his fault, and he hadn't wanted to play.

'So ho!' said his uncle, 'impenitent too! Where's the dungeon?'

We explained the dungeon, and showed him the straw pallet and the ewer and the mouldering crusts and other things.

'Very pretty and complete,' he said. 'Albert, you are more highly privileged than ever I was. No one ever made me a nice dungeon when I was your age. I think I had better leave you where you are.'

Albert began to cry again and said he was sorry, and he would be a good boy.

'And on this old familiar basis you expect me to ransom you, do you? Honestly, my nephew, I doubt whether you are worth it. Besides, the sum mentioned in this document strikes me as excessive: Albert really is *not* worth three thousand pounds. Also by a strange and unfortunate chance I haven't the money about me. Couldn't you take less?'

We said perhaps we could.

'Say eightpence,' suggested Albert-next-door's uncle, 'which is all the small change I happen to have on my person.'

'Thank you very much,' said Alice as he held it out; 'but are you sure you can spare it? Because really it was only play.'

'Quite sure. Now, Albert, the game is over. You had better run home to your mother and tell her how much you've enjoyed yourself.'

When Albert-next-door had gone his uncle sat in the Guy Fawkes armchair and took Alice on his knee, and we sat round the fire waiting till it would be time to let off our fireworks. We roasted the chestnuts he sent Dicky out for, and he told us stories till it was nearly seven. His stories are first-rate – he does all the parts in different voices. At last he said –

'Look here, young-uns. I like to see you play and enjoy yourselves, and I don't think it hurts Albert to enjoy himself too.'

'I don't think he did much,' said H. O. But I knew what Albert-next-door's uncle meant because I am much older than H. O. He went on –

'But what about Albert's mother? Didn't you think how anxious she would be at his not coming home? As it happens I saw him come in with you, so we knew it was all right. But if I hadn't, eh?'

He only talks like that when he is very serious, or even angry. Other times he talks like people in books – to us, I mean.

We none of us said anything. But I was thinking. Then Alice spoke.

Girls seem not to mind saying things that we don't

say. She put her arms round Albert-next-door's uncle's neck and said –

'We're very, very sorry. We didn't think about his mother. You see we try very hard not to think about other people's mothers because –'

Just then we heard Father's key in the door and Albert-next-door's uncle kissed Alice and put her down, and we all went down to meet Father. As we went I thought I heard Albert-next-door's uncle say something that sounded like 'Poor little beggars!'

He couldn't have meant us, when we'd been having such a jolly time, and chestnuts, and fireworks to look forward to after dinner and everything!

BEING EDITORS

It was Albert's uncle who thought of our trying a newspaper. He said he thought we should not find the bandit business a paying industry, as a permanency, and that journalism might be.

We had sold Noël's poetry and that piece of information about Lord Tottenham to the good editor, so we thought it would not be a bad idea to have a newspaper of our own. We saw plainly that editors must be very rich and powerful, because of the grand office and the man in the glass case, like a museum, and the soft carpets and big writing-table. Besides our having seen a whole handful of money that the editor pulled out quite carelessly from his trousers pocket when he gave me my five bob.

Dora wanted to be editor and so did Oswald, but he gave way to her because she is a girl, and afterwards he knew that it is true what it says in the copy-books about Virtue being its own Reward. Because you've no idea what a bother it is. Everybody wanted to put in everything just as they liked, no matter how much room there was on the page. It was simply awful! Dora put up with it as long as she could and then she said if she wasn't let alone she wouldn't go on being editor; they could be the paper's editors themselves, so there.

Then Oswald said, like a good brother: 'I will help you if you like, Dora,' and she said, 'You're more trouble than all the rest of them! Come and be editor

The time the first paper took to write out, no one would believe!

and see how you like it. I give it up to you.' But she didn't, and we did it together. We let Albert-next-door be sub-editor, because he had hurt his foot with a nail in his boot that gathered.

When it was done Albert-next-door's uncle had it copied for us in typewriting, and we sent copies to all our friends, and then of course there was no one left that we could ask to buy it. We did not think of that

87

until too late. We called the paper the *Lewisham Recorder*; Lewisham because we live there, and Recorder in memory of the good editor. I could write a better paper on my head, but an editor is not allowed to write all the paper. It is very hard, but he is not. You just have to fill up with what you can get from other writers. If I ever have time I will write a paper all by myself. It won't be patchy. We had no time to make it an illustrated paper, but I drew the ship going down with all hands for the first copy. But the typewriter can't draw ships, so it was left out in the other copies. The time the first paper took to write out no one would believe! This was the Newspaper:

The Lewisham Recorder

EDITORS: DORA AND OSWALD BASTABLE

Editorial Note

Every paper is written for some reason. Ours is because we want to sell it and get money. If what we have written brings happiness to any sad heart we shall not have laboured in vain. But we want the money too. Many papers are content with the sad heart and the happiness, but we are not like that, and it is best not to be deceitful. EDITORS.

There will be two serial stories; one by Dicky and one by all of us. In a serial story you only put in one chapter at a time. But we shall put all our serial story at once, if Dora has time to copy it. Dicky's will come later on.

Serial Story

BY US ALL

CHAPTER I – *by Dora*

The sun was setting behind a romantic-looking tower when two strangers might have been observed descending the crest of the hill. The eldest, a man in the prime of life; the other a handsome youth who reminded everybody of Quentin Durward. They approached the Castle, in which the fair Lady Alicia awaited her deliverers. She leaned from the castellated window and waved her lily hand as they approached. They returned her signal, and retired to seek rest and refreshment at a neighbouring hostelry.

CHAPTER II – *by Alice*

The Princess was very uncomfortable in the tower, because her fairy godmother had told her all sorts of horrid things would happen if she didn't catch a mouse every day, and she had caught so many mice that now there were hardly any left to catch. So she sent her carrier pigeon to ask the noble strangers if they could send her a few mice – because she would be of age in a few days and then it wouldn't matter. So the fairy godmother – (I'm very sorry, but there's no room to make the chapters any longer. ED.)

CHAPTER III – *by the Sub-Editor*

(I can't – I'd much rather not – I don't know how.)

CHAPTER IV – *by Dicky*

I must now retrace my steps and tell you something about our hero. You must know he had been to an awfully jolly school, where they had turkey and goose every day for dinner, and never any mutton, and as many helps of pudding as a fellow cared to send up his plate for – so of course they had all grown up very strong, and before he left school he challenged the Head to have it out man to man, and he gave it him, I tell you. That was the education that made him able to fight Red Indians, and to be the stranger who might have been observed in the first chapter.

CHAPTER V – *by Noël*

I think it's time something happened in this story. So then the dragon he came out, blowing fire out of his nose, and he said –

> 'Come on, you valiant man and true,
> I'd like to have a set-to along of you!'

(That's bad English. ED. I don't care; it's what the dragon said. Who told you dragons didn't talk bad English? NOËL.)

So the hero, whose name was Noeloninuris, replied –

> 'My blade is sharp, my axe is keen,
> You're not nearly as big as a good many dragons I've seen.'

(Don't put in so much poetry, Noël. It's not fair, because none of the others can do it. ED.)

And then they went at it, and he beat the dragon, just as he did the Head in Dicky's part of the story, and so he married the Princess, and they lived – (No they didn't – not till the last chapter. ED.)

CHAPTER VI – *by H. O.*

I think it's a very nice story – but what about the mice? I don't want to say any more. Dora can have what's left of my chapter.

CHAPTER VII – *by the Editors*

And so when the dragon was dead there were lots of mice, because he used to kill them for his tea; but now they rapidly multiplied and ravaged the country, so the fair lady Alicia, sometimes called the Princess, had to say she would not marry any one unless they could rid the country of this plague of mice. Then the Prince, whose real name didn't begin with N, but was Osrawalddo, waved his magic sword, and the dragon stood before them, bowing gracefully. They made him promise to be good, and then they forgave him; and when the wedding breakfast came, all the bones were saved for him. And so they were married and lived happy ever after.

(What became of the other stranger? NOËL. The dragon ate him because he asked too many questions. EDITORS.)

This is the end of the story.

Instructive

It only takes four hours and a quarter now to get from London to Manchester; but I should not think any one would if they could help it.

A dreadful warning. A wicked boy told me a very instructive thing about ginger. They had opened one of the large jars, and he happened to take out quite a lot, and he made it all right by dropping marbles in, till there was as much ginger as before. But he told me that on the Sunday, when it was coming near the part where there is only juice generally, I had no idea what his feelings were. I don't see what he could have said when they asked him. I should be sorry to act like it.

Scientific

Experiments should always be made out of doors. And don't use benzoline. DICKY.

(That was when he burnt his eyebrows off. ED.)

The earth is 2,400 miles round, and 800 through – at least I think so, but perhaps it's the other way. DICKY.

(You ought to have been sure before you began. ED.)

Scientific Column

In this so-called Nineteenth Century Science is but too little considered in the nurseries of the rich and proud. But we are not like that.

It is not generally known that if you put bits of camphor in luke-warm water it will move about. If you drop sweet oil in, the camphor will dart away and then stop moving. But don't drop any till you are tired of it, because the camphor won't any more afterwards. Much amusement and instruction is lost by not knowing things like this.

If you put a sixpence under a shilling in a wine-glass, and blow hard down the side of the glass, the sixpence will jump up and sit on the top of the shilling. At least I can't do it myself, but my cousin can. He is in the Navy.

Answers to Correspondents

Noël. You are very poetical, but I am sorry to say it will not do.

Alice. Nothing will ever make your hair curl, so it's no use. Some people say it's more important to tidy up as you go along. I don't mean you in particular, but every one.

H. O. We never said you were tubby, but the Editor does not know any cure.

Noël. If there is any of the paper over when this newspaper is finished, I will exchange it for your shut-up inkstand, or the knife that has the useful thing in it for taking stones out of horses' feet, but you can't have it without.

H. O. There are many ways how your steam engine might stop working. You might ask Dicky. He knows one of them. I think it is the way yours stopped.

Noël. If you think that by filling the garden with sand you can make crabs build their nests there you are not at all sensible.

You have altered your poem about the battle of Waterloo so often, that we cannot read it except where the Duke waves his sword and says some thing we can't read either. Why did you write it on blotting-paper with purple chalk? ED.

(Because you know who sneaked my pencil. NOËL.)

BEING EDITORS

Poetry

The Assyrian came down like a wolf on the fold,
And the way he came down was awful, I'm told;
But it's nothing to the way one of the Editors comes down on me,
If I crumble my bread-and-butter or spill my tea. NOËL.

Curious Facts

If you hold a guinea-pig up by his tail his eyes drop out.

You can't do half the things yourself that children in books do, making models or so on. I wonder why? ALICE.

If you take a date's stone out and put in an almond and eat them together, it is prime. I found this out. SUB-EDITOR.

If you put your wet hand into boiling lead it will not hurt you if you draw it out quickly enough. I have never tried this. DORA.

The Purring Class
(INSTRUCTIVE ARTICLE)

If I ever keep a school everything shall be quite different. Nobody shall learn anything they don't want to. And sometimes instead of having masters and mistresses we will have cats, and we will dress up in cat skins and learn purring.

'Now, my dears,' the old cat will say, 'one, two, three – all purr together,' and we shall purr like anything.

She won't teach us to mew, but we shall know how without teaching. Children do know some things without being taught. ALICE.

Poetry
(TRANSLATED INTO FRENCH BY DORA)

Quand j'étais jeune et j'étais fou
J'achetai un violon pour dix-huit sous
Et tous les airs que je jouai
Etait over the hills and far away.

ANOTHER PIECE OF IT

Mercie jolie vache qui fait
Bon lait pour mon déjeuner
Tous les matins tous les soirs
Mon pain je mange, ton lait je boire.

Recreations

It is a mistake to think that cats are playful. I often try to get a cat to play with me, and she never seems to care about the game, no matter how little it hurts. H. O.

Making pots and pans with clay is fun, but do not tell the grown-ups. It is better to surprise them; and then you must say at once how easily it washes off – much easier than ink. DICKY.

Sam Redfern, or the Bushranger's Burial

BY DICKY

'Well, Annie, I have bad news for you,' said Mr Ridgway, as he entered the comfortable dining-room of his cabin in the Bush. 'Sam Redfern the Bushranger is about this part of the Bush just now. I hope he will not attack us with his gang.'

'I hope not,' responded Annie, a gentle maiden of some sixteen summers.

Just then came a knock at the door of the hut, and a gruff voice asked them to open the door.

'It is Sam Redfern the Bushranger, father,' said the girl.

'The same,' responded the voice, and the next moment the hall door was smashed in, and Sam Redfern sprang in, followed by his gang.

CHAPTER II

Annie's Father was at once overpowered, and Annie herself lay bound with cords on the drawing-room sofa. Sam Redfern set a guard round the lonely hut, and all human aid was despaired of. But you never know. Far away in the Bush a different scene was being enacted.

'Must be Injuns,' said a tall man to himself as he pushed his way through the brushwood. It was Jim Carlton, the celebrated detective. 'I know them,' he added; 'they are Apaches.' Just then ten Indians in full war-paint appeared. Carlton raised his rifle and fired, and slinging their scalps on his arm he hastened towards the humble log hut where resided his affianced bride, Annie Ridgway, sometimes known as the Flower of the Bush.

Chapter III

The moon was low on the horizon, and Sam Redfern was seated at a drinking bout with some of his boon companions.

They had rifled the cellars of the hut, and the rich wines flowed like water in the golden goblets of Mr Ridgway.

But Annie had made friends with one of the gang, a noble, good-hearted man who had joined Sam Redfern by mistake, and she had told him to go and get the police as quickly as possible.

'Ha! ha!' cried Redfern, 'now I am enjoying myself.' He little knew that his doom was near upon him.

Just then Annie gave a piercing scream, and Sam Redfern got up, seizing his revolver.

'Who are you?' he cried, as a man entered.

'I am Jim Carlton, the celebrated detective,' said the new arrival.

Sam Redfern's revolver dropped from his nerveless fingers, but the next moment he had sprung upon the detective with the well-known activity of the mountain sheep, and Annie shrieked, for she had grown to love the rough Bushranger.

(*To be continued at the end of the paper if there is room.*)

Scholastic

A new slate is horrid till it is washed in milk. I like the green spots on them to draw patterns round. I know a good way to make a slate-pencil squeak, but I won't put it in because I don't want to make it common. SUB-EDITOR.

Peppermint is a great help with arithmetic. The boy who was second in the Oxford Local always did it. He gave me two. The examiner said to him, 'Are you eating peppermints?' And he said, 'No, sir.' He told me afterwards it was quite true, because he was only sucking one. I'm glad I wasn't asked. I should never have thought of that, and I should have had to say 'Yes.' OSWALD.

The Wreck of the 'Malabar'

BY NOËL

(Author of 'A Dream of Ancient Ancestors.') He isn't really – but he put it in to make it seem more real.

> Hark! what is that noise of rolling
>   Waves and thunder in the air?
> 'Tis the death-knell of the sailors
>   And officers and passengers of the good ship
>
>   Malabar.
>
> It was a fair and lovely noon
>   When the good ship put out of port
> And people said 'Ah little we think
>   How soon she will be the elements' sport.'
>
> She was indeed a lovely sight
>   Upon the billows with sails spread.
> But the captain folded his gloomy arms
>   Ah – if she had been a life-boat instead!
>
> See the captain stern yet gloomy
>   Flings his son upon a rock,
> Hoping that there his darling boy
>   May escape the wreck.
>
> Alas in vain the loud winds roared
>   And nobody was saved.
> That was the wreck of the Malabar,
>   Then let us toll for the brave. NOËL.

Gardening Notes

It is useless to plant cherry-stones in the hope of eating the fruit, because they don't!

Alice won't lend her gardening tools again, because the last time Noël left them out in the rain, and I don't like it. He said he didn't.

Seeds and Bulbs

These are useful to play at shop with, until you are ready. Not at dinner-parties, for they will not grow unless uncooked. Potatoes are not grown with seed, but with chopped-up potatoes. Apple trees are grown from twigs, which is less wasteful.

Oak trees come from acorns. Every one knows this. When Noël says he could grow one from a peach stone wrapped up in oak leaves, he shows that he knows nothing about gardening but marigolds, and when I passed by his garden I thought they seemed just like weeds now the flowers have been picked.

A boy once dared me to eat a bulb.

Dogs are very industrious and fond of gardening. Pincher is always planting bones, but they never grow up. There couldn't be a bone tree. I think this is what makes him bark so unhappily at night. He has never tried planting dog-biscuit, but he is fonder of bones, and perhaps he wants to be quite sure about them first.

Sam Redfern, or the Bushranger's Burial
BY DICKY

CHAPTER IV AND LAST

This would have been a jolly good story if they had let me finish it at the beginning of the paper as I wanted to. But now I have forgotten how I meant it to end, and I have lost my book about Red Indians, and all my *Boys of England* have been sneaked. The girls say 'Good riddance!'

so I expect they did it. They want me just to put in which Annie married, but I shan't, so they will never know.

——

We have now put everything we can think of into the paper. It takes a lot of thinking about. I don't know how

The wreck of the Malabar   O.B.

Sixpence extra for the Malabar *going down with all hands*

grown-ups manage to write all they do. It must make their heads ache, especially lesson books.

Albert-next-door only wrote one chapter of the serial story, but he could have done some more if he had wanted to. He could not write out any of the things because he cannot spell. He says he can, but it takes him such a long time he might just as well not be able. There are one or two things more. I am sick of it, but Dora says she will write them in.

Legal answer wanted. A quantity of excellent string is offered if you know whether there really is a law passed about not buying gunpowder under thirteen. DICKY.

The price of this paper is one shilling each, and sixpence extra for the picture of the *Malabar* going down with all hands. If we sell one hundred copies we will write another paper.

＝＝

And so we would have done, but we never did. Albert-next-door's uncle gave us two shillings, that was all. You can't restore fallen fortunes with two shillings!

THE G.B.

BEING editors is not the best way to wealth. We all feel this now, and highwaymen are not respected any more like they used to be.

I am sure we had tried our best to restore our fallen fortunes. We felt their fall very much, because we knew the Bastables had been rich once. Dora and Oswald can remember when Father was always bringing nice things home from London, and there used to be turkeys and geese and wine and cigars come by the carrier at Christmas-time, and boxes of candied fruit and French plums in ornamental boxes with silk and velvet and gilding on them. They were called prunes, but the prunes you buy at the grocer's are quite different. But now there is seldom anything nice brought from London, and the turkey and the prune people have forgotten Father's address.

'How *can* we restore those beastly fallen fortunes?' said Oswald. 'We've tried digging and writing and princesses and being editors.'

'And being bandits,' said H. O.

'When did you try that?' asked Dora quickly. 'You know I told you it was wrong.'

'It wasn't wrong the way we did it,' said Alice, quicker still, before Oswald could say, 'Who asked you to tell us anything about it?' which would have been rude, and he is glad he didn't. 'We only caught Albert-next-door.'

'Oh, Albert-next-door!' said Dora contemptuously, and I felt more comfortable; for even after I didn't say, 'Who asked you, and cetera,' I was afraid Dora was going to come the good elder sister over us. She does that a jolly sight too often.

Dicky looked up from the paper he was reading and said, 'This sounds likely,' and he read out –

£100 secures partnership in lucrative business for sale of useful patent. £10 weekly. No personal attendance necessary. Jobbins, 300, Old Street Road.

'I wish we could secure that partnership,' said Oswald. He is twelve, and a very thoughtful boy for his age.

Alice looked up from her painting. She was trying to paint a fairy queen's frock with green bice, and it wouldn't rub. There is something funny about green bice. It never will rub off, no matter how expensive your paintbox is – and even boiling water is very little use.

She said, 'Bother the bice! And, Oswald, it's no use thinking about that. Where are we to get a hundred pounds?'

'Ten pounds a week is five pounds to us,' Oswald went on – he had done the sum in his head while Alice was talking – 'because partnership means halves. It would be A 1.'

Noël sat sucking his pencil – he had been writing poetry as usual. I saw the first two lines –

> *I wonder why Green Bice*
> *Is never very nice.*

Suddenly he said, 'I wish a fairy would come down the chimney and drop a jewel on the table – a jewel worth just a hundred pounds.'

'She might as well give you the hundred pounds while she was about it,' said Dora.

'Or while she was about it she might as well give us five pounds a week,' said Alice.

'Or fifty,' said I.

'Or five hundred,' said Dicky.

I saw H. O. open his mouth, and I knew he was going to say, 'Or five thousand,' so I said:

'Well, she won't give us fivepence, but if you'd only do as I am always saying, and rescue a wealthy old gentleman from deadly peril he would give us a pot of money, and we could have the partnership and five pounds a week. Five pounds a week would buy a great many things.'

Then Dicky said, 'Why shouldn't we borrow it?'

So we said, 'Who from?' and then he read this out of the paper –

MONEY PRIVATELY WITHOUT FEES
THE BOND STREET BANK

Manager, Z. Rosenbaum.

Advances cash from £20 to £10,000 on ladies' or gentlemen's note of hand alone, without security. No fees. No inquiries. Absolute privacy guaranteed.

'What does it all mean?' asked H. O.

'It means that there is a kind gentleman who has a lot of money, and he doesn't know enough poor people to help, so he puts it in the paper that he will help them, by lending them his money – that's it, isn't it, Dicky?'

Dora explained this and Dicky said, 'Yes.' And H. O. said he was a Generous Benefactor, like in Miss Edgeworth. Then Noël wanted to know what a note of hand was, and Dicky knew that, because he had read it in a

book, and it was just a letter saying you will pay the
money when you can, and signed with your name.

'No inquiries!' said Alice. 'Oh – Dicky – do you
think he would?'

'Yes, I think so,' said Dicky. 'I wonder Father
doesn't go to this kind gentleman. I've seen his name
before on a circular in Father's study.'

'Perhaps he has,' said Dora.

But the rest of us were sure he hadn't, because, of
course, if he had, there would have been more money
to buy nice things. Just then Pincher jumped up and
knocked over the painting-water. He is a very careless
dog. I wonder why painting-water is always such an
ugly colour? Dora ran for a duster to wipe it up, and
H. O. dropped drops of the water on his hands and
said he had got the plague. So we played at the plague
for a bit, and I was an Arab physician with a bath-
towel turban, and cured the plague with magic acid-
drops. After that it was time for dinner, and after
dinner we talked it all over and settled that we would
go and see the Generous Benefactor the very next day.
But we thought perhaps the G. B. – it is short for
Generous Benefactor – would not like it if there were
so many of us. I have often noticed that it is the worst
of our being six – people think six a great many, when
it's children. That sentence looks wrong somehow. I
mean they don't mind six pairs of boots, or six pounds
of apples, or six oranges, especially in equations, but
they seem to think you ought not to have five brothers
and sisters. Of course Dicky was to go, because it was
his idea. Dora had to go to Blackheath to see an old
lady, a friend of Father's, so she couldn't go. Alice said
she ought to go, because it said, 'Ladies *and* gentlemen,'
and perhaps the G. B. wouldn't let us have the money
unless there were both kinds of us.

H. O. said Alice wasn't a lady; and she said *he* wasn't going, anyway. Then he called her a disagreeable cat, and she began to cry.

But Oswald always tries to make up quarrels, so he said –

'You're little sillies, both of you!'

And Dora said, 'Don't cry, Alice; he only meant you weren't a grown-up lady.'

Then H. O. said, 'What else did you think I meant, Disagreeable?'

So Dicky said, 'Don't be disagreeable yourself, H. O. Let her alone and say you're sorry, or I'll jolly well make you!'

So H. O. said he was sorry. Then Alice kissed him and said she was sorry too; and after that H. O. gave her a hug, and said, 'Now I'm *really and truly* sorry,' so it was all right.

Noël went the last time any of us went to London, so he was out of it, and Dora said she would take him to Blackheath if we'd take H. O. So as there'd been a little disagreeableness we thought it was better to take him, and we did. At first we thought we'd tear our oldest things a bit more, and put some patches of different colours on them, to show the G. B. how much we wanted money. But Dora said that would be a sort of cheating, pretending we were poorer than we are. And Dora is right sometimes, though she is our elder sister. Then we thought we'd better wear our best things, so that the G. B. might see we weren't so very poor that he couldn't trust us to pay his money back when we had it. But Dora said that would be wrong too. So it came to our being quite honest, as Dora said, and going just as we were, without even washing our faces and hands; but when I looked at H. O. in the train I wished we had not been quite so particularly honest.

Every one who reads this knows what it is like to go in the train, so I shall not tell about it – though it was rather fun, especially the part where the guard came for the tickets at Waterloo, and H. O. was under the seat and pretended to be a dog without a ticket. We went to Charing Cross, and we just went round to Whitehall to see the soldiers and then by St James's for the same reason – and when we'd looked in the shops a bit we got to Brook Street, Bond Street. It was a brass plate on a door next to a shop – a very grand place, where they sold bonnets and hats – all very bright and smart, and no tickets on them to tell you the price. We rang a bell and a boy opened the door and we asked for Mr Rosenbaum. The boy was not polite; he did not ask us in. So then Dicky gave him his visiting card; it was one of Father's really, but the name is the same, Mr Richard Bastable, and we others wrote our names underneath. I happened to have a piece of pink chalk in my pocket and we wrote them with that.

Then the boy shut the door in our faces and we waited on the step. But presently he came down and asked our business. So Dicky said –

'Money advanced, young shaver! and don't be all day about it!'

And then he made us wait again, till I was quite stiff in my legs, but Alice liked it because of looking at the hats and bonnets, and at last the door opened, and the boy said –

'Mr Rosenbaum will see you,' so we wiped our feet on the mat, which said so, and we went up stairs with soft carpets and into a room. It was a beautiful room. I wished then we had put on our best things, or at least washed a little. But it was too late now.

The room had velvet curtains and a soft, soft carpet, and it was full of the most splendid things. Black and

It was a beautiful room. I wished we had at least washed a little

gold cabinets, and china, and statues, and pictures.
There was a picture of a cabbage and a pheasant and a
dead hare that was just like life, and I would have
given worlds to have it for my own. The fur was so
natural I should never have been tired of looking at it;
but Alice liked the one of the girl with the broken jug
best. Then besides the pictures there were clocks and
candlesticks and vases, and gilt looking-glasses, and
boxes of cigars and scent and things littered all over
the chairs and tables. It was a wonderful place, and in
the middle of all the splendour was a little old gentleman with a very long black coat and a very long white
beard and a hookey nose – like a falcon. And he put on a
pair of gold spectacles and looked at us as if he knew
exactly how much our clothes were worth. And then,
while we elder ones were thinking how to begin, for we
had all said 'Good morning' as we came in, of course,
H. O. began before we could stop him. He said:

'Are you the G. B. ?'

'The *what?*' said the little old gentleman.

'The G. B.,' said H. O., and I winked at him to shut
up, but he didn't see me, and the G. B. did. He waved
his hand at *me* to shut up, so I had to, and H. O. went
on –

'It stands for Generous Benefactor.'

The old gentleman frowned. Then he said, 'Your
Father sent you here, I suppose?'

'No he didn't,' said Dicky. 'Why did you think so?'

The old gentleman held out the card, and I explained
that we took that because Father's name happens to be
the same as Dicky's.

'Doesn't he know you've come?'

'No,' said Alice, 'we shan't tell him till we've got the
partnership, because his own business worries him a
good deal and we don't want to bother him with ours

till it's settled, and then we shall give him half our share.'

The old gentleman took off his spectacles and rumpled his hair with his hands, then he said, 'Then what *did* you come for?'

'We saw your advertisement,' Dicky said, 'and we want a hundred pounds on our note of hand, and my sister came so that there should be both kinds of us; and we want it to buy a partnership with in the lucrative business for sale of useful patent. No personal attendance necessary.'

'I don't think I quite follow you,' said the G. B. 'But one thing I should like settled before entering more fully into the matter: why did you call me Generous Benefactor?'

'Well, you see,' said Alice, smiling at him to show she wasn't frightened, though I know really she was, awfully, 'we thought it was so *very* kind of you to try to find out the poor people who want money and to help them and lend them your money.'

'Hum!' said the G. B. 'Sit down.'

He cleared the clocks and vases and candlesticks off some of the chairs, and we sat down. The chairs were velvety, with gilt legs. It was like a king's palace.

'Now,' he said, 'you ought to be at school, instead of thinking about money. Why aren't you?'

We told him that we should go to school again when Father could manage it, but meantime we wanted to do something to restore the fallen fortunes of the House of Bastable. And we said we thought the lucrative patent would be a very good thing. He asked a lot of questions, and we told him everything we didn't think Father would mind our telling, and at last he said –

'You wish to borrow money. When will you repay it?'

'As soon as we've got it, of course,' Dicky said.

Then the G. B. said to Oswald, 'You seem the eldest,' but I explained to him that it was Dicky's idea, so my being eldest didn't matter. Then he said to Dicky –

'You are a minor, I presume?'

Dicky said he wasn't yet, but he had thought of being a mining engineer some day, and going to Klondike.

'Minor, not miner,' said the G. B. 'I mean you're not of age?'

'I shall be in ten years, though,' said Dicky.

'Then you might repudiate the loan,' said the G. B., and Dicky said 'What?' Of course he ought to have said 'I beg your pardon. I didn't quite catch what you said' – that is what Oswald would have said. It is more polite than 'What.'

'Repudiate the loan,' the G. B. repeated. 'I mean you might say you would not pay me back the money, and the law could not compel you to do so.'

'Oh, well, if you think we're such sneaks,' said Dicky, and he got up off his chair. But the G. B. said, 'Sit down, sit down; I was only joking.'

Then he talked some more, and at last he said –

'I don't advise you to enter into that partnership. It's a swindle. Many advertisements are. And I have not a hundred pounds by me to-day to lend you. But I will lend you a pound, and you can spend it as you like. And when you are twenty-one you shall pay me back.'

'I shall pay you back long before that,' said Dicky. 'Thanks, awfully! And what about the note of hand?'

'Oh,' said the G. B., 'I'll trust to your honour. Between gentlemen, you know – and ladies' – he made a beautiful bow to Alice – 'a word is as good as a bond.'

Then he took out a sovereign, and held it in his hand while he talked to us. He gave us a lot of good advice about not going into business too young, and about doing our lessons – just swatting a bit, on our own hook, so as not to be put in a low form when we went back to school. And all the time he was stroking the sovereign and looking at it as if he thought it very beautiful. And so it was, for it was a new one. Then at last he held it out to Dicky, and when Dicky put out his hand for it the G. B. suddenly put the sovereign back in his pocket.

'No,' he said, 'I won't give you the sovereign. I'll give you fifteen shillings, and this nice bottle of scent. It's worth far more than the five shillings I'm charging you for it. And, when you can, you shall pay me back the pound, and sixty per cent interest – sixty per cent, sixty per cent –'

'What's that?' said H. O.

The G. B. said he'd tell us that when we paid back the sovereign, but sixty per cent was nothing to be afraid of. He gave Dicky the money. And the boy was made to call a cab, and the G. B. put us in and shook hands with us all, and asked Alice to give him a kiss, so she did, and H. O. would do it too, though his face was dirtier than ever. The G. B. paid the cabman and told him what station to go to, and so we went home.

That evening Father had a letter by the seven-o'clock post. And when he had read it he came up into the nursery. He did not look quite so unhappy as usual, but he looked grave.

'You've been to Mr Rosenbaum's,' he said.

So we told him all about it. It took a long time, and Father sat in the armchair. It was jolly. He doesn't often come and talk to us now. He has to spend all his time thinking about his business. And when we'd told him all about it he said –

'You haven't done any harm this time, children;

rather good than harm, indeed. Mr Rosenbaum has written me a very kind letter.'

'Is he a friend of yours, Father?' Oswald asked.

'He is an acquaintance,' said my father, frowning a

Father said, 'You haven't done any harm this time'

little, 'we have done some business together. And this letter –' He stopped and then said: 'No; you didn't do any harm to-day; but I want you for the future not to do anything so serious as to try to buy a partnership without consulting me, that's all. I don't want to interfere with your plays and pleasures; but you will consult me about business matters, won't you?'

Of course we said we should be delighted, but then Alice, who was sitting on his knee, said, 'We didn't like to bother you.'

Father said, 'I haven't much time to be with you, for my business takes most of my time. It is an anxious business – but I can't bear to think of your being left all alone like this.'

He looked so sad we all said we liked being alone. And then he looked sadder than ever.

Then Alice said, 'We don't mean that exactly, Father. It *is* rather lonely sometimes, since Mother died.'

Then we were all quiet a little while.

Father stayed with us till we went to bed, and when he said good night he looked quite cheerful. So we told him so, and he said –

'Well, the fact is, that letter took a weight off my mind.'

I can't think what he meant – but I am sure the G. B. would be pleased if he could know he had taken a weight off somebody's mind. He is that sort of man, I think.

We gave the scent to Dora. It is not quite such good scent as we thought it would be, but we had fifteen shillings – and they were all good, so is the G. B.

And until those fifteen shillings were spent we felt almost as jolly as though our fortunes had been properly restored. You do not notice your general fortune so much, as long as you have money in your pocket. This is why so many children with regular pocket-money have never felt it their duty to seek for treasure. So, perhaps, our not having pocket-money was a blessing in disguise. But the disguise was quite

impenetrable, like the villains' in the books; and it
seemed still more so when the fifteen shillings were all
spent. Then at last the others agreed to let Oswald try
his way of seeking for treasure, but they were not at all
keen about it, and many a boy less firm than Oswald
would have chucked the whole thing. But Oswald
knew that a hero must rely on himself alone. So he
stuck to it, and presently the others saw their duty, and
backed him up.

LORD TOTTENHAM

OSWALD is a boy of firm and unswerving character, and he had never wavered from his first idea. He felt quite certain that the books were right, and that the best way to restore fallen fortunes was to rescue an old gentleman in distress. Then he brings you up as his own son: but if you preferred to go on being your own father's son I expect the old gentleman would make it up to you some other way. In the books the least thing does it – you put up the railway carriage window – or you pick up his purse when he drops it – or you say a hymn when he suddenly asks you to, and then your fortune is made.

The others, as I said, were very slack about it, and did not seem to care much about trying the rescue. They said there wasn't any deadly peril, and we should have to make one before we could rescue the old gentleman from it, but Oswald didn't see that that mattered. However, he thought he would try some of the easier ways first, by himself.

So he waited about the station, pulling up railway carriage windows for old gentlemen who looked likely – but nothing happened, and at last the porters said he was a nuisance. So that was no go. No one ever asked him to say a hymn, though he had learned a nice short one, beginning 'New every morning' – and when an old gentleman did drop a two-shilling piece just by Ellis's the hairdresser's, and Oswald picked it up, and was just thinking what he should say when he returned it, the old gentleman caught him by the collar and called him a young thief. It would have been very unpleasant for Oswald if he hadn't happened to be a very brave boy, and knew the policeman on that beat very well indeed. So the policeman backed him up, and the old gentleman said he was sorry, and offered Oswald sixpence. Oswald refused it with polite disdain, and nothing more happened at all.

When Oswald had tried by himself and it had not come off, he said to the others, 'We're wasting our time, not trying to rescue the old gentleman in deadly peril. Come – buck up! Do let's do something!'

It was dinner-time, and Pincher was going round getting the bits off the plates. There were plenty because it was cold-mutton day. And Alice said –

'It's only fair to try Oswald's way – he has tried all the things the others thought of. Why couldn't we rescue Lord Tottenham?'

Lord Tottenham is the old gentleman who walks over the Heath every day in a paper collar at three o'clock – and when he gets halfway, if there is no one about, he changes his collar and throws the dirty one into the furze-bushes.

Dicky said, 'Lord Tottenham's all right – but where's the deadly peril?'

And we couldn't think of any. There are no highwaymen on Blackheath now, I am sorry to say. And though Oswald said half of us could be highwaymen and the other half rescue party, Dora kept on saying it would be wrong to be a highwayman – and so we had to give that up.

Then Alice said, 'What about Pincher?'

And we all saw at once that it could be done.

Pincher is very well bred, and he does know one or

two things, though we never could teach him to beg. But if you tell him to hold on – he will do it, even if you only say 'Seize him!' in a whisper.

So we arranged it all. Dora said she wouldn't play; she said she thought it was wrong, and she knew it was silly – so we left her out, and she went and sat in the dining-room with a goody-book, so as to be able to say she didn't have anything to do with it, if we got into a row over it.

Alice and H. O. were to hide in the furze-bushes just by where Lord Tottenham changes his collar, and they were to whisper, 'Seize him!' to Pincher; and then when Pincher had seized Lord Tottenham we were to go and rescue him from his deadly peril. And he would say, 'How can I reward you, my noble young preservers?' and it would be all right.

So we went up to the Heath. We were afraid of being late. Oswald told the others what Procrastination was – so they got to the furze-bushes a little after two o'clock, and it was rather cold. Alice and H. O. and Pincher hid, but Pincher did not like it any more than they did, and as we three walked up and down we heard him whining. And Alice kept saying, 'I *am* so cold! Isn't he coming yet?' And H. O. wanted to come out and jump about to warm himself. But we told him he must learn to be a Spartan boy, and that he ought to be very thankful he hadn't got a beastly fox eating his inside all the time. H. O. is our little brother, and we are not going to let it be our fault if he grows up a milksop. Besides, it was not really cold. It was his knees – he wears socks. So they stayed where they were. And at last, when even the other three who were walking about were beginning to feel rather chilly, we saw Lord Tottenham's big black cloak coming along, flapping in the wind like a great bird. So we said to Alice –

'Hist! he approaches. You'll know when to set Pincher on by hearing Lord Tottenham talking to himself – he always does while he is taking off his collar.'

Then we three walked slowly away whistling to show we were not thinking of anything. Our lips were rather cold, but we managed to do it.

Lord Tottenham came striding along, talking to himself. People call him the mad Protectionist. I don't know what it means – but I don't think people ought to call a Lord such names.

As he passed us he said, 'Ruin of the country, sir! Fatal error, fatal error!' And then we looked back and saw he was getting quite near where Pincher was, and Alice and H. O. We walked on – so that he shouldn't think we were looking – and in a minute we heard Pincher's bark, and then nothing for a bit; and then we looked round, and sure enough good old Pincher had got Lord Tottenham by the trouser leg and was holding on like billy-ho, so we started to run.

Lord Tottenham had got his collar half off – it was sticking out sideways under his ear – and he was shouting, 'Help, help, murder!' exactly as if some one had explained to him beforehand what he was to do. Pincher was growling and snarling and holding on. When we got to him I stopped and said –

'Dicky, we must rescue this good old man.'

Lord Tottenham roared in his fury, 'Good old man be – ' something or othered. 'Call the dog off!'

So Oswald said, 'It is a dangerous task – but who would hesitate to do an act of true bravery?'

And all the while Pincher was worrying and snarling, and Lord Tottenham shouting to us to get the dog away. He was dancing about in the road with Pincher hanging on like grim death; and his collar flapping about, where it was undone.

Good old Pincher had got him by the trouser leg

Then Noël said, 'Haste, ere yet it be too late.' So I said to Lord Tottenham –

'Stand still, aged sir, and I will endeavour to alleviate your distress.'

He stood still, and I stooped down and caught hold of Pincher and whispered, 'Drop it, sir; drop it!'

So then Pincher dropped it, and Lord Tottenham fastened his collar again – he never does change it if there's any one looking – and he said –

'I'm much obliged, I'm sure. Nasty vicious brute! Here's something to drink my health.'

But Dicky explained that we are teetotallers, and do not drink people's healths. So Lord Tottenham said, 'Well, I'm much obliged any way. And now I come to look at you – of course, you're not young ruffians, but gentlemen's sons, eh? Still, you won't be above taking a tip from an old boy – I wasn't when I was your age,' and he pulled out half a sovereign.

It was very silly; but now we'd done it I felt it would be beastly mean to take the old boy's chink after putting him in such a funk. He didn't say anything about bringing us up as his own sons – so I didn't know what to do. I let Pincher go, and was just going to say he was very welcome, and we'd rather not have the money, which seemed the best way out of it, when that beastly dog spoiled the whole show. Directly I let him go he began to jump about at us and bark for joy, and try to lick our faces. He was so proud of what he'd done. Lord Tottenham opened his eyes and he just said, 'The dog seems to know you.'

And then Oswald saw it was all up, and he said, 'Good morning,' and tried to get away. But Lord Tottenham said –

'Not so fast!' And he caught Noël by the collar. Noël gave a howl, and Alice ran out from the bushes.

Noël is her favourite. I'm sure I don't know why. Lord Tottenham looked at her, and he said –

'So there are more of you!' And then H. O. came out.

'Do you complete the party?' Lord Tottenham asked him. And H. O. said there were only five of us this time.

Lord Tottenham turned sharp off and began to walk away, holding Noël by the collar. We caught up with him, and asked him where he was going, and he said, 'To the Police Station.' So then I said quite politely, 'Well, don't take Noël; he's not strong, and he easily gets upset. Besides, it wasn't his doing. If you want to take any one take me – it was my very own idea.'

Dicky behaved very well. He said, 'If you take Oswald I'll go too, but don't take Noël; he's such a delicate little chap.'

Lord Tottenham stopped, and he said, 'You should have thought of that before.' Noël was howling all the time, and his face was very white, and Alice said –

'Oh, do let Noël go, dear, good, kind Lord Tottenham; he'll faint if you don't, I know he will, he does sometimes. Oh, I wish we'd never done it! Dora said it was wrong.'

'Dora displayed considerable common sense,' said Lord Tottenham, and he let Noël go. And Alice put her arm round Noël and tried to cheer him up, but he was all trembly, and as white as paper.

Then Lord Tottenham said –

'Will you give me your word of honour not to try to escape?'

So we said we would.

'Then follow me,' he said, and led the way to a bench. We all followed, and Pincher too, with his tail between his legs – he knew something was wrong. Then

Lord Tottenham sat down, and he made Oswald and Dicky and H. O. stand in front of him, but he let Alice and Noël sit down. And he said –

'You set your dog on me, and you tried to make me believe you were saving me from it. And you would have taken my half-sovereign. Such conduct is most – No – you shall tell me what it is, sir, and speak the truth.'

So I had to say it was most ungentlemanly, but I said I hadn't been going to take the half-sovereign.

'Then what did you do it for?' he asked. 'The truth, mind.'

So I said, 'I see now it was very silly, and Dora said it was wrong, but it didn't seem so till we did it. We wanted to restore the fallen fortunes of our house, and in the books if you rescue an old gentleman from deadly peril, he brings you up as his own son – or if you prefer to be your father's son, he starts you in business, so that you end in wealthy affluence; and there wasn't any deadly peril, so we made Pincher into one – and so – ' I was so ashamed I couldn't go on, for it did seem an awfully mean thing. Lord Tottenham said –

'A very nice way to make your fortune – by deceit and trickery. I have a horror of dogs. If I'd been a weak man the shock might have killed me. What do you think of yourselves, eh?'

We were all crying except Oswald, and the others say he was; and Lord Tottenham went on –

'Well, well, I see you're sorry. Let this be a lesson to you; and we'll say no more about it. I'm an old man now, but I was young once.'

Then Alice slid along the bench close to him, and put her hand on his arm: her fingers were pink through the holes in her woolly gloves, and said, 'I think you're very good to forgive us, and we are really very, very sorry. But we wanted to be like the children in the books – only we never have the chances they have. Everything they do turns out all right. But we *are* sorry, very, very. And I know Oswald wasn't going to take the half-sovereign. Directly you said that about a tip from an old boy I began to feel bad inside, and I whispered to H. O. that I wished we hadn't.'

Then Lord Tottenham stood up, and he looked like the Death of Nelson, for he is clean shaved and it is a good face, and he said –

'Always remember never to do a dishonourable thing, for money or for anything else in the world.'

And we promised we would remember. Then he took off his hat, and we took off ours, and he went away, and we went home. I never felt so cheap in all my life! Dora said, 'I told you so,' but we didn't mind even that so much, though it was indeed hard to bear. It was what Lord Tottenham had said about ungentlemanly. We didn't go on to the Heath for a week after that; but at last we all went, and we waited for him by the bench. When he came along Alice said, 'Please, Lord Tottenham, we have not been on the Heath for a week, to be a punishment because you let us off. And we have brought you a present each if you will take them to show you are willing to make it up.'

He sat down on the bench, and we gave him our presents. Oswald gave him a sixpenny compass – he bought it with my own money on purpose to give him. Oswald always buys useful presents. The needle would not move after I'd had it a day or two, but Lord Tottenham used to be an admiral, so he will be able to make that go all right. Alice had made him a shaving-case, with a rose worked on it. And H. O. gave him his knife – the same one he once cut all the buttons off his best suit with. Dicky gave him his prize, *Naval Heroes*, because it was the best thing he had, and Noël gave him a piece of poetry he had made himself:

> *When sin and shame bow down the brow*
> *Then people feel just like we do now.*
> *We are so sorry with grief and pain*
> *We never will be so ungentlemanly again.*

Lord Tottenham seemed very pleased. He thanked us, and talked to us for a bit, and when he said good-bye he said —

'All's fair weather now, mates,' and shook hands.

And whenever we meet him he nods to us, and if the girls are with us he takes off his hat, so he can't really be going on thinking us ungentlemanly now.

CASTILIAN AMOROSO

ONE day when we suddenly found that we had half a crown we decided that we really ought to try Dicky's way of restoring our fallen fortunes while yet the deed was in our power. Because it might easily have happened to us never to have half a crown again. So we decided to dally no longer with being journalists and bandits and things like them, but to send for sample and instructions how to earn two pounds a week each in our spare time. We had seen the advertisement in the paper, and we had always wanted to do it, but we had never had the money to spare before, somehow. The advertisement says: 'Any lady or gentleman can easily earn two pounds a week in their spare time. Sample and instructions, two shillings. Packed free from observation.' A good deal of the half-crown was Dora's. It came from her godmother; but she said she would not mind letting Dicky have it if he would pay her back before Christmas, and if we were sure it was right to try to make our fortune that way. Of course that was quite easy, because out of two pounds a week in your spare time you can easily pay all your debts, and have almost as much left as you began with; and as to the right we told her to dry up.

Dicky had always thought that this was really the best way to restore our fallen fortunes, and we were glad that now he had a chance of trying, because of course we wanted the two pounds a week each, and besides, we were rather tired of Dicky's always saying, when our ways didn't turn out well, 'Why don't you try the sample and instructions about our spare time?'

When we found out about our half-crown we got the paper. Noël was playing admirals in it, but he had made the cocked hat without tearing the paper, and we found the advertisement, and it said just the same as ever. So we got a two-shilling postal order and a stamp, and what was left of the money it was agreed we would spend in ginger-beer to drink success to trade.

We got some nice paper out of Father's study, and Dicky wrote the letter, and we put in the money and put on the stamp, and made H. O. post it. Then we drank the ginger-beer, and then we waited for the sample and instructions. It seemed a long time coming, and the postman got quite tired of us running out and stopping him in the street to ask if it had come.

But on the third morning it came. It was quite a large parcel, and it was packed, as the advertisement said it would be, 'free from observation.' That means it was in a box; and inside the box was some stiff browny cardboard, crinkled like the galvanized iron on the tops of chicken-houses, and inside that was a lot of paper, some of it printed and same scrappy, and in the very middle of it all a bottle, not very large, and black, and sealed on the top of the cork with yellow sealing-wax.

We looked at it as it lay on the nursery table, and while all the others grabbed at the papers to see what the printing said, Oswald went to look for the cork-screw, so as to see what was inside the bottle. He found the corkscrew in the dresser drawer – it always gets there, though it is supposed to be in the sideboard drawer in the dining-room – and when he got back the others had read most of the printed papers.

'I don't think it's much good, and I don't think it's quite nice to sell wine,' Dora said; 'and besides, it's not easy to suddenly begin to sell things when you aren't used to it.'

'I don't know,' said Alice; 'I believe I could.'

They all looked rather down in the mouth, though, and Oswald asked how you were to make your two pounds a week.

'Why, you've got to get people to taste that stuff in the bottle. It's sherry – Castilian Amoroso its name is – and then you get them to buy it, and then you write to the people and tell them the other people want the wine, and then for every dozen you sell you get two shillings from the wine people, so if you sell twenty dozen a week you get your two pounds. I don't think we shall sell as much as that,' said Dicky.

'We might not the first week,' Alice said, 'but when people found out how nice it was, they would want more and more. And if we only got ten shillings a week it would be something to begin with, wouldn't it?'

Oswald said he should jolly well think it would, and then Dicky took the cork out with the corkscrew. The cork broke a good deal, and some of the bits went into the bottle. Dora got the medicine glass that has the teaspoons and tablespoons marked on it, and we agreed to have a teaspoonful each, to see what it was like.

'No one must have more than that,' Dora said, 'however nice it is.' Dora behaved rather as if it were her bottle. I suppose it was, because she had lent the money for it.

Then she measured out the teaspoonful, and she had first go, because of being the eldest. We asked at once what it was like, but Dora could not speak just then.

Then she said, 'It's like the tonic Noël had in the spring; but perhaps sherry ought to be like that.'

Then it was Oswald's turn. He thought it was very burny; but he said nothing. He wanted to see first what the others would say.

Dicky said his was simply beastly, and Alice said Noël could taste next if he liked.

Noël said it was the golden wine of the gods, but he had to put his handkerchief up to his mouth all the same, and I saw the face he made.

Then H. O. had his, and he spat it out in the fire, which was very rude and nasty, and we told him so.

Then it was Alice's turn. She said, 'Only half a tea-spoonful for me, Dora. We mustn't use it all up.' And she tasted it and said nothing.

Then Dicky said: 'Look here, I chuck this. I'm not going to hawk round such beastly stuff. Any one who likes can have the bottle. *Quis?*'

And Alice got out '*Ego*' before the rest of us. Then she said, 'I know what's the matter with it. It wants sugar.'

And at once we all saw that that was all there was the matter with the stuff. So we got two lumps of sugar and crushed it on the floor with one of the big wooden bricks till it was powdery, and mixed it with some of the wine up to the tablespoon mark, and it was quite different, and not nearly so nasty.

'You see it's all right when you get used to it,' Dicky said. I think he was sorry he had said '*Quis?*' in such a hurry.

'Of course,' Alice said, 'it's rather dusty. We must crush the sugar carefully in clean paper before we put it in the bottle.'

Dora said she was afraid it would be cheating to make one bottle nicer than what people would get when they ordered a dozen bottles, but Alice said Dora always made a fuss about everything, and really it would be quite honest.

'You see,' she said, 'I shall just tell them, quite truthfully, what we have done to it, and when their dozens come they can do it for themselves.'

So then we crushed eight more lumps, very cleanly and carefully between newspapers, and shook it up well in the bottle, and corked it up with a screw of paper, brown and not news, for fear of the poisonous printing ink getting wet and dripping down into the wine and killing people. We made Pincher have a taste, and he sneezed for ever so long, and after that he used to go under the sofa whenever we showed him the bottle.

Then we asked Alice who she would try and sell it to. She said: 'I shall ask everybody who comes to the house. And while we are doing that, we can be thinking of outside people to take it to. We must be careful: there's not much more than half of it left, even counting the sugar.'

We did not wish to tell Eliza – I don't know why. And she opened the door very quickly that day, so that the Taxes and a man who came to our house by mistake for next door got away before Alice had a chance to try them with the Castilian Amoroso. But about five Eliza slipped out for half an hour to see a friend who was making her a hat for Sunday, and while she was gone there was a knock.

Alice went, and we looked over the banisters.

When she opened the door, she said at once, 'Will you walk in, please?'

The person at the door said, 'I called to see your Pa, miss. Is he at home?'

Alice said again, 'Will you walk in, please?'

Then the person – it sounded like a man – said, 'He

is in, then?' But Alice only kept on saying, 'Will you walk in, please?' so at last the man did, rubbing his boots very loudly on the mat. Then Alice shut the front door, and we saw that it was the butcher, with an envelope in his hand. He was not dressed in blue, like when he is cutting up the sheep and things in the shop, and he wore knickerbockers. Alice says he came on a bicycle. She led the way into the dining-room, where the Castilian Amoroso bottle and the medicine glass were standing on the table all ready.

The others stayed on the stairs, but Oswald crept down and looked through the door-crack.

'Please sit down,' said Alice quite calmly, though she told me afterwards I had no idea how silly she felt. And the butcher sat down. Then Alice stood quite still and said nothing, but she fiddled with the medicine glass and put the screw of brown paper straight in the Castilian bottle.

'Will you tell your Pa I'd like a word with him?' the butcher said, when he got tired of saying nothing.

'He'll be in very soon, I think,' Alice said.

And then she stood still again and said nothing. It was beginning to look very idiotic of her, and H. O. laughed. I went back and cuffed him for it quite quietly, and I don't think the butcher heard. But Alice did, and it roused her from her stupor. She spoke suddenly, very fast indeed – so fast that I knew she had made up what she was going to say before. She had got most of it out of the circular.

She said, 'I want to call your attention to a sample of sherry wine I have here. It is called Castilian something or other, and at the price it is unequalled for flavour and bouquet.'

The butcher said, 'Well – I never!'

And Alice went on, 'Would you like to taste it?'

'Thank you very much, I'm sure, miss,' said the butcher.

Alice poured some out.

The butcher tasted a very little. He licked his lips, and we thought he was going to say how good it was. But he did not. He put down the medicine glass with nearly all the stuff left in it (we put it back in the bottle afterwards to save waste) and said, 'Excuse me, miss, but isn't it a little sweet? – for sherry I mean?'

'The *real* isn't,' said Alice. 'If you order a dozen it will come quite different to that – we like it best with sugar. I wish you *would* order some.'

The butcher asked why.

Alice did not speak for a minute, and then she said –

'I don't mind telling *you*: you are in business yourself, aren't you? We are trying to get people to buy it, because we shall have two shillings for every dozen we can make any one buy. It's called a purr something.'

'A percentage. Yes, I see,' said the butcher, looking at the hole in the carpet.

'You see there are reasons,' Alice went on, 'why we want to make our fortunes as quickly as we can.'

'Quite so,' said the butcher, and he looked at the place where the paper is coming off the wall.

'And this seems a good way,' Alice went on. 'We paid two shillings for the sample and instructions, and it says you can make two pounds a week easily in your leisure time.'

'I'm sure I hope you may, miss,' said the butcher.

And Alice said again would he buy some?

'Sherry is my favourite wine,' he said.

Alice asked him to have some more to drink.

'No, thank you, miss,' he said; 'it's my favourite wine, but it doesn't agree with me; not the least bit. But I've an uncle drinks it. Suppose I ordered him half a dozen for a Christmas present? Well, miss, here's the shilling commission, anyway,' and he pulled out a handful of money and gave her the shilling.

'But I thought the wine people paid that,' Alice said.

But the butcher said not on half-dozens they didn't. Then he said he didn't think he'd wait any longer for Father – but would Alice ask Father to write him?

Alice offered him the sherry again, but he said something about 'Not for worlds!' – and then she let him out and came back to us with the shilling, and said, 'How's that?' And we said 'A 1.'

And all the evening we talked of our fortune that we had begun to make.

Nobody came next day, but the day after a lady came to ask for money to build an orphanage for the children of dead sailors. And we saw her. I went in with Alice. And when we had explained to her that we had only a shilling and we wanted it for something else, Alice suddenly said, 'Would you like some wine?'

And the lady said, 'Thank you very much,' but she looked surprised. She was not a young lady, and she had a mantle with beads, and the beads had come off in places – leaving a browny braid showing, and she had printed papers about the dead sailors in a sealskin bag, and the seal had come off in places, leaving the skin bare.

We gave her a tablespoonful of the wine in a proper wine-glass out of the sideboard, because she was a lady. And when she had tasted it she got up in a very great hurry, and shook out her dress and snapped her bag shut, and said, 'You naughty, wicked children! What do you mean by playing a trick like this? You ought to be ashamed of yourselves! I shall write to your Mamma about it. You dreadful little girl! – you might have poisoned me. But your Mamma . . .'

Then Alice said, 'I'm very sorry; the butcher liked it, only he said it was sweet. And please don't write to Mother. It makes Father so unhappy when letters come for her!' – and Alice was very near crying.

'What do you mean, you silly child?' said the lady, looking quite bright and interested. 'Why doesn't your Father like your Mother to have letters – eh?'

And Alice said, '*Oh*, you . . .!' and began to cry, and bolted out of the room.

Then I said, 'Our Mother is dead, and will you please go away now?'

The lady looked at me a minute, and then she looked quite different, and she said, 'I'm very sorry. I didn't know. Never mind about the wine. I daresay your little sister meant it kindly.' And she looked round the room just like the butcher had done. Then she said again, 'I didn't know – I'm very sorry. . . .'

So I said, 'Don't mention it,' and shook hands with her, and let her out. Of course we couldn't have asked her to buy the wine after what she'd said. But I think she was not a bad sort of person. I do like a person to say they're sorry when they ought to be – especially a grown-up. They do it so seldom. I suppose that's why we think so much of it.

But Alice and I didn't feel jolly for ever so long afterwards. And when I went back into the dining-room I saw how different it was from when Mother was here, and we are different, and Father is different, and nothing is like it was. I am glad I am not made to think about it every day.

I went and found Alice, and told her what the lady had said, and when she had finished crying we put away the bottle and said we would not try to sell any more to people who came. And we did not tell the others – we only said the lady did not buy any – but we

went up on the Heath, and some soldiers went by and
there was a Punch-and-Judy show, and when we came
back we were better.

The bottle got quite dusty where we had put it, and
perhaps the dust of ages would have laid thick and
heavy on it, only a clergyman called when we were all
out. He was not our own clergyman – Mr Bristow is
our own clergyman, and we all love him, and we
would not try to sell sherry to people we like, and make
two pounds a week out of them in our spare time. It
was another clergyman, just a stray one; and he asked
Eliza if the dear children would not like to come to his
little Sunday school. We always spend Sunday afternoons with Father. But as he had left the name of his
vicarage with Eliza, and asked her to tell us to come,
we thought we would go and call on him, just to
explain about Sunday afternoons, and we thought we
might as well take the sherry with us.

'I won't go unless you all go too,' Alice said, 'and I
won't do the talking.'

Dora said she thought we had much better not go;
but we said 'Rot!' and it ended in her coming with us,
and I am glad she did.

Oswald said he would do the talking if the others
liked, and he learned up what to say from the printed
papers.

We went to the Vicarage early on Saturday afternoon, and rang at the bell. It is a new red house with
no trees in the garden, only very yellow mould and
gravel. It was all very neat and dry. Just before we
rang the bell we heard some one inside call 'Jane!
Jane!' and we thought we would not be Jane for anything. It was the sound of the voice that called that
made us sorry for her.

The door was opened by a very neat servant in

black, with a white apron; we saw her tying the strings as she came along the hall, through the different-coloured glass in the door. Her face was red, and I think she was Jane.

We asked if we could see Mr Mallow.

The servant said Mr Mallow was very busy with his sermon just then, but she would see.

But Oswald said, 'It's all right. He asked us to come.'

So she let us all in and shut the front door, and showed us into a very tidy room with a bookcase full of a lot of books covered in black cotton with white labels, and some dull pictures, and a harmonium. And Mr Mallow was writing at a desk with drawers, copying something out of a book. He was stout and short, and wore spectacles.

He covered his writing up when we went in – I didn't know why. He looked rather cross, and we heard Jane or somebody being scolded outside by the voice. I hope it wasn't for letting us in, but I have had doubts.

'Well,' said the clergyman, 'what is all this about?'

'You asked us to call,' Dora said, 'about your little Sunday school. We are the Bastables of Lewisham Road.'

'Oh – ah, yes,' he said; 'and shall I expect you all to-morrow?' He took up his pen and fiddled with it, and he did not ask us to sit down. But some of us did.

'We always spend Sunday afternoon with Father,' said Dora; 'but we wished to thank you for being so kind as to ask us.'

'And we wished to ask you something else!' said Oswald; and he made a sign to Alice to get the sherry ready in the glass. She did – behind Oswald's back while he was speaking.

'My time is limited,' said Mr Mallow, looking at his watch; 'but still – ' Then he muttered something about the fold, and went on: ' Tell me what is troubling you, my little man, and I will try to give you any help in my power. What is it you want?'

Then Oswald quickly took the glass from Alice, and held it out to him, and said, 'I want your opinion on that.'

'On *that*,' he said. 'What is it?'

'It is a shipment,' Oswald said; 'but it's quite enough for you to taste.' Alice had filled the glass half-full; I suppose she was too excited to measure properly.

'A shipment?' said the clergyman, taking the glass in his hand.

'Yes,' Oswald went on; 'an exceptional opportunity. Full-bodied and nutty.'

'It really does taste rather like one kind of Brazil-nut.' Alice put her oar in as usual.

The Vicar looked from Alice to Oswald, and back again, and Oswald went on with what he had learned from the printing. The clergyman held the glass at half-arm's-length, stiffly, as if he had caught cold.

'It is of a quality never before offered at the price. Old Delicate Amoro – what's its name –'

'Amorolio,' said H. O.

'Amoroso,' said Oswald. 'H. O., you just shut up – Castilian Amoroso – it's a true after-dinner wine, stimulating and yet . . .'

'*Wine?*' said Mr Mallow, holding the glass further off. 'Do you *know*,' he went on, making his voice very thick and strong (I expect he does it like that in church), 'have you never been *taught* that it is the drinking of *wine* and *spirits* – yes, and BEER, which makes half the homes in England full of *wretched* little children, and *degraded*, MISERABLE parents?'

'Not if you put sugar in it,' said Alice firmly; 'eight

135

'Wine?' said Mr Mallow, 'Have you never been taught . .'

lumps and shake the bottle. We have each had more than a teaspoonful of it, and we were not ill at all. It was something else that upset H. O. Most likely all those acorns he got out of the Park.'

The clergyman seemed to be speechless with conflicting emotions, and just then the door opened and a lady came in. She had a white cap with lace, and an ugly violet flower in it, and she was tall, and looked very strong, though thin. And I do believe she had been listening at the door.

'But why,' the Vicar was saying, 'why did you bring this dreadful fluid, this curse of our country, to *me* to taste?'

'Because we thought you might buy some,' said Dora, who never sees when a game is up. 'In books the parson loves his bottle of old port; and new sherry is just as good – with sugar – for people who like sherry. And if you would order a dozen of the wine, then we should get two shillings.'

The lady said (and it *was* the voice), 'Good gracious! Nasty, sordid little things! Haven't they any one to teach them better?'

And Dora got up and said, 'No, we are not those things you say; but we are sorry we came here to be called names. We want to make our fortune just as much as Mr Mallow does – only no one would listen to us if we preached, so it's no use our copying out sermons like him.'

And I think that was smart of Dora, even if it was rather rude.

Then I said perhaps we had better go, and the lady said, 'I should think so!' But when we were going to wrap up the bottle and glass the clergyman said, 'No; you can leave that,' and we were so upset we did, though it wasn't his after all.

We walked home very fast and not saying much, and the girls went up to their rooms. When I went to tell them tea was ready, and there was a teacake, Dora was crying like anything and Alice hugging her. I am afraid there is a great deal of crying in this chapter, but I can't help it. Girls will sometimes; I suppose it is their nature, and we ought to be sorry for their affliction.

'It's no good,' Dora was saying, 'you all hate me, and you think I'm a prig and a busybody, but I do try to do right – oh, I do! Oswald, go away; don't come here making fun of me!'

So I said, 'I'm not making fun, Sissy; don't cry, old girl.'

Mother taught me to call her Sissy when we were very little and before the others came, but I don't often somehow, now we are old. I patted her on the back, and she put her head against my sleeve, holding on to Alice all the time, and she went on. She was in that laughy-cryey state when people say things they wouldn't say at other times.

'Oh dear, oh dear – I do try, I do. And when Mother died she said, "Dora, take care of the others, and teach them to be good, and keep them out of trouble and make them happy." She said, "Take care of them for me, Dora dear." And I *have* tried, and all of you hate me for it; and to-day I let you do this, though I knew all the time it was silly.'

I hope you will not think I was a muff, but I kissed Dora for some time. Because girls like it. And I will never say again that she comes the good elder sister too much. And I have put all this in though I do hate telling about it, because I own I have been hard on Dora, but I never will be again. She is a good old sort; of course we never knew before about what Mother told her, or we wouldn't have ragged her as we did. We did not tell the little ones, but I got Alice to speak to Dicky, and we three can sit on the others if requisite.

This made us forget all about the sherry; but about eight o'clock there was a knock, and Eliza went, and we saw it was poor Jane, if her name was Jane, from the Vicarage. She handed in a brown-paper parcel and a letter. And three minutes later Father called us into his study.

On the table was the brown-paper parcel, open, with our bottle and glass on it, and Father had a letter in his hand. He pointed to the bottle and sighed, and said, 'What have you been doing now?' The letter in his hand was covered with little black writing, all over the four large pages.

So Dicky spoke up, and he told Father the whole thing, as far as he knew it, for Alice and I had not told about the dead sailors' lady.

And when he had done, Alice said, 'Has Mr Mallow written to you to say he will buy a dozen of the sherry after all? It is really not half bad with sugar in it.'

Father said no, he didn't think clergymen could afford such expensive wine; and he said *he* would like to taste it. So we gave him what there was left, for we had decided coming home that we would give up trying for the two pounds a week in our spare time.

Father tasted it, and then he acted just as H. O. had done when he had his teaspoonful, but of course we did not say anything. Then he laughed till I thought he would never stop.

I think it was the sherry, because I am sure I have read somewhere about 'wine that maketh glad the heart of man'. He had only a very little, which shows that it was a good after-dinner wine, stimulating, and yet . . . I forget the rest.

But when he had done laughing he said, 'It's all

right, kids. Only don't do it again. The wine trade is overcrowded; and besides, I thought you promised to consult me before going into business?'

'Before buying one I thought you meant,' said Dicky. 'This was only on commission.' And Father laughed again. I am glad we got the Castilian Amoroso, because it did really cheer Father up, and you cannot always do that, however hard you try, even if you make jokes, or give him a comic paper.

THE NOBLENESS OF OSWALD

THE part about his nobleness only comes at the end, but you would not understand it unless you knew how it began. It began, like nearly everything about that time, with treasure-seeking.

Of course as soon as we had promised to consult my Father about business matters we all gave up wanting to go into business. I don't know how it is, but having to consult about a thing with grown-up people, even the bravest and the best, seems to make the thing not worth doing afterwards.

We don't mind Albert's uncle chipping in sometimes when the thing's going on, but we are glad he never asked us to promise to consult him about anything. Yet Oswald saw that my Father was quite right; and I daresay if we had had that hundred pounds we should have spent it on the share in that lucrative business for the sale of useful patent, and then found out afterwards that we should have done better to spend the money in some other way. My Father says so, and he ought to know. We had several ideas about that time, but having so little chink always stood in the way. This was the case with H. O.'s idea of setting up a coconut-shy on this side of the Heath, where there are none generally. We had no sticks or wooden balls, and the greengrocer said he could not book so many as twelve dozen coconuts without Mr Bastable's written order. And as we did not wish to consult my Father it was decided to drop it. And when Alice dressed up Pincher in some of the dolls' clothes and we made up our minds to take him round with an organ as soon as we had taught him to dance, we were stopped at once by Dicky's remembering how he had once heard that an organ cost seven hundred pounds. Of course this was the big church kind, but even the ones on three legs can't be got for one-and-sevenpence, which was all we had when we first thought of it. So we gave that up too.

It was a wet day, I remember, and mutton hash for dinner – very tough with pale gravy with lumps in it. I think the others would have left a good deal on the sides of their plates, although they know better, only Oswald said it was a savoury stew made of the red deer that Edward shot. So then we were the Children of the New Forest, and the mutton tasted much better. No one in the New Forest minds venison being tough and the gravy pale.

Then after dinner we let the girls have a dolls' tea-party, on condition they didn't expect us boys to wash up; and it was when we were drinking the last of the liquorice water out of the little cups that Dicky said –

'This reminds me.'

So we said, 'What of?'

Dicky answered us at once, though his mouth was full of bread with liquorice stuck in it to look like cake. You should not speak with your mouth full, even to your own relations, and you shouldn't wipe your mouth on the back of your hand, but on your handkerchief, if you have one. Dicky did not do this. He said –

'Why, you remember when we first began about treasure-seeking, I said I had thought of something, only I could not tell you because I hadn't finished thinking about it.'

We said 'Yes.'

'Well, this liquorice water –'

'Tea,' said Alice softly.

'Well, tea then – made me think.' He was going on to say what it made him think, but Noël interrupted and cried out, 'I say; let's finish off this old tea-party and have a council of war.'

So we got out the flags and the wooden sword and the drum, and Oswald beat it while the girls washed up, till Eliza came up to say she had the jumping toothache, and the noise went through her like a knife. So of course Oswald left off at once. When you are polite to Oswald he never refuses to grant your requests.

When we were all dressed up we sat down round the camp fire, and Dicky began again.

'Every one in the world wants money. Some people get it. The people who get it are the ones who see things. I have seen one thing.'

Dicky stopped and smoked the pipe of peace. It is the pipe we did bubbles with in the summer, and somehow it has not got broken yet. We put tea-leaves in it for the pipe of peace, but the girls are not allowed to have any. It is not right to let girls smoke. They get to think too much of themselves if you let them do everything the same as men.

Oswald said, 'Out with it.'

'I see that glass bottles only cost a penny. H. O., if you dare to snigger I'll send you round selling old bottles, and you shan't have any sweets except out of the money you get for them. And the same with you, Noël.'

'Noël wasn't sniggering,' said Alice in a hurry; 'it is only his taking so much interest in what you were saying makes him look like that. Be quiet, H. O., and don't you make faces, either. Do go on, Dicky dear.'

So Dicky went on.

'There must be hundreds of millions of bottles of medicines sold every year. Because all the different medicines say, "Thousands of cures daily," and if you only take that as two thousand, which it must be, at least, it mounts up. And the people who sell them must make a great deal of money by them because they are nearly always two-and-ninepence the bottle, and three-and-six for one nearly double the size. Now the bottles, as I was saying, don't cost anything like that.'

'It's the medicine costs the money,' said Dora; 'look how expensive jujubes are at the chemist's, and pepper-mints too.'

'That's only because they're nice,' Dicky explained; 'nasty things are not so dear. Look what a lot of brim-stone you get for a penny, and the same with alum. We would not put the nice kinds of chemist's things in our medicine.'

Then he went on to tell us that when we had invented our medicine we would write and tell the editor about it, and he would put it in the paper, and then people would send their two-and-ninepence and three-and-six for the bottle nearly double the size, and then when the medicine had cured them they would write to the paper and their letters would be printed, saying how they had been suffering for years, and never thought to get about again, but thanks to the blessing of our ointment –

Dora interrupted and said, 'Not ointment – it's so messy.' And Alice thought so too. And Dicky said he did not mean it, he was quite decided to let it be in bottles. So now it was all settled, and we did not see at the time that this would be a sort of going into business, but afterwards when Albert's uncle showed us we saw it, and we were sorry. We only had to invent the medicine. You might think that was easy, because of the number of them you see every day in the paper, but it is much harder than you think. First we had to decide what sort of illness we should like to cure, and a 'heated discussion ensued', like in Parliament.

Dora wanted it to be something to make the complexion of dazzling fairness, but we remembered how her face came all red and rough when she used the Rosabella soap that was advertised to make the darkest complexion fair as the lily, and she agreed that perhaps it was better not. Noël wanted to make the medicine first and then find out what it would cure, but Dicky thought not, because there are so many more medicines than there are things the matter with us, so it would be easier to choose the disease first.

Oswald would have liked wounds. I still think it was a good idea, but Dicky said, 'Who has wounds, especially now there aren't any wars? We shouldn't sell a bottle a day!' So Oswald gave in because he knows what manners are, and it was Dicky's idea. H. O. wanted a cure for the uncomfortable feeling that they give you powders for, but we explained to him that grown-up people do not have this feeling, however much they eat, and he agreed. Dicky said he did not care a straw what the loathsome disease was, as long as we hurried up and settled on something. Then Alice said –

'It ought to be something very common, and only one thing. Not the pains in the back and all the hundreds of things the people have in somebody's syrup. What's the commonest thing of all?'

And at once we said, 'Colds.'

So that was settled.

Then we wrote a label to go on the bottle. When it was written it would not go on the vinegar bottle that we had got, but we knew it would go small when it was printed. It was like this:

BASTABLE'S
CERTAIN CURE FOR COLDS

Coughs, Asthma, Shortness of Breath, and all infections
of the Chest

One dose gives immediate relief
It will cure your cold in one bottle
Especially the larger size at 3s. 6d.
Order at once of the Makers
To prevent disappointment

Makers:

D., O., R., A., N., & H. O. BASTABLE
150 Lewisham Road, s.e.
(*A halfpenny for all bottles returned*)

—

Of course the next thing was for one of us to catch a cold and try what cured it; we all wanted to be the one, but it was Dicky's idea, and he said he was not going to be done out of it, so we let him. It was only fair. He left off his undershirt that very day, and next morning he stood in a draught in his nightgown for quite a long time. And we damped his day-shirt with the nail-brush before he put it on. But all was vain. They always tell you that these things will give you cold, but we found it was not so.

So then we all went over to the Park, and Dicky went right into the water with his boots on, and stood there as long as he could bear it, for it was rather cold, and we stood and cheered him on. He walked home in his wet clothes, which they say is a sure thing, but it was no go, though his boots were quite spoiled. And three days after Noël began to cough and sneeze.

So then Dicky said it was not fair.

'I can't help it,' Noël said. 'You should have caught it yourself, then it wouldn't have come to me.'

And Alice said she had known all along Noël oughtn't to have stood about on the bank cheering in the cold.

Noël had to go to bed, and then we began to make the medicines; we were sorry he was out of it, but he had the fun of taking the things.

We made a great many medicines. Alice made herb tea. She got sage and thyme and savory and marjoram and boiled them all up together with salt and water, but she would put parsley in too. Oswald is sure parsley is not a herb. It is only put on the cold meat and you are not supposed to eat it. It kills parrots to eat parsley, I believe. I expect it was the parsley that disagreed so with Noël. The medicine did not seem to do the cough any good.

Oswald got a pennyworth of alum, because it is so cheap, and some turpentine which every one knows is good for colds, and a little sugar and an aniseed ball. These were mixed in a bottle with water, but Eliza threw it away and said it was nasty rubbish, and I hadn't any money to get more things with.

Dora made him some gruel, and he said it did his chest good; but of course that was no use, because you cannot put gruel in bottles and say it is medicine. It would not be honest, and besides nobody would believe you.

Dick mixed up lemon-juice and sugar and a little of the juice of the red flannel that Noël's throat was done up in. It comes out beautifully in hot water. Noël took this and he liked it. Noël's own idea was liquorice-water, and we let him have it, but it is too plain and black to sell in bottles at the proper price.

Noël liked H. O.'s medicine the best, which was silly of him, because it was only peppermints melted in hot water, and a little cobalt to make it look blue. It was all right, because H. O.'s paint-box is the French kind, with *Couleurs non Vénéneuses* on it. This means you may suck your brushes if you want to, or even your paints if you are a very little boy.

It was rather jolly while Noël had that cold. He had a fire in his bedroom which opens out of Dicky's and Oswald's, and the girls used to read aloud to Noël all day; they will not read aloud to you when you are well. Father was away at Liverpool on business, and Albert's uncle was at Hastings. We were rather glad of this, because we wished to give all the medicines a fair trial, and grown-ups are but too fond of interfering. As if we should have given him anything poisonous!

His cold went on – it was bad in his head, but it was not one of the kind when he has to have poultices and can't sit up in bed. But when it had been in his head nearly a week, Oswald happened to tumble over Alice on the stairs. When we got up she was crying.

'Don't cry silly!' said Oswald; 'you know I didn't hurt you.' I was very sorry if I had hurt her, but you ought not to sit on the stairs in the dark and let other people tumble over you. You ought to remember how beastly it is for them if they do hurt you.

'Oh, it's not that, Oswald,' Alice said. 'Don't be a pig! I am so miserable. Do be kind to me.'

So Oswald thumped her on the back and told her to shut up.

'It's about Noël,' she said. 'I'm sure he's very ill; and playing about with medicines is all very well, but I know he's ill, and Eliza won't send for the doctor: she says it's only a cold. And I know the doctor's bills are awful. I heard Father telling Aunt Emily so in the summer. But he *is* ill, and perhaps he'll die or something.'

Then she began to cry again. Oswald thumped her again, because he knows how a good brother ought to behave, and said, 'Cheer up.' If we had been in a book Oswald would have embraced his little sister tenderly, and mingled his tears with hers.

Then Oswald said, 'Why not write to Father?' And she cried more and said, 'I've lost the paper with the address. H. O. had it to draw on the back of, and I can't find it now; I've looked everywhere. I'll tell you what I'm going to do. No I won't. But I'm going out. Don't tell the others. And I say, Oswald, do pretend I'm in if Eliza asks. Promise.'

'Tell me what you're going to do,' I said. But she said 'No'; and there was a good reason why not. So I said I wouldn't promise if it came to that. Of course I meant to all right. But it did seem mean of her not to tell me.

So Alice went out by the side door while Eliza was setting tea, and she was a long time gone; she was not in to tea. When Eliza asked Oswald where she was he said he did not know, but perhaps she was tidying her corner drawer. Girls often do this, and it takes a long time. Noël coughed a good bit after tea, and asked for Alice. Oswald told him she was doing something and it was a secret. Oswald did not tell any lies even to save his sister. When Alice came back she was very quiet, but she whispered to Oswald that it was all right. When it was rather late Eliza said she was going out to post a letter. This always takes her an hour, because she will go to the post-office across the Heath instead of the pillar-box, because once a boy dropped fusees in our pillar-box and burnt the letters. It was not any of us; Eliza told us about it. And when there was a knock

... the Presence had a cold in its head

at the door a long time after we thought it was Eliza
come back, and that she had forgotten the back-door
key. We made H. O. go down to open the door,
because it is his place to run about: his legs are younger
than ours. And we heard boots on the stairs besides
H. O.'s, and we listened spell-bound till the door
opened, and it was Albert's uncle. He looked very tired.

'I am glad you've come,' Oswald said. 'Alice began
to think Noël –'

Alice stopped me, and her face was very red, her nose was shiny too, with having cried so much before tea.

She said, 'I only said I thought Noël ought to have the doctor. Don't you think he ought?' She got hold of Albert's uncle and held on to him.

'Let's have a look at you, young man,' said Albert's uncle, and he sat down on the edge of the bed. It is a rather shaky bed, the bar that keeps it steady underneath got broken when we were playing burglars last winter. It was our crowbar. He began to feel Noël's pulse, and went on talking.

'It was revealed to the Arab physician as he made merry in his tents on the wild plains of Hastings that the Presence had a cold in its head. So he immediately seated himself on the magic carpet, and bade it bear him hither, only pausing in the flight to purchase a few sweetmeats in the bazaar.'

He pulled out a jolly lot of chocolate and some butter-scotch, and grapes for Noël. When we had all said thank you, he went on.

'The physician's are the words of wisdom: it's high time this kid was asleep. I have spoken. Ye have my leave to depart.'

So we bunked, and Dora and Albert's uncle made Noël comfortable for the night.

Then they came to the nursery which we had gone down to, and he sat down in the Guy Fawkes chair and said, ' Now then.'

Alice said, 'You may tell them what I did. I daresay they'll all be in a wax, but I don't care.'

'I think you were very wise,' said Albert's uncle, pulling her close to him to sit on his knee. 'I am very glad you telegraphed.'

So then Oswald understood what Alice's secret was.

She had gone out and sent a telegram to Albert's uncle at Hastings. But Oswald thought she might have told him. Afterwards she told me what she had put in the telegram. It was, 'Come home. We have given Noël a cold, and I think we are killing him.' With the address it came to tenpence-halfpenny.

Then Albert's uncle began to ask questions, and it all came out, how Dicky had tried to catch the cold, but the cold had gone to Noël instead, and about the medicines and all. Albert's uncle looked very serious.

'Look here,' he said, 'you're old enough not to play the fool like this. Health is the best thing you've got; you ought to know better than to risk it. You might have killed your little brother with your precious medicines. You've had a lucky escape, certainly. But poor Noël!'

'Oh, do you think he's going to die?' Alice asked that, and she was crying again.

'No, no,' said Albert's uncle; 'but look here. Do you see how silly you've been? And I thought you promised your Father –' And then he gave us a long talking-to. He can make you feel most awfully small. At last he stopped, and we said we were very sorry, and he said, 'You know I promised to take you all to the panto-mime?'

So we said, 'Yes,' and knew but too well that now he wasn't going to. Then he went on –

'Well, I will take you if you like, or I will take Noël to the sea for a week to cure his cold. Which is it to be?'

Of course he knew we should say, 'Take Noël' and we did; but Dicky told me afterwards he thought it was hard on H. O.

Albert's uncle stayed till Eliza came in, and then he

said good night in a way that showed us that all was forgiven and forgotten.

And we went to bed. It must have been the middle of the night when Oswald woke up suddenly, and there was Alice with her teeth chattering, shaking him to wake him.

'Oh, Oswald!' she said, 'I am so unhappy. Suppose I should die in the night!'

Oswald told her to go to bed and not gas. But she said, 'I must tell you; I wish I'd told Albert's uncle. I'm a thief, and if I die to-night I know where thieves go to.'

So Oswald saw it was no good and he sat up in bed and said –

'Go ahead.'

So Alice stood shivering and said –

'I hadn't enough money for the telegram, so I took the bad sixpence out of the exchequer. And I paid for it with that and the fivepence I had. And I wouldn't tell you, because if you'd stopped me doing it I couldn't have borne it; and if you'd helped me you'd have been a thief too. Oh, what shall I do?'

Oswald thought a minute, and then he said –

'You'd better have told me. But I think it will be all right if we pay it back. Go to bed. Cross with you? No, stupid! Only another time you'd better not keep secrets.' So she kissed Oswald, and he let her, and she went back to bed. The next day Albert's uncle took Noël away, before Oswald had time to persuade Alice that we ought to tell him about the sixpence. Alice was very unhappy, but not so much as in the night: you can be very miserable in the night if you have done anything wrong and you happen to be awake. I know this for a fact.

None of us had any money except Eliza, and she wouldn't give us any unless we said what for; and of course we could not do that because of the honour of the family. And Oswald was anxious to get the sixpence to give to the telegraph people because he feared that the badness of that sixpence might have been found out, and that the police might come for Alice at any moment. I don't think I ever had such an unhappy day. Of course we could have written to Albert's uncle, but it would have taken a long time, and every moment of delay added to Alice's danger. We thought and thought, but we couldn't think of any way to get that sixpence. It seems a small sum, but you see Alice's liberty depended on it. It was quite late in the afternoon when I met Mrs Leslie on the Parade. She had a brown fur coat and a lot of yellow flowers in her hands. She stopped to speak to me, and asked me how the Poet was. I told her he had a cold, and I wondered whether she would lend me sixpence if I asked her, but I could not make up my mind how to begin to say it. It is a hard thing to say – much harder than you would think. She talked to me for a bit, and then she suddenly got into a cab, and said –

'I'd no idea it was so late,' and told the man where to go. And just as she started she shoved the yellow flowers through the window and said, 'For the sick poet, with my love,' and was driven off.

Gentle reader, I will not conceal from you what Oswald did. He knew all about not disgracing the family, and he did not like doing what I am going to say: and they were really Noël's flowers, only he could not have sent them to Hastings, and Oswald knew he would say 'Yes' if Oswald asked him. Oswald sacrificed his family pride because of his little sister's danger. I do not say he was a noble boy – I just tell you what he did, and you can decide for yourself about the nobleness.

I wondered whether she could lend me sixpence, but could not make up my mind how to say it

He put on his oldest clothes – they're much older than any you would think he had if you saw him when he was tidy – and he took those yellow chrysanthemums and he walked with them to Greenwich Station and waited for the trains bringing people from London. He sold those flowers in penny bunches and got tenpence. Then he went to the telegraph office at Lewisham, and said to the lady there:

'A little girl gave you a bad sixpence yesterday. Here are six good pennies.'

The lady said she had not noticed it, and never mind, but Oswald knew that 'Honesty is the best Policy', and he refused to take back the pennies. So at last she said she should put them in the plate on Sunday. She is a very nice lady. I like the way she does her hair.

Then Oswald went home to Alice and told her, and she hugged him, and said he was a dear, good, kind boy, and he said 'Oh, it's all right.'

We bought peppermint bullseyes with the fourpence I had over, and the others wanted to know where we got the money, but we would not tell.

Only afterwards when Noël came home we told him, because they were his flowers, and he said it was quite right. He made some poetry about it. I only remember one bit of it.

> *The noble youth of high degree*
> *Consents to play a menial part,*
> *All for his sister Alice's sake,*
> *Who was so dear to his faithful heart.*

But Oswald himself has never bragged about it.

We got no treasure out of this, unless you count the peppermint bullseyes.

THE ROBBER AND THE BURGLAR

A DAY or two after Noël came back from Hastings there was snow; it was jolly. And we cleared it off the path. A man to do it is sixpence at least, and you should always save when you can. A penny saved is a penny earned. And then we thought it would be nice to clear it off the top of the portico, where it lies so thick, and the edges as if they had been cut with a knife. And just as we had got out of the landing-window on to the portico, the Water Rates came up the path with his book that he tears the thing out of that says how much you have got to pay, and the little ink-bottle hung on to his buttonhole in case you should pay him. Father says the Water Rates is a sensible man, and knows it is always well to be prepared for whatever happens, however unlikely. Alice said afterwards that she rather liked the Water Rates, really, and Noël said he had a face like a good vizier, or the man who rewards the honest boy for restoring the purse, but we did not think about these things at the time, and as the Water Rates came up the steps, we shovelled down a great square slab of snow like an avalanche – and it fell right on his head. Two of us thought of it at the same moment, so it was quite a large avalanche. And when the Water Rates had shaken himself he rang the bell. It was Saturday, and Father was at home. We know now that it is very wrong and ungentlemanly to shovel snow off porticoes on to the Water Rates, or any other person, and we hope he did not catch a cold, and we are very sorry. We apologized to the Water Rates when Father told us to. We were all sent to bed for it.

We all deserved the punishment, because the others would' have shovelled down snow just as we did if they'd thought of it – only they are not so quick at thinking of things as we are. And even quite wrong things sometimes lead to adventures; as every one knows who has ever read about pirates or highwaymen.

Eliza hates us to be sent to bed early, because it means her having to bring meals up, and it means lighting the fire in Noël's room ever so much earlier than usual. He had to have a fire because he still had a bit of a cold. But this particular day we got Eliza into a good temper by giving her a horrid brooch with pretending amethysts in it, that an aunt once gave to Alice, so Eliza brought up an extra scuttle of coals, and when the greengrocer came with the potatoes (he is always late on Saturdays) she got some chestnuts from him. So that when we heard Father go out after his dinner, there was a jolly fire in Noël's room, and we were able to go in and be Red Indians in blankets most comfortably. Eliza had gone out; she says she gets things cheaper on Saturday nights. She has a great friend, who sells fish at a shop, and he is very generous, and lets her have herrings for less than half the natural price.

So we were all alone in the house; Pincher was out with Eliza, and we talked about robbers. And Dora thought it would be a dreadful trade, but Dicky said –

'I think it would be very interesting. And you would only rob rich people, and be very generous to the poor and needy, like Claude Duval.'

Dora said, 'It is wrong to be a robber.'

'Yes,' said Alice, 'you would never know a happy

hour. Think of trying to sleep with the stolen jewels under your bed, and remembering all the quantities of policemen and detectives that there are in the world!'

'There are ways of being robbers that are not wrong,' said Noël; 'if you can rob a robber it is a right act.'

'But you can't,' said Dora; 'he is too clever, and besides, it's wrong anyway.'

'Yes you can, and it isn't; and murdering him with boiling oil is a right act, too, so there!' said Noël. 'What about Ali Baba? Now then!' And we felt it was a score for Noël.

'What would you do if there *was* a robber?' said Alice.

H. O. said he would kill him with boiling oil; but Alice explained that she meant a real robber – now – this minute – in the house.

Oswald and Dicky did not say; but Noël said he thought it would only be fair to ask the robber quite politely and quietly to go away, and then if he didn't you could deal with him.

Now what I am going to tell you is a very strange and wonderful thing, and I hope you will be able to believe it. I should not, if a boy told me, unless I knew him to be a man of honour, and perhaps not then unless he gave his sacred word. But it is true, all the same, and it only shows that the days of romance and daring deeds are not yet at an end.

Alice was just asking Noël *how* he would deal with the robber who wouldn't go if he was asked politely and quietly, when we heard a noise downstairs – quite a plain noise, not the kind of noise you fancy you hear. It was like somebody moving a chair. We held our breath and listened – and then came another noise, like some one poking a fire. Now, you remember there was no one *to* poke a fire or move a chair downstairs, because Eliza and Father were both out. They could not have come in without our hearing them, because the front door is as hard to shut as the back one, and whichever you go in by you have to give a slam that you can hear all down the street.

H. O. and Alice and Dora caught hold of each other's blankets and looked at Dicky and Oswald, and every one was quite pale. And Noël whispered –

'It's ghosts, I know it is' – and then we listened again, but there was no more noise. Presently Dora said in a whisper –

'Whatever shall we do? Oh, whatever shall we do – what *shall* we do?'

And she kept on saying it till we had to tell her to shut up.

O reader, have you ever been playing Red Indians in blankets round a bedroom fire in a house where you thought there was no one but you – and then suddenly heard a noise like a chair, and a fire being poked, downstairs? Unless you have you will not be able to imagine at all what it feels like. It was not like in books; our hair did not stand on end at all, and we never said 'Hist!' once, but our feet got very cold, though we were in blankets by the fire, and the insides of Oswald's hands got warm and wet, and his nose was cold like a dog's, and his ears were burning hot.

The girls said afterwards that they shivered with terror, and their teeth chattered, but we did not see or hear this at the time.

'Shall we open the window and call police?' said Dora; and then Oswald suddenly thought of something, and he breathed more freely and he said –

'I *know* it's not ghosts, and I don't believe it's robbers. I expect it's a stray cat got in when the coals came this morning, and she's been hiding in the cellar, and now she's moving about. Let's go down and see.'

The girls wouldn't, of course; but I could see that they breathed more freely too. But Dicky said, 'All right; I will if you will.'

H. O. said, 'Do you think it's *really* a cat?' So we said he had better stay with the girls. And of course after that we had to let him and Alice both come. Dora said if we took Noël down with his cold, she would scream 'Fire!' and 'Murder!' and she didn't mind if the whole street heard.

So Noël agreed to be getting his clothes on, and the rest of us said we would go down and look for the cat.

Now Oswald *said* that about the cat, and it made it easier to go down, but in his inside he did not feel at all sure that it might not be robbers after all. Of course, we had often talked about robbers before, but it is very different when you sit in a room and listen and listen and listen; and Oswald felt somehow that it would be easier to go down and see what it was, than to wait, and listen, and wait, and wait, and listen, and wait, and then perhaps to hear *It*, whatever it was, come creeping slowly up the stairs as softly as *It* could with *Its* boots off, and the stairs creaking, towards the room where we were with the door open in case of Eliza coming back suddenly, and all dark on the landings. And then it would have been just as bad, and it would have lasted longer, and you would have known you were a coward besides. Dicky says he felt all these same things. Many people would say we were young heroes to go down as we did; so I have tried to explain, because no young hero wishes to have more credit than he deserves.

The landing gas was turned down low – just a blue bead – and we four went out very softly, wrapped in our blankets, and we stood on the top of the stairs a good long time before we began to go down. And we listened and listened till our ears buzzed.

And Oswald whispered to Dicky, and Dicky went into our room and fetched the large toy pistol that is a foot long, and that has the trigger broken, and I took it because I am the eldest; and I don't think either of us thought it was the cat now. But Alice and H. O. did. Dicky got the poker out of Noël's room, and told Dora it was to settle the cat with when we caught her.

Then Oswald whispered, 'Let's play at burglars; Dicky and I are armed to the teeth, we will go first. You keep a flight behind us, and be a reinforcement if we are attacked. Or you can retreat and defend the women and children in the fortress, if you'd rather.'

But they said they would be a reinforcement.

Oswald's teeth chattered a little when he spoke. It was not with anything else except cold.

So Dicky and Oswald crept down, and when we got to the bottom of the stairs, we saw Father's study door just ajar, and the crack of light. And Oswald was so pleased to see the light, knowing that burglars prefer the dark, or at any rate the dark lantern, that he felt really sure it *was* the cat after all, and then he thought it would be fun to make the others upstairs think it was really a robber. So he cocked the pistol – you can cock it, but it doesn't go off – and he said, 'Come on, Dick!' and he rushed at the study door and burst into the room, crying, 'Surrender! you are discovered! Surrender, or I fire! Throw up your hands!'

And, as he finished saying it, he saw before him, standing on the study hearthrug, a Real Robber. There was no mistake about it. Oswald was sure it was a robber, because it had a screwdriver in its hands, and was standing near the cupboard door that H. O. broke the lock off, and there were gimlets and screws and things on the floor. There is nothing in that cupboard but old ledgers and magazines and the tool chest, but of course, a robber could not know that beforehand.

When Oswald saw that there really was a robber, and that he was so heavily armed with the screw-driver, he did not feel comfortable. But he kept the pistol pointed at the robber, and – you will hardly believe it, but it is true – the robber threw down the screwdriver clattering on the other tools, and he *did* throw up his hands, and said –

'I surrender; don't shoot me! How many of you are there?'

So Dicky said, 'You are outnumbered. Are you armed?'

And the robber said, 'No, not in the least.'

And Oswald said, still pointing the pistol, and feeling very strong and brave and as if he was in a book, 'Turn out your pockets.'

The robber did: and while he turned them out, we looked at him. He was of the middle height, and clad in a black frock-coat and grey trousers. His boots were a little gone at the sides, and his shirt-cuffs were a bit frayed, but otherwise he was of gentlemanly demeanour. He had a thin, wrinkled face, with big, light eyes that sparkled, and then looked soft very queerly, and a short beard. In his youth it must have been of a fair golden colour, but now it was tinged with grey. Oswald was sorry for him, especially when he saw that one of his pockets had a large hole in it, and that he had nothing in his pockets but letters and string and three boxes of matches, and a pipe and a handkerchief and a thin tobacco pouch and two pennies. We made him put all the things on the table, and then he said –

'Well, you've caught me; what are you going to do with me? Police?'

Alice and H. O. had come down to be reinforcements, when they heard a shout, and when Alice saw that it was a Real Robber, and that he had surrendered, she clapped her hands and said, 'Bravo, boys!' and so did H. O. And now she said, 'If he gives his word of honour not to escape, I shouldn't call the police: it seems a pity. Wait till Father comes home.'

The robber agreed to this, and gave his word of honour, and asked if he might put on a pipe, and we said 'Yes,' and he sat in Father's armchair and warmed his boots, which steamed, and I sent H. O. and Alice to put on some clothes and tell the others, and bring down Dicky's and my knickerbockers, and the rest of the chestnuts.

And they all came, and we sat round the fire, and it was jolly. The robber was very friendly, and talked to us a great deal.

'I wasn't always in this low way of business,' he said, when Noël said something about the things he had turned out of his pockets. 'It's a great come-down to a man like me. But, if I must be caught, it's something to be caught by brave young heroes like you. My stars! How you did bolt into the room, – "Surrender, and up with your hands!" You might have been born and bred to the thief-catching.'

Oswald is sorry if it was mean, but he could not own up just then that he did not think there was any one in the study when he did that brave if rash act. He has told since.

'And what made you think there was any one in the house?' the robber asked, when he had thrown his head back, and laughed for quite half a minute. So we told him. And he applauded our valour, and Alice and H. O. explained that they would have said 'Surrender,' too, only they were reinforcements.

The robber ate some of the chestnuts – and we sat and wondered when Father would come home, and what he would say to us for our intrepid conduct. And the robber told us of all the things he had done before he began to break into houses. Dicky picked up the tools from the floor, and suddenly he said –

'Why, this is Father's screwdriver and his gimlets, and all! Well, I do call it jolly cheek to pick a man's locks with his own tools!'

'True, true,' said the robber. 'It is cheek, of the jolliest! But you see I've come down in the world. I was a highway robber once, but horses are so expensive to hire – five shillings an hour, you know – and I couldn't afford to keep them. The highwayman business isn't what it was.'

'What about a bike?' said H. O.

But the robber thought cycles were low – and besides you couldn't go across country with them when occasion arose, as you could with a trusty steed. And he talked of highwaymen as if he knew just how we liked hearing it.

Then he told us how he had been a pirate captain – and how he had sailed over waves mountains high, and gained rich prizes – and how he *did* begin to think that here he had found a profession to his mind.

'I don't say there are no ups and downs in it,' he said, 'especially in stormy weather. But what a trade! And a sword at your side, and the Jolly Roger flying at the peak, and a prize in sight. And all the black mouths of your guns pointed at the laden trader – and the wind in your favour, and your trusty crew ready to live and die for you! Oh – but it's a grand life!'

I did feel so sorry for him. He used such nice words, and he had a gentleman's voice.

'I'm sure you weren't brought up to be a pirate,' said

Dora. She had dressed even to her collar – and made Noël do it too – but the rest of us were in blankets with just a few odd things put on anyhow underneath.

The robber frowned and sighed.

'No,' he said, 'I was brought up to the law. I was at Balliol, bless your hearts, and that's true anyway.' He sighed again, and looked hard at the fire.

'That was my Father's college,' H. O. was beginning, but Dicky said –

'Why did you leave off being a pirate?'

'A pirate?' he said, as if he had not been thinking of such things. 'Oh, yes; why I gave it up because – because I could not get over the dreadful sea-sickness.'

'Nelson was sea-sick,' said Oswald.

'Ah,' said the robber; 'but I hadn't his luck or his pluck, or something. He stuck to it and won Trafalgar, didn't he? "Kiss me, Hardy" – and all that, eh? *I* couldn't stick to it – I had to resign. And nobody kissed *me*.'

I saw by his understanding about Nelson that he was really a man who had been to a good school as well as to Balliol.

Then we asked him, 'And what did you do then?'

And Alice asked if he was ever a coiner, and we told him how we had thought we'd caught the desperate gang next door, and he was very much interested and said he was glad he had never taken to coining. 'Besides, the coins are so ugly nowadays,' he said, 'no one could really find any pleasure in making them. And it's a hole-and-corner business at the best, isn't it? – and it must be a very thirsty one – with the hot metal and furnaces and things.'

And again he looked at the fire.

Oswald forgot for a minute that the interesting stranger was a robber, and asked him if he wouldn't have a drink. Oswald has heard Father do this to his friends, so he knows it is the right thing. The robber said he didn't mind if he did. And that is right, too.

And Dora went and got a bottle of Father's ale – the Light Sparkling Family – and a glass, and we gave it to the robber. Dora said she would be responsible.

Then when he had had a drink he told us about bandits, but he said it was so bad in wet weather. Bandits' caves were hardly ever properly weathertight. And bush-ranging was the same.

'As a matter of fact,' he said, 'I was bush-ranging this afternoon, among the furze-bushes on the Heath, but I had no luck. I stopped the Lord Mayor in his gilt coach, with all his footmen in plush and gold lace, smart as cockatoos. But it was no go. The Lord Mayor hadn't a stiver in his pockets. One of the footmen had six new pennies: the Lord Mayor always pays his servants' wages in new pennies. I spent fourpence of that in bread and cheese, that on the table's the tuppence. Ah, it's a poor trade!' And then he filled his pipe again.

We had turned out the gas, so that Father should have a jolly good surprise when he did come home, and we sat and talked as pleasant as could be. I never liked a new man better than I liked that robber. And I felt so sorry for him. He told us he had been a war-correspondent and an editor, in happier days, as well as a horse-stealer and a colonel of dragoons.

And quite suddenly, just as we were telling him about Lord Tottenham and our being highwaymen ourselves, he put up his hand and said 'Shish!' and we were quiet and listened.

There was a scrape, scrape, scraping noise; it came from downstairs.

'They're filing something,' whispered the robber,

'here – shut up, give me that pistol, and the poker. There *is* a burglar now, and no mistake.'

'It's only a toy one and it won't go off,' I said, 'but you can cock it.'

Then we heard a snap.

'There goes the window bar,' said the robber softly. 'Jove! what an adventure! You kids stay here, I'll tackle it.'

But Dicky and I said we should come. So he let us go as far as the bottom of the kitchen stairs, and we took the tongs and shovel with us. There was a light in the kitchen; a very little light. It is curious we never thought, any of us, that this might be a plant of our robber's to get away. We never thought of doubting his word of honour. And we were right.

That noble robber dashed the kitchen door open, and rushed in with the big toy pistol in one hand and the poker in the other, shouting out just like Oswald had done –

'Surrender! You are discovered! Surrender, or I'll fire! Throw up your hands!' And Dicky and I rattled the tongs and shovel so that he might know there were more of us, all bristling with weapons.

And we heard a husky voice in the kitchen saying –

'All right, governor! Stow that scent sprinkler. I'll give in. Blowed if I ain't pretty well sick of the job, anyway.'

Then we went in. Our robber was standing in the grandest manner with his legs very wide apart, and the pistol pointing at the cowering burglar. The burglar was a large man who did not mean to have a beard, I think, but he had got some of one, and a red comforter, and a fur cap, and his face was red and his voice was thick. How different from our own robber! The burglar had a dark lantern, and he was standing by the plate-

He scowled and said, 'Well, go on: why don't yer fetch the pleece?'

basket. When we had lit the gas we all thought he was very like what a burglar ought to be. He did not look as if he could ever have been a pirate or a highwayman, or anything really dashing or noble, and he scowled and shuffled his feet and said: 'Well, go on: why don't yer fetch the pleeee?'

'Upon my word, I don't know,' said our robber, rubbing his chin. 'Oswald, why don't we fetch the police?'

It is not every robber that I would stand Christian names from, I can tell you; but just then I didn't think of that. I just said –

'Do you mean I'm to fetch one?'

Our robber looked at the burglar and said nothing.

Then the burglar began to speak very fast, and to look different ways with his hard, shiny little eyes.

'Lookee 'ere, governor,' he said, 'I was stony broke, so help me, I was. And blessed if I've nicked a haporth of your little lot. You know yourself there ain't much to tempt a bloke,' he shook the plate-basket as if he was angry with it, and the yellowy spoons and forks rattled. 'I was just a-looking through this 'ere Bank-ollerday show, when you come. Let me off, sir. Come now, I've got kids of my own at home, strike me if I ain't – same as yours – I've got a nipper just about 'is size, and what'll come of them if I'm lagged? I ain't been in it long, sir, and I ain't 'andy at it.'

'No,' said our robber; 'you certainly are not.'

Alice and the others had come down by now to see what was happening. Alice told me afterwards they thought it really was the cat this time.

'No, I ain't 'andy, as you say, sir, and if you let me off this once I'll chuck the whole blooming bizz; rake my civvy, I will. Don't be hard on a cove, mister; think of the missis and the kids. I've got one just the cut of little missy there; bless 'er pretty 'eart.'

'Your family certainly fits your circumstances very nicely,' said our robber.

Then Alice said –

'Oh, do let him go! If he's got a little girl like me, whatever will she do? Suppose it was Father!'

'I don't think he's got a little girl like you, my dear,' said our robber, 'and I think he'll be safer under lock and key.'

'You ask yer Father to let me go, miss,' said the burglar; ' 'e won't 'ave the 'art to refuse you.'

'If I do,' said Alice, 'will you promise never to come back?'

'Not me, miss,' the burglar said very earnestly, and he looked at the plate-basket again, as if that alone would be enough to keep him away, our robber said afterwards.

'And will you be good and not rob any more?' said Alice.

'I'll turn over a noo leaf, miss, so help me.'

Then Alice said –

'Oh, do let him go! I'm sure he'll be good.'

But our robber said no, it wouldn't be right; we must wait till Father came home.

Then H. O. said, very suddenly and plainly:

'I don't think it's at all fair, when you're a robber yourself.'

The minute he'd said it the burglar said, 'Kidded, by gum!' – and then our robber made a step towards him to catch hold of him, and before you had time to think 'Hullo!' the burglar knocked the pistol up with one hand and knocked our robber down with the other, and was off out of the window like a shot, though Oswald and Dicky did try to stop him by holding on to his legs.

And that burglar had the cheek to put his head in at the window and say, 'I'll give yer love to the kids and the missis' – and he was off like winking, and there were Alice and Dora trying to pick up our robber, and asking him whether he was hurt, and where. He wasn't hurt at all, except a lump at the back of his head. And he got up, and we dusted the kitchen floor off him. Eliza is a dirty girl.

Then he said, 'Let's put up the shutters. It never rains but it pours. Now you've had two burglars I daresay you'll have twenty.' So we put up the shutters, which Eliza has strict orders to do before she goes out, only she never does, and we went back to Father's study, and the robber said, 'What a night we are having!' and put his boots back in the fender to go on steaming, and then we all talked at once. It was the most wonderful adventure we ever had, though it wasn't treasure-seeking – at least not ours. I suppose it was the burglar's treasure-seeking, but he didn't get much – and our robber said he didn't believe a word about those kids that were so like Alice and me.

And then there was the click of the gate, and we said, 'Here's Father,' and the robber said, 'And now for the police.'

Then we all jumped up. We did like him so much, and it seemed so unfair that he should be sent to prison, and the horrid, lumping big burglar not.

And Alice said, 'Oh, *no* – run! Dicky will let you out at the back door. Oh, do go, go *now*.'

And we all said, 'Yes, *go*,' and pulled him towards the door, and gave him his hat and stick and the things out of his pockets.

But Father's latchkey was in the door, and it was too late.

Father came in quickly, purring with the cold, and began to say, 'It's all right, Foulkes, I've got –' And then he stopped short and stared at us. Then he said, in the voice we all hate, 'Children, what is the meaning of all this?'

And for a minute nobody spoke.

Then my Father said, 'Foulkes, I must really apologize for these very naughty —'

And then our robber rubbed his hands and laughed, and cried out: 'You're mistaken, my dear sir, I'm not Foulkes; I'm a robber, captured by these young people in the most gallant manner. "Hands up, surrender, or I fire," and all the rest of it. My word, Bastable, but you've got some kids worth having! I wish my Denny had their pluck.'

Then we began to understand, and it was like being knocked down, it was so sudden. And our robber told us he wasn't a robber after all. He was only an old college friend of my Father's, and he had come after dinner, when Father was just trying to mend the lock H. O. had broken, to ask Father to get him a letter to a doctor about his little boy Denny, who was ill. And Father had gone over the Heath to Vanbrugh Park to see some rich people he knows and get the letter. And he had left Mr Foulkes to wait till he came back, because it was important to know at once whether Father could get the letter, and if he couldn't Mr Foulkes would have had to try some one else directly.

We were dumb with amazement.

Our robber told my Father about the other burglar, and said he was sorry he'd let him escape, but my Father said, 'Oh, it's all right: poor beggar; if he really had kids at home: you never can tell — forgive us our debts, don't you know; but tell me about the first business. It must have been moderately entertaining.'

Then our robber told my Father how I had rushed into the room with a pistol, crying out .. but you know all about that. And he laid it on so thick and fat about plucky young-uns, and chips of old blocks, and things like that, that I felt I was purple with shame, even under the blanket. So I swallowed that thing that tries to prevent you speaking when you ought to, and I said, 'Look here, Father, I didn't really think there was any one in the study. We thought it was a cat at first, and then I thought there was no one there, and I was just larking. And when I said surrender and all that, it was just the game, don't you know?'

Then our robber said, 'Yes, old chap; but when you found there really *was* some one there, you dropped the pistol and bunked, didn't you, eh?'

And I said, 'No; I thought, "Hullo! here's a robber! Well, it's all up, I suppose, but I may as well hold on and see what happens." '

And I was glad I'd owned up, for Father slapped me on the back, and said I was a young brick, and our robber said I was no funk anyway, and though I got very hot under the blanket I liked it, and I explained that the others would have done the same if they had thought of it.

Then Father got up some more beer, and laughed about Dora's responsibility, and he got out a box of figs he had bought for us, only he hadn't given it to us because of the Water Rates, and Eliza came in and brought up the bread and cheese, and what there was left of the neck of mutton — cold wreck of mutton, Father called it – and we had a feast – like a picnic – all sitting anywhere, and eating with our fingers. It was prime. We sat up till past twelve o'clock, and I never felt so pleased to think I was not born a girl. It was hard on the others; they would have done just the same if they'd thought of it. But it does make you feel jolly when your pater says you're a young brick!

When Mr Foulkes was going, he said to Alice, 'Good-bye, Hardy.'

And Alice understood, of course, and kissed him as hard as she could.

And she said, 'I wanted to, when you said no one kissed you when you left off being a pirate captain.'

And he said, 'I know you did, my dear.'

And Dora kissed him too, and said, 'I suppose none of these tales were true?'

And our robber just said, 'I tried to play the part properly, my dear.'

And he jolly well did play it, and no mistake. We have often seen him since, and his boy Denny, and his girl Daisy, but that comes in another story.

And if any of you kids who read this ever had two such adventures in one night you can just write and tell me. That's all.

CHAPTER 14

THE DIVINING-ROD

You have no idea how uncomfortable the house was on the day when we sought for gold with the divining-rod. It was like a spring-cleaning in the winter-time. All the carpets were up, because Father had told Eliza to make the place decent as there was a gentleman coming to dinner the next day. So she got in a char-woman, and they slopped water about, and left brooms and brushes on the stairs for people to tumble over. H. O. got a big bump on his head in that way, and when he said it was too bad, Eliza said he should keep in the nursery then, and not be where he'd no business. We bandaged his head with a towel, and then he stopped crying and played at being England's wounded hero dying in the cockpit, while every man was doing his duty, as the hero had told them to, and Alice was Hardy, and I was the doctor, and the others were the crew. Playing at Hardy made us think of our own dear robber, and we wished he was there, and wondered if we should ever see him any more.

We were rather astonished at Father's having any-one to dinner, because now he never seems to think of anything but business. Before Mother died people often came to dinner, and Father's business did not take up so much of his time and was not the bother it is now. And we used to see who could go furthest down in our nightgowns and get nice things to eat, without being seen, out of the dishes as they came out of the dining-room. Eliza can't cook very nice things. She told Father she was a good plain cook, but he says it was a fancy portrait. We stayed in the nursery till the char-woman came in and told us to be off – she was going to make one job of it, and have our carpet up as well as all the others, now the man was here to beat them. It came up, and it was very dusty — and under it we found my threepenny-bit that I lost ages ago, which shows what Eliza is. H. O. had got tired of being the wounded hero, and Dicky was so tired of doing nothing that Dora said she knew he'd begin to tease Noël in a minute; then of course Dicky said he wasn't going to tease anybody – he was going out to the Heath. He said he'd heard that nagging women drove a man from his home, and now he found it was quite true. Oswald always tries to be a peace-maker, so he told Dicky to shut up and not make an ass of himself. And Alice said, 'Well, Dora began –' And Dora tossed her chin up and said it wasn't any business of Oswald's any way, and no one asked Alice's opinion. So we all felt very uncomfortable till Noël said, 'Don't let's quarrel about nothing. You know let dogs delight – and I made up another piece while you were talking –

> *Quarrelling is an evil thing,*
> *It fills with gall life's cup;*
> *For when once you begin*
> *It takes such a long time to make it up.'*

We all laughed then and stopped jawing at each other. Noël is very funny with his poetry. But that piece happened to come out quite true. You begin to quarrel and then you can't stop; often, long before the others are ready to cry and make it up, I see how silly it is, and I want to laugh; but it doesn't do to say so – for it only makes the others crosser than they were before. I wonder why that is?

Alice said Noël ought to be poet laureate, and she actually went out in the cold and got some laurel leaves – the spotted kind – out of the garden, and Dora made a crown and we put it on him. He was quite pleased; but the leaves made a mess, and Eliza said, 'Don't.' I believe that's a word grown-ups use more than any other. Then suddenly Alice thought of that old idea of hers for finding treasure, and she said –

'Do let's try the divining-rod.'

So Oswald said, 'Fair priestess, we do greatly desire to find gold beneath our land, therefore we pray thee practise with the divining-rod, and tell us where we can find it.'

'Do ye desire to fashion of it helms and hauberks?' said Alice.

'Yes,' said Noël; 'and chains and ouches.'

'I bet you don't know what an "ouch" is,' said Dicky.

'Yes I do, so there!' said Noël. 'It's a carcanet. I looked it out in the dicker, now then!'

We asked him what a carcanet was, but he wouldn't say.

'And we want to make fair goblets of the gold,' said Oswald.

'Yes, to drink coconut milk out of,' said H. O.

'And we desire to build fair palaces of it,' said Dicky.

'And to buy things,' said Dora; 'a great many things. New Sunday frocks and hats and kid gloves and –'

She would have gone on for ever so long only we reminded her that we hadn't found the gold yet.

By this Alice had put on the nursery tablecloth, which is green, and tied the old blue and yellow antimacassar over her head, and she said –

'If your intentions are correct, fear nothing and follow me.'

And she went down into the hall. We all followed chanting 'Heroes.' It is a gloomy thing the girls learnt at the High School, and we always use it when we want a priestly chant.

Alice stopped short by the hat-stand, and held up her hands as well as she could for the table-cloth, and said –

'Now, great altar of the golden idol, yield me the divining-rod that I may use it for the good of the suffering people.'

The umbrella-stand was the altar of the golden idol, and it yielded her the old school umbrella. She carried it between her palms.

'Now,' she said, 'I shall sing the magic chant. You mustn't say anything, but just follow wherever I go – like follow my leader, you know – and when there is gold underneath the magic rod will twist in the hand of the priestess like a live thing that seeks to be free. Then you will dig, and the golden treasure will be revealed. H. O., if you make that clatter with your boots they'll come and tell us not to. Now come on all of you.'

So she went upstairs and down and into every room. We followed her on tiptoe, and Alice sang as she went. What she sang is not out of a book – Noël made it up while she was dressing up for the priestess.

> *Ashen rod cold*
> *That here I hold,*
> *Teach me where to find the gold.*

When we came to where Eliza was, she said, 'Get along with you'; but Dora said it was only a game, and we wouldn't touch anything, and our boots were quite clean, and Eliza might as well let us. So she did.

Ashen rod cold
That here I hold,
Teach me where to find the gold

180

It was all right for the priestess, but it was a little dull for the rest of us, because she wouldn't let us sing, too; so we said we'd had enough of it, and if she couldn't find the gold we'd leave off and play something else. The priestess said, 'All right, wait a minute,' and went on singing. Then we all followed her back into the nursery, where the carpet was up and the boards smelt of soft soap. Then she said, 'It moves, it moves! Once more the choral hymn!' So we sang 'Heroes' again, and in the middle the umbrella dropped from her hands.

'The magic rod has spoken,' said Alice; 'dig here, and that with courage and despatch.' We didn't quite see how to dig, but we all began to scratch on the floor with our hands, but the priestess said, 'Don't be so silly! It's the place where they come to do the gas. The board's loose. Dig an you value your lives, for ere sundown the dragon who guards this spoil will return in his fiery fury and make you his unresisting prey.'

So we dug – that is, we got the loose board up. And Alice threw up her arms and cried –

'See the rich treasure – the gold in thick layers, with silver and diamonds stuck in it!'

'Like currants in cake,' said H. O.

'It's a lovely treasure,' said Dicky yawning. 'Let's come back and carry it away another day.'

But Alice was kneeling by the hole.

'Let me feast my eyes on the golden splendour,' she said, 'hidden these long centuries from the human eye. Behold how the magic rod has led us to treasures more – Oswald, don't push so! – more bright than ever monarch – I say, there *is* something down there, really. I saw it shine!'

We thought she was kidding, but when she began to try to get into the hole, which was much too small, we saw she meant it, so I said, 'Let's have a squint,' and I looked, but I couldn't see anything, even when I lay down on my stomach. The others lay down on their stomachs too and tried to see, all but Noël, who stood and looked at us and said we were the great serpents come down to drink at the magic pool. He wanted to be the knight and slay the great serpents with his good sword – he even drew the umbrella ready – but Alice said, 'All right, we will in a minute. But now – I'm sure I saw it; do get a match, Noël, there's a dear.'

'What did you see?' asked Noël, beginning to go for the matches very slowly.

'Something bright, away in the corner under the board against the beam.'

'Perhaps it was a rat's eye,' Noël said, 'or a snake's,' and we did not put our heads quite so close to the hole till he came back with the matches.

Then I struck a match, and Alice cried, 'There it is!'

And there it was, and it was a half-sovereign, partly dusty and partly bright. We think perhaps a mouse, disturbed by the carpets being taken up, may have brushed the dust of years from part of the half-sovereign with his tail. We can't imagine how it came there, only Dora thinks she remembers once when H. O. was very little Mother gave him some money to hold, and he dropped it, and it rolled all over the floor. So we think perhaps this was part of it. We were very glad. H. O. wanted to go out at once and buy a mask he had seen for fourpence. It had been a shilling mask, but now it was going very cheap because Guy Fawkes' Day was over, and it was a little cracked at the top. But Dora said, 'I don't know that it's our money. Let's wait and ask Father.'

But H. O. did not care about waiting, and I felt for

him. Dora is rather like grown-ups in that way; she does not seem to understand that when you want a thing you do want it, and that you don't wish to wait, even a minute.

So we went and asked Albert-next-door's uncle. He was pegging away at one of the rotten novels he has to write to make his living, but he said we weren't interrupting him at all.

'My hero's folly has involved him in a difficulty,' he said. 'It is his own fault. I will leave him to meditate on the incredible fatuity – the hare-brained recklessness – which have brought him to this pass. It will be a lesson to him. I, meantime, will give myself unreservedly to the pleasures of your conversation.'

That's one thing I like Albert's uncle for. He always talks like a book, and yet you can always understand what he means. I think he is more like us, inside of his mind, than most grown-up people are. He can pretend beautifully. I never met any one else so good at it, except our robber, and we began it, with him. But it was Albert's uncle who first taught us how to make people talk like books when you're playing things, and he made us learn to tell a story straight from the beginning, not starting in the middle like most people do. So now Oswald remembered what he had been told, as he generally does, and began at the beginning, but when he came to where Alice said she was the priestess, Albert's uncle said –

'Let the priestess herself set forth the tale in fitting speech.'

So Alice said, 'O high priest of the great idol, the humblest of thy slaves took the school umbrella for a divining-rod, and sang the song of inver – what's-it's-name?'

'Invocation perhaps?' said Albert's uncle.

'Yes; and then I went about and about and the others got tired, so the divining-rod fell on a certain spot, and I said, "Dig", and we dug – it was where the loose board is for the gas men – and then there really and truly was a half-sovereign lying under the boards, and here it is.'

Albert's uncle took it and looked at it.

'The great high priest will bite it to see if it's good,' he said, and he did. 'I congratulate you,' he went on; 'you are indeed among those favoured by the Immortals. First you find half-crowns in the garden, and now this. The high priest advises you to tell your Father, and ask if you may keep it. My hero has become penitent, but impatient. I must pull him out of this scrape. Ye have my leave to depart.'

Of course we know from Kipling that that means, 'You'd better bunk, and be sharp about it,' so we came away. I do like Albert's uncle. I shall be like that when I'm a man. He gave us our Jungle books, and he is awfully clever, though he does have to write grown-up tales.

We told Father about it that night. He was very kind. He said we might certainly have the half-sovereign, and he hoped we should enjoy ourselves with our treasure-trove.

Then he said, 'Your dear Mother's Indian Uncle is coming to dinner here to-morrow night. So will you not drag the furniture about overhead, please, more than you're absolutely obliged; and H. O. might wear slippers or something. I can always distinguish the note of H. O.'s boots.'

We said we would be very quiet, and Father went on –

'This Indian Uncle is not used to children, and he is coming to talk business with me. It is really important that he should be quiet. Do you think, Dora, that perhaps bed at six for H. O. and Noël –'

But H. O. said, 'Father, I really and truly won't make a noise. I'll stand on my head all the evening sooner than disturb the Indian Uncle with my boots.'

And Alice said Noël never made a row anyhow.

So Father laughed and said, 'All right.' And he said we might do as we liked with the half-sovereign. 'Only for goodness' sake don't try to go in for business with it,' he said. 'It's always a mistake to go into business with an insufficient capital.'

We talked it over all that evening, and we decided that as we were not to go into business with our half-sovereign it was no use not spending it at once, and so we might as well have a right royal feast. The next day we went out and bought the things. We got figs, and almonds and raisins, and a real raw rabbit, and Eliza promised to cook it for us if we would wait till to-morrow, because of the Indian Uncle coming to dinner. She was very busy cooking nice things for him to eat. We got the rabbit because we are so tired of beef and mutton, and Father hasn't a bill at the poultry shop. And we got some flowers to go on the dinner-table for Father's party. And we got hardbake and raspberry noyau and peppermint rock and oranges and a coconut, with other nice things. We put it all in the top long drawer. It is H. O.'s play drawer, and we made him turn his things out and put them in Father's old portmanteau. H. O. is getting old enough now to learn to be unselfish, and besides, his drawer wanted tidying very badly. Then we all vowed by the honour of the ancient House of Bastable that we would not touch any of the feast till Dora gave the word next day. And we gave H. O. some of the hardbake, to make it easier for him to keep his vow. The next day was the most rememorable day in all our lives, but we didn't know that then. But that is another story. I think that is such a useful way to know when you can't think how to end up a chapter. I learnt it from another writer named Kipling. I've mentioned him before, I believe, but he deserves it!

'LO, THE POOR INDIAN!'

It was all very well for Father to ask us not to make a row because the Indian Uncle was coming to talk business, but my young brother's boots are not the only things that make a noise. We took his boots away and made him wear Dora's bath slippers, which are soft and woolly, and hardly any soles to them; and of course we wanted to see the Uncle, so we looked over the banisters when he came, and we were as quiet as mice – but when Eliza had let him in she went straight down to the kitchen and made the most awful row you ever heard, it sounded like the Day of Judgement, or all the saucepans and crockery in the house being kicked about the floor, but she told me afterwards it was only the tea-tray and one or two cups and saucers, that she had knocked over in her flurry. We heard the Uncle say, 'God bless my soul!' and then he went into Father's study and the door was shut – we didn't see him properly at all that time.

I don't believe the dinner was very nice. Something got burned I'm sure – for we smelt it. It was an extra smell, besides the mutton. I know *that* got burned. Eliza wouldn't have any of us in the kitchen except Dora – till dinner was over. Then we got what was left of the dessert, and had it on the stairs – just round the corner where they can't see you from the hall, unless the first landing gas is lighted. Suddenly the study door opened and the Uncle came out and went and felt in

his greatcoat pocket. It was his cigar-case he wanted.
We saw that afterwards. We got a much better view of
him then. He didn't look like an Indian but just like a
kind of brown, big Englishman, and of course he didn't
see us, but we heard him mutter to himself –

'Shocking bad dinner! Eh! – what?' When he went
back to the study he didn't shut the door properly.
That door has always been a little tiresome since the
day we took the lock off to get out the pencil sharpener
H. O. had shoved into the keyhole. We didn't listen –
really and truly – but the Indian Uncle has a very big
voice, and Father was not going to be beaten by a poor
Indian in talking or anything else – so he spoke up too,
like a man, and I heard him say it was a very good
business, and only wanted a little capital – and he said
it as if it was an imposition he had learned, and he
hated having to say it. The Uncle said, 'Pooh, pooh!'
to that, and then he said he was afraid that what that
same business wanted was not capital but management.
Then I heard my Father say, 'It is not a pleasant
subject: I am sorry I introduced it. Suppose we change
it, sir. Let me fill your glass.' Then the poor Indian
said something about vintage – and that a poor,
broken-down man like he was couldn't be too careful.
And then Father said, 'Well, whisky then,' and afterwards they talked about Native Races and Imperial
something or other and it got very dull.

So then Oswald remembered that you must not hear
what people do not intend you to hear – even if you are
not listening; and he said, 'We ought not to stay here
any longer. Perhaps they would not like us to hear –'

Alice said, 'Oh, do you think it could possibly
matter?' and went and shut the study door softly but
quite tight. So it was no use staying there any longer,
and we went to the nursery.

Then Noël said, 'Now I understand. Of course my Father is making a banquet for the Indian, because he is a poor, broken-down man. We might have known that from "Lo, the poor Indian!" you know.'

We all agreed with him, and we were glad to have the thing explained, because we had not understood before what Father wanted to have people to dinner for – and not let us come in.

'Poor people are very proud,' said Alice, 'and I expect Father thought the Indian would be ashamed, if all of us children knew how poor he was.'

Then Dora said, 'Poverty is no disgrace. We should honour honest Poverty.'

And we all agreed that that was so.

'I wish his dinner had not been so nasty,' Dora said, while Oswald put lumps of coal on the fire with his fingers, so as not to make a noise. He is a very thoughtful boy, and he did not wipe his fingers on his trouser leg as perhaps Noël or H. O. would have done, but he just rubbed them on Dora's handkerchief while she was talking. 'I am afraid the dinner was horrid.' Dora went on, 'The table looked very nice with the flowers we got. I set it myself, and Eliza made me borrow the silver spoons and forks from Albert-next-door's Mother.'

'I hope the poor Indian is honest,' said Dicky gloomily, 'when you are a poor, broken-down man silver spoons must be a great temptation.'

Oswald told him not to talk such tommy-rot because the Indian was a relation, so of course he couldn't do anything dishonourable. And Dora said it was all right any way, because she had washed up the spoons and forks herself and counted them, and they were all there, and she had put them into their wash-leather bag, and taken them back to Albert-next-door's Mother.

'And the brussels sprouts were all wet and swimmy,' she went on, 'and the potatoes looked grey – and there were bits of black in the gravy – and the mutton was bluey-red and soft in the middle. I saw it when it came out. The apple-pie looked very nice – but it wasn't quite done in the apply part. The other thing that was burnt – you must have smelt it, was the soup.'

'It is a pity,' said Oswald; 'I don't suppose he gets a good dinner every day.'

'No more do we,' said H. O., 'but we shall to-morrow.'

I thought of all the things we had bought with our half-sovereign – the rabbit and the sweets and the almonds and raisins and figs and the coconut: and I thought of the nasty mutton and things, and while I was thinking about it all Alice said –

'Let's ask the poor Indian to come to dinner with *us* to-morrow.' I should have said it myself if she had given me time.

We got the little ones to go to bed by promising to put a note on their dressing-table saying what had happened, so that they might know the first thing in the morning, or in the middle of the night if they happened to wake up, and then we elders arranged everything.

I waited by the back door, and when the Uncle was beginning to go Dicky was to drop a marble down between the banisters for a signal, so that I could run round and meet the Uncle as he came out.

This seems like deceit, but if you are a thoughtful and considerate boy you will understand that we could not go down and say to the Uncle in the hall under Father's eye, 'Father has given you a beastly, nasty dinner, but if you will come to dinner with us to-morrow, we will show you our idea of good things to eat.' You will see, if you think it over, that this would not have been at all polite to Father.

So when the Uncle left, Father saw him to the door and let him out, and then went back to the study, looking very sad, Dora says.

As the poor Indian came down our steps he saw me there at the gate. I did not mind his being poor, and I said, 'Good evening, Uncle,' just as politely as though he had been about to ascend into one of the gilded chariots of the rich and affluent, instead of having to walk to the station a quarter of a mile in the mud, unless he had the money for a tram fare.

'Good evening, Uncle.' I said it again, for he stood staring at me. I don't suppose he was used to politeness from boys – some boys are anything but – especially to the Aged Poor.

So I said, 'Good evening, Uncle,' yet once again. Then he said –

'Time you were in bed, young man. Eh! – what?'

Then I saw I must speak plainly with him, man to man. So I did. I said –

'You've been dining with my Father, and we couldn't help hearing you say the dinner was shocking. So we thought as you're an Indian, perhaps you're very poor' – I didn't like to tell him we had heard the dreadful truth from his own lips, so I went on, 'because of "Lo, the poor Indian" – you know – and you can't get a good dinner every day. And we are very sorry if you're poor; and won't you come and have dinner with us to-morrow – with us children, I mean? It's a very, very good dinner – rabbit, and hardbake, and coconut – and you needn't mind us knowing you're poor, because we know honourable poverty is no disgrace, and –' I could have gone on much longer, but he interrupted me to say –

'Upon my word! And what's *your* name, eh?'

'Oswald Bastable,' I said; and I do hope you people who are reading this story have not guessed before that I was Oswald all the time.

'Oswald Bastable, eh? Bless my soul!' said the poor Indian. 'Yes, I'll dine with you, Mr Oswald Bastable, with all the pleasure in life. Very kind and cordial invitation, I'm sure. Good night, sir. At one o'clock, I presume?'

'Yes, at one,' I said. 'Good night, sir.'

Then I went in and told the others, and we wrote a paper and put it on the boy's dressing-table, and it said –

'The poor Indian is coming at one. He seemed very grateful to me for my kindness.'

We did not tell Father that the Uncle was coming to dinner with us, for the polite reason that I have explained before. But we had to tell Eliza; so we said a friend was coming to dinner and we wanted everything very nice. I think she thought it was Albert-next-door, but she was in a good temper that day, and she agreed to cook the rabbit and to make a pudding with currants in it. And when one o'clock came the Indian Uncle came too. I let him in and helped him off with his greatcoat, which was all furry inside, and took him straight to the nursery. We were to have dinner there as usual, for we had decided from the first that he would enjoy himself more if he was not made a stranger of. We agreed to treat him as one of ourselves, because if we were too polite, he might think it was our pride because he was poor.

He shook hands with us all and asked our ages, and what schools we went to, and shook his head when we said we were having a holiday just now. I felt rather uncomfortable – I always do when they talk about

schools – and I couldn't think of anything to say to
show him we meant to treat him as one of ourselves. I
did ask if he played cricket. He said he had not played
lately. And then no one said anything till dinner came
in. We had all washed our faces and hands and brushed
our hair before he came in, and we all looked very nice,
especially Oswald, who had had his hair cut that very
morning. When Eliza had brought in the rabbit and
gone out again, we looked at each other in silent
despair, like in books. It seemed as if it were going to
be just a dull dinner like the one the poor Indian had
had the night before; only, of course, the things to eat
would be nicer. Dicky kicked Oswald under the table
to make him say something – and he had his new boots
on, too! – but Oswald did not kick back; then the
Uncle asked –

'Do you carve, sir, or shall I?'

Suddenly Alice said –

'Would you like grown-up dinner, Uncle, or play-
dinner?'

He did not hesitate a moment, but said, 'Play-
dinner, by all means. Eh! – what?' and then we knew
it was all right.

So we at once showed the Uncle how to be a dauntless hunter. The rabbit was the deer we had slain in the
green forest with our trusty yew bows, and we toasted
the joints of it, when the Uncle had carved it, on bits of
firewood sharpened to a point. The Uncle's piece got a
little burnt, but he said it was delicious, and he said
game was always nicer when you had killed it yourself.
When Eliza had taken away the rabbit bones and
brought in the pudding, we waited till she had gone out
and shut the door, and then we put the dish down on
the floor and slew the pudding in the dish in the good
old-fashioned way. It was a wild boar at bay, and very

The uncle was very fierce indeed with the pudding

hard indeed to kill, even with forks. The Uncle was very fierce indeed with the pudding, and jumped and howled when he speared it, but when it came to his turn to be helped, he said, 'No, thank you; think of my liver. Eh! – what?'

But he had some almonds and raisins – when we had climbed to the top of the chest of drawers to pluck them from the boughs of the great trees; and he had a fig from the cargo that the rich merchants brought in their ship – the long drawer was the ship – and the rest of us had the sweets and the coconut. It was a very glorious and beautiful feast, and when it was over we said we hoped it was better than the dinner last night. And he said:

'I never enjoyed a dinner more.' He was too polite to say what he really thought about Father's dinner. And we saw that though he might be poor, he was a true gentleman.

He smoked a cigar while we finished up what there was left to eat, and told us about tiger shooting and about elephants. We asked him about wigwams, and wampum, and mocassins, and beavers, but he did not seem to know, or else he was shy about talking of the wonders of his native land.

We liked him very much indeed, and when he was going at last, Alice nudged me, and I said –

'There's one and threepence farthing left out of our half-sovereign. Will you take it, please, because we do like you very much indeed, and we don't want it, really; and we would rather you had it.' And I put the money into his hand.

'I'll take the threepenny-bit,' he said, turning the money over and looking at it, 'but I couldn't rob you of the rest. By the way, where did you get the money for this most royal spread – half a sovereign you said – eh, what?'

We told him all about the different ways we had looked for treasure, and when we had been telling some time he sat down, to listen better; and at last we told him how Alice had played at divining-rod, and how it really had found a half-sovereign. Then he said he would like to see her do it again. But we explained that the rod would only show gold and silver, and that we were quite sure there was no more gold in the house, because we happened to have looked very carefully.

'Well, silver, then,' said he; 'let's hide the plate-basket, and little Alice shall make the divining-rod find it. Eh! – what?'

'There isn't any silver in the plate-basket now,' Dora said. 'Eliza asked me to borrow the silver spoons and forks for your dinner last night from Albert-next-door's Mother. Father never notices, but she thought it would be nicer for you. Our own silver went to have the dents taken out; and I don't think Father could afford to pay the man for doing it, for the silver hasn't come back.'

'Bless my soul!' said the Uncle again, looking at the hole in the big chair that we burnt when we had Guy Fawkes' Day indoors. 'And how much pocket-money do you get? Eh! – what?'

'We don't have any now,' said Alice; 'but indeed we don't want the other shilling. We'd much rather you had it, wouldn't we?'

And the rest of us said, 'Yes.' The Uncle wouldn't take it, but he asked a lot of questions, and at last he went away. And when he went he said –

'Well, youngsters, I've enjoyed myself very much. I shan't forget your kind hospitality. Perhaps the poor Indian may be in a position to ask you all to dinner some day.'

Oswald said if he ever could we should like to come very much, but he was not to trouble to get such a nice dinner as ours, because we could do very well with cold mutton and rice pudding. We do not like these things, but Oswald knows how to behave. Then the poor Indian went away.

We had not got any treasure by this party, but we had had a very good time, and I am sure the Uncle enjoyed himself.

We were so sorry he was gone that we could none of us eat much tea; but we did not mind, because we had pleased the poor Indian and enjoyed ourselves too. Besides, as Dora said, 'A contented mind is a continual feast,' so it did not matter about not wanting tea.

Only H. O. did not seem to think a continual feast was a contented mind, and Eliza gave him a powder in what was left of the red-currant jelly Father had for the nasty dinner.

But the rest of us were quite well, and I think it must have been the coconut with H. O. We hoped nothing had disagreed with the Uncle, but we never knew.

THE END OF THE
TREASURE-SEEKING

Now it is coming near the end of our treasure-seeking, and the end was so wonderful that now nothing is like it used to be. It is like as if our fortunes had been in an earthquake, and after those, you know, everything comes out wrong-way up.

The day after the Uncle speared the pudding with us opened in gloom and sadness. But you never know. It was destined to be a day when things happened. Yet no sign of this appeared in the early morning. Then all was misery and upsetness. None of us felt quite well; I don't know why: and Father had one of his awful colds, so Dora persuaded him not to go to London, but to stay cosy and warm in the study, and she made him some gruel. She makes it better than Eliza does; Eliza's gruel is all little lumps, and when you suck them it is dry oatmeal inside.

We kept as quiet as we could, and I made H. O. do some lessons, like the G. B. had advised us to. But it was very dull. There are some days when you seem to have got to the end of all the things that could ever possibly happen to you, and you feel you will spend all the rest of your life doing dull things just the same way. Days like this are generally wet days. But, as I said, you never know.

Then Dicky said if things went on like this he should run away to sea, and Alice said she thought it would be rather nice to go into a convent. H. O. was a little disagreeable because of the powder Eliza had given him, so he tried to read two books at once, one with each eye, just because Noël wanted one of the books, which was very selfish of him, so it only made his headache worse. H. O. is getting old enough to learn by experience that it is wrong to be selfish, and when he complained about his head Oswald told him whose fault it was, because I am older than he is, and it is my duty to show him where he is wrong. But he began to cry, and then Oswald had to cheer him up because of Father wanting to be quiet. So Oswald said –

'They'll eat H. O. if you don't look out!'

And Dora said Oswald was too bad.

Of course Oswald was not going to interfere again, so he went to look out of the window and see the trams go by, and by and by H. O. came and looked out too, and Oswald, who knows when to be generous and forgiving, gave him a piece of blue pencil and two nibs, as good as new, to keep.

As they were looking out at the rain splashing on the stones in the street they saw a four-wheeled cab come lumbering up from the way the station is. Oswald called out –

'Here comes the coach of the Fairy Godmother. It'll stop here, you see if it doesn't!'

So they all came to the window to look. Oswald had only said that about stopping and he was stricken with wonder and amaze when the cab really did stop. It had boxes on the top and knobby parcels sticking out of the window, and it was something like going away to the seaside and something like the gentleman who takes things about in a carriage with the wooden shutters up, to sell to the drapers' shops. The cabman got down, and some one inside handed out ever so many parcels of different shapes and sizes, and the cabman stood holding them in his arms and grinning over them.

Dora said, 'It is a pity some one doesn't tell him this isn't the house.' And then from inside the cab some one put out a foot feeling for the step, like a tortoise's foot coming out from under his shell when you are holding him off the ground, and then a leg came and more parcels, and then Noël cried –

'It's the poor Indian!'

And it was.

Eliza opened the door, and we were all leaning over the banisters. Father heard the noise of parcels and boxes in the hall, and he came out without remembering how bad his cold was. If you do that yourself when you have a cold they call you careless and naughty. Then we heard the poor Indian say to Father –

'I say, Dick, I dined with your kids yesterday – as I daresay they've told you. Jolliest little cubs I ever saw! Why didn't you let me see them the other night? The eldest is the image of poor Janey – and as to young Oswald, he's a man! If he's not a man, I'm a nigger! Eh! – what? And Dick, I say, I shouldn't wonder if I could find a friend to put a bit into that business of yours – eh?'

Then he and Father went into the study and the door was shut – and we went down and looked at the parcels. Some were done up in old, dirty newspapers, and tied with bits of rag, and some were in brown paper and string from the shops, and there were boxes. We wondered if the Uncle had come to stay and this was his luggage, or whether it was to sell. Some of it smelt of spices, like merchandise – and one bundle Alice felt certain was a bale. We heard a hand on the knob of the study door after a bit, and Alice said –

'Fly!' and we all got away but H. O., and the Uncle

caught him by the leg as he was trying to get upstairs after us.

'Peeping at the baggage, eh?' said the Uncle, and the rest of us came down because it would have been dishonourable to leave H. O. alone in a scrape, and we wanted to see what was in the parcels.

'I didn't touch,' said H. O. 'Are you coming to stay? I hope you are.'

'No harm done if you did touch,' said the good, kind, Indian man to all of us. 'For all these parcels are *for you.*'

I have several times told you about our being dumb with amazement and terror and joy, and things like that, but I never remember us being dumber than we were when he said this.

The Indian Uncle went on: 'I told an old friend of mine what a pleasant dinner I had with you, and about the threepenny-bit, and the divining-rod, and all that, and he sent all these odds and ends as presents for you. Some of the things came from India.'

'Have you come from India, Uncle?' Noël asked; and when he said 'Yes' we were all very much surprised, for we never thought of his being that sort of Indian. We thought he was the Red kind, and of course his not being accounted for his ignorance of beavers and things.

He got Eliza to help, and we took all the parcels into the nursery and he undid them and undid them and undid them, till the papers lay thick on the floor. Father came too and sat in the Guy Fawkes chair. I cannot begin to tell you all the things that kind friend of Uncle's had sent us. He must be a very agreeable person.

There were toys for the kids and model engines for Dick and me, and a lot of books, and Japanese china tea-sets for the girls, red and white and gold – there were

sweets by the pound and by the box – and long yards
and yards of soft silk from India, to make frocks for the
girls – and a real Indian sword for Oswald and a book
of Japanese pictures for Noël, and some ivory chessmen
for Dicky: the castles of the chessmen are elephant-
and-castles. There is a railway station called that; I
never knew what it meant before. The brown paper
and string parcels had boxes of games in them – and big
cases of preserved fruits and things. And the shabby
old newspaper parcels and the boxes had the Indian
things in. I never saw so many beautiful things before.
There were carved fans and silver bangles and strings
of amber beads, and necklaces of uncut gems –
turquoises and garnets, the Uncle said they were – and
shawls and scarves of silk, and cabinets of brown and
gold, and ivory boxes and silver trays, and brass things.
The Uncle kept saying, 'This is for you, young man,' or
'Little Alice will like this fan,' or 'Miss Dora would look
well in this green silk, I think. Eh! – what?'

And Father looked on as if it was a dream, till the
Uncle suddenly gave him an ivory paper-knife and a
box of cigars, and said, 'My old friend sent you these,
Dick; he's an old friend of yours too, he says.' And he
winked at my Father, for H. O. and I saw him. And
my Father winked back, though he has always told us
not to.

That was a wonderful day. It was a treasure, and
no mistake! I never saw such heaps and heaps of
presents, like things out of a fairy-tale – and even Eliza
had a shawl. Perhaps she deserved it, for she did cook
the rabbit and the pudding; and Oswald says it is not
her fault if her nose turns up and she does not brush
her hair. I do not think Eliza likes brushing things. It
is the same with the carpets. But Oswald tries to make
allowances even for people who do not wash their ears.

The Indian Uncle came to see us often after that, and his friend always sent us something. Once he tipped us a sovereign each – the Uncle brought it; and once he sent us money to go to the Crystal Palace, and the Uncle took us; and another time to a circus; and when Christmas was near the Uncle said –

'You remember when I dined with you, some time ago, you promised to dine with me some day, if I could ever afford to give a dinner-party. Well, I'm going to have one – a Christmas party. Not on Christmas Day, because every one goes home then – but on the day after. Cold mutton and rice pudding. You'll come? Eh! – what?'

We said we should be delighted, if Father had no objection, because that is the proper thing to say, and the poor Indian, I mean the Uncle, said, 'No, your Father won't object – he's coming too, bless your soul!'

We all got Christmas presents for the Uncle. The girls made him a handkerchief case and a comb bag, out of some of the pieces of silk he had given them. I got him a knife with three blades; H. O. got a siren whistle, a very strong one, and Dicky joined with me in the knife, and Noël would give the Indian ivory box that Uncle's friend had sent on the wonderful Fairy Cab day. He said it was the very nicest thing he had, and he was sure Uncle wouldn't mind his not having bought it with his own money.

I think Father's business must have got better – perhaps Uncle's friend put money in it and that did it good, like feeding the starving. Anyway we all had new suits, and the girls had the green silk from India made into frocks, and on Boxing Day we went in two cabs – Father and the girls in one, and us boys in the other.

We wondered very much where the Indian Uncle

203

lived, because we had not been told. And we thought
when the cab began to go up the hill towards the
Heath that perhaps the Uncle lived in one of the poky
little houses up at the top of Greenwich. But the cab
went right over the Heath and in at some big gates, and
through a shrubbery all white with frost like a fairy
forest, because it was Christmas time. And at last we
stopped before one of those jolly, big, ugly red houses
with a lot of windows, that are so comfortable inside,
and on the steps was the Indian Uncle, looking very
big and grand, in a blue cloth coat and yellow sealskin
waistcoat, with a bunch of seals hanging from it.

'I wonder whether he has taken a place as butler
here?' said Dicky. 'A poor, broken-down man –'

Noël thought it was very likely, because he knew that
in these big houses there were always thousands of
stately butlers.

The Uncle came down the steps and opened the cab
door himself, which I don't think butlers would expect
to have to do. And he took us in. It was a lovely hall,
with bear and tiger skins on the floor, and a big clock
with the faces of the sun and moon dodging out when
it was day or night, and Father Time with a scythe
coming out at the hours, and the name on it was
'Flint. Ashford. 1776'; and there was a fox eating a
stuffed duck in a glass case, and horns of stags and other
animals over the doors.

'We'll just come into my study first,' said the Uncle,
'and wish each other a Merry Christmas.' So then we
knew he wasn't the butler, but it must be his own
house, for only the master of the house has a study.

His study was not much like Father's. It had hardly
any books, but swords and guns and newspapers and a
great many boots, and boxes half unpacked, with more
Indian things bulging out of them.

The uncle looked at Father, and Father said, 'You tell them'

We gave him our presents and he was awfully pleased. Then he gave us his Christmas presents. You must be tired of hearing about presents, but I must remark that all the Uncle's presents were watches; there was a watch for each of us, with our names engraved inside, all silver except H. O.'s, and that was a Waterbury, 'To match his boots,' the Uncle said. I don't know what he meant.

Then the Uncle looked at Father, and Father said, 'You tell them, sir.'

So the Uncle coughed and stood up and made a speech. He said –

'Ladies and gentlemen, we are met together to discuss an important subject which has for some weeks engrossed the attention of the honourable member opposite and myself.'

I said, 'Hear, hear,' and Alice whispered, 'What happened to the guinea-pig?' Of course you know the answer to that.

The Uncle went on –

'I am going to live in this house, and as it's rather big for me, your Father has agreed that he and you shall come and live with me. And so, if you're agreeable, we're all going to live here together, and, please God, it'll be a happy home for us all. Eh! – what?'

He blew his nose and kissed us all round. As it was Christmas I did not mind, though I am much too old for it on other dates. Then he said, 'Thank you all very much for your presents; but I've got a present here I value more than anything else I have.'

I thought it was not quite polite of him to say so, till I saw that what he valued so much was a threepenny-bit on his watch-chain, and, of course, I saw it must be the one we had given him.

He said, 'You children gave me that when you thought I was the poor Indian, and I'll keep it as long as I live. And I've asked some friends to help us to be jolly, for this is our house-warming. Eh! – what?'

Then he shook Father by the hand, and they blew their noses; and then Father said, 'Your Uncle has been most kind – most –'

But Uncle interrupted by saying, 'Now, Dick, no nonsense!'

Then H. O. said, 'Then you're not poor at all?' as if he were very disappointed.

The Uncle replied, 'I have enough for my simple wants, thank you, H. O.; and your Father's business will provide him with enough for yours. Eh! – what?'

Then we all went down and looked at the fox thoroughly, and made the Uncle take the glass off so that we could see it all round; and then the Uncle took us all over the house, which is the most comfortable one I have ever been in. There is a beautiful portrait of Mother in Father's sitting-room. The Uncle must be very rich indeed. This ending is like what happens in Dickens's books; but I think it was much jollier to happen like a book, and it shows what a nice man the Uncle is, the way he did it all.

Think how flat it would have been if the Uncle had said, when we first offered him the one and threepence farthing, 'Oh, I don't want your dirty one and threepence! I'm very rich indeed.' Instead of which he saved up the news of his wealth till Christmas, and then told us all in one glorious burst. Besides, I can't help it if it is like Dickens, because it happens this way. Real life is often something like books.

Presently, when we had seen the house, we were

taken into the drawing-room, and there was Mrs Leslie, who gave us the shillings and wished us good hunting, and Lord Tottenham, and Albert-next-door's Uncle – and Albert-next-door, and his Mother (I'm not very fond of her), and best of all our own Robber and his two kids, and our Robber had a new suit on. The Uncle told us he had asked the people who had been kind to us, and Noël said, 'Where is my noble editor that I wrote the poetry to?'

The Uncle said he had not had the courage to ask a strange editor to dinner; but Lord Tottenham was an old friend of Uncle's, and he had introduced Uncle to Mrs Leslie, and that was how he had the pride and pleasure of welcoming her to our house-warming. And he made her a bow like you see on a Christmas card.

Then Alice asked, 'What about Mr Rosenbaum? He was kind; it would have been a pleasant surprise for him.'

But everybody laughed, and Uncle said –

'Your father has paid him the sovereign he lent you. I don't think he could have borne another pleasant surprise.'

And I said there was the butcher, and he was really kind; but they only laughed, and Father said you could not ask all your business friends to a private dinner.

Then it was dinner-time, and we thought of Uncle's talk about cold mutton and rice. But it was a beautiful dinner, and I never saw such a dessert! We had ours on plates to take away into another sitting-room, which was much jollier than sitting round the table with the grown-ups. But the Robber's kids stayed with their Father. They were very shy and frightened, and said hardly anything, but looked all about with very bright eyes. H. O. thought they were like white mice; but afterwards we got to know them very well, and in the end they were not so mousy. And there is a good deal of interesting stuff to tell about them; but I shall put all that in another book, for there is no room for it in this one. We played desert islands all the afternoon and drank Uncle's health in ginger wine. It was H. O. that upset his over Alice's green silk dress, and she never even rowed him. Brothers ought not to have favourites, and Oswald would never be so mean as to have a favourite sister, or, if he had, wild horses should not make him tell who it was.

And now we are to go on living in the big house on the Heath, and it is very jolly.

Mrs Leslie often comes to see us, and our own Robber and Albert-next-door's uncle. The Indian Uncle likes him because he has been in India too and is brown; but our Uncle does not like Albert-next-door. He says he is a muff. And I am to go to Rugby, and so are Noël and H. O., and perhaps to Balliol afterwards. Balliol is my Father's college. It has two separate coats of arms, which many other colleges are not allowed. Noël is going to be a poet and Dicky wants to go into Father's business.

The Uncle is a real good old sort; and just think, we should never have found him if we hadn't made up our minds to be Treasure Seekers!

Noël made a poem about it –

> *Lo! the poor Indian from lands afar,*
> *Comes where the treasure seekers are;*
> *We looked for treasure, but we find*
> *The best treasure of all is the Uncle good and kind.*

I thought it was rather rot, but Alice would show it to the Uncle, and he liked it very much. He kissed

Alice and he smacked Noël on the back, and he said,
'I don't think *I've* done so badly either, if you come to
that, though I was never a regular professional treasure
seeker. Eh! – what?'

THE
WOULDBEGOODS

BEING THE FURTHER
ADVENTURES OF THE
TREASURE SEEKERS

To

MY DEAR SON

FABIAN BLAND

CONTENTS

THE JUNGLE

CHILDREN are like jam: all very well in the proper place, but you can't stand them all over the shop – eh, what?

These were the dreadful words of our Indian uncle. They made us feel very young and angry; and yet we could not be comforted by calling him names to ourselves, as you do when nasty grown-ups say nasty things, because he is not nasty, but quite the exact opposite when not irritated. And we could not think it ungentlemanly of him to say we were like jam, because, as Alice says, jam is very nice indeed – only not on furniture and improper places like that. My father said, 'Perhaps they had better go to boarding-school.' And that was awful, because we know Father disapproves of boarding-schools. And he looked at us and said, 'I am ashamed of them, sir!'

Your lot is indeed a dark and terrible one when your father is ashamed of you. And we all knew this, so that we felt in our chests just as if we had swallowed a hardboiled egg whole. At least, this is what Oswald felt, and Father said once that Oswald, as the eldest, was the representative of the family, so, of course, the others felt the same.

And then everybody said nothing for a short time. At last Father said –

'You may go – but remember . . .' The words that followed I am not going to tell you. It is no use telling you what you know before – as they do in schools. And you must all have had such words said to you many times. We went away when it was over. The girls cried, and we boys got out books and began to read, so that nobody should think we cared. But we felt it deeply in our interior hearts, especially Oswald, who is the eldest and the representative of the family.

We felt it all the more because we had not really meant to do anything wrong. We only thought perhaps the grown-ups would not be quite pleased if they knew, and that is quite different. Besides, we meant to put all the things back in their proper places when we had done with them before anyone found out about it. But I must not anticipate (that means telling the end of the story before the beginning. I tell you this because it is so sickening to have words you don't know in a story, and to be told to look it up in the dicker).

We are the Bastables – Oswald, Dora, Dicky, Alice, Noël, and H. O. If you want to know why we call our youngest brother H. O. you can jolly well read *The Treasure Seekers* and find out. We were the Treasure Seekers, and we sought it high and low, and quite regularly, because we particularly wanted to find it. And at last we did not find it, but we were found by a good, kind Indian uncle, who helped Father with his business, so that Father was able to take us all to live in a jolly big red house on Blackheath, instead of in the Lewisham Road, where we lived when we were only poor but honest Treasure Seekers. When we were poor but honest we always used to think that if only Father had plenty of business, and we did not have to go short of pocket money and wear shabby clothes (I don't mind this myself, but the girls do), we should be happy and very, very good.

And when we were taken to the beautiful big Blackheath house we thought now all would be well, because it was a house with vineries and pineries, and gas and water, and shrubberies and stabling, and replete with every modern convenience, like it says in Dyer & Hilton's list of Eligible House Property. I read all about it, and I have copied the words quite right.

It is a beautiful house, all the furniture solid and strong, no casters off the chairs, and the tables not scratched, and the silver not dented; and lots of servants, and the most decent meals every day – and lots of pocket-money.

But it is wonderful how soon you get used to things, even the things you want most. Our watches, for instance. We wanted them frightfully; but when I had mine a week or two, after the mainspring got broken and was repaired at Bennett's in the village, I hardly cared to look at the works at all, and it did not make me feel happy in my heart any more, though, of course, I should have been very unhappy if it had been taken away from me. And the same with new clothes and nice dinners and having enough of everything. You soon get used to it all, and it does not make you extra happy, although, if you had it all taken away, you would be very dejected. (That is a good word, and one I have never used before.) You get used to everything, as I said, and then you want something more. Father says this is what people mean by the deceitfulness of riches; but Albert's uncle says it is the spirit of progress, and Mrs Leslie said some people called it 'divine discontent'. Oswald asked them all what they thought one Sunday at dinner. Uncle said it was rot, and what we wanted was bread and water and a licking; but he meant it for a joke. This was in the Easter holidays.

We went to live at the Red House at Christmas. After the holidays the girls went to the Blackheath High

School, and we boys went to the Prop. (that means the Proprietary School). And we had to swot rather during term; but about Easter we knew the deceitfulness of riches in the vac., when there was nothing much on, like pantomimes and things. Then there was the summer term, and we swotted more than ever; and it was boiling hot, and masters' tempers got short and sharp, and the girls used to wish the exams came in cold weather. I can't think why they don't. But I suppose schools don't think of sensible thinks like that. They teach botany at girls' schools.

Then the Midsummer holidays came, and we breathed again – but only for a few days. We began to feel as if we had forgotten something, and did not know what it was. We wanted something to happen – only we didn't exactly know what. So we were very pleased when Father said –

'I've asked Mr Foulkes to send his children here for a week or two. You know – the kids who came at Christmas. You must be jolly to them, and see that they have a good time, don't you know.'

We remembered them right enough – they were little pinky, frightened things, like white mice, with very bright eyes. They had not been to our house since Christmas, because Denis, the boy, had been ill, and they had been with an aunt at Ramsgate.

Alice and Dora would have liked to get the bedrooms ready for the honoured guests, but a really good house-maid is sometimes more ready to say 'Don't' than even a general. So the girls had to chuck it. Jane only let them put flowers in the pots on the visitors' mantelpieces, and then they had to ask the gardener which kind they might pick, because nothing worth gathering happened to be growing in our own gardens just then.

Their train got in at 12.27. We all went to meet them.

Afterwards I thought that was a mistake, because their aunt was with them, and she wore black with beady things and a tight bonnet, and she said, when we took our hats off –

'Who are you?' quite crossly.

We said, 'We are the Bastables; we've come to meet Daisy and Denny.'

The aunt is a very rude lady, and it made us sorry for Daisy and Denny when she said to them –

'*Are* these the children? Do you remember them?'

We weren't very tidy, perhaps, because we'd been playing brigands in the shrubbery; and we knew we should have to wash for dinner as soon as we got back, anyhow. But still –

Denny said he thought he remembered us. But Daisy said, 'Of course they are,' and then looked as if she was going to cry.

So then the aunt called a cab, and told the man where to drive, and put Daisy and Denny in, and then she said –

'You two little girls may go too, if you like, but you little boys must walk.'

So the cab went off, and we were left. The aunt turned to us to say a few last words. We knew it would have been about brushing your hair and wearing gloves, so Oswald said, 'Good-bye', and turned haughtily away, before she could begin, and so did the others. No one but that kind of black beady tight lady would say 'little boys'. She is like Miss Murdstone in *David Copperfield*. I should like to tell her so; but she would not understand. I don't suppose she has ever read anything but *Markham's History* and *Mangnall's Questions* – improving books like that.

When we got home we found all four of those who had ridden in the cab sitting in our sitting-room – we don't call it nursery now – looking very thoroughly washed, and our girls were asking polite questions and the others were saying 'Yes' and 'No', and 'I don't know'. We boys did not say anything. We stood at the window and looked out till the gong went for our dinner. We felt it was going to be awful – and it was. The newcomers would never have done for knight-errants, or to carry the Cardinal's sealed message through the heart of France on a horse; they would never have thought of anything to say to throw the enemy off the scent when they got into a tight place.

They said 'Yes, please', and 'No, thank you'; and they ate very neatly, and always wiped their mouths before they drank, as well as after, and never spoke with them full.

And after dinner it got worse and worse.

We got out all our books and they said 'Thank you', and didn't look at them properly. And we got out all our toys, and they said 'Thank you, it's very nice' to everything. And it got less and less pleasant, and towards teatime it came to nobody saying anything except Noël and H. O. – and they talked to each other about cricket.

After tea Father came in, and he played 'Letters' with them and the girls, and it was a little better; but while late dinner was going on – I shall never forget it. Oswald felt like the hero of a book – 'almost at the end of his resources'. I don't think I was ever glad of bed-time before, but that time I was.

When they had gone to bed (Daisy had to have all her strings and buttons undone for her, Dora told me, though she is nearly ten, and Denny said he couldn't sleep without the gas being left a little bit on) we held a council in the girls' room. We all sat on the bed – it is a mahogany fourposter with green curtains very good for

tents, only the housekeeper doesn't allow it, and
Oswald said –

'This is jolly nice, isn't it?'

'They'll be better to-morrow,' Alice said, 'they're
only shy.'

Dicky said shy was all very well, but you needn't
behave like a perfect idiot.

'They're frightened. You see we're all strange to
them,' Dora said.

'We're not wild beasts or Indians; we shan't eat them.
What have they got to be frightened of?' Dicky said
this.

Noël told us he thought they were an enchanted
prince and princess who'd been turned into white
rabbits, and their bodies had got changed back but not
their insides.

But Oswald told him to dry up.

'It's no use making things up about them,' he said.
'The thing is: what are we going to *do*? We can't have
our holidays spoiled by these snivelling kids.'

'No,' Alice said, 'but they can't possibly go on
snivelling for ever. Perhaps they've got into the habit of
it with that Murdstone aunt. She's enough to make anyone snivel.'

'All the same,' said Oswald, 'we jolly well aren't
going to have another day like today. We must do
something to rouse them from their snivelling leth –
what's its name? – something sudden and – what is
it? – decisive.'

'A booby trap,' said H. O., 'the first thing when they
get up, and an apple-pie bed at night.'

But Dora would not hear of it, and I own she was
right.

'Suppose,' she said, 'we could get up a good play –
like we did when we were Treasure Seekers.'

We said, well what? But she did not say.

'It ought to be a good long thing – to last all day,' Dicky said, 'and if they like they can play, and if they don't – '

'If they don't, I'll read to them,' Alice said.

But we all said 'No, you don't — if you begin that way you'll have to go on.' And Dicky added, 'I wasn't going to say that at all. I was going to say if they didn't like it they could jolly well do the other thing.'

We all agreed that we must think of something, but we none of us could, and at last the council broke up in confusion because Mrs Blake – she is the housekeeper – came up and turned off the gas.

But next morning when we were having breakfast, and the two strangers were sitting there so pink and clean, Oswald suddenly said –

'I know; we'll have a jungle in the garden.'

And the others agreed, and we talked about it till brek was over. The little strangers only said 'I don't know' whenever we said anything to them.

After brekker Oswald beckoned his brothers and sisters mysteriously apart and said –

'Do you agree to let me be captain today, because I thought of it?'

And they said they would.

Then he said, 'We'll play *Jungle Book*, and I shall be Mowgli. The rest of you can be what you like – Mowgli's father and mother, or any of the beasts.'

'I don't suppose they know the book,' said Noël. 'They don't look as if they read anything, except at lesson times.'

'Then they can go on being beasts all the time,' Oswald said. 'Anyone can be a beast.'

So it was settled.

And now Oswald – Albert's uncle has sometimes said he is clever at arranging things – began to lay his plans for the jungle. The day was indeed well chosen. Our Indian uncle was away; Father was away; Mrs Blake was going away, and the housemaid had an afternoon off. Oswald's first conscious act was to get rid of the white mice – I mean the little good visitors. He explained to them that there would be a play in the afternoon, and they could be what they liked, and gave them the *Jungle Book* to read the stories he told them to – all the ones about Mowgli. He led the strangers to a secluded spot among the sea-kale pots in the kitchen garden and left them. Then he went back to the others, and we had a jolly morning under the cedar talking about what we would do when Blakie was gone. She went just after our dinner.

When we asked Denny what he would like to be in the play, it turned out he had not read the stories Oswald told him at all, but only the 'White Seal' and 'Rikki Tikki'.

We then agreed to make the jungle first and dress up for our parts afterwards. Oswald was a little uncomfortable about leaving the strangers alone all the morning, so he said Denny should be his aide-de-camp, and he was really quite useful. He is rather handy with his fingers, and things that he does up do not come untied. Daisy might have come too, but she wanted to go on reading, so we let her, which is the truest manners to a visitor. Of course the shrubbery was to be the jungle, and the lawn under the cedar a forest glade, and then we began to collect the things. The cedar lawn is just nicely out of the way of the windows. It was a jolly hot day – the kind of day when the sunshine is white and the shadows are dark grey, not black like they are in the evening.

Up to now all was not

We all thought of different things. Of course first we dressed up pillows in the skins of beasts and set them about on the grass to look as natural as we could. And then we got Pincher, and rubbed him all over with powdered slate-pencil, to make him the right colour for Grey Brother. But he shook it all off, and it had taken an awful time to do. Then Alice said –

'Oh, I know!' and she ran off to Father's dressing-room, and came back with the tube of *crème d'amande pour la barbe et les mains*, and we squeezed it on Pincher and rubbed it in, and then the slate-pencil stuff stuck all right, and he rolled in the dust-bin of his own accord, which made him just the right colour. He is a very clever dog, but soon after he went off and we did not

lost beyond recall

find him till quite late in the afternoon. Denny helped
with Pincher, and with the wild-beast skins, and when
Pincher was finished he said –

'Please, may I make some paper birds to put in the
trees? I know how.'

And of course we said 'Yes', and he only had red ink
and newspapers, and quickly he made quite a lot of
large paper birds with red tails. They didn't look half
bad on the edge of the shrubbery.

While he was doing this he suddenly said, or rather
screamed, 'Oh?'

And we looked, and it was a creature with great
horns and a fur rug – something like a bull and
something like a minotaur – and I don't wonder

Denny was frightened. It was Alice, and it was first-class.

Up to now all was not yet lost beyond recall. It was the stuffed fox that did the mischief – and I am sorry to own it was Oswald who thought of it. He is not ashamed of having *thought* of it. That was rather clever of him. But he knows now that it is better not to take other people's foxes and things without asking, even if you live in the same house with them.

It was Oswald who undid the back of the glass case in the hall and got out the fox with the green and grey duck in its mouth, and when the others saw how awfully like life they looked on the lawn, they all rushed off to fetch the other stuffed things. Uncle has a tremendous lot of stuffed things. He shot most of them himself – but not the fox, of course. There was another fox's mask, too, and we hung that in a bush to look as if the fox was peeping out. And the stuffed birds we fastened on to the trees with string. The duck-bill – what's its name? – looked very well sitting on his tail with the otter snarling at him. Then Dicky had an idea; and though not nearly so much was said about it afterwards as there was about the stuffed things, I think myself it was just as bad, though it was a good idea, too. He just got the hose and put the end over a branch of the cedar-tree. Then we got the steps they clean windows with, and let the hose rest on the top of the steps and run. It was to be a waterfall, but it ran between the steps and was only wet and messy; so we got Father's mackintosh and uncle's and covered the steps with them, so that the water ran down all right and was glorious, and it ran away in a stream across the grass where we had dug a little channel for it – and the otter and the duck-bill-thing were as if in their native haunts. I hope all this is not very dull to read about. I know it was jolly good fun to do. Taking one thing with another, I don't know that we ever had a better time while it lasted.

We got all the rabbits out of the hutches and put pink paper tails on to them, and hunted them with horns made out of *The Times*. They got away somehow, and before they were caught next day they had eaten a good many lettuces and other things. Oswald is very sorry for this. He rather likes the gardener.

Denny wanted to put paper tails on the guinea-pigs, and it was no use our telling him there was nothing to tie the paper on to. He thought we were kidding until we showed him, and then he said, 'Well, never mind', and got the girls to give him bits of the blue stuff left over from their dressing-gowns.

'I'll make them sashes to tie round their little middles,' he said. And he did, and the bows stuck up on the tops of their backs. One of the guinea-pigs was never seen again, and the same with the tortoise when we had done his shell with vermilion paint. He crawled away and returned no more. Perhaps someone collected him and thought he was an expensive kind unknown in these cold latitudes.

The lawn under the cedar was transformed into a dream of beauty, what with the stuffed creatures and the paper-tailed things and the waterfall. And Alice said –

'I wish the tigers did not look so flat.' For of course with pillows you can only pretend it is a sleeping tiger getting ready to make a spring out at you. It is difficult to prop up tiger-skins in a life-like manner when there are no bones inside them, only pillows and sofa cushions. 'What about the beer-stands?' I said. And we got two out of the cellar. With bolsters and string we fastened insides to the tigers – and they were really fine. The legs of the beer-stands did for tigers' legs. It was indeed the finishing touch.

Then we boys put on just our bathing drawers and vests – so as to be able to play with the waterfall without hurting our clothes. I think this was thoughtful. The girls only tucked up their frocks and took their shoes and stockings off. H. O. painted his legs and his hands with Condy's fluid – to make him brown, so that he might be Mowgli, although Oswald was captain and had plainly said he was going to be Mowgli himself. Of course the others weren't going to stand that. So Oswald said –

'Very well. Nobody asked you to brown yourself like that. But now you've done it, you've simply got to go and be a beaver, and live in the dam under the waterfall till it washes off.'

He said he didn't want to be beavers. And Noël said –

'Don't make him. Let him be the bronze statue in the palace gardens that the fountain plays out of.'

So we let him have the hose and hold it up over his head. It made a lovely fountain, only he remained brown. So then Dicky and Oswald and I did ourselves brown too, and dried H. O. as well as we could with our handkerchiefs, because he was just beginning to snivel. The brown did not come off any of us for days.

Oswald was to be Mowgli, and we were just beginning to arrange the different parts. The rest of the hose that was on the ground was Kaa, the Rock Python, and Pincher was Grey Brother, only we couldn't find him. And while most of us were talking, Dicky and Noël got messing about with the beer-stand tigers.

And then a really sad event instantly occurred, which was not really our fault, and we did not mean to.

That Daisy girl had been mooning indoors all the afternoon with the *Jungle Books*, and now she came suddenly out, just as Dicky and Noël had got under the tigers and were shoving them along to fright each other. Of course, this is not in the Mowgli book at all: but they did look jolly like real tigers, and I am very far from wishing to blame the girl, though she little knew what would be the awful consequence of her rash act. But for her we might have got out of it all much better than we did.

What happened was truly horrid.

As soon as Daisy saw the tigers she stopped short, and uttering a shriek like a railway whistle she fell flat on the ground.

'Fear not, gentle Indian maid,' Oswald cried, thinking with surprise that perhaps after all she did know how to play, 'I myself will protect thee.' And he sprang forward with the native bow and arrows out of uncle's study.

The gentle Indian maiden did not move.

'Come hither,' Dora said, 'let us take refuge in yonder covert while this good knight does battle for us.'

Dora might have remembered that we were savages, but she did not. And that is Dora all over. And still the Daisy girl did not move.

Then we were truly frightened. Dora and Alice lifted her up, and her mouth was a horrid violet-colour and her eyes half shut. She looked horrid. Not at all like fair fainting damsels, who are always of an interesting pallor. She was green, like a cheap oyster on a stall.

We did what we could, a prey to alarm as we were. We rubbed her hands and let the hose play gently but perseveringly on her unconscious brow. The girls loosened her dress, though it was only the kind that comes down straight without a waist. And we were all doing what we could as hard as we could, when we heard the click of the front gate. There was no mistake about it.

'I hope whoever it is will go straight to the front

door,' said Alice. But whoever it was did not. There were feet on the gravel, and there was the uncle's voice, saying in his hearty manner –

'This way. This way. On such a day as this we shall find our young barbarians all at play somewhere about the grounds.'

And then, without further warning, the uncle, three other gentlemen and two ladies burst upon the scene.

We had no clothes on to speak of – I mean us boys. We were all wet through. Daisy was in a faint or a fit, or dead, none of us then knew which. And all the stuffed animals were there staring the uncle in the face. Most of them had got a sprinkling, and the otter and the duck-bill brute were simply soaked. And three of us were dark brown. Concealment, as so often happens, was impossible.

The quick brain of Oswald saw, in a flash, exactly how it would strike the uncle, and his brave young blood ran cold in his veins. His heart stood still.

'What's all this – eh, what?' said the tones of the wronged uncle.

Oswald spoke up and said it was jungles we were playing, and he didn't know what was up with Daisy. He explained as well as anyone could, but words were now in vain.

The uncle had a Malacca cane in his hand, and we were but ill prepared to meet the sudden attack. Oswald and H. O. caught it worst. The other boys were under the tigers – and of course my uncle would not strike a girl. Denny was a visitor and so got off. But it was bread and water for us for the next three days, and our own rooms. I will not tell you how we sought to vary the monotonousness of imprisonment. Oswald thought of taming a mouse, but he could not find one. The reason of the wretched captives might have given way but for the gutter that you can crawl along from our room to the girls'. But I will not dwell on this because you might try it yourselves, and it really is dangerous. When my father came home we got the talking to, and we said we were sorry – and we really were – especially about Daisy, though she had behaved with muffishness, and then it was settled that we were to go into the country and stay till we had grown into better children.

Albert's uncle was writing a book in the country; we were to go to his house. We were glad of this – Daisy and Denny too. This we bore nobly. We knew we had deserved it. We were all very sorry for everything, and we resolved that for the future we *would* be good.

I am not sure whether we kept this resolution or not. Oswald thinks now that perhaps we made a mistake in trying so very hard to be good all at once. You should do everything by degrees.

P.S. – It turned out Daisy was not really dead at all. It was only fainting – so like a girl.

N.B. – Pincher was found on the drawing-room sofa.

Appendix. – I have not told you half the things we did for the jungle – for instance, about the elephants' tusks and the horse-hair sofa-cushions, and uncle's fishing-boots.

THE WOULDBEGOODS

WHEN we were sent down into the country to learn to
be good we felt it was rather good business, because we
knew our being sent there was really only to get us out
of the way for a little while, and we knew right enough
that it wasn't a punishment, though Mrs Blake said it
was, because we had been punished thoroughly for
taking the stuffed animals out and making a jungle on
the lawn with them, and the garden hose. And you
cannot be punished twice for the same offence. This is
the English law; at least I think so. And at any rate no
one would punish you three times, and we had had the
Malacca cane and the solitary confinement; and the
uncle had kindly explained to us that all ill-feeling
between him and us was wiped out entirely by the bread
and water we had endured. And what with the bread
and water and being prisoners, and not being able to
tame any mice in our prisons, I quite feel that we had
suffered it up thoroughly, and now we could start fair.

I think myself that descriptions of places are generally
dull, but I have sometimes thought that was because
the authors do not tell you what you truly want to
know. However, dull or not, here goes – because you
won't understand anything unless I tell you what the
place was like.

The Moat House was the one we went to stay at.
There has been a house there since Saxon times. It is a
manor, and a manor goes on having a house on it

whatever happens. The Moat House was burnt down once or twice in ancient centuries – I don't remember which – but they always built a new one, and Cromwell's soldiers smashed it about, but it was patched up again. It is a very odd house: the front door opens

The Moat House with a brick bridge leading to the front door

straight into the dining-room, and there are red curtains and a black-and-white marble floor like a chess-board, and there is a secret staircase, only it is not secret now – only rather rickety. It is not very big, but there is a watery moat all round it with a brick bridge that leads to the front door. Then, on the other side of the moat there is the farm, with barns and oast houses and stables, or things like that. And the other way the garden lawn goes on till it comes to the churchyard. The churchyard is not divided from the garden at all except by a little grass bank. In the front of the house there is more garden, and the big fruit garden is at the back.

The man the house belongs to likes new houses, so he built a big one with conservatories and a stable with a clock in a turret on the top, and he left the Moat House. And Albert's uncle took it, and my father was to come down sometimes from Saturday to Monday, and Albert's uncle was to live with us all the time, and he would be writing a book, and we were not to bother him, but he would give an eye to us. I hope all this is plain. I have said it as short as I can.

We got down rather late, but there was still light enough to see the big bell hanging at the top of the house. The rope belonging to it went right down the house, through our bedroom to the dining-room. H. O. saw the rope and pulled it while he was washing his hands for supper, and Dicky and I let him, and the bell tolled solemnly. Father shouted to him not to, and we went down to supper. But presently there were many feet trampling on the gravel, and Father went out to see. When he came back he said –

'The whole village, or half of it, has come up to see why the bell rang. It's only rung for fire or burglars. Why can't you kids let things alone?'

Albert's uncle said –

'Bed follows supper as the fruit follows the flower. They'll do no more mischief to-night, sir. To-morrow I will point out a few of the things to be avoided in this bucolic retreat.'

So it was bed directly after supper, and that was why we did not see much that night.

But in the morning we were all up rather early, and we seemed to have awakened in a new world rich in surprises beyond the dreams of anybody, as it says in the quotation.

We went everywhere we could in the time, but when it was breakfast-time we felt we had not seen half or a quarter. The room we had breakfast in was exactly like in a story – black oak panels and china in corner cupboards with glass doors. These doors were locked. There were green curtains, and honeycomb for breakfast. After brekker my father went back to town, and Albert's uncle went too, to see publishers. We saw them to the station, and Father gave us a long list of what we weren't to do. It began with 'Don't pull ropes unless you're quite sure what will happen at the other end,' and it finished with 'For goodness sake, try to keep out of mischief till I come down on Saturday'. There were lots of other things in between.

We all promised we would. And we saw them off, and waved till the train was quite out of sight. Then we started to walk home. Daisy was tired so Oswald carried her home on his back. When we got home she said –

'I do like you, Oswald.'

She is not a bad little kid; and Oswald felt it was his duty to be nice to her because she was a visitor. Then we looked all over everything. It was a glorious place. You did not know where to begin.

We were all a little tired before we found the hayloft, but we pulled ourselves together to make a fort with the trusses of hay – great square things – and we were having a jolly good time, all of us, when suddenly a trap-door opened and a head bobbed up with a straw in its mouth. We knew nothing about the country then, and the head really did scare us rather, though, of course, we found out directly that the feet belonging to it were standing on the bar of the loose-box underneath. The head said –

'Don't you let the governor catch you a-spoiling of that there hay, that's all.' And it spoke thickly because of the straw.

It is strange to think how ignorant you were in the past. We can hardly believe now that once we really did not know that it spoiled hay to mess about with it. Horses don't like to eat it afterwards. Always remember this.

When the head had explained a little more it went away, and we turned the handle of the chaff-cutting machine, and nobody got hurt, though the head *had* said we should cut our fingers off if we touched it.

And then we sat down on the floor, which is dirty with the nice clean dirt that is more than half chopped hay, and those there was room for hung their legs down out of the top door, and we looked down at the farm-yard, which is very slushy when you get down into it, but most interesting.

Then Alice said –

'Now we're all here, and the boys are tired enough to sit still for a minute, I want to have a council.'

We said what about? And she said, 'I'll tell you. H. O., don't wriggle so; sit on my frock if the straws tickle your legs.'

You see he wears socks, and so he can never be quite as comfortable as anyone else.

'Promise not to laugh,' Alice said, getting very red, and looking at Dora, who got red too.

We did, and then she said: 'Dora and I have talked this over, and Daisy too, and we have written it down because it is easier than saying it. Shall I read it? or will you, Dora?'

Dora said it didn't matter; Alice might. So Alice read it, and though she gabbled a bit we all heard it. I copied it afterwards. This is what she read:

'NEW SOCIETY FOR BEING GOOD IN

'I, Dora Bastable, and Alice Bastable, my sister, being of sound mind and body, when we were shut up with bread and water on that jungle day, we thought a great deal about our naughty sins, and we made our minds up to be good for ever after. And we talked to Daisy about it, and she had an idea. So we want to start a society for being good in. It is Daisy's idea, but we think so too.'

'You know,' Dora interrupted, 'when people want to do good things they always make a society. There are thousands – there's the Missionary Society.'

'Yes,' Alice said, 'and the Society for the Prevention of something or other, and the Young Men's Mutual Improvement Society, and the S.P.G.'

'What's S.P.G.?' Oswald asked.

'Society for the Propagation of the Jews, of course,' said Noël, who cannot always spell.

'No, it isn't; but do let me go on.'

Alice did go on.

'We propose to get up a society, with a chairman and a treasurer and secretary, and keep a journal-book saying what we've done. If that doesn't make us good it won't be my fault.

'The aim of the society is nobleness and goodness, and great and unselfish deeds. We wish not to be such a nuisance to grown-up people and to perform prodigies of real goodness. We wish to spread our wings' – here Alice read very fast. She told me afterwards Daisy had helped her with that part, and she thought when she came to the wings they sounded rather silly – 'to spread our wings and rise above the kind of interesting things that you ought not to do, but to do kindnesses to all, however low and mean.'

Denny was listening carefully. Now he nodded three or four times.

> '*Little words of kindness*' (he said),
> '*Little deeds of love,*
> *Make this earth an eagle*
> *Like the one above.*'

This did not sound right, but we let it pass, because an eagle *does* have wings, and we wanted to hear the rest of what the girls had written. But there was no rest.

'That's all,' said Alice, and Daisy said –

'Don't you think it's a good idea?'

'That depends,' Oswald answered, 'who is president and what you mean by being good.' Oswald did not care very much for the idea himself, because being good is not the sort of thing he thinks it is proper to talk about, especially before strangers. But the girls and Denny seemed to like it, so Oswald did not say exactly what he thought, especially as it was Daisy's idea. This was true politeness.

'I think it would be nice,' Noël said, 'if we made it a sort of play. Let's do the *Pilgrim's Progress*.'

We talked about that for some time, but it did not come to anything, because we all wanted to be Mr Greatheart, except H. O., who wanted to be the lions, and you could not have lions in a Society for Goodness.

Dicky said he did not wish to play if it meant reading books about children who die; he really felt just as Oswald did about it, he told me afterwards. But the girls were looking as if they were in Sunday school, and we did not wish to be unkind.

At last Oswald said, 'Well, let's draw up the rules of

the society, and choose the president and settle the name.'

Dora said Oswald should be president, and he modestly consented. She was secretary, and Denny treasurer if we ever had any money.

Making the rules took us all the afternoon. They were these:

RULES

1. Every member is to be as good as possible.
2. There is to be no more jaw than necessary about being good. (Oswald and Dicky put that rule in.)
3. No day must pass without our doing some kind action to a suffering fellow-creature.
4. We are to meet every day, or as often as we like.
5. We are to do good to people we don't like as often as we can.
6. No one is to leave the Society without the consent of all the rest of us.
7. The Society is to be kept a profound secret from all the world except us.
8. The name of our Society is –

And when we got as far as that we all began to talk at once. Dora wanted it called the Society for Humane Improvement; Denny said the Society for Reformed Outcast Children; but Dicky said, No, we really were not so bad as all that. Then H. O. said, 'Call it the Good Society.'

'Or the Society for Being Good In,' said Daisy.

'Or the Society of Goods,' said Noël.

'That's priggish,' said Oswald; 'besides, we don't know whether we shall be so very.'

'You see,' Alice explained, 'we only said if we *could* we would be good.'

'Well, then,' Dicky said, getting up and beginning to dust the chopped hay off himself, 'call it the Society of the Wouldbegoods and have done with it.'

Oswald thinks Dicky was getting sick of it and wanted to make himself a little disagreeable. If so, he was doomed to disappointment. For everyone else clapped hands and called out, 'That's the very thing!' Then the girls went off to write out the rules, and took H. O. with them, and Noël went to write some poetry to put in the minute book. That's what you call the book that a society's secretary writes what it does in. Denny went with him to help. He knows a lot of poetry. I think he went to a lady's school where they taught nothing but that. He was rather shy of us, but he took to Noël. I can't think why. Dicky and Oswald walked round the garden and told each other what they thought of the new society.

'I'm not sure we oughtn't to have put our foot down at the beginning,' Dicky said. 'I don't see much in it, anyhow.'

'It pleases the girls,' Oswald said, for he is a kind brother.

'But we're not going to stand jaw, and "words in season", and "loving sisterly warnings". I tell you what it is, Oswald, we'll have to run this thing our way, or it'll be jolly beastly for everybody.'

Oswald saw this plainly.

'We must do something,' Dicky said; 'it's very very hard, though. Still, there must be *some* interesting things that are not wrong.'

'I suppose so,' Oswald said, 'but being good is so much like being a muff, generally. Anyhow I'm not going to smooth the pillows of the sick, or read to the aged poor, or any rot out of *Ministering Children*.'

'No more am I,' Dicky said. He was chewing a straw

like the head had in its mouth, 'but I suppose we must play the game fair. Let's begin by looking out for something useful to do – something like mending things or cleaning them, not just showing off.'

'The boys in books chop kindling wood and save their pennies to buy tea and tracts.'

'Little beasts!' said Dick. 'I say, let's talk about something else.' And Oswald was glad to, for he was beginning to feel jolly uncomfortable.

We were all rather quiet at tea, and afterwards Oswald played draughts with Daisy and the others yawned. I don't know when we've had such a gloomy evening. And everyone was horribly polite, and said 'Please' and 'Thank you' far more than requisite.

Albert's uncle came home after tea. He was jolly, and told us stories, but he noticed us being a little dull, and asked what blight had fallen on our young lives. Oswald could have answered and said, 'It is the Society of the Wouldbegoods that is the blight,' but of course he didn't; and Albert's uncle said no more, but he went up and kissed the girls when they were in bed, and asked them if there was anything wrong. And they told him no, on their honour.

The next morning Oswald awoke early. The refreshing beams of the morning sun shone on his narrow white bed and on the sleeping forms of his dear little brothers and Denny, who had got the pillow on top of his head and was snoring like a kettle when it sings. Oswald could not remember at first what was the matter with him, and then he remembered the Wouldbegoods, and wished he hadn't. He felt at first as if there was nothing you could do, and even hesitated to buzz a pillow at Denny's head. But he soon saw that this could not be. So he chucked his boot and caught Denny right in the waistcoat part, and thus the day began more brightly than he had expected.

Oswald had not done anything out of the way good the night before, except that when no one was looking he polished the brass candlestick in the girls' bedroom with one of his socks. And he might just as well have let it alone, for the servants cleaned it again with the other things in the morning, and he could never find the sock afterwards. There were two servants. One of them had to be called Mrs Pettigrew instead of Jane and Eliza like others. She was cook and managed things.

After breakfast Albert's uncle said –

'I now seek the retirement of my study. At your peril violate my privacy before 1.30 sharp. Nothing short of bloodshed will warrant the intrusion, and nothing short of man – or rather boy – slaughter shall avenge it.'

So we knew he wanted to be quiet, and the girls decided that we ought to play out of doors so as not to disturb him; we should have played out of doors anyhow on a jolly fine day like that.

But as we were going out Dicky said to Oswald –

'I say, come along here a minute, will you?'

So Oswald came along, and Dicky took him into the other parlour and shut the door, and Oswald said –

'Well, spit it out: what is it?' He knows that is vulgar, and he would not have said it to anyone but his own brother.

Dicky said –

'It's a pretty fair nuisance. I told you how it would be.'

And Oswald was patient with him, and said –

'What is? Don't be all day about it.'

Dicky fidgeted about a bit, and then he said –

'Well, I did as I said. I looked about for something useful to do. And you know that dairy window that wouldn't open – only a little bit like that? Well, I mended the catch with wire and whipcord and it opened wide.'

'And I suppose they didn't want it mended,' said Oswald. He knew but too well that grown-up people sometimes like to keep things far different from what we would, and you catch it if you try to do otherwise.

'I shouldn't have minded *that*,' Dicky said, 'because I could easily have taken it all off again if they'd only said so. But the sillies went and propped up a milk-pan against the window. They never took the trouble to notice I had mended it. So the wretched thing pushed the window open all by itself directly they propped it up, and it's tumbled through into the moat, and they are most awfully waxy. All the men are out in the fields and they haven't any spare milk-pans. If I were a farmer, I must say I wouldn't stick at an extra milk-pan or two. Accidents must happen sometimes. I call it mean.'

Dicky spoke in savage tones. But Oswald was not so unhappy, first because it wasn't his fault, and next because he is a far-seeing boy.

'Never mind,' he said kindly. 'Keep your tail up. We'll get the beastly milk-pan out all right. Come on.'

He rushed hastily to the garden and gave a low, signifying whistle, which the others know well enough to mean something extra being up.

And when they were all gathered round him he spoke.

'Fellow countrymen,' he said, 'we're going to have a rousing good time.'

'It's nothing naughty, is it,' Daisy asked, 'like the last time you had that was rousingly good?'

Alice said 'Shish', and Oswald pretended not to hear.

'A precious treasure,' he said, 'has inadvertently been laid low in the moat by one of us.'

'The rotten thing tumbled in by itself,' Dicky said.

Oswald waved his hand and said, 'Anyhow, it's there. It's our duty to restore it to its sorrowing owners. I say, look here – we're going to drag the moat.'

Everyone brightened up at this. It was our duty and it was interesting too. This is very uncommon.

So we went out to where the orchard is, at the other side of the moat. There were gooseberries and things on the bushes, but we did not take any till we had asked if we might. Alice went and asked. Mrs Pettigrew said, 'Law! I suppose so; you'd eat 'em anyhow, leave or no leave.'

She little knows the honourable nature of the house of Bastable. But she has much to learn.

The orchard slopes gently down to the dark waters of the moat. We sat there in the sun and talked about dragging the moat, till Denny said, 'How *do* you drag moats?'

And we were speechless, because, though we had read many times about a moat being dragged for missing heirs and lost wills, we really had never thought about exactly how it was done.

'Grappling-irons are right, I believe,' Denny said, 'but I don't suppose they'd have any at the farm.'

And we asked, and found they had never even heard of them. I think myself he meant some other word, but he was quite positive.

So then we got a sheet off Oswald's bed, and we all took our shoes and stockings off, and we tried to see if the sheet would drag the bottom of the moat, which is shallow at that end. But it would keep floating on the top of the water, and when we tried sewing stones into one end of it, it stuck on something in the bottom, and when we got it up it was torn. We were very sorry, and the sheet was in an awful mess; but the girls said they were sure they could wash it in the basin in their room, and we thought as we had torn it anyway, we might as well go on. That washing never came off.

'No human being,' Noël said, 'knows half the treasures hidden in this dark tarn.'

And we decided we would drag a bit more at that end, and work gradually round to under the dairy window where the milk-pan was. We could not see that part very well, because of the bushes that grow between the cracks of the stones where the house goes down into the moat. And opposite the dairy window the barn goes straight down into the moat too. It is like pictures of Venice; but you cannot get opposite the dairy window anyhow.

We got the sheet down again when we had tied the torn parts together in a bunch with string, and Oswald was just saying –

'Now then, my hearties, pull together, pull with a will! One, two, three,' when suddenly Dora dropped her bit of the sheet with a piercing shriek and cried out –

'Oh! it's all wormy at the bottom. I felt them wriggle.' And she was out of the water almost before the words were out of her mouth. The other girls all scuttled out too, and they let the sheet go in such a hurry that we had no time to steady ourselves, and one of us went right in, and the rest got wet up to our waistbands. The one who went right in was only H. O.; but Dora made an awful fuss and said it was our fault. We told her what we thought, and it ended in the girls going in with H. O. to change his things. We had some more gooseberries while they were gone. Dora was in an awful wax when she went away, but she is not of a sullen disposition though sometimes hasty, and when they all came back we saw it was all right, so we said –

'What shall we do now?'

Alice said, 'I don't think we need drag any more. It *is* wormy. I felt it when Dora did. And besides, the milk-pan is sticking a bit of itself out of the water. I saw it through the dairy window.'

'Couldn't we get it up with fish-hooks?' Noël said. But Alice explained that the dairy was now locked up and the key taken out.

So then Oswald said –

'Look here, we'll make a raft. We should have to do it some time, and we might as well do it now. I saw an old door in that corner stable that they don't use. You know. The one where they chop the wood.'

We got the door.

We had never made a raft, any of us, but the way to make rafts is better described in books, so we knew what to do.

We found some nice little tubs stuck up on the fence of the farm garden, and nobody seemed to want them for anything just then, so we took them. Denny had a box of tools someone had given him for his last birthday; they were rather rotten little things, but the gimlet worked all right, so we managed to make holes in the edges of the tubs and fasten them with string under the four corners of the old door. This took us a long time. Albert's uncle asked us at dinner what we had been playing at, and we said it was a secret, and it was nothing wrong. You see we wished to atone for Dicky's mistake before anything more was said. The house has no windows in the side that faces the orchard.

The rays of the afternoon sun were beaming along the orchard grass when at last we launched the raft. She floated out beyond reach with the last shove of the launching. But Oswald waded out and towed her back; he is not afraid of worms. Yet if he had known of the other things that were in the bottom of that moat he would have kept his boots on. So would the others, especially Dora, as you will see.

At last the gallant craft rode upon the waves. We manned her, though not up to our full strength, because if more than four got on the water came up too near our knees, and we feared she might founder if over-manned.

Daisy and Denny did not want to go on the raft, white mice that they were, so that was all right. And as H.O. had been wet through once he was not very keen. Alice promised Noël her best paint-brush if he'd give up and not go, because we knew well that the voyage was fraught with deep dangers, though the exact danger that lay in wait for us under the dairy window we never even thought of.

So we four elder ones got on the raft very carefully; and even then, every time we moved the water swished up over the raft and hid our feet. But I must say it was a jolly decent raft.

Dicky was captain, because it was his adventure. We had hop-poles from the hop-garden beyond the orchard to punt with. We made the girls stand together in the middle and hold on to each other to keep steady. Then we christened our gallant vessel. We called it the *Richard*, after Dicky, and also after the splendid admiral who used to eat wine-glasses and died after the Battle of the *Revenge* in Tennyson's poetry.

Then those on shore waved a fond adieu as well as they could with the dampness of their handkerchiefs, which we had had to use to dry our legs and feet when we put on our stockings for dinner, and slowly and stately the good ship moved away from shore, riding on the waves as though they were her native element.

We kept her going with the hop-poles, and we kept her steady in the same way, but we could not always keep her steady enough, and we could not always keep her in the wind's eye. That is to say, she went where we did not want, and once she bumped her corner against the barn wall, and all the crew had to sit down suddenly to avoid falling overboard into a watery grave. Of course then the waves swept her decks, and when we got up again we said that we should have to change completely before tea.

But we pressed on undaunted, and at last our saucy craft came into port, under the dairy window and there was the milk-pan, for whose sake we had endured such hardships and privations, standing up on its edge quite quietly.

The girls did not wait for orders from the captain, as they ought to have done; but they cried out, 'Oh, here it is!' and then both reached out to get it. Anyone who has pursued a naval career will see that of course the raft capsized. For a moment it felt like standing on the roof of the house, and the next moment the ship stood up on end and shot the whole crew into the dark waters.

We boys can swim all right. Oswald has swum three times across the Ladywell Swimming Baths at the shallow end, and Dicky is nearly as good; but just then we did not think of this; though, of course, if the water had been deep we should have.

As soon as Oswald could get the muddy water out of his eyes he opened them on a horrid scene.

Dicky was standing up to his shoulders in the inky waters; the raft had righted itself, and was drifting gently away towards the front of the house, where the bridge is, and Dora and Alice were rising from the deep,

A great noise of splashing, and 'Lord love the children!'

with their hair all plastered over their faces – like Venus in the Latin verses.

There was a great noise of splashing. And besides that a feminine voice, looking out of the dairy window and screaming –

'Lord love the children!'

It was Mrs Pettigrew. She disappeared at once, and we were sorry we were in such a situation that she would be able to get at Albert's uncle before we could. Afterwards we were not so sorry.

Before a word could be spoken about our desperate position Dora staggered a little in the water, and suddenly shrieked, 'Oh, my foot! oh, it's a shark! I know it is – or a crocodile!'

The others on the bank could hear her shrieking, but they could not see us properly; they did not know what was happening. Noël told me afterwards he never could care for that paint-brush.

Of course we knew it could not be a shark, but I thought of pike, which are large and very angry always, and I caught hold of Dora. She screamed without stopping. I shoved her along to where there was a ledge of brickwork, and shoved her up, till she could sit on it, then she got her foot out of the water, still screaming.

It was indeed terrible. The thing she thought was a shark came up with her foot, and it was a horrid, jagged, old meat-tin, and she had put her foot right into it. Oswald got it off, and directly he did so blood began to pour from the wounds. The tin edges had cut it in several spots. It was very pale blood, because her foot was wet, of course.

She stopped screaming, and turned green, and I thought she was going to faint, like Daisy did on the Jungle day.

Oswald held her up as well as he could, but it really was one of the least agreeable moments in his life. For the raft was gone, and she couldn't have waded back anyway, and we didn't know how deep the moat might be in other places.

But Mrs Pettigrew had not been idle. She is not a bad sort really.

Just as Oswald was wondering whether he could swim after the raft and get it back, a boat's nose shot out from under a dark archway a little further up under the house. It was the boathouse, and Albert's uncle had got the punt and took us back in it. When we had regained the dark arch where the boat lives we had to go up the cellar stairs. Dora had to be carried.

There was but little said to us that day. We were sent to bed – those who had not been on the raft the same as the others, for they owned up all right, and Albert's uncle is the soul of justice.

Next day but one was Saturday. Father gave us a talking to – with other things.

The worst was when Dora couldn't get her shoe on, so they sent for the doctor, and Dora had to lie down for ever so long. It was indeed poor luck.

When the doctor had gone Alice said to me –

'It *is* hard lines, but Dora's very jolly about it. Daisy's been telling her about how we should all go to her with our little joys and sorrows and things, and about the sweet influence from a sick bed that can be felt all over the house, like in *What Katy Did*, and Dora said she hoped she might prove a blessing to us all while she's laid up.'

Oswald said he hoped so, but he was not pleased. Because this sort of jaw was exactly the sort of thing he and Dicky didn't want to have happen.

The thing we got it hottest for was those little tubs

off the garden railings. They turned out to be butter-tubs that had been put out there 'to sweeten'.

But as Denny said, 'After the mud in that moat not all the perfumes of somewhere or other could make them fit to use for butter again.'

I own this was rather a bad business. Yet we did not do it to please ourselves, but because it was our duty. But that made no difference to our punishment when Father came down. I have known this mistake occur before.

BILL'S TOMBSTONE

THERE were soldiers riding down the road, on horses two and two. That is the horses were two and two, and the men not. Because each man was riding one horse and leading another. To exercise them. They came from Chatham Barracks. We all drew up in a line outside the churchyard wall, and saluted as they went by, though we had not read *Toady Lion* then. We have since. It is the only decent book I have ever read written by *Toady Lion*'s author. The others are mere piffle. But many people like them.

In *Sir Toady Lion* the officer salutes the child.

There was only a lieutenant with those soldiers, and he did not salute me. He kissed his hand to the girls; and a lot of the soldiers behind kissed theirs too. We waved ours back.

Next day we made a Union Jack out of pocket-handkerchiefs and part of a red flannel petticoat of the White Mouse's, which she did not want just then, and some blue ribbon we got at the village shop.

Then we watched for the soldiers, and after three days they went by again, by twos and twos as before. It was A1.

We waved our flag, and we shouted. We gave them three cheers. Oswald can shout loudest. So as soon as the first man was level with us (not the advance guard, but the first of the battery) – he shouted –

'Three cheers for the Queen and the British Army!'

255

And then we waved the flag, and bellowed. Oswald stood on the wall to bellow better, and Denny waved the flag because he was a visitor, and so politeness made us let him enjoy the fat of whatever there was going.

The soldiers did not cheer that day; they only grinned and kissed their hands.

The next day we all got up as much like soldiers as we could. H. O. and Noël had tin swords, and we asked Albert's uncle to let us wear some of the real arms that are on the wall in the dining-room. And he said, 'Yes', if we would clean them up afterwards. But we jolly well cleaned them up first with Brooke's soap and brick dust and vinegar, and the knife polish (invented by the great and immortal Duke of Wellington in his spare time when he was not conquering Napoleon. Three cheers for our Iron Duke!), and with emery paper and wash leather and whitening. Oswald wore a cavalry sabre in its sheath. Alice and the Mouse had pistols in their belts, large old flint-locks, with bits of red flannel behind the flints. Denny had a naval cutlass, a very beautiful blade, and old enough to have been at Trafalgar. I hope it was. The others had French sword-bayonets that were used in the Franco-German war. They are very bright when you get them bright, but the sheaths are hard to polish. Each sword-bayonet has the name on the blade of the warrior who once wielded it. I wonder where they are now. Perhaps some of them died in the war. Poor chaps! But it is a very long time ago.

I should like to be a soldier. It is better than going to the best schools, and to Oxford afterwards, even if it is Balliol you go to. Oswald wanted to go to South Africa for a bugler, but father would not let him. And it is true that Oswald does not yet know how to bugle, though he can play the infantry 'advance', and the 'charge' and the 'halt' on a penny whistle. Alice taught

them to him with the piano, out of the red book Father's
cousin had when he was in the Fighting Fifth. Oswald
cannot play the 'retire', and he would scorn to do
so. But I suppose a bugler has to play what he is
told, no matter how galling to the young boy's proud
spirit.

The next day, being thoroughly armed, we put on
everything red, white and blue that we could think of
-- night-shirts are good for white, and you don't know
what you can do with red socks and blue jerseys till you
try -- and we waited by the churchyard wall for the
soldiers. When the advance guard (or whatever you
call it of artillery -- it's that for infantry, I know) came
by, we got ready, and when the first man of the first
battery was level with us Oswald played on his penny
whistle the 'advance' and the 'charge' -- and then
shouted --

'Three cheers for the Queen and the British Army!'

This time they had the guns with them. And every
man of the battery cheered too. It was glorious. It made
you tremble all over. The girls said it made them want
to cry -- but no boy would own to this, even if it were
true. It is babyish to cry. But it was glorious, and Oswald
felt differently to what he ever did before.

Then suddenly the officer in front said, 'Battery!
Halt!' and all the soldiers pulled their horses up, and
the great guns stopped too. Then the officer said, 'Sit at
ease,' and something else, and the sergeant repeated it,
and some of the men got off their horses and lit their
pipes, and some sat down on the grass edge of the road,
holding their horses' bridles.

We could see all the arms and accoutrements as
plain as plain.

Then the officer came up to us. We were all standing
on the wall that day, except Dora, who had to sit,

because her foot was bad, but we let her have the three-edged rapier to wear, and the blunderbuss to hold as well – it has a brass mouth and is like in Mr Caldecott's pictures.

He was a beautiful man the officer. Like a Viking. Very tall and fair, with moustaches very long, and bright blue eyes.

He said –

'Good morning.'

So did we.

Then he said –

'You seem to be a military lot.'

We said we wished we were.

'And patriotic,' said he.

Alice said she should jolly well think so.

Then he said he had noticed us there for several days, and he had halted the battery because he thought we might like to look at the guns.

Alas! there are but too few grown-up people so far-seeing and thoughtful as this brave and distinguished officer.

We said, 'Oh, yes', and then we got off the wall, and that good and noble man showed us the string that moves the detonator and the breech-block (when you take it out and carry it away the gun is in vain to the enemy, even if he takes it); and he let us look down the gun to see the rifling, all clean and shiny; and he showed us the ammunition boxes, but there was nothing in them. He also told us how the gun was unlimbered (this means separating the gun from the ammunition carriage), and how quick it could be done – but he did not make the men do this then, because they were resting. There were six guns. Each had painted on the carriage, in white letters, 15 Pr., which the captain told us meant fifteen-pounder.

'I should have thought the gun weighed more than fifteen pounds,' Dora said. 'It would if it was beef, but I suppose wood and gun are lighter.'

And the officer explained to her very kindly and patiently that 15 Pr. meant the gun could throw a *shell* weighing fifteen pounds.

When we had told him how jolly it was to see the soldiers go by so often, he said –

'You won't see us many more times. We're ordered to the front; and we sail on Tuesday week; and the guns will be painted mud-colour, and the men will wear mud-colour too, and so shall I.'

The men looked very nice, though they were not wearing their busbies, but only Tommy caps, put on all sorts of ways.

We were very sorry they were going, but Oswald, as well as others, looked with envy on those who would soon be allowed – being grown up, and no nonsense about your education – to go and fight for their Queen and country.

Then suddenly Alice whispered to Oswald, and he said –

'All right; but tell him yourself.'

So Alice said to the captain –

'Will you stop next time you pass?'

He said, 'I'm afraid I can't promise that.'

Alice said, 'You might; there's a particular reason.'

He said, 'What?' which was a natural remark; not rude, as it is with children.

Alice said –

'We want to give the soldiers a keepsake and will write to ask my father. He is very well off just now. Look here – if we're not on the wall when you come by, don't stop; but if we are, *please*, PLEASE do!'

The officer pulled his moustache and looked as if he

He showed us all the cuts, thrusts, and guards

did not quite know; but at last he said 'Yes', and we were very glad, though but Alice and Oswald knew the dark but pleasant scheme at present fermenting in their youthful nuts.

The captain talked a lot to us. At last Noël said –

'I think you are like Diarmid of the Golden Collar. But I should like to see your sword out, and shining in the sun like burnished silver.'

The captain laughed and grasped the hilt of his good blade. But Oswald said hurriedly –

'Don't. Not yet. We shan't ever have a chance like this. If you'd only show us the pursuing practice! Albert's uncle knows it; but he only does it on an arm-chair, because he hasn't a horse.'

And that brave and swagger captain did really do it. He rode his horse right into our gate when we opened it, and showed us all the cuts, thrusts, and guards. There are four of each kind. It was splendid. The morning sun shone on his flashing blade, and his good steed stood with all its legs far apart and stiff on the lawn. Then we opened the paddock gate, and he did it again, while the horse galloped as if upon the bloody battlefield among the fierce foes of his native land, and this was far more ripping still.

Then we thanked him very much, and he went away, taking his men with him. And the guns of course.

Then we wrote to my father, and he said 'Yes', as we knew he would, and next time the soldiers came by – but they had no guns this time, only the captive Arabs of the desert – we had the keepsakes ready in a wheelbarrow, and we were on the churchyard wall.

And the bold captain called an immediate halt.

Then the girls had the splendid honour and pleasure of giving a pipe and four whole ounces of tobacco to each soldier.

Then we shook hands with the captain, and the sergeant and the corporals, and the girls kissed the captain – I can't think why girls will kiss everybody – and we all cheered for the Queen.

It was grand. And I wish my father had been there

to see how much you can do with £12 if you order the things from the Stores.

We have never seen those brave soldiers again.

I have told you all this to show you how we got so keen about soldiers, and why we sought to aid and abet the poor widow at the white cottage in her desolate and oppressedness.

Her name was Simpkins, and her cottage was just beyond the churchyard, on the other side from our house. On the different military occasions which I have remarked upon this widow woman stood at her garden gate and looked on. And after the cheering she rubbed her eyes with her apron. Alice noticed this slight but signifying action.

We feel quite sure Mrs Simpkins liked soldiers, and so we felt friendly to her. But when we tried to talk to her she would not. She told us to go along with us, do, and not bother her. And Oswald, with his usual delicacy and good breeding, made the others do as she said.

But we were not to be thus repulsed with impunity. We made complete but cautious inquiries, and found out that the reason she cried when she saw soldiers was that she had only one son, a boy. He was twenty-two, and he had gone to the War last April. So that she thought of him when she saw the soldiers, and that was why she cried. Because when your son is at the wars you always think he is being killed. I don't know why. A great many of them are not. If I had a son at the wars I should never think he was dead till I heard he was, and perhaps not then, considering everything.

After we had found this out we held a council.

Dora said, 'We must do something for the soldier's widowed mother.'

We all agreed, but added 'What?'

Alice said, 'The gift of money might be deemed an insult by that proud, patriotic spirit. Besides, we haven't more than eighteenpence among us.'

We had put what we had to father's £12 to buy the baccy and pipes.

The Mouse then said, 'Couldn't we make her a flannel petticoat and leave it without a word upon her doorstep?'

But everyone said, 'Flannel petticoats in this weather?' so that was no go.

Noël said he would write her a poem, but Oswald had a deep, inward feeling that Mrs Simpkins would not understand poetry. Many people do not.

H. O. said, 'Why not sing "Rule Britannia" under her window after she had gone to bed, like waits,' but no one else thought so.

Denny thought we might get up a subscription for her among the wealthy and affluent, but we said again that we knew money would be no balm to the haughty mother of a brave British soldier.

'What we want,' Alice said, 'is something that will be a good deal of trouble to us and some good to her.'

'A little help is worth a deal of poetry,' said Denny. I should not have said that myself. Noël did look sick.

'What *does* she do that we can help in?' Dora asked. 'Besides, she won't let us help.'

H. O. said, 'She does nothing but work in the garden. At least if she does anything inside you can't see it, because she keeps the door shut.'

Then at once we saw. And we agreed to get up the very next day, ere yet the rosy dawn had flushed the east, and have a go at Mrs Simpkins's garden.

We got up. We really did. But too often when you mean to, overnight, it seems so silly to do it when you come to waking in the dewy morn. We crept downstairs with our boots in our hands. Denny is rather unlucky, though a most careful boy. It was he who dropped his boot, and it went blundering down the stairs, echoing like thunderbolts, and waking up Albert's uncle. But when we explained to him that we were going to do some gardening he let us, and went back to bed.

Everything is very pretty and different in the early morning, before people are up. I have been told this is because the shadows go a different way from what they do in the awake part of the day. But I don't know. Noël says the fairies have just finished tidying up then. Anyhow it all feels quite otherwise.

We put on our boots in the porch, and we got our gardening tools and we went down to the white cottage. It is a nice cottage, with a thatched roof, like in the drawing copies you get at girls' schools, and you do the thatch – if you can – with a B.B. pencil. If you cannot, you just leave it. It looks just as well, somehow, when it is mounted and framed.

We looked at the garden. It was very neat. Only one patch was coming up thick with weeds. I could see groundsel and chickweed, and others that I did not know. We set to work with a will. We used all our tools – spades, forks, hoes, and rakes – and Dora worked with the trowel, sitting down, because her foot was hurt. We cleared the weedy patch beautifully, scraping off all the nasty weeds and leaving the nice clean brown dirt. We worked as hard as ever we could. And we were happy, because it was unselfish toil, and no one thought then of putting it in the Book of Golden Deeds, where we had agreed to write down our virtuous actions and the good doings of each other, when we happen to notice them.

We had just done, and we were looking at the beautiful production of our honest labour, when the cottage door burst open, and the soldier's widowed mother came out like a wild tornado, and her eyes looked like upas trees – death to the beholder.

'You wicked, meddlesome, nasty children!' she said, 'ain't you got enough of your own good ground to runch up and spoil, but you must come into *my* little lot?'

Some of us we were deeply alarmed, but we stood firm.

'We have only been weeding your garden,' Dora said; 'we wanted to do something to help you.'

'Dratted little busybodies,' she said. It was indeed hard, but everyone in Kent says 'dratted' when they are cross. 'It's my turnips,' she went on, 'you've hoed up, and my cabbages. My turnips that my boy sowed afore he went. There, get along with you do, afore I come at you with my broom-handle.'

She did come at us with her broom-handle as she spoke, and even the boldest turned and fled. Oswald was even the boldest.

'They looked like weeds right enough,' he said.

And Dicky said, 'It all comes of trying to do golden deeds.'

This was when we were out in the road.

As we went along, in a silence full of gloomy remorse, we met the postman. He said –

'Here's the letters for the Moat,' and passed on hastily. He was a bit late.

When we came to look through the letters, which were nearly all for Albert's uncle, we found there was a postcard that had got stuck in a magazine wrapper. Alice pulled it out. It was addressed to Mrs Simpkins. We honourably only looked at the address, although it is allowed by the rules of honourableness to read postcards that come to your house if you like, even if they are not for you.

After a heated discussion, Alice and Oswald said they were not afraid, whoever was, and they retraced their steps, Alice holding the postcard right way up, so that we should not look at the lettery part of it, but only the address.

With quickly-beating heart, but outwardly unmoved, they walked up to the white cottage door.

It opened with a bang when we knocked.

'Well?' Mrs Simpkins said, and I think she said it what people in books call 'sourly'.

Oswald said, 'We are very, very sorry we spoiled your turnips, and we will ask my father to try and make it up to you some other way.'

She muttered something about not wanting to be beholden to anybody.

'We came back,' Oswald went on, with his always unruffled politeness, 'because the postman gave us a postcard in mistake with our letters, and it is addressed to you.'

'We haven't read it,' Alice said quickly. I think she needn't have said that. Of course we hadn't. But perhaps girls know better than we do what women are likely to think you capable of.

The soldier's mother took the postcard (she snatched it really, but 'took' is a kinder word, considering everything) and she looked at the address a long time. Then she turned it over and read what was on the back. Then she drew her breath in as far as it would go, and caught hold of the door-post. Her face got awful. It was like the wax face of a dead king I saw once at Madame Tussaud's.

Alice understood. She caught hold of the soldier's mother's hand and said –

'Oh, *no* – it's *not* your boy Bill!'

And the woman said nothing, but shoved the postcard into Alice's hand, and we both read it – and it *was* her boy Bill.

Alice gave her back the card. She had held on to the woman's hand all the time, and now she squeezed the hand, and held it against her face. But she could not say a word because she was crying so. The soldier's mother took the card again and she pushed Alice away, but it was not an unkind push, and she went in and shut the door; and as Alice and Oswald went down the road Oswald looked back, and one of the windows of the cottage had a white blind. Afterwards the other windows had too. There were no blinds really to the cottage. It was aprons and things she had pinned up.

Alice cried most of the morning, and so did the other girls. We wanted to do something for the soldier's mother, but you can do nothing when people's sons are shot. It is the most dreadful thing to want to do something for people who are unhappy, and not to know what to do.

It was Noël who thought of what we *could* do at last.

He said, 'I suppose they don't put up tombstones to soldiers when they die in war. But there – I mean —'

Oswald said, 'Of course not.'

Noël said, 'I daresay you'll think it's silly, but I don't care. Don't you think she'd like it, if we put one up to *him*? Not in the churchyard, of course, because we shouldn't be let, but in our garden, just where it joins on to the churchyard?'

And we all thought it was a first-rate idea.

This is what we meant to put on the tombstone:

'Here lies

BILL SIMPKINS

Who died fighting for Queen
and Country.'

———

'*A faithful son,*
A son so dear,
A soldier brave
Lies buried here.'

Then we remembered that poor brave Bill was really buried far away in the Southern hemisphere, if at all.

So we altered it to –

'*A soldier brave*
We weep for here.'

Then we looked out a nice flagstone in the stable-yard, and we got a cold chisel out of the Dentist's tool-box, and began.

But stone-cutting is difficult and dangerous work.

Oswald went at it a bit, but he chipped his thumb, and it bled so he had to chuck it. Then Dicky tried, and then Denny, but Dicky hammered his finger, and Denny took all day over every stroke, so that by tea-time we had only done the H, and about half the E – and the E was awfully crooked. Oswald chipped his thumb over the H.

We looked at it the next morning, and even the most sanguinary of us saw that it was a hopeless task.

Then Denny said, 'Why not wood and paint?' and he showed us how. We got a board and two stumps from the carpenter's in the village, and we painted it all white, and when that was dry Denny did the words on it.

It was something like this:

'IN MEMORY OF
BILL SIMPKINS
DEAD FOR QUEEN AND COUNTRY.
HONOUR TO HIS NAME AND ALL
OTHER BRAVE SOLDIERS.'

We could not get in what we meant to at first, so we had to give up the poetry.

We fixed it up when it was dry. We had to dig jolly deep to get the posts to stand up, but the gardener helped us.

Then the girls made wreaths of white flowers, roses and canterbury bells, and lilies and pinks, and sweet-peas and daisies, and put them over the posts. And I think if Bill Simpkins had known how sorry we were, he would have been glad. Oswald only hopes if *he* falls on the wild battlefield, which is his highest ambition, that somebody will be as sorry about him as he was about Bill, that's all!

When all was done, and what flowers there were over from the wreaths scattered under the tombstone between the posts, we wrote a letter to Mrs Simpkins, and said –

DEAR MRS SIMPKINS – We are very, very sorry about the turnips and things, and we beg your pardon humbly. We have put up a tombstone to your brave son.

And we signed our names.

Alice took the letter.

The soldier's mother read it, and said something about our oughting to know better than to make fun of people's troubles with our tombstones and tomfoolery.

Alice told me she could not help crying.

She said –

'It's *not!* it's NOT! Dear, *dear* Mrs Simpkins, do come with me and see! You don't know how sorry we are about Bill. Do come and see. We can go through the churchyard, and the others have all gone in, so as to leave it quiet for you. Do come.'

And Mrs Simpkins did. And when she read what we had put up, and Alice told her the verse we had not had room for, she leant against the wall by the grave – I mean the tombstone – and Alice hugged her, and they both cried bitterly. The poor soldier's mother was very, very pleased, and she forgave us about the turnips, and we were friends after that, but she always liked Alice the best. A great many people do, somehow.

After that we used to put fresh flowers every day on Bill's tombstone, and I do believe his mother *was* pleased, though she got us to move it away from the churchyard edge and put it in a corner of our garden under a laburnum, where people could not see it from the church. But you could from the road, though I think she thought you couldn't. She came every day to look at the new wreaths. When the white flowers gave out we put coloured, and she liked it just as well.

About a fortnight after the erecting of the tombstone the girls were putting fresh wreaths on it when a soldier in a red coat came down the road, and he stopped and looked at us. He walked with a stick, and he had a bundle in a blue cotton handkerchief, and one arm in a sling.

And he looked again, and he came nearer, and he leaned on the wall, so that he could read the black printing on the white paint.

And he grinned all over his face, and he said –

'Well, I *am* blessed!'

And he read it all out in a sort of half whisper, and when he came to the end, where it says, 'and all such brave soldiers', he said –

'Well, I really *am*!' I suppose he meant he really was blessed.

Oswald thought it was like the soldier's cheek, so he said –

'I daresay you aren't so very blessed as you think. What's it to do with you, anyway, eh, Tommy?'

Of course Oswald knew from Kipling that an infantry soldier is called that. The soldier said –

'Tommy yourself, young man. That's *me*!' and he pointed to the tombstone.

We stood rooted to the spot. Alice spoke first.

'Then you're Bill, and you're not dead,' she said. 'Oh, Bill, I am so glad! Do let *me* tell your mother.'

She started running, and so did we all. Bill had to go slowly because of his leg, but I tell you he went as fast as ever he could.

We all hammered at the soldier's mother's door, and shouted –

'Come out! come out!' and when she opened the door we were going to speak, but she pushed us away, and went tearing down the garden path like winking. I never saw a grown-up woman run like it, because she saw Bill coming.

She met him at the gate, running right into him, and caught hold of him, and she cried much more than when she thought he was dead.

And we all shook his hand and said how glad we were.

The soldier's mother kept hold of him with both hands, and I couldn't help looking at her face. It was like wax that had been painted on both pink cheeks, and the eyes shining like candles. And when we had all said how glad we were, she said –

'Thank the dear Lord for His mercies,' and she took her boy Bill into the cottage and shut the door.

We went home and chopped up the tombstone with the wood-axe and had a blazing big bonfire, and cheered till we could hardly speak.

The postcard was a mistake; he was only missing. There was a pipe and a whole pound of tobacco left over from our keepsake to the other soldiers. We gave it to Bill. Father is going to have him for under-gardener when his wounds get well. He'll always be a bit lame, so he cannot fight any more.

THE TOWER OF MYSTERY

IT was very rough on Dora having her foot bad, but we took it in turns to stay in with her, and she was very decent about it. Daisy was most with her. I do not dislike Daisy, but I wish she had been taught how to play. Because Dora is rather like that naturally, and sometimes I have thought that Daisy makes her worse.

I talked to Albert's uncle about it one day, when the others had gone to church, and I did not go because of ear-ache, and he said it came from reading the wrong sort of books partly – she has read *Ministering Children*, and *Anna Ross, or The Orphan of Waterloo*, and *Ready Work for Willing Hands*, and *Elsie, or Like a Little Candle*, and even a horrid little blue book about the something or other of Little Sins. After this conversation Oswald took care she had plenty of the right sort of books to read, and he was surprised and pleased when she got up early one morning to finish *Monte Cristo*. Oswald felt that he was really being useful to a suffering fellow-creature when he gave Daisy books that were not all about being good.

A few days after Dora was laid up, Alice called a council of the Wouldbegoods, and Oswald and Dicky attended with darkly-clouded brows. Alice had the minute-book, which was an exercise-book that had not much written in it. She had begun at the other end. I hate doing that myself, because there is so little room at the top compared with right way up.

Dora and a sofa had been carried out on to the lawn, and we were on the grass. It was very hot and dry. We had sherbet. Alice read:

' "Society of the Wouldbegoods.
' "We have not done much. Dicky mended a window, and we got the milk-pan out of the moat that dropped through where he mended it. Dora, Oswald, Dicky and me got upset in the moat. This was not goodness. Dora's foot was hurt. We hope to do better next time." '
Then came Noël's poem:

> *We are the Wouldbegoods Society,*
> *We are not good yet, but we mean to try,*
> *And if we try, and if we don't succeed,*
> *It must mean we are very bad indeed.'*

This sounded so much righter than Noël's poetry generally does, that Oswald said so, and Noël explained that Denny had helped him.

'He seems to know the right length for lines of poetry. I suppose it comes of learning so much at school,' Noël said.

Then Oswald proposed that anybody should be allowed to write in the book if they found out anything good that anyone else had done, but not things that were public acts; and nobody was to write about themselves, or anything other people told them, only what they found out.

After a brief jaw the others agreed, and Oswald felt, not for the first time in his young life, that he would have made a good diplomatic hero to carry despatches and outwit the other side. For now he had put it out of the minute-book's power to be the kind of thing readers of *Ministering Children* would have wished.

'And if anyone tells other people any good thing he's done he is to go to Coventry for the rest of the day.' And Denny remarked, 'We shall do good by stealth, and blush to find it shame.'

After that nothing was written in the book for some time. I looked about, and so did the others, but I never caught anyone in the act of doing anything extra; though several of the others have told me since of things they did at this time, and really wondered nobody had noticed.

I think I said before that when you tell a story you cannot tell everything. It would be silly to do it. Because ordinary kinds of play are dull to read about; and the only other thing is meals, and to dwell on what you eat is greedy and not like a hero at all. A hero is always contented with a venison pasty and a horn of sack. All the same, the meals *were* very interesting; with things you do not get at home – Lent pies with custard and currants in them, sausage rolls and flede cakes, and raisin cakes and apple turnovers, and honeycomb and syllabubs, besides as much new milk as you cared about, and cream now and then, and cheese always on the table for tea. Father told Mrs Pettigrew to get what meals she liked, and she got these strange but attractive foods.

In a story about Wouldbegoods it is not proper to tell of times when only some of us were naughty, so I will pass lightly over the time when Noël got up the kitchen chimney and brought three bricks and an old starling's nest and about a ton of soot down with him when he fell. They never use the big chimney in the summer, but cook in the wash-house. Nor do I wish to dwell on what H. O. did when he went into the dairy. I do not know what his motive was. But Mrs Pettigrew said *she* knew; and she locked him in, and said if it was cream he wanted he should have enough, and she wouldn't let him out till tea-time. The cat had also got into the dairy for some reason of her own, and when H. O. was tired of whatever he went in for he poured all the milk into the churn and tried to teach the cat to swim in it. He must have been desperate. The cat did not even try to learn, and H. O. had the scars on his hands for weeks. I do not wish to tell tales of H. O., for he is very young, and whatever he does he always catches it for; but I will just allude to our being told not to eat the greengages in the garden. And we did not. And whatever H. O. did was Noël's fault – for Noël told H. O. that greengages would grow again all right if you did not bite as far as the stone, just as wounds are not mortal except when you are pierced through the heart. So the two of them bit bites out of every greengage they could reach. And of course the pieces did not grow again.

Oswald did not do things like these, but then he is older than his brothers. The only thing he did just about then was making a booby-trap for Mrs Pettigrew when she had locked H. O. up in the dairy, and unfortunately it was the day she was going out in her best things, and part of the trap was a can of water. Oswald was not willingly vicious; it was but a light and thoughtless act which he had every reason to be sorry for afterwards. And he is sorry even without those reasons, because he knows it is ungentlemanly to play tricks on women.

I remember Mother telling Dora and me when we were little that you ought to be very kind and polite to servants, because they have to work very hard, and do not have so many good times as we do. I used to think about Mother more at the Moat House than I did at Blackheath, especially in the garden. She was very fond of flowers, and she used to tell us about the big garden where she used to live; and I remember Dora and I helped her to plant seeds. But it is no use wishing. She would have liked that garden, though.

The girls and the white mice did not do anything boldly wicked – though of course they used to borrow Mrs Pettigrew's needles, which made her very nasty. Needles that are borrowed might just as well be stolen. But I say no more.

I have only told you these things to show the kind of events which occurred on the days I don't tell you about. On the whole, we had an excellent time.

It was on the day we had the pillow-fight that we went for the long walk. Not the Pilgrimage – that is another story. We did not mean to have a pillow-fight. It is not usual to have them after breakfast, but Oswald had come up to get his knife out of the pocket of his Etons, to cut some wire we were making rabbit snares of. It is a very good knife, with a file in it, as well as a cork-screw and other things – and he did not come down at once, because he was detained by having to make an apple-pie bed for Dicky. Dicky came up after him to see what we was up to, and when he did see he buzzed a pillow at Oswald, and the fight began. The others, hearing the noise of battle from afar, hastened to the field of action, all except Dora, who couldn't because of being laid up with her foot, and Daisy, because she is a little afraid of us still, when we are all together. She thinks we are rough. This comes of having only one brother.

Well, the fight was a very fine one. Alice backed me up, and Noël and H. O. backed Dicky, and Denny heaved a pillow or two; but he cannot shy straight, so I don't know which side he was on.

And just as the battle raged most fiercely, Mrs Pettigrew came in and snatched the pillows away, and shook those of the warriors who were small enough for it. *She* was rough if you like. She also used language I should have thought she would be above. She said, 'Drat you!' and 'Drabbit you!' The last is a thing I have never heard said before. She said –

'There's no peace of your life with you children. Drat your antics! And that poor, dear, patient gentleman right underneath, with his headache and his handwriting: and you rampaging about over his head like young bull-calves. I wonder you haven't more sense, a great girl like you.'

She said this to Alice, and Alice answered gently, as we are told to do –

'I really am awfully sorry; we forgot about the headache. Don't be cross, Mrs Pettigrew; we didn't mean to; we didn't think.'

'You never do,' she said, and her voice, though grumpy, was no longer violent. 'Why on earth you can't take yourselves off for the day I don't know.'

We all said, 'But may we?'

She said, 'Of course you may. Now put on your boots and go for a good long walk. And I'll tell you what – I'll put you up a snack, and you can have an egg to your tea to make up for missing your dinner. Now don't go clattering about the stairs and passages, there's good children. See if you can't be quiet this once, and give the good gentleman a chance with his copying.'

She went off. Her bark is worse than her bite. She does not understand anything about writing books, though. She thinks Albert's uncle copies things out of printed books, when he is really writing new ones. I wonder how she thinks printed books get made first of all. Many servants are like this.

She gave us the 'snack' in a basket, and sixpence to

buy milk with. She said any of the farms would let us have it, only most likely it would be skim. We thanked her politely, and she hurried us out of the front door as if we'd been chickens on a pansy bed.

(I did not know till after I had left the farm gate open, and the hens had got into the garden, that these feathered bipeds display a great partiality for the young buds of plants of the genus *viola*, to which they are extremely destructive. I was told that by the gardener. I looked it up in the gardening book afterwards to be sure he was right. You do learn a lot of things in the country.)

We went through the garden as far as the church, and then we rested a bit in the porch, and just looked into the basket to see what the 'snack' was. It proved to be sausage rolls and queen cakes, and a Lent pie in a round tin dish, and some hard-boiled eggs, and some apples. We all ate the apples at once, so as not to have to carry them about with us. The churchyard smells awfully good. It is the wild thyme that grows on the graves. This is another thing we did not know before we came into the country.

Then the door of the church tower was ajar, and we all went up; it had always been locked before when we had tried it.

We saw the ringers' loft where the ends of the bell-ropes hang down with long, furry handles to them like great caterpillars, some red, and some blue and white, but we did not pull them. And then we went up to where the bells are, very big and dusty among large dirty beams; and four windows with no glass, only shutters like Venetian blinds, but they won't pull up. There were heaps of straws and sticks on the window ledges. We think they were owls' nests, but we did not see any owls.

Then the tower stairs got very narrow and dark, and we went on up, and we came to a door and opened it suddenly, and it was like being hit in the face, the light was so sudden. And there we were on the top of the tower, which is flat, and people have cut their names on it, and a turret at one corner, and a low wall all round, up and down, like castle battlements. And we looked down and saw the roof of the church, and the leads, and the churchyard, and our garden, and the Moat House, and the farm, and Mrs Simpkins's cottage, looking very small, and other farms looking like toy things out of boxes, and we saw corn-fields and meadows and pastures. A pasture is not the same thing as a meadow, whatever you may think. And we saw the tops of trees and hedges, looking like the map of the United States, and villages, and a tower that did not look very far away standing by itself on the top of a hill.

Alice pointed to it, and said –

'What's that?'

'It's not a church,' said Noël, 'because there's no churchyard. Perhaps it's a tower of mystery that covers the entrance to a subterranean vault with treasure in it.'

Dicky said, 'Subterranean fiddlestick!' and 'A water-works, more likely.'

Alice thought perhaps it was a ruined castle, and the rest of its crumbling walls were concealed by ivy, the growth of years.

Oswald could not make his mind up what it was, so he said, 'Let's go and see! We may as well go there as anywhere.'

So we got down out of the church tower and dusted ourselves, and set out.

The Tower of Mystery showed quite plainly from the road, now that we knew where to look for it, because it was on the top of a hill. We began to walk. But the tower did not seem to get any nearer. And it was very hot.

So we sat down in a meadow where there was a stream in the ditch and ate the 'snack'. We drank the pure water from the brook out of our hands, because there was no farm to get milk at just there, and it was too much fag to look for one – and, besides, we thought we might as well save the sixpence.

Then we started again, and still the tower looked as far off as ever. Denny began to drag his feet, though he had brought a walking-stick which none of the rest of us had, and said –

'I wish a cart would come along. We might get a lift.'

He knew all about getting lifts, of course, from having been in the country before. He is not quite the white mouse we took him for at first. Of course when you live in Lewisham or Blackheath you learn other things. If you asked for a lift in Lewisham, High Street, your only reply would be jeers. We sat down on a heap of stones, and decided that we would ask for a lift from the next cart, whichever way it was going. It was while we were waiting that Oswald found out about plantain seeds being good to eat.

When the sound of wheels came we remarked with joy that the cart was going towards the Tower of Mystery. It was a cart a man was going to fetch a pig home in. Denny said –

'I say, you might give us a lift. Will you?'

The man who was going for the pig said –

'What, all that little lot?' but he winked at Alice, and we saw that he meant to aid us on our way. So we climbed up, and he whipped up the horse and asked us where we were going. He was a kindly old man, with a face like a walnut shell, and white hair and beard like a jack-in-the-box.

'We want to get to the tower,' Alice said. 'Is it a ruin, or not?'

'It ain't no ruin,' the man said; 'no fear of that! The man wot built it he left so much a year to be spent on repairing of it! Money that might have put bread in honest folks' mouths.'

We asked was it a church then, or not.

'Church?' he said. 'Not it. It's more of a tombstone, from all I can make out. They do say there was a curse on him that built it, and he wasn't to rest in earth or sea. So he's buried half-way up the tower – if you can call it buried.'

'Can you go up it?' Oswald asked.

'Lord love you! yes; a fine view from the top they say. I've never been up myself, though I've lived in sight of it, boy and man, these sixty-three years come harvest.'

Alice asked whether you had to go past the dead and buried person to get to the top of the tower, and could you see the coffin.

'No, no,' the man said; 'that's all hid away behind a slab of stone, that is, with reading on it. You've no call to be afraid, missy. It's daylight all the way up. But I wouldn't go there after dark, so I wouldn't. It's always open, day and night, and they say tramps sleep there now and again. Anyone who likes can sleep there, but it wouldn't be me.'

We thought that it would not be us either, but we wanted to go more than ever, especially when the man said –

'My own great-uncle of the mother's side, he was one of the masons that set up the stone slab. Before then it was thick glass, and you could see the dead man lying inside, as he'd left it in his will. He was lying there in a glass coffin with his best clothes – blue satin and silver, my uncle said, such as was all the go in his day, with his wig on, and his sword beside him, what he used to wear. My uncle said his hair had grown out from under his wig, and his beard was down to the toes of him. My uncle he always upheld that that dead man was no deader than you and me, but was in a sort of fit, a transit, I think they call it, and looked for him to waken into life again some day. But the doctor said not. It was only something done to him like Pharaoh in the Bible afore he was buried.'

Alice whispered to Oswald that we should be late for tea, and wouldn't it be better to go back now directly. But he said –

'If you're afraid, say so; and you needn't come in anyway – but I'm going on.'

The man who was going for the pig put us down at a gate quite near the tower – at least it looked so until we began to walk again. We thanked him, and he said –

'Quite welcome,' and drove off.

We were rather quiet going through the wood. What we had heard made us very anxious to see the tower – all except Alice, who would keep talking about tea, though not a greedy girl by nature. None of the others encouraged her, but Oswald thought himself that we had better be home before dark.

As we went up the path through the wood we saw a poor wayfarer with dusty bare feet sitting on the bank.

He stopped us and said he was a sailor, and asked for a trifle to help him to get back to his ship.

I did not like the look of him much myself, but Alice said, 'Oh, the poor man, do let's help him, Oswald.' So we held a hurried council, and decided to give him the

milk sixpence. Oswald had it in his purse, and he had to
empty the purse into his hand to find the sixpence, for
that was not all the money he had, by any means.
Noël said afterwards that he saw the wayfarer's eyes
fastened greedily upon the shining pieces as Oswald
returned them to his purse. Oswald has to own that he
purposely let the man see that he had more money, so
that the man might not feel shy about accepting so large
a sum as sixpence.

The man blessed our kind hearts and we went on.

The sun was shining very brightly, and the Tower of
Mystery did not look at all like a tomb when we got to
it. The bottom storey was on arches, all open, and ferns
and things grew underneath. There was a round stone
stair going up in the middle. Alice began to gather ferns
while we went up, but when we had called out to her
that it was as the pig-man had said, and daylight all the
way up, she said –

'All right. I'm not afraid. I'm only afraid of being
late home,' and came up after us. And perhaps, though
not downright manly truthfulness, this was as much as
you could expect from a girl.

There were holes in the little tower of the staircase to
let light in. At the top of it was a thick door with iron
bolts. We shot these back, and it was not fear but caution
that made Oswald push open the door so very slowly
and carefully.

Because, of course, a stray dog or cat might have got
shut up there by accident, and it would have startled
Alice very much if it had jumped out on us.

When the door was opened we saw that there was no
such thing. It was a room with eight sides. Denny says
it is the shape called octagenarian; because a man
named Octagius invented it. There were eight large
arched windows with no glass, only stone-work, like in

churches. The room was full of sunshine, and you could see the blue sky through the windows, but nothing else, because they were so high up It was so bright we began to think the pig-man had been kidding us. Under one of the windows was a door. We went through, and there was a little passage and then a turret-twisting stair, like in the church, but quite light with windows. When we had gone some way up this, we came to a sort of landing, and there was a block of stone let into the wall – polished – Denny said it was Aberdeen graphite, with gold letters cut in it. It said –

'Here lies the body of Mr Richard Ravenal
Born 1720. Died 1779.'

and a verse of poetry:

> *'Here lie I, between earth and sky,*
> *Think upon me, dear passers-by,*
> *And you who do my tombstone see*
> *Be kind to say a prayer for me.'*

'How horrid!' Alice said. 'Do let's get home.'

'We may as well go to the top,' Dicky said, 'just to say we've been.'

And Alice is no funk – so she agreed; though I could see she did not like it.

Up at the top it was like the top of the church tower, only octagenarian in shape, instead of square.

Alice got all right there; because you cannot think much about ghosts and nonsense when the sun is shining bang down on you at four o'clock in the afternoon, and you can see red farm-roofs between the trees, and the safe white roads, with people in carts like black ants crawling.

It was very jolly, but we felt we ought to be getting

back, because tea is at five, and we could not hope to find lifts both ways.

So we started to go down. Dicky went first, then Oswald, then Alice – and H. O. had just stumbled over the top step and saved himself by Alice's back, which nearly upset Oswald and Dicky, when the hearts of all stood still, and then went on by leaps and bounds, like the good work in missionary magazines.

For, down below us, in the tower where the man whose beard grew down to his toes after he was dead was buried, there was a noise – a loud noise. And it was like a door being banged and bolts fastened. We tumbled over each other to get back into the open sun-shine on the top of the tower, and Alice's hand got jammed between the edge of the doorway and H. O.'s boot; it was bruised black and blue, and another part bled, but she did not notice it till long after.

We looked at each other, and Oswald said in a firm voice (at least, I hope it was) –

'What was that?'

'He *has* waked up,' Alice said. 'Oh, I know he has. Of course there is a door for him to get out by when he wakes. He'll come up here. I know he will.'

Dicky said, and his voice was not at all firm (I noticed that at the time), 'It doesn't matter, if he's *alive.*'

'Unless he's come to life a raving lunatic,' Noël said, and we all stood with our eyes on the doorway of the turret – and held our breath to hear.

But there was no more noise.

Then Oswald said – and nobody ever put it in the Golden Deed book, though they own that it was brave and noble of him – he said –

'Perhaps it was only the wind blowing one of the doors to. I'll go down and see, if you will, Dick.'

Dicky only said –

'*I'm not afraid. I'll go and see*'

'The wind doesn't shoot bolts.'

'A bolt from the blue,' said Denny to himself, looking up at the sky. His father is a sub-editor. He had gone very red, and he was holding on to Alice's hand. Suddenly he stood up quite straight and said –

'I'm not afraid. I'll go and see.'

This was afterwards put in the Golden Deed book. It ended in Oswald and Dicky and Denny going. Denny went first because he said he would rather – and Oswald understood this and let him. If Oswald had pushed first it would have been like Sir Lancelot refusing to let a young knight win his spurs. Oswald took good care to go second himself, though. The others never understood this. You don't expect it from girls; but I did think father would have understood without Oswald telling him, which of course he never could.

We all went slowly.

At the bottom of the turret stairs we stopped short. Because the door there was bolted fast and would not yield to shoves, however desperate and united.

Only now somehow we felt that Mr Richard Ravenal was all right and quiet, but that some one had done it for a lark, or perhaps not known about anyone being up there. So we rushed up, and Oswald told the others in a few hasty but well-chosen words, and we all leaned over between the battlements, and shouted, 'Hi! you there!'

Then from under the arches of the quite-downstairs part of the tower a figure came forth – and it was the sailor who had had our milk sixpence. He looked up and he spoke to us. He did not speak loud, but he spoke loud enough for us to hear every word quite plainly. He said –

'Drop that.'

Oswald said, 'Drop what?'

He said, 'That row.'

Oswald said, 'Why?'

He said, 'Because if you don't I'll come up and make you, and pretty quick too, so I tell you.'

Dicky said, 'Did you bolt the door?'

The man said, 'I did so, my young cock.'

Alice said – and Oswald wished to goodness she had held her tongue, because he saw right enough the man was not friendly – 'Oh, do come and let us out – do, please.'

While she was saying it Oswald suddenly saw that he did not want the man to come up. So he scurried down the stairs because he thought he had seen something on the door on the top side, and sure enough there were two bolts, and he shot them into their sockets. This bold act was not put in the Golden Deed book, because when Alice wanted to, the others said it was not *good* of Oswald to think of this, but only *clever*. I think sometimes, in moments of danger and disaster, it is as good to be clever as it is to be good. But Oswald would never demean himself to argue about this.

When he got back the man was still standing staring up. Alice said –

'Oh, Oswald, he says he won't let us out unless we give him all our money. And we might be here for days and days and all night as well. No one knows where we are to come and look for us. Oh, do let's give it him *all*.'

She thought the lion of the English nation, which does not know when it is beaten, would be ramping in her brother's breast. But Oswald kept calm. He said –

'All right,' and he made the others turn out their pockets. Denny had a bad shilling, with a head on both sides, and three halfpence. H. O. had a halfpenny. Noël had a French penny, which is only good for chocolate machines at railway stations. Dicky had tenpence-half-penny, and Oswald had a two-shilling piece of his own that he was saving up to buy a gun with. Oswald tied the whole lot up in his handkerchief, and looking over the battlements, he said –

'You are an ungrateful beast. We gave you sixpence freely of our own will.'

The man did look a little bit ashamed, but he mumbled something about having his living to get.

Then Oswald said –

'Here you are. Catch!' and he flung down the hand-kerchief with the money in it.

The man muffed the catch – butter-fingered idiot! – but he picked up the handkerchief and undid it, and when he saw what was in it he swore dreadfully. The cad!

'Look here,' he called out, 'this won't do, young shaver. I want those there shiners I see in your pus! Chuck 'em along!'

Then Oswald laughed. He said –

'I shall know you again anywhere, and you'll be put in prison for this. Here are the *shiners*.' And he was so angry he chucked down purse and all. The shiners were not real ones, but only card-counters that looked like sovereigns on one side. Oswald used to carry them in his purse so as to look affluent. He does not do this now.

When the man had seen what was in the purse he disappeared under the tower, and Oswald was glad of what he had done about the bolts – and he hoped they were as strong as the ones on the other side of the door.

They were.

We heard the man kicking and pounding at the door,

and I am not ashamed to say that we were all holding on to each other very tight. I am proud, however, to relate that nobody screamed or cried.

After what appeared to be long years, the banging stopped, and presently we saw the brute going away among the trees.

Then Alice did cry, and I do not blame her.

Then Oswald said –

'It's no use. Even if he's undone the door, he may be in ambush. We must hold on here till somebody comes.'

Then Alice said, speaking chokily because she had not quite done crying –

'Let's wave a flag.'

By the most fortunate accident she had on one of her Sunday petticoats, though it was Monday. This petticoat is white. She tore it out at the gathers, and we tied it to Denny's stick, and took turns to wave it. We had laughed at his carrying a stick before, but we were very sorry now that we had done so.

And the tin dish the Lent pie was baked in we polished with our handkerchiefs, and moved it about in the sun so that the sun might strike on it and signal our distress to some of the outlying farms.

This was perhaps the most dreadful adventure that had then ever happened to us. Even Alice had now stopped thinking of Mr Richard Ravenal, and thought only of the lurker in ambush.

We all felt our desperate situation keenly. I must say Denny behaved like anything but a white mouse. When it was the others' turn to wave, he sat on the leads of the tower and held Alice's and Noël's hands, and said poetry to them – yards and yards of it. By some strange fatality it seemed to comfort them. It wouldn't have me.

He said 'The Battle of the Baltic', and 'Gray's

Elegy', right through, though I think he got wrong in places, and the 'Revenge', and Macaulay's thing about Lars Porsena and the Nine Gods. And when it was his turn he waved like a man.

I will try not to call him a white mouse any more. He was a brick that day, and no mouse.

The sun was low in the heavens, and we were sick of waving and very hungry, when we saw a cart in the road below. We waved like mad, and shouted, and Denny screamed exactly like a railway whistle, a thing none of us had known before that he could do.

And the cart stopped. And presently we saw a figure with a white beard among the trees. It was our Pig-man.

We bellowed the awful truth to him, and when he had taken it in – he thought at first we were kidding – he came up and let us out.

He had got the pig; luckily it was a very small one – and we were not particular. Denny and Alice sat on the front of the cart with the Pig-man, and the rest of us got in with the pig, and the man drove us right home. You may think we talked it over on the way. Not us. We went to sleep, among the pig, and before long the Pig-man stopped and got us to make room for Alice and Denny. There was a net over the cart. I never was so sleepy in my life, though it was not more than bed-time.

Generally, after anything exciting, you are punished – but this could not be, because we had only gone for a walk, exactly as we were told.

There was a new rule made, though. No walks except on the high-roads, and we were always to take Pincher and either Lady, the deer-hound, or Martha, the bull-dog. We generally hate rules, but we did not mind this one.

Father gave Denny a gold pencil-case because he was first to go down into the tower. Oswald does not grudge Denny this, though some might think he deserved at least a silver one.

But Oswald is above such paltry jealousies.

THE WATERWORKS

THIS is the story of one of the most far-reaching and influentially naughty things we ever did in our lives. We did not mean to do such a deed. And yet we did do it. These things will happen with the best-regulated consciences.

The story of this rash and fatal act is intimately involved – which means all mixed up anyhow – with a private affair of Oswald's, and the one cannot be revealed without the other. Oswald does not particularly want his story to be remembered, but he wishes to tell the truth, and perhaps it is what father calls a wholesome discipline to lay bare the awful facts.

It was like this.

On Alice's and Noël's birthday we went on the river for a picnic. Before that we had not known that there was a river so near us. Afterwards father said he wished we had been allowed to remain on our pristine ignorance, whatever that is. And perhaps the dark hour did dawn when we wished so too. But a truce to vain regrets.

It was rather a fine thing in birthdays. The uncle sent a box of toys and sweets, things that were like a vision from another and a brighter world. Besides that Alice had a knife, a pair of shut-up scissors, a silk handkerchief, a book – it was *The Golden Age* and is A1 except where it gets mixed with grown-up nonsense. Also a work-case lined with pink plush, a boot-bag, which no one in their senses would use because it had flowers in wool all over it. And she had a box of chocolates and a musical box that played 'The Man who broke' and two other tunes, and two pairs of kid gloves for church, and a box of writing-paper pink – with 'Alice' on it in gold writing, and an egg coloured red that said 'A. Bastable' in ink on one side. These gifts were the offerings of Oswald, Dora, Dicky, Albert's uncle, Daisy, Mr Foulkes (our own robber), Noël, H. O., father and Denny. Mrs Pettigrew gave the egg. It was a kindly housekeeper's friendly token.

I shall not tell you about the picnic on the river because the happiest times form but dull reading when they are written down. I will merely state that it was prime. Though happy, the day was uneventful. The only thing exciting enough to write about was in one of the locks, where there was a snake – a viper. It was asleep in a warm sunny corner of the lock gate, and when the gate was shut it fell off into the water.

Alice and Dora screamed hideously. So did Daisy, but her screams were thinner.

The snake swam round and round all the time our boat was in the lock. It swam with four inches of itself – the head end – reared up out of the water, exactly like Kaa in the *Jungle Book* – so we know Kipling is a true author and no rotter. We were careful to keep our hands well inside the boat. A snake's eyes strike terror into the boldest breast.

When the lock was full father killed the viper with a boat-hook. I was sorry for it myself. It was indeed a venomous serpent. But it was the first we had ever seen, except at the Zoo. And it did swim most awfully well.

Directly the snake had been killed H. O. reached out for its corpse, and the next moment the body of our little brother was seen wriggling conclusively on the boat's edge. This exciting spectacle was not of a lasting nature. He went right in. Father clawed him out. He is very unlucky with water.

Being a birthday, but little was said. H. O. was wrapped in everybody's coats, and did not take any cold at all.

This glorious birthday ended with an iced cake and ginger wine, and drinking healths. Then we played whatever we liked. There had been rounders during the afternoon. It was a day to be for ever marked by memory's brightest what's-its-name.

I should not have said anything about the picnic but for one thing. It was the thin edge of the wedge. It was the all-powerful lever that moved but too many events. You see, *we were now no longer strangers to the river.*

And we went there whenever we could. Only we had to take the dogs, and to promise no bathing without grown-ups. But paddling in back waters was allowed. I say no more.

I have not numerated Noël's birthday presents because I wish to leave something to the imagination of my young readers. (The best authors always do this.) If you will take the large, red catalogue of the Army and Navy Stores, and just make a list of about fifteen of the things you would like best – prices from 2s. to 25s. – you will get a very good idea of Noël's presents, and it will help you to make up your mind in case you are asked just before your next birthday what you really *need*.

One of Noël's birthday presents was a cricket ball. He cannot bowl for nuts, and it was a first-rate ball. So some days after the birthday Oswald offered him to exchange it for a coconut he had won at the fair, and two pencils (new), and a brand-new note-book. Oswald thought, and he still thinks, that this was a fair exchange, and so did Noël at the time, and he agreed to it, and was quite pleased till the girls said it wasn't fair, and Oswald had the best of it. And then that young beggar Noël wanted the ball back, but Oswald, though not angry, was firm.

'You said it was a bargain, and you shook hands on it,' he said, and he said it quite kindly and calmly.

Noël said he didn't care. He wanted his cricket ball back.

And the girls said it was a horrid shame.

If they had not said that, Oswald might yet have consented to let Noël have the beastly ball, but now, of course, he was not going to. He said –

'Oh, yes, I daresay. And then you would be wanting the coconut and things again the next minute.'

'No, I shouldn't,' Noël said. It turned out afterwards he and H. O. had eaten the coconut, which only made it worse. And it made them worse too – which is what the book calls poetic justice.

Dora said, 'I don't think it was fair,' and even Alice said –

'Do let him have it back, Oswald.' I wish to be just to Alice. She did not know then about the coconut having been secretly wolfed up.

We were in the garden. Oswald felt all the feelings of the hero when the opposing forces gathered about him are opposing as hard as ever they can. He knew he was not unfair, and he did not like to be jawed at just because Noël had eaten the coconut and wanted the ball back. Though Oswald did not know then about the eating of the coconut, but he felt the injustice in his soul all the same.

Noël said afterwards he meant to offer Oswald something else to make up for the coconut, but he said nothing about this at the time.

'Give it me, I say.' Noël said.

And Oswald said, 'Shan't!'

Then Noël called Oswald names, and Oswald did not answer back but just kept smiling pleasantly, and carelessly throwing up the ball and catching it again with an air of studied indifference.

It was Martha's fault that what happened happened. She is the bull-dog, and very stout and heavy. She had just been let loose and she came bounding along in her clumsy way, and jumped up on Oswald, who is beloved by all dumb animals. (You know how sagacious they are.) Well, Martha knocked the ball out of Oswald's hands, and it fell on the grass, and Noël pounced on it like a hooded falcon on its prey. Oswald would scorn to deny that he was not going to stand this, and the next moment the two were rolling over on the grass, and very soon Noël was made to bite the dust. And serve him right. He is old enough to know his own mind.

Then Oswald walked slowly away with the ball, and the others picked Noël up, and consoled the beaten, but Dicky would not take either side.

And Oswald went up into his own room and lay on his bed, and reflected gloomy reflections about unfairness.

Presently he thought he would like to see what the others were doing without their knowing he cared. So he went into the linen-room and looked out of its window, and he saw they were playing Kings and Queens – and Noël had the biggest paper crown and the longest stick sceptre.

Oswald turned away without a word, for it really was sickening.

Then suddenly his weary eyes fell upon something they had not before beheld. It was a square trap-door in the ceiling of the linen-room.

Oswald never hesitated. He crammed the cricket ball into his pocket and climbed up the shelves and unbolted the trap-door, and shoved it up, and pulled himself up through it. Though above all was dark and smelt of spiders, Oswald fearlessly shut the trap-door down again before he struck a match. He always carries matches. He is a boy fertile in every subtle expedient. Then he saw he was in the wonderful, mysterious place between the ceiling and the roof of the house. The roof is beams and tiles. Slits of light show through the tiles here and there. The ceiling, on its other and top side, is made of rough plaster and beams. If you walk on the beams it is all right – if you walk on the plaster you go through with your feet. Oswald found this out later, but some fine instinct now taught the young explorer where he ought to tread and where not. It was splendid. He was still very angry with the others and he was glad he had found out a secret they jolly well didn't know.

He walked along a dark, narrow passage. Every now and then cross-beams barred his way, and he had to creep under them. At last a small door loomed before him with cracks of light under and over. He drew back the rusty bolts and opened it. It opened straight on to the leads, a flat place between two steep red roofs, with a parapet two feet high back and front, so that no one could see you. It was a place no one could have invented better than, if they had tried, for hiding in.

Oswald spent the whole afternoon there. He happened to have a volume of *Percy's Anecdotes* in his pocket, the one about lawyers, as well as a few apples. While he read he fingered the cricket ball, and presently it rolled away, and he thought he would get it by-and-by.

When the tea-bell rang he forgot the ball and went

hurriedly down, for apples do not keep the inside from the pangs of hunger.

Noël met him on the landing, got red in the face, and said –

'It wasn't *quite* fair about the ball, because H. O. and I had eaten the coconut. *You* can have it.'

'I don't want your beastly ball,' Oswald said, 'only I hate unfairness. However, I don't know where it is just now. When I find it you shall have it to bowl with as often as you want.'

'Then you're not waxy?'

And Oswald said 'No' and they went in to tea together. So that was all right. There were raisin cakes for tea.

Next day we happened to want to go down to the river quite early. I don't know why; this is called Fate, or Destiny. We dropped in at the 'Rose and Crown' for some ginger-beer on our way. The landlady is a friend of ours and lets us drink it in her back parlour, instead of in the bar, which would be improper for girls.

We found her awfully busy, making pies and jellies, and her two sisters were hurrying about with great hams, and pairs of chickens, and rounds of cold beef and lettuces, and pickled salmon and trays of crockery and glasses.

'It's for the angling competition,' she said.

We said, 'What's that?'

'Why,' she said, slicing cucumber like beautiful machinery while she said it, 'a lot of anglers come down some particular day and fish one particular bit of the river. And the one that catches most fish gets the prize. They're fishing the pen above Stoneham Lock. And they all come here to dinner. So I've got my hands full and a trifle over.'

We said, 'Couldn't we help?'

But she said, 'Oh, no, thank you. Indeed not, please. I really am so I don't know which way to turn. Do run along, like dears.'

So we ran along like these timid but graceful animals.

Need I tell the intellectual reader that we went straight off to the pen above Stoneham Lock to see the anglers competing? Angling is the same thing as fishing.

I am not going to try and explain locks to you. If you've never seen a lock you could never understand even if I wrote it in words of one syllable and pages and pages long. And if you have, you'll understand without my telling you. It is harder than Euclid if you don't know beforehand. But you might get a grown-up person to explain it to you with books or wooden bricks.

I will tell you what a pen is because that is easy. It is the bit of river between one lock and the next. In some rivers 'pens' are called 'reaches', but pen is the proper word.

We went along the towing-path; it is shady with willows, aspens, alders, elders, oaks and other trees. On the banks are flowers – yarrow, meadow-sweet, willow herb, loosestrife, and lady's bed-straw. Oswald learned the names of all these trees and plants on the day of the picnic. The others didn't remember them, but Oswald did. He is a boy of what they call relenting memory.

The anglers were sitting here and there on the shady bank among the grass and the different flowers I have named. Some had dogs with them, and some umbrellas, and some had only their wives and families.

We should have liked to talk to them and ask how they liked their lot, and what kinds of fish there were, and whether they were nice to eat, but we did not like to.

Denny had seen anglers before and he knew they

liked to be talked to, but though he spoke to them quite like to equals he did not ask the things we wanted to know. He just asked whether they'd had any luck, and what bait they used.

And they answered him back politely. I am glad I am not an angler. It is an immovable amusement, and, as often as not, no fish to speak of after all.

Daisy and Dora had stayed at home: Dora's foot was nearly well but they seem really to like sitting still. I think Dora likes to have a little girl to order about. Alice never would stand it. When we got to Stoneham Lock Denny said he should go home and fetch his fishing-rod. H. O. went with him. This left four of us – Oswald, Alice, Dicky, and Noël. We went on down the towing-path.

The lock shuts up (that sounds as if it was like the lock on a door, but it is very otherwise) between one pen of the river and the next; the pen where the anglers were was full right up over the roots of the grass and flowers.

But the pen below was nearly empty.

'You can see the poor river's bones,' Noël said.

And so you could.

Stones and mud and dried branches, and here and there an old kettle or a tin pail with no bottom to it, that some bargee had chucked in.

From walking so much along the river we knew many of the bargees. Bargees are the captains and crews of the big barges that are pulled up and down the river by slow horses. The horses do not swim. They walk on the towing-path, with a rope tied to them, and the other end to the barge. So it gets pulled along. The bargees we knew were a good friendly sort, and used to let us go all over the barges when they were in a good temper. They were not at all the sort of bullying, cowardly fiends in human form that the young hero at Oxford fights a crowd of, single-handed, in books.

The river does not smell nice when its bones are showing. But we went along down, because Oswald wanted to get some cobbler's wax in Falding village for a bird-net he was making.

But just above Falding Lock, where the river is narrow and straight, we saw a sad and gloomy sight – a big barge sitting flat on the mud because there was not water enough to float her.

There was no one on board, but we knew by a red flannel waistcoat that was spread out to dry on top that the barge belonged to friends of ours.

Then Alice said, 'They have gone to find the man who turns on the water to fill the pen. I daresay they won't find him. He's gone to his dinner, I shouldn't wonder. What a lovely surprise it would be if they came back to find their barge floating high and dry on a lot of water! *Do* let's do it. It's a long time since any of us did a kind action deserving of being put in the Book of Golden Deeds.'

We had given that name to the minute-book of that beastly 'Society of the Wouldbegoods'. Then you could think of the book if you wanted to without remembering the Society. I always tried to forget both of them.

Oswald said, 'But how? *You* don't know how. And if you did we haven't got a crowbar.'

I cannot help telling you that locks are opened with crowbars. You push and push till a thing goes up and the water runs through. It is rather like the little sliding door in the big door of a hen-house.

'I know where the crowbar is,' Alice said. 'Dicky and I were down here yesterday when you were su –' She was going to say sulking, I know, but she remembered

manners ere too late so Oswald bears her no malice.
She went on: 'Yesterday, when you were upstairs. And
we saw the water-tender open the lock and the weir
sluices. It's quite easy, isn't it, Dicky?'

'As easy as kiss your hand,' said Dicky; 'and what's
more, I know where he keeps the other thing he opens
the sluices with. I votes we do.'

'Do let's, if we can,' Noël said, 'and the bargees will
bless the names of their unknown benefactors. They
might make a song about us, and sing it on winter
nights as they pass round the wassail bowl in front of the
cabin fire.'

Noël wanted to very much; but I don't think it was
altogether for generousness, but because he wanted to
see how the sluices opened. Yet perhaps I do but wrong
the boy.

We sat and looked at the barge a bit longer, and then
Oswald said, well, he didn't mind going back to the lock
and having a look at the crowbars. You see Oswald did
not propose this; he did not even care very much about
it when Alice suggested it.

But when we got to Stoneham Lock, and Dicky
dragged the two heavy crowbars from among the elder
bushes behind a fallen tree, and began to pound away
at the sluice of the lock, Oswald felt it would not be
manly to stand idly apart. So he took his turn.

It was very hard work but we opened the lock sluices,
and we did not drop the crowbar into the lock either,
as I have heard of being done by older and sillier
people.

The water poured through the sluices all green and
solid, as if it had been cut with a knife, and where it fell
on the water underneath the white foam spread like a
moving counterpane. When we had finished the lock we
did the weir – which is wheels and chains – and the

water pours through over the stones in a magnificent waterfall and sweeps out all round the weir-pool.

The sight of the foaming waterfalls was quite enough reward for our heavy labours, even without the thought of the unspeakable gratitude that the bargees would feel to us when they got back to their barge and found her no longer a stick-in-the-mud, but bounding on the free bosom of the river.

When we had opened all the sluices we gazed awhile on the beauties of Nature, and then went home, because we thought it would be more truly noble and good not to wait to be thanked for our kind and devoted action – and besides, it was nearly dinner-time and Oswald thought it was going to rain.

On the way home we agreed not to tell the others, because it would be like boasting of our good acts.

'They will know all about it,' Noël said, 'when they hear us being blessed by the grateful bargees, and the tale of the Unknown Helpers is being told by every village fireside. And then they can write it in the Golden Deed book.'

So we went home. Denny and H. O. had thought better of it, and they were fishing in the moat. They did not catch anything.

Oswald is very weather-wise – at least, so I have heard it said, and he had thought there would be rain. There was. It came on while we were at dinner – a great, strong, thundering rain, coming down in sheets – the first rain we had had since we came to the Moat House.

We went to bed as usual. No presentiment of the coming awfulness clouded our young mirth. I remember Dicky and Oswald had a wrestling match, and Oswald won.

In the middle of the night Oswald was awakened by

a hand on his face. It was a wet hand and very cold. Oswald hit out, of course, but a voice said, in a hoarse, hollow whisper –

'Don't be a young ass! Have you got any matches? My bed's full of water; it's pouring down from the ceiling.'

Oswald's first thoughts was that perhaps by opening those sluices we had flooded some secret passage which communicated with the top of Moat House, but when he was properly awake he saw that this could not be, on account of the river being so low.

He had matches. He is, as I said before, a boy full of resources. He struck one and lit a candle, and Dicky, for it was indeed he, gazed with Oswald at the amazing spectacle.

Our bedroom floor was all wet in patches. Dicky's bed stood in a pond, and from the ceiling water was dripping in rich profusion at a dozen different places. There was a great wet patch in the ceiling, and that was blue, instead of white like the dry part, and the water dripped from different parts of it.

In a moment Oswald was quite unmanned.

'Krikey!' he said, in a heart-broken tone, and remained an instant plunged in thought.

'What on earth are we to do?' Dicky said.

And really for a short time even Oswald did not know. It was a blood-curdling event, a regular facer. Albert's uncle had gone to London that day to stay till the next. Yet something must be done.

The first thing was to rouse the unconscious others from their deep sleep, because the water was beginning to drip on to their beds, and though as yet they knew it not, there was quite a pool on Noël's bed, just in the hollow behind where his knees were doubled up, and one of H. O.'s boots was full of water, that surged wildly out when Oswald happened to kick it over.

We woke them – a difficult task, but we did not shrink from it.

Then we said, 'Get up, there is a flood! Wake up, or you will be drowned in your beds! And it's half past two by Oswald's watch.'

They awoke slowly and very stupidly. H. O. was the slowest and stupidest.

The water poured faster and faster from the ceiling.

We looked at each other and turned pale, and Noël said –

'Hadn't we better call Mrs Pettigrew?'

But Oswald simply couldn't consent to this. He could not get rid of the feeling that this was our fault somehow for meddling with the river, though of course the clear star of reason told him it could not possibly be the case.

We all devoted ourselves, heart and soul, to the work before us. We put the bath under the worst and wettest place, and the jugs and basins under lesser streams, and we moved the beds away to the dry end of the room. Ours is a long attic that runs right across the house.

But the water kept coming in worse and worse. Our nightshirts were wet through, so we got into our other shirts and knickerbockers, but preserved bareness in our feet. And the floor kept on being half an inch deep in water, however much we mopped it up.

We emptied the basins out of the window as fast as they filled, and we baled the bath with a jug without pausing to complain how hard the work was. All the same, it was more exciting than you can think. But in Oswald's dauntless breast he began to see that they would *have* to call Mrs Pettigrew.

A new waterfall broke out between the fire-grate and the mantelpiece, and spread in devastating floods.

Oswald is full of ingenious devices. I think I have said this before, but it is quite true; and perhaps even truer this time than it was last time I said it.

He got a board out of the box-room next door, and rested one end in the chink between the fireplace and the mantelpiece, and laid the other end on the back of a chair, then we stuffed the rest of the chink with our nightgowns, and laid a towel along the plank, and behold, a noble stream poured over the end of the board right into the bath we put there ready. It was like Niagara, only not so round in shape. The first lot of water that came down the chimney was very dirty. The wind whistled outside. Noël said, 'If it's pipes burst, and not the rain, it will be nice for the water-rates.' Perhaps it was only natural after this for Denny to begin with his everlasting poetry. He stopped mopping up the water to say:

> *'By this the storm grew loud apace,*
> *The water-rats were shrieking,*
> *And in the howl of Heaven each face*
> *Grew black as they were speaking.'*

Our faces were black, and our hands too, but we did not take any notice; we only told him not to gas but to go on mopping. And he did. And we all did.

But more and more water came pouring down. You would not believe so much could come off one roof.

When at last it was agreed that Mrs Pettigrew must be awakened at all hazards, we went and woke Alice to do the fatal errand.

When she came back, with Mrs Pettigrew in a night-cap and red flannel petticoat, we held our breath.

But Mrs Pettigrew did not even say, 'What on earth have you children been up to *now?*' as Oswald had feared.

Up all night, with water pouring through the roof

She simply sat down on my bed and said –

'Oh, dear! oh, dear! oh, dear!' ever so many times.

Then Denny said, 'I once saw holes in a cottage roof. The man told me it was done when the water came through the thatch. He said if the water lies all about on the top of the ceiling, it breaks it down, but if you make holes the water will only come through the holes and you can put pails under the holes to catch it.'

So we made nine holes in the ceiling with the poker, and put pails, baths and tubs under, and now there was not so much water on the floor. But we had to keep on working like niggers, and Mrs Pettigrew and Alice worked the same.

About five in the morning the rain stopped; about seven the water did not come in so fast, and presently it only dripped slowly. Our task was done.

This is the only time I was ever up all night. I wish it happened oftener. We did not go back to bed then, but dressed and went down. We all went to sleep in the afternoon, though. Quite without meaning to.

Oswald went up on the roof, before breakfast, to see if he could find the hole where the rain had come in. He did not find any hole, but he found the cricket ball jammed in the top of a gutter pipe which he afterwards knew ran down inside the wall of the house and ran into the moat below. It seems a silly dodge, but so it was.

When the men went up after breakfast to see what had caused the flood they said there must have been a good half-foot of water on the leads the night before for it to have risen high enough to go above the edge of the lead, and of course when it got above the lead there was nothing to stop it running down under it, and soaking through the ceiling. The parapet and the roofs kept it from tumbling off down the sides of the house in the natural way. They said there must have been some obstruction in the pipe which ran down into the house, but whatever it was the water had washed it away, for they put wires down, and the pipe was quite clear.

While we were being told this Oswald's trembling fingers felt at the wet cricket ball in his pocket. And he *knew*, but he *could* not tell. He heard them wondering what the obstruction could have been, and all the time he had the obstruction in his pocket, and never said a single word.

I do not seek to defend him. But it really was an awful thing to have been the cause of; and Mrs Pettigrew is but harsh and hasty. But this, as Oswald knows too well, is no excuse for his silent conduct.

That night at tea Albert's uncle was rather silent too. At last he looked upon us with a glance full of intelligence, and said –

'There was a queer thing happened yesterday. You know there was an angling competition. The pen was kept full on purpose. Some mischievous busybody went and opened the sluices and let all the water out. The anglers' holiday was spoiled. No, the rain wouldn't have spoiled it anyhow, Alice; anglers *like* rain. The 'Rose and Crown' dinner was half of it wasted because the anglers were so furious that a lot of them took the next train to town. And this is the worst of all – a barge, that was on the mud in the pen below, was lifted and jammed across the river and the water tilted her over, and her cargo is on the river bottom. It was coals.'

During this speech there were four of us who knew not where to turn our agitated glances. Some of us tried bread-and-butter, but it seemed dry and difficult, and those who tried tea choked and spluttered and were sorry they had not let it alone.

When the speech stopped Alice said, 'It was us.'

And with deepest feelings she and the rest of us told

all about it. Oswald did not say much. He was turning the obstruction round and round in his pocket, and wishing with all his sentiments that he had owned up like a man when Albert's uncle asked him before tea to tell him all about what had happened during the night.

When they had told all, Albert's uncle told us four still more plainly, and exactly, what we had done, and how much pleasure we had spoiled, and how much of my father's money we had wasted – because he would have to pay for the coals being got up from the bottom of the river, if they could be, and if not, for the price of the coals. And we saw it *all*.

And when he had done Alice burst out crying over her plate and said –

'It's no use! We *have* tried to be good since we've been down here. You don't know how we've tried! And it's all no use. I believe we are the wickedest children in the whole world, and I wish we were all dead!'

This was a dreadful thing to say, and of course the rest of us were all very shocked. But Oswald could not help looking at Albert's uncle to see how he would take it.

He said very gravely, 'My dear kiddie, you ought to be sorry, and I wish you to be sorry for what you've done. And you will be punished for it.' (We were; our pocket-money was stopped and we were forbidden to go near the river, besides impositions miles long.) 'But,' he went on, 'you mustn't give up trying to be good. You are extremely naughty and tiresome, as you know very well.'

Alice, Dicky, and Noël began to cry at about this time.

'But you are not the wickedest children in the world by any means.'

Then he stood up and straightened his collar, and put his hands in his pockets.

'You're very unhappy now,' he said, 'and you deserve to be. But I will say one thing to you.'

Then he said a thing which Oswald at least will never forget (though but little he deserved it, with the obstruction in his pocket, unowned up to all the time).

He said, 'I have known you all for four years – and you know as well as I do how many scrapes I've seen you in and out of – but I've never known one of you tell a lie, and I've never known one of you do a mean or dishonourable action. And when you have done wrong you are always sorry. Now this is something to stand firm on. You'll learn to be good in the other ways some day.'

He took his hands out of his pockets, and his face looked different, so that three of the four guilty creatures knew he was no longer adamant, and they threw themselves into his arms. Dora, Denny, Daisy, and H. O., of course, were not in it, and I think they thanked their stars.

Oswald did not embrace Albert's uncle. He stood there and made up his mind he would go for a soldier. He gave the wet ball one last squeeze, and took his hand out of his pocket, and said a few words before going to enlist. He said –

'The others may deserve what you say. I hope they do, I'm sure. But I don't, because it was my rotten cricket ball that stopped up the pipe and caused the midnight flood in our bedroom. And I knew it quite early this morning. And I didn't own up.'

Oswald stood there covered with shame, and he could feel the hateful cricket ball heavy and cold against the top of his leg, through the pocket.

Albert's uncle said – and his voice made Oswald hot all over, but not with shame – he said –

I shall not tell you what he said. It is no one's business but Oswald's; only I will own it made Oswald not quite so anxious to run away for a soldier as he had been before.

That owning up was the hardest thing I ever did. They did put that in the Book of Golden Deeds, though it was not a kind or generous act, and did no good to anyone or anything except Oswald's own inside feelings. I must say I think they might have let it alone. Oswald would rather forget it. Especially as Dicky wrote it in and put this:

'Oswald acted a lie, which, he knows, is as bad as telling one. But he owned up when he needn't have, and this condones his sin. We think he was a thorough brick to do it.'

Alice scratched this out afterwards and wrote the record of the incident in more flattering terms. But Dicky had used Father's ink, and she used Mrs Pettigrew's, so anyone can read *his* underneath the scratching outs.

The others were awfully friendly to Oswald, to show they agreed with Albert's uncle in thinking I deserved as much share as anyone in any praise there might be going.

It was Dora who said it all came from my quarrelling with Noël about that rotten cricket ball; but Alice, gently yet firmly, made her shut up.

I let Noël have the ball. It had been thoroughly soaked, but it dried all right. But it could never be the same to me after what *it* had done and what I had done.

I hope you will try to agree with Albert's uncle and not think foul scorn of Oswald because of this story. Perhaps you have done things nearly as bad yourself

sometimes. If you have, you will know how 'owning up'
soothes the savage breast and alleviates the gnawings
of remorse.

If you have never done naughty acts I expect it is
only because you never had the sense to think of anything.

THE CIRCUS

THE ones of us who had started the Society of the Wouldbegoods began, at about this time, to bother.

They said we had not done anything really noble – not worth speaking of, that is – for over a week, and that it was high time to begin again – 'with earnest endeavour', Daisy said. So then Oswald said –

'All right; but there ought to be an end to everything. Let's each of us think of one really noble and unselfish act, and the others shall help to work it out, like we did when we were Treasure Seekers. Then when everybody's had their go-in we'll write every single thing down in the Golden Deed book, and we'll draw two lines in red ink at the bottom, like Father does at the end of an account. And after that, if anyone wants to be good they can jolly well be good on our own, if at all.'

The ones who had made the Society did not welcome this wise idea, but Dicky and Oswald were firm.

So they had to agree. When Oswald is really firm, opposingness and obstinacy have to give way.

Dora said, 'It would be a noble action to have all the school-children from the village and give them tea and games in the paddock. They would think it so nice and good of us.'

But Dicky showed her that this would not be *our* good act, but Father's, because he would have to pay for the tea, and he had already stood us the keepsakes for the soldiers, as well as having to stump up heavily over the coal barge. And it is in vain being noble and generous when someone else is paying for it all the time, even if it happens to be your father. Then three others had ideas at the same time and began to explain what they were.

We were all in the dining-room, and perhaps we were making a bit of a row. Anyhow, Oswald for one, does not blame Albert's uncle for opening his door and saying

'I suppose I must not ask for complete silence. That were too much. But if you could whistle, or stamp with your feet, or shriek or howl – anything to vary the monotony of your well-sustained conversation.'

Oswald said kindly, 'We're awfully sorry. Are you busy?'

'Busy?' said Albert's uncle. 'My heroine is now hesitating on the verge of an act which, for good or ill, must influence her whole subsequent career. You wouldn't like her to decide in the middle of such a row that she can't hear herself think?'

We said, 'No, we wouldn't.'

Then he said, 'If any outdoor amusement should commend itself to you this bright mid-summer day.'

So we all went out.

Then Daisy whispered to Dora – they always hang together. Daisy is not nearly so white-micey as she was at first, but she still seems to fear the deadly ordeal of public speaking. Dora said –

'Daisy's idea is a game that'll take us all day. She thinks keeping out of the way when he's making his heroine decide right would be a noble act, and fit to write in the Golden Book; and we might as well be playing something at the same time.'

We all said 'Yes, but what?'

There was a silent interval.

'Speak up, Daisy, my child.' Oswald said; 'fear not to lay bare the utmost thoughts of that faithful heart.'

Daisy giggled. Our own girls never giggle; they laugh right out or hold their tongues. Their kind brothers have taught them this. Then Daisy said –

'If we could have a sort of play to keep us out of the way. I once read a story about an animal race. Everybody had an animal, and they had to go how they liked, and the one that got in first got the prize. There was a tortoise in it, and a rabbit, and a peacock, and sheep, and dogs, and a kitten.'

This proposal left us cold, as Albert's uncle says, because we knew there could not be any prize worth bothering about. And though you may be ever ready and willing to do anything for nothing, yet if there's going to be a prize there must *be* a prize and there's an end of it.

Thus the idea was not followed up. Dicky yawned and said, 'Let's go into the barn and make a fort.'

So we did, with straw. It does not hurt straw to be messed about with like it does hay.

The downstairs – I mean down-ladder – part of the barn was fun too, especially for Pincher. There was as good ratting there as you could wish to see. Martha tried it, but she could not help running kindly beside the rat, as if she was in double harness with it. This is the noble bull-dog's gentle and affectionate nature coming out. We all enjoyed the ratting that day, but it ended, as usual, in the girls crying because of the poor rats. Girls cannot help this; we must not be waxy with them on account of it, they have their nature, the same as bull-dogs have, and it is this that makes them so useful in smoothing the pillows of the sick-bed and tending wounded heroes.

However, the forts, and Pincher, and the girls crying, and having to be thumped on the back, passed the time very agreeably till dinner. There was roast mutton with onion sauce, and a roly-poly pudding.

Albert's uncle said we had certainly effaced ourselves effectually, which means we hadn't bothered.

So we determined to do the same during the afternoon, for he told us his heroine was by no means out of the wood yet.

And at first it was easy. Jam roly gives you a peaceful feeling and you do not at first care if you never play any runabout game ever any more. But after a while the torpor begins to pass away. Oswald was the first to recover from his.

He had been lying on his front part in the orchard, but now he turned over on his back and kicked his legs up, and said –

'I say, look here; let's do something.'*

Daisy looked thoughtful. She was chewing the soft yellow parts of grass, but I could see she was still thinking about that animal race. So I explained to her that it would be very poor fun without a tortoise and a peacock, and she saw this, though not willingly.

It was H. O. who said –

'Doing anything with animals is prime! if they only will. Let's have a circus!'

At the word the last thought of the pudding faded from Oswald's memory, and he stretched himself, sat up, and said –

'Bully for H. O. Let's!'

The others also threw off the heavy weight of memory, and sat up and said 'Let's!' too.

Never, never in all our lives had we had such a gay galaxy of animals at our command. The rabbits and the

* See p. 336 for short story.

guinea-pigs, and even all the bright, glass-eyed, stuffed denizens of our late-lamented Jungle paled into insignificance before the number of live things on the farm.

(I hope you do not think that the words I use are getting too long. I know they are the right words. And Albert's uncle says your style is always altered a bit by what you read. And I have been reading the Vicomte de Bragelonne. Nearly all my new words come out of those.)

'The worst of a circus is,' Dora said, 'that you've got to teach the animals things. A circus where the performing creatures hadn't learned performing would be a bit silly. Let's give up a week to teaching them and then have the circus.'

Some people have no idea of the value of time. And Dora is one of those who do not understand that when you want to do a thing you *do* want to, and not to do something else, and perhaps your own thing, a week later.

Oswald said the first thing was to collect the performing animals.

'Then perhaps,' he said, 'we may find that they have hidden talents hitherto unsuspected by their harsh masters.'

So Denny took a pencil and wrote a list of the animals required.

This is it:

LIST OF ANIMALS REQUISITE FOR THE CIRCUS WE ARE GOING TO HAVE

1 Bull for bull-fight.
1 Horse for ditto (if possible).
1 Goat to do Alpine feats of daring.
1 Donkey to play see-saw.

2 White pigs – one to be Learned, and the other to play with the clown.

Turkeys, as many as possible, because they can make a noise that sounds like an audience applauding.

The dogs, for any odd parts.

1 Large black pig – to be the Elephant in the procession.

Calves (several) to be camels, and to stand on tubs.

Daisy ought to have been captain because it was partly her idea, but she let Oswald be, because she is of a retiring character. Oswald said –

'The first thing is to get all the creatures together; the paddock at the side of the orchard is the very place, because the hedge is good all round. When we've got the performers all there we'll make a programme, and then dress for our parts. It's a pity there won't be any audience but the turkeys.'

We took the animals in their right order, according to Denny's list. The bull was the first. He is black. He does not live in the cowhouse with the other horned people; he has a house all to himself two fields away. Oswald and Alice went to fetch him. They took a halter to lead the bull by, and a whip, not to hurt the bull with, but just to make him mind.

The others were to try to get one of the horses while we were gone.

Oswald as usual was full of bright ideas.

'I daresay,' he said, 'the bull will be shy at first, and he'll have to be goaded into the arena.'

'But goads hurt,' Alice said.

'They don't hurt the bull,' Oswald said; 'his powerful hide is too thick.'

'Then why does he attend to it,' Alice asked, 'if it doesn't hurt?'

'Properly-brought-up bulls attend because they know they ought,' Oswald said. 'I think I shall ride the bull,' the brave boy went on. 'A bull-fight, where an intrepid rider appears on the bull, sharing its joys and sorrows. It would be something quite new.'

'You can't ride bulls,' Alice said; 'at least, not if their backs are sharp like cows.'

But Oswald thought he could. The bull lives in a house made of wood and prickly furze bushes, and he has a yard to his house. You cannot climb on the roof of his house at all comfortably.

When we got there he was half in his house and half out in his yard, and he was swinging his tail because of the flies which bothered. It was a very hot day.

'You'll see,' Alice said, 'he won't want a goad. He'll be so glad to get out for a walk he'll drop his head in my hand like a tame fawn, and follow me lovingly all the way.'

Oswald called to him. He said, 'Bull! Bull! Bull! Bull!' because we did not know the animal's real name. The bull took no notice; then Oswald picked up a stone and threw it at the bull, not angrily, but just to make it pay attention. But the bull did not pay a farthing's worth of it. So then Oswald leaned over the iron gate of the bull's yard and just flicked the bull with the whip-lash. And then the bull *did* pay attention. He started when the lash struck him, then suddenly he faced round, uttering a roar like that of the wounded King of Beasts, and putting his head down close to his feet he ran straight at the iron gate where we were standing.

Alice and Oswald mechanically turned away; they did not wish to annoy the bull any more, and they ran as fast as they could across the field so as not to keep the others waiting.

As they ran across the field Oswald had a dream-like fancy that perhaps the bull had rooted up the gate with one paralysing blow, and was now tearing across the field after him and Alice, with the broken gate balanced on its horns. We climbed the stile quickly and looked back; the bull was still on the right side of the gate.

Oswald said, 'I think we'll do without the bull. He did not seem to want to come. We must be kind to dumb animals.'

Alice said, between laughing and crying –

'Oh, Oswald, how can you!' But we did do without the bull, and we did not tell the others how we had hurried to get back. We just said, 'The bull didn't seem to care about coming.'

The others had not been idle. They had got old Clover, the cart-horse, but she would do nothing but graze, so we decided not to use her in the bull-fight, but to let her be the Elephant. The Elephant's is a nice quiet part, and she was quite big enough for a young one. Then the black pig could be Learned, and the other two could be something else. They had also got the goat; he was tethered to a young tree.

The donkey was there. Denny was leading him in the halter.

The dogs were there, of course – they always are.

So now we only had to get the turkeys for the applause and the calves and pigs.

The calves were easy to get, because they were in their own house. There were five. And the pigs were in their houses too. We got them out after long and patient toil, and persuaded them that they wanted to go into the paddock, where the circus was to be. This is done by pretending to drive them the other way. A pig only knows two ways – the way you want him to go, and the other. But the turkeys knew thousands of different ways, and tried them all. They made such an awful row, we had to drop all ideas of ever hearing applause from their lips, so we came away and left them.

'Never mind,' H. O. said, 'they'll be sorry enough afterwards, nasty, unobliging things, because now they won't see the circus. I hope the other animals will tell them about it.'

While the turkeys were engaged in baffling the rest of us, Dicky had found three sheep who seemed to wish to join the glad throng, so we let them.

Then we shut the gate of the paddock, and left the dumb circus performers to make friends with each other while we dressed.

Oswald and H. O. were to be clowns. It is quite easy with Albert's uncle's pyjamas, and flour on your hair and face, and the red they do the brick-floors with.

Alice had very short pink and white skirts, and roses in her hair and round her dress. Her dress was the pink calico and white muslin stuff off the dressing-table in the girls' room fastened with pins and tied round the waist with a small bath towel. She was to be the Dauntless Equestrienne, and to give her enhancing act a bare-backed daring, riding either a pig or a sheep, whichever we found was freshest and most skittish. Dora was dressed for the *Haute École*, which means a riding-habit and a high hat. She took Dick's topper that he wears with his Etons, and a skirt of Mrs Pettigrew's. Daisy, dressed the same as Alice, taking the muslin from Mrs Pettigrew's dressing-table without saying anything beforehand. None of us would have advised this, and indeed we were thinking of trying to put it back, when Denny and Noël, who were wishing to look like high-waymen, with brown-paper top-boots and slouch hats and Turkish towel cloaks, suddenly stopped dressing and gazed out of the window.

'Krikey!' said Dick, 'come on, Oswald!' and he bounded like an antelope from the room.

Oswald and the rest followed, casting a hasty glance

through the window. Noël had got brown-paper boots too, and a Turkish towel cloak. H. O. had been waiting for Dora to dress him up for the other clown. He had only his shirt and knickerbockers and his braces on. He came down as he was – as indeed we all did. And no wonder, for in the paddock, where the circus was to be, a blood-thrilling thing had transpired. The dogs were chasing the sheep. And we had now lived long enough in the country to know the fell nature of our dogs' improper conduct.

We all rushed into the paddock, calling to Pincher, and Martha, and Lady. Pincher came almost at once. He is a well-brought-up dog – Oswald trained him. Martha did not seem to hear. She is awfully deaf, but she did not matter so much, because the sheep could walk away from her easily. She has no pace and no wind. But Lady is a deer-hound. She is used to pursuing that fleet and antlered pride of the forest – the stag – and she can go like billyo. She was now far away in a distant region of the paddock, with a fat sheep just before her in full flight. I am sure if ever anybody's eyes did start out of their heads with horror, like in narratives of adventure, ours did then.

There was a moment's pause of speechless horror. We expected to see Lady pull down her quarry, and we know what a lot of money a sheep costs, to say nothing of its own personal feelings.

Then we started to run for all we were worth. It is hard to run swiftly as the arrow from the bow when you happen to be wearing pyjamas belonging to a grown-up person – as I was – but even so I beat Dicky. He said afterwards it was because his brown-paper boots came undone and tripped him up. Alice came in third. She held on the dressing-table muslin and ran jolly well. But ere we reached the fatal spot all was very nearly up with the sheep. We heard a plop; Lady stopped and looked round. She must have heard us bellowing to her as we ran. Then she came towards us, prancing with happiness, but we said 'Down!' and 'Bad dog!' and ran sternly on.

When we came to the brook which forms the northern boundary of the paddock we saw the sheep struggling in the water. It is not very deep, and I believe the sheep could have stood up, and been well in its depth, if it had liked, but it would not try.

It was a steepish bank. Alice and I got down and stuck our legs into the water, and then Dicky came down, and the three of us hauled that sheep up by its shoulders till it could rest on Alice and me as we sat on the bank. It kicked all the time we were hauling. It gave one extra kick at last, that raised it up, and I tell you that sopping wet, heavy, panting, silly donkey of a sheep sat there on our laps like a pet dog; and Dicky got his shoulder under it at the back and heaved constantly to keep it from flumping off into the water again, while the others fetched the shepherd.

When the shepherd came he called us every name you can think of, and then he said –

'Good thing master didn't come along. He would ha' called you some tidy names.'

He got the sheep out, and took it and the others away. And the calves too. He did not seem to care about the other performing animals.

Alice, Oswald and Dick had had almost enough circus for just then, so we sat in the sun and dried ourselves and wrote the programme of the circus. This was it:

PROGRAMME

1. Startling leap from the lofty precipice by the performing sheep. Real water, and real precipice. The

gallant rescue. O. A. and D. Bastable. (We thought we might as well put that in though it was over and had happened accidentally.)

2. Graceful bare-backed equestrienne act on the trained pig, Eliza. A. Bastable.

3. Amusing clown interlude, introducing trained dog, Pincher, and the other white pig. H. O. and O. Bastable.

4. The See-Saw. Trained donkeys. (H. O. said we had only one donkey, so Dicky said H. O. could be the other. When peace was restored we went on to 5.)

5. Elegant equestrian act by D. Bastable. *Haute École*, on Clover, the incomparative trained elephant from the plains of Venezuela.

6. Alpine feat of daring. The climbing of the Andes, by Billy, the well-known acrobatic goat. (We thought we could make the Andes out of hurdles and things, and so we could have but for what always happens. (This is the unexpected. (This is a saying Father told me – but I see I am three deep in brackets so I will close them before I get into any more).).).

7. The Black but Learned Pig. ('I daresay he knows something,' Alice said, 'if we can only find out what.' We *did* find out all too soon.)

We could not think of anything else, and our things were nearly dry – all except Dick's brown-paper top-boots, which were mingled with the gurgling waters of the brook.

We went back to the seat of action – which was the iron trough where the sheep have their salt put – and began to dress up the creatures. We had just tied the Union Jack we made out of Daisy's flannel petticoat and cetera, when we gave the soldiers the baccy, round the waist of the Black and Learned Pig, when we heard screams from the back part of the house; and suddenly we saw that Billy, the acrobatic goat, had got loose from the tree we had tied him to. (He had eaten all the parts of its bark that he could get at, but we did not notice it until next day, when led to the spot by a grown-up.)

The gate of the paddock was open. The gate leading to the bridge that goes over the moat to the back door was open too. We hastily proceeded in the direction of the screams, and, guided by the sound, threaded our way into the kitchen. As we went, Noël, ever fertile in melancholy ideas, said he wondered whether Mrs Pettigrew was being robbed, or only murdered.

In the kitchen we saw that Noël was wrong as usual. It was neither. Mrs Pettigrew, screaming like a steam-siren and waving a broom, occupied the foreground. In the distance the maid was shrieking in a hoarse and monotonous way, and trying to shut herself up inside a clothes-horse on which washing was being aired. On the dresser – which he had ascended by a chair – was Billy, the acrobatic goat, doing his Alpine daring act. He had found out his Andes for himself, and even as we gazed he turned and tossed his head in a way that showed us some mysterious purpose was hidden beneath his calm exterior. The next moment he put his off-horn neatly behind the end plate of the next to the bottom row, and ran it along against the wall. The plates fell crashing on to the soup tureen and vegetable dishes which adorned the lower range of the Andes.

Mrs Pettigrew's screams were almost drowned in the discording crash and crackle of the falling avalanche of crockery.

Oswald, though stricken with horror and polite regret, preserved the most dauntless coolness.

Disregarding the mop which Mrs Pettigrew kept on poking at the goat in a timid yet cross way, he sprang forward, crying out to his trusty followers, 'Stand by to catch him!'

He put his horn neatly behind the end plate and
ran it along against the wall

But Dick had thought of the same thing, and ere
Oswald could carry out his long-cherished and general-
like design, Dicky had caught the goat's legs and tripped
it up. The goat fell against another row of plates, righted
itself hastily in the gloomy ruins of the soup tureen and
the sauce-boats, and then fell again, this time towards
Dicky. The two fell heavily on the ground together.
The trusty followers had been so struck by the daring of
Dicky and his lion-hearted brother, that they had not
stood by to catch anything. The goat was not hurt, but
Dicky had a sprained thumb and a lump on his head
like a black marble door-knob. He had to go to bed.

I will draw a veil and asterisks over what Mrs Pettigrew said. Also Albert's uncle, who was brought to the scene of ruin by her screams. Few words escaped our lips. There are times when it is not wise to argue; however, little what has occurred is really our fault.

When they had said what they deemed enough and we were let go, we all went out. Then Alice said distractedly, in a voice which she vainly strove to render firm –

'Let's give up the circus. Let's put the toys back in the boxes – no, I don't mean that – the creatures in their places – and drop the whole thing. I want to go and read to Dicky.'

Oswald has a spirit that no reverses can depreciate. He hates to be beaten. But he gave in to Alice, as the others said so too, and we went out to collect the performing troop and sort it out into its proper places.

Alas! we came too late. In the interest we had felt about whether Mrs Pettigrew was the abject victim of burglars or not, we had left both gates open again. The old horse – I mean the trained elephant from Venezuela – was there all right enough. The dogs we had beaten and tied up after the first act, when the intrepid sheep bounded, as it says in the programme. The two white pigs were there, but the donkey was gone. We heard his hoofs down the road, growing fainter and fainter, in the direction of the 'Rose and Crown'. And just round the gatepost we saw a flash of red and white and blue and black that told us, with dumb signification, that the pig was off in exactly the opposite direction. Why couldn't they have gone the same way? But no, one was a pig and the other was a donkey, as Denny said afterwards.

Daisy and H. O. started after the donkey; the rest of us, with one accord, pursued the pig – I don't know why. It trotted quietly down the road; it looked very black against the white road, and the ends on the top, where the Union Jack was tied, bobbed brightly as it trotted. At first we thought it would be easy to catch up to it. This was an error.

When we ran faster it ran faster; when we stopped it stopped and looked round at us, and nodded. (I daresay you won't swallow this, but you may safely. It's as true as true, and so's all that about the goat. I give you my sacred word of honour.) I tell you the pig nodded as much as to say –

'Oh, yes. You think you will, but you won't!' and then as soon as we moved again off it went. That pig led us on and on, o'er miles and miles of strange country. One thing, it did keep to the roads. When we met people, which wasn't often, we called out to them to help us, but they only waved their arms and roared with laughter. One chap on a bicycle almost tumbled off his machine, and then he got off it and propped it against a gate and sat down in the hedge to laugh properly. You remember Alice was still dressed up as the gay equestrienne in the dressing-table pink and white, with rosy garlands, now very droopy, and she had no stockings on, only white sand-shoes, because she thought they would be easier than boots for balancing on the pig in the graceful bare-backed act.

Oswald was attired in red paint and flour and pyjamas, for a clown. It is really *impossible* to run speedfully in another man's pyjamas, so Oswald had taken them off, and wore his own brown knickerbockers belonging to his Norfolks. He had tied the pyjamas round his neck, to carry them easily. He was afraid to leave them in a ditch, as Alice suggested, because he did not know the roads, and for aught he recked they might have been infested with footpads. If it had been his own pyjamas it would have been different. (I'm going to ask for pyjamas next winter, they are so useful in many ways.)

Noël was a highwayman in brown-paper gaiters and bath towels and a cocked hat of newspaper. I don't know how he kept it on. And the pig was encircled by the dauntless banner of our country. All the same, I think if I had seen a band of youthful travellers in bitter distress about a pig I should have tried to lend a helping hand and not sat roaring in the hedge, no matter how the travellers and the pig might have been dressed.

It was hotter than anyone would believe who has never had occasion to hunt the pig when dressed for quite another part. The flour got out of Oswald's hair into his eyes and his mouth. His brow was wet with what the village blacksmith's was wet with, and not his fair brow alone. It ran down his face and washed the red off in streaks, and when he rubbed his eyes he only made it worse. Alice had to run holding the equestrienne skirts on with both hands, and I think the brown-paper boots bothered Noël from the first. Dora had her skirt over her arm and carried the topper in her hand. It was no use to tell ourselves it was a wild boar hunt – we were long past that.

At last we met a man who took pity on us. He was a kind-hearted man. I think, perhaps, he had a pig of his own – or, perhaps, children, Honour to his name!

He stood in the middle of the road and waved his arms. The pig right-wheeled through a gate into a private garden and cantered up the drive. We followed. What else were we to do, I should like to know?

The Learned Black Pig seemed to know its way. It turned first to the right and then to the left, and emerged on a lawn.

'Now, all together!' cried Oswald, mustering his failing voice to give the word of command. 'Surround him! – cut off his retreat!'

We almost surrounded him. He edged off towards the house.

'Now we've got him!' cried the crafty Oswald, as the pig got on to a bed of yellow pansies close against the red house wall.

All would even then have been well, but Denny, at the last, shrank from meeting the pig face to face in a manly way. He let the pig pass him, and the next moment, with a squeak that said 'There now!' as plain as words, the pig bolted into a French window. The pursuers halted not. This was no time for trivial ceremony. In another moment the pig was a captive. Alice and Oswald had their arms round him under the ruins of a table that had had teacups on it, and around the hunters and their prey stood the startled members of a parish society for making clothes for the poor heathen, that that pig had led us into the very midst of. They were reading a missionary report or something when we ran our quarry to earth under their table. Even as he crossed the threshold I heard something about 'black brothers being already white to the harvest'. All the ladies had been sewing flannel things for the poor blacks while the curate read aloud to them. You think they screamed when they saw the Pig and Us? You are right.

On the whole, I cannot say that the missionary people behaved badly. Oswald explained that it was entirely the pig's doing, and asked pardon quite properly for any alarm the ladies had felt; and Alice said how sorry we were but really it was *not* our fault this time. The curate looked a bit nasty, but the presence of ladies made him keep his hot blood to himself.

When we had explained, we said, 'Might we go?'

The curate said, 'The sooner the better.' But the Lady of the House asked for our names and addresses, and said she should write to our Father. (She did, and we heard of it too.) They did not do anything to us, as Oswald at one time believed to be the curate's idea. They let us go.

And we went, after we had asked for a piece of rope to lead the pig by.

'In case it should come back into your nice room,' Alice said. 'And that would be such a pity, wouldn't it?'

A little girl in a starched pinafore was sent for the rope. And as soon as the pig had agreed to let us tie it round his neck we came away. The scene in the drawing-room had not been long.

The pig went slowly,

'Like the meandering brook,'

Denny said. Just by the gate the shrubs rustled and opened, and the little girl came out. Her pinafore was full of cake.

'Here,' she said. 'You must be hungry if you've come all that way. I think they might have given you some tea after all the trouble you've had.'

We took the cake with correct thanks.

'I wish *I* could play at circuses,' she said. 'Tell me about it.'

We told her while we ate the cake; and when we had done she said perhaps it was better to hear about than do, especially the goat's part and Dicky's.

'But I do wish auntie had given you tea,' she said.

We told her not to be too hard on her aunt, because you have to make allowances for grown-up people.

When we parted she said she would never forget us,

333

and Oswald gave her his pocket button-hook and cork-screw combined for a keepsake.

Dicky's act with the goat (which is true, and no kid) was the only thing out of that day that was put in the Golden Deed book, and he put that in himself while we were hunting the pig.

Alice and me capturing the pig was never put in. We would scorn to write our own good actions, but I suppose Dicky was dull with us all away; and you must pity the dull, and not blame them.

I will not seek to unfold to you how we got the pig home, or how the donkey was caught (that was poor sport compared to the pig). Nor will I tell you a word of all that was said and done to the intrepid hunters of the Black and Learned. I have told you all the interesting part. Seek not to know the rest. It is better buried in obliquity.

BEING BEAVERS; OR, THE YOUNG EXPLORERS (ARCTIC OR OTHERWISE)

You read in books about the pleasures of London, and about how people who live in the country long for the gay whirl of fashion in town because the country is so dull. I do not agree with this at all. In London, or at any rate Lewisham, nothing happens unless you make it happen; or if it happens it doesn't happen to you, and you don't know the people it does happen to. But in the country the most interesting events occur quite freely, and they seem to happen to you as much as to anyone else. Very often quite without your doing anything to help.

The natural and right ways of earning your living in the country are much jollier than town ones, too; sowing and reaping, and doing things with animals, are much better sport than fishmongering or bakering or oil-shopping, and those sort of things, except, of course, a plumber's and gasfitter's, and he is the same in town or country – most interesting and like an engineer.

I remember what a nice man it was that came to cut the gas off once at our old house in Lewisham, when my father's business was feeling so poorly. He was a true gentleman, and gave Oswald and Dicky over two yards and a quarter of good lead piping, and a brass tap that only wanted a washer, and a whole handful of screws to do what we liked with. We screwed the back door up with the screws, I remember, one night when Eliza was out without leave. There was an awful row. We did not mean to get her into trouble. We only thought it would be amusing for her to find the door screwed up when she came down to take in the milk in the morning. But I must not say any more about the Lewisham house. It is only the pleasures of memory, and nothing to do with being beavers, or any sort of exploring.

I think Dora and Daisy are the kind of girls who will grow up very good, and perhaps marry missionaries. I am glad Oswald's destiny looks at present as if it might be different.

We made two expeditions to discover the source of the Nile (or the North Pole), and owing to their habit of sticking together and doing dull and praiseable things, like sewing, and helping with the cooking, and taking invalid delicacies to the poor and indignant, Daisy and Dora were wholly out of it both times, though Dora's foot was now quite well enough to have gone to the North Pole or the Equator either. They said they did not mind the first time, because they like to keep themselves clean; it is another of their queer ways. And they said they had had a better time than us. (It was only a clergyman and his wife who called, and hot cakes for tea.) The second time they said they were lucky not to have been in it. And perhaps they were right. But let me to my narrating. I hope you will like it. I am going to try to write it a different way, like the books they give you for a prize at a girls' school – I mean a 'young ladies' school', of course – not a high school. High schools are not nearly so silly as some other kinds. Here goes:

'"Ah, me!" sighed a slender maiden of twelve summers, removing her elegant hat and passing her tapery fingers lightly through her fair tresses, "how sad it is – is it not? – to see able-bodied youths and young ladies wasting the precious summer hours in idleness and luxury."

'The maiden frowned reproachingly, but yet with earnest gentleness, at the group of youths and maidens who sat beneath an umbragipeaous beech tree and ate black currants.

' "Dear brothers and sisters," the blushing girl went on, "could we not, even now, at the eleventh hour, turn to account these wasted lives of ours, and seek some occupation at once improving and agreeable?"

' 'I do not quite follow your meaning, dear sister," replied the cleverest of her brothers, on whose brow – '

It's no use. I can't write like these books. I wonder how the books' authors can keep it up.

What really happened was that we were all eating black currants in the orchard, out of a cabbage leaf, and Alice said –

'I say, look here, let's do something. It's simply silly to waste a day like this. It's just on eleven. Come on!'

And Oswald said, 'Where to?'

This was the beginning of it.

The moat that is all round our house is fed by streams. One of them is a sort of open overflow pipe from a good-sized stream that flows at the other side of the orchard.

It was this stream that Alice meant when she said –

'Why not go and discover the source of the Nile?'

Of course Oswald knows quite well that the source of the real live Egyptian Nile is no longer buried in that mysteriousness where it lurked undisturbed for such a long time. But he was not going to say so. It is a great thing to know when not to say things.

'Why not have it an Arctic expedition?' said Dicky;

'then we could take an ice-axe, and live on blubber and things. Besides, it sounds cooler.'

'Vote! vote!' cried Oswald. So we did.

Oswald, Alice, Noël, and Denny voted for the river of the ibis and the crocodile. Dicky, H. O., and the other girls for the region of perennial winter and rich blubber.

So Alice said, 'We can decide as we go. Let's start anyway.'

The question of supplies had now to be gone into. Everybody wanted to take something different, and nobody thought the other people's things would be the slightest use. It is sometimes thus even with grown-up expeditions. So then Oswald, who is equal to the hardest emergency that ever emerged yet, said –

'Let's each get what we like. The secret storehouse can be the shed in the corner of the stableyard where we got the door for the raft. Then the captain can decide who's to take what.'

This was done. You may think it but the work of a moment to fit out an expedition, but this is not so, especially when you know not whether your exploring party is speeding to Central Africa or merely to the world of icebergs and the Polar bear.

Dicky wished to take the wood-axe, the coal hammer, a blanket, and a mackintosh.

H. O. brought a large faggot in case we had to light fires, and a pair of old skates he had happened to notice in the box-room, in case the expedition turned out icy.

Noël had nicked a dozen boxes of matches, a spade, and a trowel, and had also obtained – I know not by what means – a jar of pickled onions.

Denny had a walking-stick – we can't break him of walking with it – a book to read in case he got tired of being a discoverer, a butterfly net and a box with a cork in it, a tennis ball, if we happened to want to play rounders in the pauses of exploring, two towels and an umbrella in the event of camping or if the river got big enough to bathe in or to be fallen into.

Alice had a comforter for Noël in case we got late, a pair of scissors and needle and cotton, two whole candles in case of caves. And she had thoughtfully brought the tablecloth off the small table in the dining-room, so that we could make all the things up into one bundle and take it in turns to carry it.

Oswald had fastened his master mind entirely on grub. Nor had the others neglected this.

All the stores for the expedition were put down on the tablecloth and the corners tied up. Then it was more than even Oswald's muscley arms could raise from the ground, so we decided not to take it, but only the best-selected grub. The rest we hid in the straw loft, for there are many ups and downs in life, and grub *is* grub at any time, and so are stores of all kinds. The pickled onions we had to leave, but not for ever.

Then Dora and Daisy came along with their arms round each other's necks as usual, like a picture on a grocer's almanac, and said they weren't coming.

It was, as I have said, a blazing hot day, and there were differences of opinion among the explorers about what eatables we ought to have taken, and H. O. had lost one of his garters and wouldn't let Alice tie it up with her handkerchief, which the gentle sister was quite willing to do. So it was a rather gloomy expedition that set off that bright sunny day to seek the source of the river where Cleopatra sailed in Shakespeare (or the frozen plains Mr Nansen wrote that big book about).

But the balmy calm of peaceful Nature soon made the others less cross – Oswald had not been cross exactly but only disinclined to do anything the others wanted – and by the time we had followed the stream a little way, and had seen a water-rat and shied a stone or two at him, harmony was restored. We did not hit the rat.

You will understand that we were not the sort of people to have lived so long near a stream without plumbing its depths. Indeed it was the same stream the sheep took its daring jump into the day we had the circus. And of course we had often paddled in it – in the shallower parts. But now our hearts were set on exploring. At least they ought to have been, but when we got to the place where the stream goes under a wooden sheep-bridge, Dicky cried, 'A camp! a camp!' and we were all glad to sit down at once. Not at all like real explorers, who know no rest, day or night, till they have got there (whether it's the North Pole, or the central point of the part marked *Desert of Sahara* on old-fashioned maps).

The food supplies obtained by various members were good and plenty of it. Cake, hard eggs, sausage-rolls, currants, lemon cheese-cakes, raisins, and cold apple dumplings. It was all very decent, but Oswald could not help feeling that the source of the Nile (or North Pole) was a long way off, and perhaps nothing much when you got there.

So he was not wholly displeased when Denny said, as he lay kicking into the bank when the things to eat were all gone –

'I believe this is clay: did you ever make huge platters and bowls out of clay and dry them in the sun? Some people did in a book called *Foul Play*, and I believe they baked turtles, or oysters, or something, at the same time.'

He took up a bit of clay and began to mess it about, like you do putty when you get hold of a bit. And at once the heavy gloom that had hung over the explorers became expelled, and we all got under the shadow of the bridge and messed about with clay.

'It will be jolly!' Alice said, 'and we can give the huge platters to poor cottagers who are short of the usual sorts of crockery. That would really be a very golden deed.'

It is harder than you would think when you read about it, to make huge platters with clay. It flops about as soon as you get it any size, unless you keep it much too thick, and then when you turn up the edges they crack. Yet we did not mind the trouble. And we had all got our shoes and stockings off. It is impossible to go on being cross when your feet are in cold water; and there is something in the smooth messiness of clay, and not minding how dirty you get, that would soothe the savagest breast that ever beat.

After a bit, though, we gave up the idea of the huge platter and tried little things. We made some platters – they were like flower-pot saucers; and Alice made a bowl by doubling up her fists and getting Noël to slab the clay on outside. Then they smoothed the thing inside and out with wet fingers, and it was a bowl – at least they said it was. When we'd made a lot of things we set them in the sun to dry, and then it seemed a pity not to do the thing thoroughly. So we made a bonfire, and when it had burnt down we put our pots on the soft, white, hot ashes among the little red sparks, and kicked the ashes over them and heaped more fuel over the top. It was a fine fire.

Then tea-time seemed as if it ought to be near, and we decided to come back next day and get our pots.

As we went home across the fields Dicky looked back and said –

'The bonfire's going pretty strong.'

We looked. It was. Great flames were rising to heaven against the evening sky. And we had left it a smouldering flat heap.

There is something in the smoothness of clay . . .

'The clay must have caught alight.' H. O. said. 'Perhaps it's the kind that burns. I know I've heard of fireclay. And there's another sort you can eat.'

'Oh, shut up!' Dicky said with anxious scorn.

With one accord we turned back. We all felt *the* feeling – the one that means something fatal being up and it being your fault.

'Perhaps,' Alice said, 'a beautiful young lady in a muslin dress was passing by, and a spark flew on to her, and now she is rolling in agony enveloped in flames.'

We could not see the fire now, because of the corner of the wood, but we hoped Alice was mistaken.

But when we got in sight of the scene of our pottering industry we saw it was as bad nearly as Alice's wild dream. For the wooden fence leading up to the bridge had caught fire, and it was burning like billy oh.

Oswald started to run; so did the others. As he ran he said to himself, 'This is no time to think about your clothes. Oswald, be bold!'

And he was.

Arrived at the site of the conflagration, he saw that caps or straw hats full of water, however quickly and perseveringly given, would never put the bridge out, and his eventful past life made him know exactly the sort of wigging you get for an accident like this.

So he said, 'Dicky, soak your jacket and mine in the stream and chuck them along. Alice, stand clear, or your silly girl's clothes'll catch as sure as fate.'

Dicky and Oswald tore off their jackets, so did Denny, but we would not let him and H. O. wet theirs. Then the brave Oswald advanced warily to the end of the burning rails and put his wet jacket over the end bit, like a linseed poultice on the throat of a suffering invalid who has got bronchitis. The burning wood hissed and smouldered, and Oswald fell back, almost choked with the smoke.

But at once he caught up the other wet jacket and put it on another place, and of course it did the trick as he had known it would do. But it was a long job, and the smoke in his eyes made the young hero obliged to let Dicky and Denny take a turn as they had bothered to do from the first. At last all was safe; the devouring element was conquered. We covered up the beastly bonfire with clay to keep it from getting into mischief again, and then Alice said –

'Now we must go and tell.'

'Of course,' Oswald said shortly. He had meant to tell all the time.

So we went to the farmer who has the Moat House Farm, and we went at once, because if you have any news like that to tell it only makes it worse if you wait about. When we had told him he said –

'You little – .' I shall not say what he said besides that, because I am sure he must have been sorry for it next Sunday when he went to church, if not before.

We did not take any notice of what he said, but just kept on saying how sorry we were; and he did not take our apology like a man, but only said he daresayed, just like a woman does. Then he went to look at his bridge, and we went in to our tea. The jackets were never quite the same again.

Really great explorers would never be discouraged by the daresaying of a farmer, still less by his calling them names he ought not to. Albert's uncle was away so we got no double slating; and next day we started again to discover the source of the river of cataracts (or the region of mountain-like icebergs).

We set out, heavily provisioned with a large cake Daisy and Dora had made themselves, and six bottles of ginger-beer. I think real explorers most likely have their ginger-beer in something lighter to carry than stone bottles. Perhaps they have it by the cask, which would come cheaper; and you could make the girls carry it on their back, like in pictures of the daughters of regiments.

We passed the scene of the devouring conflagration, and the thought of the fire made us so thirsty we decided to drink the ginger-beer and leave the bottles in a place of concealment. Then we went on, determined to reach our destination, Tropic or Polar, that day.

Denny and H. O. wanted to stop and try to make a fashionable watering-place at that part where the stream spreads out like a small-sized sea, but Noël said, 'No.' We did not like fashionableness.

'*You* ought to, at any rate,' Denny said. 'A Mr Collins wrote an Ode to the Fashions, and he was a great poet.'

'The poet Milton wrote a long book about Satan,' Noël said, 'but I'm not bound to like *him*.' I think it was smart of Noël.

'People aren't obliged to like everything they write about even, let alone read,' Alice said. 'Look at "Ruin seize thee, ruthless king!" and all the pieces of poetry about war, and tyrants, and slaughtered saints – and the one you made yourself about the black beetle, Noël.'

By this time we had got by the pondy place and the danger of delay was past; but the others went on talking about poetry for quite a field and a half, as we walked along by the banks of the stream. The stream was broad and shallow at this part, and you could see the stones and gravel at the bottom, and millions of baby fishes, and a sort of skating-spiders walking about on the top of the water. Denny said the water must be ice for them to be able to walk on it, and this showed we were getting near the North Pole. But Oswald had seen a kingfisher by the wood, and he said it was an ibis, so this was even.

When Oswald had had as much poetry as he could bear he said, 'Let's be beavers and make a dam.'

And everybody was so hot they agreed joyously, and soon our clothes were tucked up as far as they could go and our legs looked green through the water, though they were pink out of it.

Making a dam is jolly good fun, though laborious, as books about beavers take care to let you know.

Dicky said it must be Canada if we were beavers, and so it was on the way to the Polar system, but Oswald pointed to his heated brow, and Dicky owned it was warm for Polar regions. He had brought the ice-axe (it is called the wood chopper sometimes), and Oswald, ever ready and able to command, set him and Denny to cut turfs from the bank while we heaped stones across the stream. It was clayey here, or of course dam making would have been vain, even for the best-trained beaver.

When we had made a ridge of stones we laid turfs against them – nearly across the stream, leaving about two feet for the water to go through – then more stones, and then lumps of clay stamped down as hard as we could. The industrious beavers spent hours over it, with only one easy to eat cake in. And at last the dam rose to the level of the bank. Then the beavers collected a great heap of clay, and four of them lifted it and dumped it down in the opening where the water was running. It did splash a little, but a true-hearted beaver knows better than to mind a bit of a wetting, as Oswald told Alice at the time. Then with more clay the work was completed. We must have used tons of clay; there was quite a big long hole in the bank above the dam where we had taken it out.

When our beaver task was performed we went on, and Dicky was so hot he had to take his jacket off and shut up about icebergs.

I cannot tell you about all the windings of the stream; it went through fields and woods and meadows. and at last the banks got steeper and higher, and the trees overhead darkly arched their mysterious branches, and we felt like the princes in a fairy tale who go out to seek their fortunes.

And then we saw a thing that was well worth coming all that way for; the stream suddenly disappeared under a dark stone archway, and however much you stood in the water and stuck your head down between your knees you could not see any light at the other end.

The stream was much smaller than where we had been beavers.

Gentle reader, you will guess in a moment who it was that said –

'Alice, you've got a candle. Let's explore.'

This gallant proposal met but a cold response.

The others said they didn't care much about it, and what about tea?

I often think the way people try to hide their cowardliness behind their teas is simply beastly.

Oswald took no notice. He just said, with that dignified manner, not at all like sulking, which he knows so well how to put on –

'All right. *I'm* going. If you funk it you'd better cut along home and ask your nurses to put you to bed.'

So then, of course, they agreed to go. Oswald went first with the candle. It was not comfortable; the architect of that dark subterranean passage had not imagined anyone would ever be brave enough to lead a band of beavers into its inky recesses, or he would have built it high enough to stand upright in. As it was, we were bent almost at a right angle, and this is very awkward if for long.

But the leader pressed dauntlessly on, and paid no attention to the groans of his faithful followers, nor to what they said about their backs.

It really was a very long tunnel, though, and even Oswald was not sorry to say, 'I see daylight.' The followers cheered as well as they could as they splashed after him. The floor was stone as well as the roof, so it was easy to walk on. I think the followers would have turned back if it had been sharp stones or gravel.

And now the spot of daylight at the end of the tunnel grew larger and larger, and presently the intrepid leader found himself blinking in the full sun, and the candle he carried looked simply silly. He emerged, and the others too, and they stretched their backs and the word 'krikey' fell from more than one lip. It had indeed been a cramping adventure. Bushes grew close to the mouth of the tunnel, so we could not see much landscape, and when we had stretched our backs we went on up-stream and nobody said they'd had jolly well enough of it, though in more than one young heart this was thought.

It was jolly to be in the sunshine again. I never knew before how cold it was underground. The stream was getting smaller and smaller.

Dicky said, 'This can't be the way. I expect there was a turning to the North Pole inside the tunnel, only we missed it. It was cold enough there.'

But here a twist in the stream brought us out from the bushes, and Oswald said –

'Here is strange, wild, tropical vegetation in the richest profusion. Such blossoms as these never opened in a frigid what's-its-name.'

It was indeed true. We had come out into a sort of marshy, swampy place like I think, a jungle is, that the stream ran through, and it was simply crammed with queer plants, and flowers we never saw before or since. And the stream was quite thin. It was torridly hot, and softish to walk on. There were rushes and reeds and small willows, and it was all tangled over with different sorts of grasses – and pools here and there. We saw no wild beasts, but there were more different kinds of wild flies and beetles than you could believe anybody could bear, and dragon-flies and gnats. The girls picked a lot of flowers. I know the names of some of them, but I will not tell you them because this is not meant to be instructing. So I will only name meadow-sweet, yarrow, loose-strife, lady's bed-straw and willow herb – both the larger and the lesser.

Everyone now wished to go home. It was much hotter there than in natural fields. It made you want to tear all your clothes off and play at savages, instead of keeping respectable in your boots.

But we had to bear the boots because it was so brambly.

It was Oswald who showed the others how flat it would be to go home the same way we came; and he pointed out the telegraph wires in the distance and said –

'There must be a road there, let's make for it,' which was quite a simple and ordinary thing to say, and he does not ask for any credit for it.

So we sloshed along, scratching our legs with the brambles, and the water squelched in our boots, and Alice's blue muslin frock was torn all over in those criss-cross tears which are considered so hard to darn.

We did not follow the stream any more. It was only a trickle now, so we knew we had tracked it to its source. And we got hotter and hotter and hotter, and the dews of agony stood in beads on our brows and rolled down our noses and off our chins. And the flies buzzed, and

the gnats stung, and Oswald bravely sought to keep up
Dicky's courage, when he tripped on a snag and came
down on a bramble bush, by saying –

'*You* see it *is* the source of the Nile we've discovered.
What price North Poles now?'

Alice said, 'Ah, but think of ices! I expect Oswald
wishes it *had* been the Pole, anyway –'

Oswald is naturally the leader, especially when
following up what is his own idea, but he knows that
leaders have other duties besides just leading. One is to
assist weak or wounded members of the expedition,
whether Polar or Equatorish.

So the others had got a bit ahead through Oswald
lending the tottering Denny a hand over the rough
places. Denny's feet hurt him, because when he was a
beaver his stockings had dropped out of his pocket, and
boots without stockings are not a bed of luxuriousness.
And he is often unlucky with his feet.

Presently we came to a pond, and Denny said –

'Let's paddle.'

Oswald likes Denny to have ideas; he knows it is
healthy for the boy, and generally he backs him up, but
just now it was getting late and the others were ahead,
so he said –

'Oh, rot! come on.'

Generally the Dentist would have; but even worms
will turn if they are hot enough, and if their feet are
hurting them.

'I don't care, I shall!' he said.

Oswald overlooked the mutiny and did not say who
was leader. He just said –

'Well don't be all day about it,' for he is a kind-
hearted boy and can make allowances.

So Denny took off his boots and went into the pool.

'Oh, it's ripping!' he said. 'You ought to come in.'

'It looks beastly muddy,' said his tolerating leader.

'It is a bit,' Denny said, 'but the mud's just as cool as the water, and so soft, it squeezes between your toes quite different to boots.'

And so he splashed about, and kept asking Oswald to come along in.

But some unseen influence prevented Oswald doing this; or it may have been because both his bootlaces were in hard knots.

Oswald had cause to bless the unseen influence, or the bootlaces, or whatever it was.

Denny had got to the middle of the pool, and he was splashing about, and getting his clothes very wet indeed, and altogether you would have thought his was a most envious and happy state. But alas! the brightest cloud had a waterproof lining. He was just saying –

'You *are* a silly, Oswald. You'd much better – ' when he gave a blood-piercing scream, and began to kick about.

'What's up?' cried the ready Oswald; he feared the worst from the way Denny screamed, but he knew it could not be an old meat tin in this quiet and jungular spot, like it was in the moat when the shark bit Dora.

'I don't know, it's biting me. Oh, it's biting me all over my legs! Oh, what shall I do? Oh, it does hurt! Oh! oh! oh!' remarked Denny, among his screams, and he splashed towards the bank. Oswald went into the water and caught hold of him and helped him out. It is true that Oswald had his boots on, but I trust he would not have funked the unknown terrors of the deep, even without his boots, I am almost sure he would not have.

When Denny had scrambled and been hauled ashore, we saw with horror and amaze that his legs were stuck all over with large black, slug-looking things. Denny

turned green in the face – and even Oswald felt a bit
queer, for he knew in a moment what the black dread-
fulnesses were. He had read about them in a book called
Magnet Stories, where there was a girl called Theodosia,
and she could play brilliant trebles on the piano in
duets, but the other girl knew all about leeches which is
much more useful and golden deedy. Oswald tried to
pull the leeches off, but they wouldn't, and Denny
howled so he had to stop trying. He remembered from
the *Magnet Stories* how to make the leeches begin biting
– the girl did it with cream – but he could not remember
how to stop them, and they had not wanted any showing
how to begin.

'Oh, what shall I do? What shall I do? Oh, it does
hurt! Oh, oh!' Denny observed, and Oswald said –

'Be a man! Buck up! If you won't let me take them
off you'll just have to walk home in them.'

At this thought the unfortunate youth's tears fell fast.
But Oswald gave him an arm, and carried his boots for
him, and he consented to buck up, and the two struggled
on towards the others, who were coming back, attracted
by Denny's yells. He did not stop howling for a moment,
except to breathe. No one ought to blame him till they
have had eleven leeches on their right leg and six on
their left, making seventeen in all, as Dicky said, at
once.

It was lucky he did yell, as it turned out, because a
man on the road – where the telegraph wires were –
was interested by his howls, and came across the marsh
to us as hard as he could.

When he saw Denny's legs he said –

'Blest if I didn't think so,' and he picked Denny up
and carried him under one arm, where Denny went on
saying 'Oh!' and 'It does hurt' as hard as ever.

Our rescuer, who proved to be a fine big young man

in the bloom of youth, and a farm-labourer by trade, in corduroys, carried the wretched sufferer to the cottage where he lived with his aged mother; and then Oswald found that what he had forgotten about the leeches was *salt*. The young man in the bloom of youth's mother put salt on the leeches, and they squirmed off, and fell with sickening, slug-like flops on the brick floor.

Then the young man in corduroys and the bloom, etc., carried Denny home on his back, after his legs had been bandaged up, so that he looked like 'wounded warriors returning'.

It was not far by the road, though such a long distance by the way the young explorers had come.

He was a good young man, and though, of course, acts of goodness are their own reward, still I was glad he had the two half-crowns Albert's uncle gave him, as well as his own good act. But I am not sure Alice ought to have put him in the Golden Deed book which was supposed to be reserved for Us.

Perhaps you will think this was the end of the source of the Nile (or North Pole). If you do, it only shows how mistaken the gentlest reader may be.

The wounded explorer was lying with his wounds and bandages on the sofa, and we were all having our tea, with raspberries and white currants, which we richly needed after our torrid adventures, when Mrs Pettigrew, the housekeeper, put her head in at the door and said –

'Please could I speak to you half a moment, sir?' to Albert's uncle. And her voice was the kind that makes you look at each other when the grown-up has gone out, and you are silent, with your bread-and-butter half-way to the next bite, or your teacup in mid flight to your lips.

It was as we suppose. Albert's uncle did not come back

353

for a long while. We did not keep the bread-and-butter on the wing all that time, of course, and we thought we might as well finish the raspberries and white currants. We kept some for Albert's uncle, of course, and they were the best ones too; but when he came back he did not notice our thoughtful unselfishness.

He came in, and his face wore the look that means bed, and very likely no supper.

He spoke, and it was the calmness of white-hot iron, which is something like the calmness of despair. He said –

'You have done it again. What on earth possessed you to make a dam?'

'We were being beavers,' said H. O., in proud tones He did not see as we did where Albert's uncle's tone pointed to.

'No doubt,' said Albert's uncle, rubbing his hands through his hair. 'No doubt! no doubt! Well, my beavers, you may go and build dams with your bolsters. Your dam stopped the stream; the clay you took for it left a channel through which it has run down and ruined about seven pounds' worth of freshly-reaped barley. Luckily the farmer found it out in time or you might have spoiled seventy 'pounds' worth. And you burned a bridge yesterday.'

We said we were sorry. There was nothing else to say, only Alice added, 'We didn't *mean* to be naughty.'

'Of course not,' said Albert's uncle, 'you never do. Oh, yes, I'll kiss you – but it's bed and it's two hundred lines to-morrow, and the line is – "Beware of Being Beavers and Burning Bridges. Dread Dams." It will be a capital exercise in capital B's and D's.'

We knew by that that, though annoyed, he was not furious; we went to bed.

I got jolly sick of capital B's and D's before sunset on

the morrow. That night, just as the others were falling asleep, Oswald said –

'I say.'

'Well,' retorted his brother.

'There is one thing about it,' Oswald went on, 'it does show it was a rattling good dam anyhow.'

And filled with this agreeable thought, the weary beavers (or explorers, Polar or otherwise) fell asleep.

THE HIGH-BORN BABE

IT really was not such a bad baby – for a baby. Its face was round and quite clean, which babies' faces are not always, as I daresay you know by your own youthful relatives; and Dora said its cape was trimmed with real lace, whatever that may be – I don't see myself how one kind of lace can be realler than another. It was in a very swagger sort of perambulator when we saw it; and the perambulator was standing quite by itself in the lane that leads to the mill.

'I wonder whose baby it is,' Dora said. 'Isn't it a darling, Alice?'

Alice agreed to its being one, and said she thought it was most likely the child of noble parents stolen by gipsies.

'These two, as likely as not,' Noël said. 'Can't you see something crime-like in the very way they're lying?'

They were two tramps, and they were lying on the grass at the edge of the lane on the shady side fast asleep, only a very little further on than where the Baby was. They were very ragged, and their snores did have a sinister sound.

'I expect they stole the titled heir at dead of night, and they've been travelling hot-foot ever since, so now they're sleeping the sleep of exhaustedness,' Alice said. 'What a heart-rending scene when the patrician mother wakes in the morning and finds the infant aristocrat isn't in bed with his mamma.'

The Baby was fast asleep or else the girls would have kissed it. They are strangely fond of kissing. The author never could see anything in it himself.

'If the gipsies *did* steal it,' Dora said 'perhaps they'd sell it to us. I wonder what they'd take for it.'

'What could you do with it if you'd got it?' H. O. asked.

'Why, adopt it, of course,' Dora said. 'I've often thought I should enjoy adopting a baby. It would be a golden deed, too. We've hardly got any in the book yet.'

'I should have thought there were enough of us,' Dicky said.

'Ah, but you're none of you babies,' said Dora.

'Unless you count H. O. as a baby: he behaves jolly like one sometimes.'

This was because of what had happened that morning when Dicky found H. O. going fishing with a box of worms, and the box was the one Dicky keeps his silver studs in, and the medal he got at school, and what is left of his watch and chain. The box is lined with red velvet and it was not nice afterwards. And then H. O. said Dicky had hurt him, and he was a beastly bully, and he cried. We thought all this had been made up, and were sorry to see it threaten to break out again. So Oswald said –

'Oh, bother the Baby! Come along, do!'

And the others came.

We were going to the miller's with a message about some flour that hadn't come, and about a sack of sharps for the pigs.

After you go down the lane you come to a cloverfield, and then a cornfield, and then another lane, and then it is the mill. It is a jolly fine mill: in fact it is two – water and wind ones – one of each kind – with a house and farm buildings as well. I never saw a mill like it, and I don't believe you have either.

If we had been in a story-book the miller's wife would have taken us into the neat sanded kitchen where the old oak settle was black with time and rubbing, and dusted chairs for us – old brown Windsor chairs – and given us each a glass of sweet-scented cowslip wine and a thick slice of rich home-made cake. And there would have been fresh roses in an old china bowl on the table. As it was, she asked us all into the parlour and gave us Eiffel Tower lemonade and Marie biscuits. The chairs in her parlour were 'bent wood', and no flowers, except some wax ones under a glass shade, but she was very kind, and we were very much obliged to her. We got out to the miller, though, as soon as we could; only Dora and Daisy stayed with her, and she talked to them about her lodgers and about her relations in London.

The miller is a MAN. He showed us all over the mills – both kinds – and let us go right up into the very top of the wind-mill, and showed us how the top moved round so that the sails could catch the wind, and the great heaps of corn, some red and some yellow (the red is English wheat), and the heaps slice down a little bit at a time into a square hole and go down to the mill-stones. The corn makes a rustling soft noise that is very jolly – something like the noise of the sea – and you can hear it through all the other mill noises.

Then the miller let us go all over the water-mill. It is fairy palaces inside a mill. Everything is powdered over white, like sugar on pancakes when you are allowed to help yourself. And he opened a door and showed us the great water-wheel working on slow and sure, like some great, round, dripping giant, Noël said, and then he asked us if we fished.

'Yes,' was our immediate reply.

'Then why not try the mill-pool?' he said, and we replied politely; and when he was gone to tell his man something we owed to each other that he was a trump.

He did the thing thoroughly. He took us out and cut us ash saplings for rods; he found us in lines and hooks, and several different sorts of bait, including a handsome handful of meal-worms, which Oswald put loose in his pocket.

When it came to bait, Alice said she was going home with Dora and Daisy. Girls are strange, mysterious, silly things. Alice always enjoys a rat hunt until the rat is caught, but she hates fishing from beginning to end. We boys have got to like it. We don't feel now as we did when we turned off the water and stopped the competition of the competing anglers. We had a grand day's fishing that day. I can't think what made the miller so kind to us. Perhaps he felt a thrill of fellow-feeling in his manly breast for his fellow-sportsmen, for he was a noble fisherman himself.

We had glorious sport – eight roach, six dace, three eels, seven perch, and a young pike, but he was so very young the miller asked us to put him back, and of course we did.

'He'll live to bite another day,' said the miller.

The miller's wife gave us bread and cheese and more Eiffel Tower lemonade, and we went home at last, a little damp, but full of successful ambition, with our fish on a string.

It had been a strikingly good time – one of those times that happen in the country quite by themselves. Country people are much more friendly than town people. I suppose they don't have to spread their friendly feelings out over so many persons, so it's thicker, like a pound of butter on one loaf is thicker than on a dozen. Friendliness in the country is not scrape,

like it is in London. Even Dicky and H. O. forgot the
affair of honour that had taken place in the morning.
H. O. changed rods with Dicky because H. O.'s was
the best rod, and Dicky baited H. O.'s hook for him,
just like loving, unselfish brothers in Sunday School
magazines.

We were talking fishlikely as we went along down the
lane and through the cornfield and the cloverfield, and
then we came to the other lane where we had seen the
Baby. The tramps were gone, and the perambulator
was gone, and, of course, the Baby was gone too.

'I wonder if those gipsies *had* stolen the Baby?' Noël
said dreamily. He had not fished much, but he had made
a piece of poetry. It was this:

> *How I wish*
> *I was a fish.*
> *I would not look*
> *At your hook,*
> *But lie still and be cool*
> *At the bottom of the pool*
> *And when you went to look*
> *At your cruel hook,*
> *You would not find me there,*
> *So there!'*

'If they did steal the Baby,' Noël went on, 'they will
be tracked by the lordly perambulator. You can disguise a baby in rags and walnut juice, but there isn't
any disguise dark enough to conceal a perambulator's
person.'

'You might disguise it as a wheel-barrow,' said
Dicky.

'Or cover it with leaves,' said H. O., 'like the robins.'

We told him to shut up and not gibber, but afterwards we had to own that even a young brother may
sometimes talk sense by accident.

For we took the short cut home from the lane – it begins with a large gap in the hedge and the grass and weeds trodden down by the hasty feet of persons who were late for church and in too great a hurry to go round by the road. Our house is next to the church, as I think I have said before, some time.

The short cut leads to a stile at the edge of a bit of wood (the Parson's Shave, they call it, because it belongs to him). The wood has not been shaved for some time, and it has grown out beyond the stile; and here, among the hazels and chestnuts and young dog-wood bushes, we saw something white. We felt it was our duty to investigate, even if the white was only the under side of the tail of a dead rabbit caught in a trap. It was not – it was part of the perambulator. I forget whether I said that the perambulator was enamelled white – not the kind of enamelling you do at home with Aspinall's and the hairs of the brush come out and it is gritty-looking, but smooth, like the handles of ladies' very best lace parasols. And whoever had abandoned the helpless perambulator in that lonely spot had done exactly as H. O. said, and covered it with leaves, only they were green and some of them had dropped off.

The others were wild with excitement. Now or never, they thought, was a chance to be real detectives. Oswald alone retained a calm exterior. It was he who would not go straight to the police station.

He said: 'Let's try and ferret out something for ourselves before we tell the police. They always have a clue directly they hear about the finding of the body. And besides, we might as well let Alice be in anything there is going. And besides, we haven't had our dinners yet.'

This argument of Oswald's was so strong and powerful – his arguments are often that, as I daresay you have

'*The clue is always left exactly as it is found till the police have seen it*'

noticed – that the others agreed. It was Oswald, too, who showed his artless brothers why they had much better not take the deserted prambulator home with them.

'The dead body, or whatever the clue is, is always left exactly as it is found,' he said, 'till the police have seen it, and the coroner, and the inquest, and the doctor, and the sorrowing relations. Besides, suppose someone saw us with the beastly thing, and thought we had stolen it; then they would say, "*What have you done with the Baby?*" and then where should we be?'

Oswald's brothers could not answer this question, but once more Oswald's native eloquence and far-seeing discerningness conquered.

'Anyway,' Dicky said, 'let's shove the derelict a little further under cover.'

So we did.

Then we went on home. Dinner was ready and so were Alice and Daisy, but Dora was not there.

'She's got a – well, she's not coming to dinner anyway,' Alice said when we asked. 'She can tell you herself afterwards what it is she's got.'

Oswald thought it was headache, or pain in the temper, or in the pinafore, so he said no more, but as soon as Mrs Pettigrew had helped us and left the room he began the thrilling tale of the forsaken perambulator. He told it with the greatest thrillingness anyone could have, but Daisy and Alice seemed almost unmoved. Alice said –

'Yes, very strange,' and things like that, but both the girls seemed to be thinking of something else. They kept looking at each other and trying not to laugh, so Oswald saw they had got some silly secret and he said –

'Oh, all right! I don't care about telling you.' I only

thought you'd like to be in it. It's going to be a really big thing, with policemen in it, and perhaps a judge.'

'In what?' H. O. said; 'the perambulator?'

Daisy choked and then tried to drink, and spluttered and got purple, and had to be thumped on the back. But Oswald was not appeased. When Alice said, 'Do go on, Oswald. I'm sure we all like it very much,' he said –

'Oh, no, thank you,' very politely. 'As it happens,' he went on, 'I'd just as soon go through with this thing without having any girls in it.'

'In the perambulator?' said H. O. again.

'It's a man's job,' Oswald went on, without taking any notice of H. O.

'Do you really think so,' said Alice, 'when there's a baby in it?'

'But there isn't,' said H. O., 'if you mean in the perambulator.'

'Blow you and your perambulator,' said Oswald, with gloomy forbearance.

Alice kicked Oswald under the table and said –

'Don't be waxy, Oswald. Really and truly Daisy and I *have* got a secret, only it's Dora's secret, and she wants to tell you herself. If it was mine or Daisy's we'd tell you this minute, wouldn't we, Mouse?'

'This very second,' said the White Mouse.

And Oswald consented to take their apologies.

Then the pudding came in, and no more was said except asking for things to be passed – sugar and water, and bread and things.

Then when the pudding was all gone, Alice said –
'Come on.'

And we came on. We did not want to be disagreeable, though really we were keen on being detectives and sifting that perambulator to the very dregs. But boys have to try to take an interest in their sisters' secrets, however silly. This is part of being a good brother.

Alice led us across the field where the sheep once fell into the brook, and across the brook by the plank. At the other end of the next field there was a sort of wooden house on wheels, that the shepherd sleeps in at the time of year when lambs are being born, so that he can see that they are not stolen by gipsies before the owners have counted them.

To this hut Alice now led her kind brothers and Daisy's kind brother.

'Dora is inside,' she said, 'with the Secret. We were afraid to have it in the house in case it made a noise.'

The next moment the Secret was a secret no longer, for we all beheld Dora, sitting on a sack on the floor of the hut, with the Secret in her lap.

It was the High-born Babe!

Oswald was so overcome that he sat down suddenly, just like Betsy Trotwood did in *David Copperfield*, which just shows what a true author Dickens is.

'You've done it this time,' he said. 'I suppose you know you're a baby-stealer?'

'I'm not,' Dora said. 'I've adopted him.'

'Then it was you,' Dicky said, 'who scuttled the perambulator in the wood?'

'Yes,' Alice said; 'we couldn't get it over the stile unless Dora put down the Baby, and we were afraid of the nettles for his legs. His name is to be Lord Edward.'

'But, Dora – really, don't you think – '

'If you'd been there you'd have done the same,' said Dora firmly. 'The gipsies had gone. Of course something had frightened them and they fled from justice. And the little darling was awake and held out his arms to me. No, he hasn't cried a bit, and I know all about babies;

I've often nursed Mrs Simpkins's daughter's baby when she brings it up on Sundays. They have bread and milk to eat. You take him, Alice, and I'll go and get some bread and milk for him.'

Alice took the noble brat. It was horribly lively, and squirmed about in her arms, and wanted to crawl on the floor. She could only keep it quiet by saying things to it a boy would be ashamed even to think of saying, such as 'Goo goo', and 'Did ums was', and 'Ickle ducksums, then'.

When Alice used these expressions the Baby laughed and chuckled and replied –

'Daddadda', 'Bababa', or 'Glueglue'.

But if Alice stopped her remarks for an instant the thing screwed its face up as if it was going to cry, but she never gave it time to begin.

It was a rummy little animal.

Then Dora came back with the bread and milk, and they fed the noble infant. It was greedy and slobbery, but all three girls seemed unable to keep their eyes and hands off it. They looked at it exactly as if it was pretty.

We boys stayed watching them. There was no amusement left for us now, for Oswald saw that Dora's Secret knocked the bottom out of the perambulator.

When the infant aristocrat had eaten a hearty meal it sat on Alice's lap and played with the amber heart she wears that Albert's uncle brought her from Hastings after the business of the bad sixpence and the nobleness of Oswald.

'Now,' said Dora, 'this is a council, so I want to be business-like. The Duckums Darling has been stolen away; its wicked stealers have deserted the Precious. We've got it. Perhaps its ancestral halls are miles and miles away. I vote we keep the little Lovey Duck till it's advertised for.'

'If Albert's uncle lets you,' said Dicky darkly.

'Oh, don't say "you" like that,' Dora said; 'I want it to be all of our baby. It will have five fathers and three mothers, and a grandfather and a great Albert's uncle, and a great grand-uncle. I'm sure Albert's uncle will let us keep it – at any rate till it's advertised for.'

'And suppose it never is,' Noël said.

'Then so much the better,' said Dora, 'the little Duckywux.'

She began kissing the baby again. Oswald, ever thoughtful, said –

'Well, what about your dinner?'

'Bother dinner!' Dora said – so like a girl. 'Will you all agree to be his fathers and mothers?'

'Anything for a quiet life,' said Dicky, and Oswald said –

'Oh, yes, if you like. But you'll see we shan't be allowed to keep it.'

'You talk as if he was rabbits or white rats,' said Dora, 'and he's not – he's a little man, he is.'

'All right, he's no rabbit, but a man. Come on and get some grub, Dora.' rejoined the kind-hearted Oswald, and Dora did, with Oswald and the other boys. Only Noël stayed with Alice. He really seemed to like the baby. When I looked back he was standing on his head to amuse it, but the baby did not seem to like him any better whichever end of him was up.

Dora went back to the shepherd's house on wheels directly she had had her dinner. Mrs Pettigrew was very cross about her not being in to it, but she had kept her some mutton hot all the same. She is a decent sort. And there were stewed prunes. We had some to keep Dora company. Then we boys went fishing again in the moat, but we caught nothing.

Just before tea-time we all went back to the hut,

and before we got half across the last field we could hear the howling of the Secret.

'Poor little beggar,' said Oswald, with manly tenderness. 'They must be sticking pins in it.'

We found the girls and Noël looking quite pale and breathless. Daisy was walking up and down with the Secret in her arms. It looked like Alice in Wonderland nursing the baby that turned into a pig. Oswald said so, and added that its screams were like it too.

'What on earth is the matter with it?' he said.

'I don't know,' said Alice. 'Daisy's tired, and Dora and I are quite worn out. He's been crying for hours and hours. *You* take him a bit.'

'Not me,' replied Oswald, firmly, withdrawing a pace from the Secret.

Dora was fumbling with her waistband in the furthest corner of the hut.

'I think he's cold,' she said. 'I thought I'd take off my flannelette petticoat, only the horrid strings got into a hard knot. Here, Oswald, let's have your knife.'

With the word she plunged her hand into Oswald's jacket pocket, and next moment she was rubbing her hand like mad on her dress, and screaming almost as loud as the Baby. Then she began to laugh and to cry at the same time. This is called hysterics.

Oswald was sorry, but he was annoyed too. He had forgotten that his pocket was half full of the mealworms the miller had kindly given him. And, anyway, Dora ought to have known that a man always carries his knife in his trousers pocket and not in his jacket one.

Alice and Daisy rushed to Dora. She had thrown herself down on the pile of sacks in the corner. The titled infant delayed its screams for a moment to listen to Dora's, but almost at once it went on again.

'Oh, get some water!' said Alice. 'Daisy, run!'

The White Mouse, ever docile and obedient, shoved the baby into the arms of the nearest person, who had to take it or it would have fallen a wreck to the ground. This nearest person was Oswald. He tried to pass it on to the others, but they wouldn't. Noël would have, but he was busy kissing Dora and begging her not to.

So our hero, for such I may perhaps term him, found himself the degraded nursemaid of a small but furious kid.

He was afraid to lay it down, for fear in its rage it should beat its brains out against the hard earth, and he did not wish, however innocently, to be the cause of its hurting itself at all. So he walked earnestly up and down with it, thumping it unceasingly on the back, while the others attended to Dora, who presently ceased to yell.

Suddenly it struck Oswald that the High-born also had ceased to yell. He looked at it, and could hardly believe the glad tidings of his faithful eyes. With bated breath he hastened back to the sheep-house.

The others turned on him, full of reproaches about the meal-worms and Dora, but he answered without anger.

'Shut up,' he said in a whisper of imperial command. 'Can't you see it's *gone to sleep*?'

As exhausted as if they had all taken part in all the events of a very long Athletic Sports, the youthful Bastables and their friends dragged their weary limbs back across the fields. Oswald was compelled to go on holding the titled infant, for fear it should wake up if it changed hands, and begin to yell again. Dora's flannelette petticoat had been got off somehow – how I do not seek to inquire – and the Secret was covered with it. The others surrounded Oswald as much as possible, with a view to concealment if we met Mrs

Pettigrew. But the coast was clear. Oswald took the Secret up into his bedroom. Mrs Pettigrew doesn't come there much, it's too many stairs.

With breathless precaution Oswald laid it down on his bed. It sighed, but did not wake. Then we took it in turns to sit by it and see that it did not get up and fling itself out of bed, which, in one of its furious fits, it would just as soon have done as not.

We expected Albert's uncle every minute.

At last we heard the gate, but he did not come in, so we looked out and saw that there he was talking to a distracted-looking man on a piebald horse – one of the miller's horses.

A shiver of doubt coursed through our veins. We could not remember having done anything wrong at the miller's. But you never know. And it seemed strange his sending a man up on his own horse. But when we had looked a bit longer our fears went down and our curiosity got up. For we saw that the distracted one was a gentleman.

Presently he rode off, and Albert's uncle came in. A deputation met him at the door – all the boys and Dora, because the baby was her idea.

'We've found something,' Dora said, 'and we want to know whether we may keep it.'

The rest of us said nothing. We were not so very extra anxious to keep it after we had heard how much and how long it could howl. Even Noël had said he had no idea a baby could yell like it. Dora said it only cried because it was sleepy, but we reflected that it would certainly be sleepy once a day, if not oftener.

'What is it?' said Albert's uncle. 'Let's see this treasure-trove. Is it a wild beast?'

'Come and see,' said Dora, and we led him to our room.

Alice turned down the pink flannelette petticoat with silly pride, and showed the youthful heir fatly and pinkly sleeping.

'A baby!' said Albert's uncle. '*The* Baby! Oh, my cat's alive!'

That is an expression which he uses to express despair unmixed with anger.

'Where did you? – but that doesn't matter. We'll talk of this later.'

He rushed from the room, and in a moment or two we saw him mount his bicycle and ride off.

Quite shortly he returned with the distracted horseman.

It was *his* baby, and not titled at all. The horseman and his wife were the lodgers at the mill. The nursemaid was a girl from the village.

She *said* she only left the Baby five minutes while she went to speak to her sweetheart who was gardener at the Red House. But *we* knew she left it over an hour, and nearly two.

I never saw anyone so pleased as the distracted horseman.

When we were asked we explained about having thought the Baby was the prey of gipsies, and the distracted horseman stood hugging the Baby, and actually thanked us.

But when he had gone we had a brief lecture on minding our own business. But Dora still thinks she was right. As for Oswald and most of the others, they agreed that they would rather mind their own business all their lives than mind a baby for a single hour.

If you have never had to do with a baby in the frenzied throes of sleepiness you can have no idea what its screams are like.

If you have been through such a scene you will

understand how we managed to bear up under having no baby to adopt.

Oswald insisted on having the whole thing written in the Golden Deed book. Of course his share could not be put in without telling about Dora's generous adopting of the forlorn infant outcast, and Oswald could not and cannot forget that he was the one who did get that baby to sleep.

What a time Mr and Mrs Distracted Horseman must have of it, though – especially now they've sacked the nursemaid.

If Oswald is ever married – I suppose he must be some day – he will have ten nurses to each baby. Eight is not enough. We know that because we tried, and the whole eight of us were not enough for the needs of that deserted infant who was not so extra high-born after all.

HUNTING THE FOX

IT is idle to expect everyone to know everything in the world without being told. If we had been brought up in the country we should have known that it is not done – to hunt the fox in August. But in the Lewisham Road the most observing boy does not notice the dates when it is proper to hunt foxes.

And there are some things you cannot bear to think that anybody would think you would do; that is why I wish to say plainly at the very beginning that none of us would have shot a fox on purpose even to save our skins. Of course, if a man were at bay in a cave, and had to defend girls from the simultaneous attack of a herd of savage foxes it would be different. A man is bound to protect girls and take care of them – they can jolly well take care of themselves really it seems to me – still, this is what Albert's uncle calls one of the 'rules of the game', so we are bound to defend them and fight for them to the death, if needful.

Denny knows a quotation which says –

> '*What dire offence from harmless causes springs,*
> *What mighty contests rise from trefoil things.*'

He says this means that all great events come from three things – threefold, like the clover or trefoil, and the causes are always harmless. Trefoil is short for threefold.

There were certainly three things that led up to the adventure which is now going to be told you. The first was our Indian uncle coming down to the country to see us. The second was Denny's tooth. The third was only our wanting to go hunting; but if you count it in it makes the thing about the trefoil come right. And all these causes were harmless.

It is a flattering thing to say, and it was not Oswald who said it, but Dora. She said she was certain our uncle missed us, and that he felt he could no longer live without seeing his dear ones (that was us).

Anyway, he came down, without warning, which is one of the few bad habits that excellent Indian man has, and this habit has ended in unpleasantness more than once, as when we played Jungles.

However, this time it was all right. He came on rather a dull kind of day, when no one had thought of anything particularly amusing to do. So that, as it happened to be dinner-time and we had just washed our hands and faces, we were all spotlessly clean (compared with what we are sometimes, I mean, of course).

We were just sitting down to dinner, and Albert's uncle was just plunging the knife into the hot heart of the steak pudding, when there was the rumble of wheels, and the station fly stopped at the garden gate. And in the fly, sitting very upright, with his hands on his knees, was our Indian relative so much beloved. He looked very smart, with a rose in his buttonhole. How different from what he looked in other days when he helped us to pretend that our currant pudding was a wild boar we were killing with our forks. Yet, though tidier, his heart still beat kind and true. You should not judge people harshly because their clothes are tidy. He had dinner with us, and then we showed him round the place, and told him everything we thought he would like to hear, and about the Tower of Mystery, and he said –

'It makes my blood boil to think of it.'

Noël said he was sorry for that, because everyone else we had told it to had owned, when we asked them, that it froze their blood.

'Ah,' said the Uncle, 'but in India we learn how to freeze our blood and boil it at the same time.'

In those hot longitudes, perhaps, the blood is always near boiling-point, which accounts for Indian tempers, though not for the curry and pepper they eat. But I must not wander; there is no curry at all in this story. About temper I will not say.

Then Uncle let us all go with him to the station when the fly came back for him; and when we said good-bye he tipped us all half a quid, without any insidious distinctions about age or considering whether you were a boy or a girl. Our Indian uncle is a true-born Briton, with no nonsense about him.

We cheered him like one man as the train went off, and then we offered the fly-driver a shilling to take us back to the four cross-roads, and the grateful creature did it for nothing because, he said, the gent had tipped him something like. How scarce is true gratitude! So we cheered the driver too for this rare virtue, and then went home to talk about what we should do with our money.

I cannot tell you all that we did with it, because money melts away 'like snow-wreaths in thaw-jean', as Denny says, and somehow the more you have the more quickly it melts. We all went into Maidstone, and came back with the most beautiful lot of brown-paper parcels, with things inside that supplied long-felt wants. But none of them belongs to this narration, except what Oswald and Denny clubbed to buy.

This was a pistol, and it took all the money they both had, but when Oswald felt the uncomfortable inside sensation that reminds you who it is and his money that are soon parted he said to himself –

'I don't care. We ought to have a pistol in the house, and one that will go off, too – not those rotten flintlocks. Suppose there should be burglars and us totally unarmed?'

We took it in turns to have the pistol, and we decided always to practise with it far from the house, so as not to frighten the grown-ups, who are always much nervouser about firearms than we are.

It was Denny's idea getting it; and Oswald owns it surprised him, but the boy was much changed in his character. We got it while the others were grubbing at the pastry-cook's in the High Street, and we said nothing till after tea, though it was hard not to fire at the birds on the telegraph wires as we came home in the train.

After tea we called a council in the straw-loft, and Oswald said –

'Denny and I have got a secret.'

'I know what it is,' Dicky said contemptibly. 'You've found out that shop in Maidstone where peppermint rock is four ounces a penny. H. O. and I found it out before you did.'

Oswald said, 'You shut up. If you don't want to hear the secret you'd better bunk. I'm going to administer the secret oath.'

This is a very solemn oath, and only used about real things, and never for pretending ones, so Dicky said –

'Oh, all right; go ahead! I thought you were only rotting.'

So they all took the secret oath. Noël made it up long before, when he had found the first thrush's nest we ever saw in the Blackheath garden:

'I will not tell, I will not reveal,
I will not touch, or try to steal;
And may I be called a beastly sneak,
If this great secret I ever repeat.'

It is a little wrong about the poetry, but it is a very binding promise. They all repeated it, down to H. O.

'Now then,' Dicky said, 'what's up?'

Oswald, in proud silence, drew the pistol from his breast and held it out, and there was a murmur of awful amazement and respect from every one of the council. The pistol was not loaded, so we let even the girls have it to look at.

And then Dicky said, 'Let's go hunting.'

And we decided that we would. H. O. wanted to go down to the village and get penny horns at the shop for the huntsmen to wind, like in the song, but we thought it would be more modest not to wind horns or anything noisy, at anyrate not until we had run down our prey. But his talking of the song made us decide that it was the fox we wanted to hunt. We had not been particular which animal we hunted before that.

Oswald let Denny have first go with the pistol, and when we went to bed he slept with it under his pillow, but not loaded, for fear he should have a nightmare and draw his fell weapon before he was properly awake.

Oswald let Denny have it, because Denny had tooth-ache, and a pistol is consoling though it does not actually stop the pain of the tooth. The toothache got worse, and Albert's uncle looked at it, and said it was very loose, and Denny owned he had tried to crack a peach-stone with it. Which accounts. He had creosote and camphor, and went to bed early, with his tooth tied up in red flannel.

Oswald knows it is right to be very kind when people

are ill, and he forbore to wake the sufferer next morning
by buzzing a pillow at him, as he generally does.
He got up and went over to shake the invalid,
but the bird had flown and the nest was cold. The
pistol was not in the nest either, but Oswald found
it afterwards under the looking-glass on the dressing-
table. He had just awakened the others (with a hair-
brush because they had not got anything the matter
with their teeth), when he heard wheels, and, looking
out, beheld Denny and Albert's uncle being driven from
the door in the farmer's high cart with the red wheels.

We dressed extra quick, so as to get downstairs to
the bottom of the mystery. And we found a note
from Albert's uncle. It was addressed to Dora, and
said –

'Denny's toothache got him up in the small hours.
He's off to the dentist to have it out with him, man to
man. Home to dinner.'

Dora said, 'Denny's gone to the dentist.'

'I expect it's a relation,' H. O. said. 'Denny must be
short for Dentist.'

I suppose he was trying to be funny – he really does
try very hard. He wants to be a clown when he grows
up. The others laughed.

'I wonder,' said Dicky, 'whether he'll get a shilling
or half-a-crown for it.'

Oswald had been meditating in gloomy silence, now
he cheered up and said –

'Of course! I'd forgotten that. He'll get his tooth
money, and the drive too. So it's quite fair for us to have
the fox-hunt while he's gone. I was thinking we should
have to put it off.'

The others agreed that it would not be unfair.

378

'We can have another one another time if he wants to,' Oswald said.

We know foxes are hunted in red coats and on horseback – but we could not do this – but H. O. had the old red football jersey that was Albert's uncle's when he was at Loretto. He was pleased.

'But I do wish we'd had horns,' he said grievingly. 'I should have liked to wind the horn.'

'We can pretend horns,' Dora said; but he answered, 'I didn't want to pretend. I wanted to wind something.'

'Wind your watch,' Dicky said. And that was unkind, because we all know H. O.'s watch is broken, and when you wind it, it only rattles inside without going in the least.

We did not bother to dress up much for the hunting expedition – just cocked hats and lath swords; and we tied a card on to H. O.'s chest with 'Moat House Fox-Hunters' on it; and we tied red flannel round all the dogs' necks to show they were fox-hounds. Yet it did not seem to show it plainly; somehow it made them look as if they were not fox-hounds, but their own natural breeds – only with sore throats.

Oswald slipped the pistol and a few cartridges into his pocket. He knew, of course, that foxes are not shot; but as he said –

'Who knows whether we may not meet a bear or a crocodile.'

We set off gaily. Across the orchard and through two cornfields, and along the hedge of another field, and so we got into the wood, through a gap we had happened to make a day or two before, playing 'follow my leader'.

The wood was very quiet and green; the dogs were happy and most busy. Once Pincher started a rabbit. We said, 'View Halloo!' and immediately started in pursuit; but the rabbit went and hid, so that even Pincher could not find him, and we went on. But we saw no foxes.

So at last we made Dicky be a fox, and chased him down the green rides. A wide walk in a wood is called a ride, even if people never do anything but walk in it.

We had only three hounds – Lady, Pincher and Martha – so we joined the glad throng and were being hounds as hard as we could, when we suddenly came barking round a corner in full chase and stopped short, for we saw that our fox had stayed his hasty flight. The fox was stooping over something reddish that lay beside the path, and he cried –

'I say, look here!' in tones that thrilled us throughout.

Our fox – whom we must now call Dicky, so as not to muddle the narration – pointed to the reddy thing that the dogs were sniffing at.

'It's a real live fox,' he said. And so it was. At least it was real – only it was quite dead – and when Oswald lifted it up its head was bleeding. It had evidently been shot through the brain and expired instantly. Oswald explained this to the girls when they began to cry at the sight of the poor beast; I do not say he did not feel a bit sorry himself.

The fox was cold, but its fur was so pretty, and its tail and its little feet. Dicky strung the dogs on the leash; they were so much interested we thought it was better.

'It does seem horrid to think it'll never see again out of its poor little eyes,' Dora said, blowing her nose.

'And never run about through the wood again, lend me your hanky, Dora,' said Alice.

'And never be hunted or get into a hen-roost or a trap or anything exciting, poor little thing,' said Dicky.

The girls began to pick green chestnut leaves to cover up the poor fox's fatal wound, and Noël began to walk up and down making faces, the way he always does when he's making poetry. He cannot make one without the other. It works both ways, which is a comfort.

'What are we going to do now?' H. O. said; 'the huntsman ought to cut off its tail, I'm quite certain. Only, I've broken the big blade of my knife, and the other never was any good.'

The girls gave H. O. a shove, and even Oswald said, 'Shut up', for somehow we all felt we did not want to play fox-hunting any more that day. When his deadly wound was covered the fox hardly looked dead at all.

'Oh, I wish it wasn't true!' Alice said.

Daisy had been crying all the time, and now she said, 'I should like to pray God to make it not true.'

But Dora kissed her, and told her that was no good – only she might pray God to take care of the fox's poor little babies, if it had had any, which I believe she has done ever since.

'If only we could wake up and find it was a horrid dream,' Alice said. It seems silly that we should have cared so much when we had really set out to hunt foxes with dogs, but it is true. The fox's feet looked so helpless. And there was a dusty mark on its side that I know would not have been there if it had been alive and able to wash itself.

Noël now said, 'This is the piece of poetry':

> *'Here lies poor Reynard who is slain,*
> *He will not come to life again.*
> *I never will the huntsman's horn*
> *Wind since the day that I was born*
> *Until the day I die.*
> *For I don't like hunting, and this is why.'*

'Let's have a funeral,' said H. O. This pleased everybody, and we got Dora to take off her petticoat to wrap the fox in, so that we could carry it to our garden and bury it without bloodying our jackets. Girls' clothes are silly in one way, but I think they are useful too. A boy cannot take off more than his jacket and waistcoat in any emergency, or he is at once entirely undressed. But I have known Dora take off two petticoats for useful purposes and look just the same outside afterwards.

We boys took it in turns to carry the fox. It was very heavy. When we got near the edge of the wood Noël said –

'It would be better to bury it here, where the leaves can talk funeral songs over its grave for ever, and the other foxes can come and cry if they want to.' He dumped the fox down on the moss under a young oak tree as he spoke.

'If Dicky fetched the spade and fork we could bury it here, and then he could tie up the dogs at the same time.'

'You're sick of carrying it,' Dicky remarked, 'that's what it is.' But he went on condition the rest of us boys went too.

While we were gone the girls dragged the fox to the edge of the wood; it was a different edge to the one we went in by – close to a lane – and while they waited for the digging or fatigue party to come back, they collected a lot of moss and green things to make the fox's long home soft for it to lie in. There are no flowers in the woods in August, which is a pity.

When we got back with the spade and fork we dug a hole to bury the fox in. We did not bring the dogs back, because they were too interested in the funeral to behave with real, respectable calmness.

The ground was loose and soft and easy to dig when we had scraped away the broken bits of sticks and the dead leaves and the wild honeysuckle; Oswald used the fork and Dicky had the spade. Noël made faces and poetry – he was struck so that morning – and the girls sat stroking the clean parts of the fox's fur till the grave was deep enough. At last it was; then Daisy threw in the leaves and grass, and Alice and Dora took the poor dead fox by his two ends and we helped to put him in the grave. We could not lower him slowly – he was dropped in, really. Then we covered the furry body with leaves, and Noël said the Burial Ode he had made up. He says this was it, but it sounds better now than it did then, so I think he must have done something to it since:

THE FOX'S BURIAL ODE

'*Dear Fox, sleep here, and do not wake,*
We picked these leaves for your sake.
You must not try to rise or move,
We give you this with our love.
Close by the wood where once you grew
Your mourning friends have buried you.
If you had lived you'd not have been
(Been proper friends with us, I mean),
But now you're laid upon the shelf,
Poor fox, you cannot help yourself,
So, as I say, we are your loving friends
And here your Burial Ode, dear Foxy, ends.
P.S. – When in the moonlight bright
The foxes wander of a night,
They'll pass your grave and fondly think of you,
Exactly like we mean to always do.
So now, dear fox, adieu!
Your friends are few
But true
To you.
Adieu!'

When this had been said we filled in the grave and covered the top if it with dry leaves and sticks to make it look like the rest of the wood. People might think it was a treasure, and dig it up, if they thought there was anything buried there, and we wished the poor fox to sleep sound and not to be disturbed.

The interring was over. We folded up Dora's blood-stained pink cotton petticoat, and turned to leave the sad spot.

We had not gone a dozen yards down the lane when we heard footsteps and a whistle behind us, and a scrabbling and whining, and a gentleman with two fox-terriers had called a halt just by the place where we had laid low the 'little red rover'.

The gentleman stood in the lane, but the dogs were digging – we could see their tails wagging and see the dust fly. And we *saw where*. We ran back.

'Oh, please, do stop your dogs digging there!' Alice said.

The gentleman said 'Why?'

'Because we've just had a funeral, and that's the grave.'

The gentleman whistled, but the fox-terriers were not trained like Pincher, who was brought up by Oswald. The gentleman took a stride through the hedge gap.

'What have you been burying – pet dicky bird, eh?' said the gentleman, kindly. He had riding breeches and white whiskers.

We did not answer, because now, for the first time, it came over all of us, in a rush of blushes and uncomfortableness, that burying a fox is a suspicious act. I don't know why we felt this, but we did.

Noël said dreamily –

> '*We found his murdered body in the wood,*
> *And dug a grave by which the mourners stood.*'

But no one heard him except Oswald, because Alice

and Dora and Daisy were all jumping about with the jumps of unrestrained anguish, and saying, 'Oh, call them off! Do! do! – oh, don't, don't! Don't let them dig.'

Alas! Oswald was, as usual, right. The ground of the grave had not been trampled down hard enough, and he had said so plainly at the time, but his prudent counsels had been overruled. Now these busy-bodying, meddling, mischief-making fox-terriers (how different from Pincher, who minds his own business unless told otherwise) had scratched away the earth and laid bare the reddish tip of the poor corpse's tail.

We all turned to go without a word, it seemed to be no use staying any longer.

But in a moment the gentleman with the whiskers had got Noël and Dicky each by an ear – they were nearest him. H. O. hid in the hedge. Oswald, to whose noble breast sneakishness is, I am thankful to say, a stranger, would have scorned to escape, but he ordered his sisters to bunk in a tone of command which made refusal impossible.

'And bunk sharp, too,' he added sternly. 'Cut along home.'

So they cut.

The white-whiskered gentleman now encouraged his mangy fox-terriers, by every means at his command, to continue their vile and degrading occupation; holding on all the time to the ears of Dicky and Noël, who scorned to ask for mercy. Dicky got purple and Noël got white. It was Oswald who said –

'Don't hang on to them, sir. We won't cut. I give you my word of honour.'

'*Your* word of honour,' said the gentleman, in tones for which, in happier days, when people drew their bright blades and fought duels, I would have had his heart's dearest blood. But now Oswald remained calm and polite as ever.

'Yes, on my honour,' he said, and the gentleman dropped the ears of Oswald's brothers at the sound of his firm, unswerving tones. He dropped the ears and pulled out the body of the fox and held it up. The dogs jumped up and yelled.

'Now,' he said, 'you talk very big about words of honour. Can you speak the truth?'

Dickie said, 'If you think we shot it, you're wrong. We know better than that.'

The white-whiskered one turned suddenly to H. O. and pulled him out of the hedge.

'And what does that mean?' he said, and he was pink with fury to the ends of his large ears, as he pointed to the card on H. O.'s breast, which said, 'Moat House Fox-Hunters'.

Then Oswald said, 'We *were* playing at fox-hunting, but we couldn't find anything but a rabbit that hid, so my brother was being the fox; and then we found the fox shot dead, and I don't know who did it; and we were sorry for it and we buried it – and that's all.'

'Not quite,' said the riding-breeches gentleman, with what I think you call a bitter smile, 'not quite. This is my land and I'll have you up for trespass and damage. Come along now, no nonsense! I'm a magistrate and I'm Master of the Hounds. A vixen, too! What did you shoot her with? You're too young to have a gun. Sneaked your Father's revolver, I suppose?'

Oswald thought it was better to be goldenly silent. But it was vain. The Master of the Hounds made him empty his pockets, and there was the pistol and the cartridges.

The magistrate laughed a harsh laugh of successful disagreeableness.

'All right,' said he, 'where's your licence? You come with me. A week or two in prison.'

I don't believe now he could have done it, but we all thought then he could and would, what's more.

So H. O. began to cry, but Noël spoke up. His teeth were chattering yet he spoke up like a man.

He said, 'You don't know us. You've no right not to believe us till you've found us out in a lie. We don't tell lies. You ask Albert's uncle if we do.'

'Hold your tongue,' said the White-Whiskered.

But Noël's blood was up.

'If you do put us in prison without being sure,' he said, trembling more and more, 'you are a horrible tyrant like Caligula, and Herod, or Nero, and the Spanish Inquisition, and I will write a poem about it in prison, and people will curse you for ever.'

'Upon my word,' said White Whiskers. 'We'll see about that,' and he turned up the lane with the fox hanging from one hand and Noël's ear once more reposing in the other.

I thought Noël would cry or faint. But he bore up nobly – exactly like an early Christian martyr.

The rest of us came along too. I carried the spade and Dicky had the fork. H. O. had the card, and Noël had the magistrate. At the end of the lane there was Alice. She had bunked home, obeying the orders of her thoughtful brother, but she had bottled back again like a shot, so as not to be out of the scrape. She is almost worthy to be a boy for some things.

She spoke to Mr Magistrate and said –

'Where are you taking him?'

The outraged majesty of the magistrate said, 'To prison, you naughty little girl.'

Alice said, 'Noël will faint. Somebody once tried to take him to prison before – about a dog. Do please come to our house and see our uncle – at least he's not – but it's the same thing. We didn't kill the fox, if that's what you think – indeed we didn't. Oh, dear, I do wish you'd think of your own little boys and girls if you've got any, or else about when you were little. You wouldn't be so horrid if you did.'

I don't know which, if either, of these objects the fox-hound master thought of, but he said –

'Well, lead on,' and he let go Noël's ear and Alice snuggled up to Noël and put her arm round him.

It was a frightened procession, whose cheeks were pale with alarm – except those between white whiskers, and they were red – that wound in at our gate and into the hall among the old oak furniture, and black and white marble floor and things.

Dora and Daisy were at the door. The pink petticoat lay on the table, all stained with the gore of the departed. Dora looked at us all, and she saw that it was serious. She pulled out the big oak chair and said, 'Won't you sit down?' very kindly to the white-whiskered magistrate.

He grunted, but did as she said.

Then he looked about him in a silence that was not comforting, and so did we.

At last he said –

'Come, you didn't try to bolt. Speak the truth, and I'll say no more.'

We said we had.

Then he laid the fox on the table, spreading out the petticoat under it, and he took out a knife and the girls hid their faces. Even Oswald did not care to look. Wounds in battle are all very well, but it's different to see a dead fox cut into with a knife.

Next moment the magistrate wiped something on his handkerchief and then laid it on the table, and put one of my cartridges besides it. It was the bullet that had killed the fox.

'Look here!' he said. And it was too true. The bullets were the same.

A thrill of despair ran through Oswald. He knows now how a hero feels when he is innocently accused of a crime and the judge is putting on the black cap, and the evidence is convulsive and all human aid is despaired of.

'I can't help it,' he said, 'we didn't kill it, and that's all there is to it.'

The white-whiskered magistrate may have been master of the fox-hounds, but he was not master of his temper, which is more important, I should think, than a lot of beastly dogs.

He said several words which Oswald would never repeat, much less in his own conversing, and besides that he called us 'obstinate little beggars'.

Then suddenly Albert's uncle entered in the midst of a silence freighted with despairing reflections. The M.F.H. got up and told his tale: it was mainly lies, or, to be more polite, it was hardly any of it true, though I supposed he believed it.

'I am very sorry, sir,' said Albert's uncle, looking at the bullets. 'You'll excuse my asking for the children's version?'

'Oh, certainly, sir, certainly,' fuming, the fox-hound magistrate replied.

Then Albert's uncle said, 'Now Oswald, I know I can trust you to speak the exact truth.'

So Oswald did.

Then the white-whiskered fox-master laid the bullets before Albert's uncle, and I felt this would be a trial to his faith far worse than the rack or the thumbscrew in the days of the Armada.

And then Denny came in. He looked at the fox on the table.

'You found it, then?' he said.

The M.F.H. would have spoken but Albert's uncle said, 'One moment, Denny; you've seen this fox before?'

'Rather,' said Denny; 'I –'

But Albert's uncle said, 'Take time. Think before you speak and say the exact truth. No, don't whisper to Oswald. This boy,' he said to the injured fox-master, 'has been with me since seven this morning. His tale, whatever it is, will be independent evidence.'

But Denny would not speak, though again and again Albert's uncle told him to.

'I can't till I've asked Oswald something,' he said at last.

White Whiskers said, 'That looks bad – eh?'

But Oswald said, 'Don't whisper, old chap. Ask me whatever you like, but speak up.'

So Denny said, 'I can't without breaking the secret oath.'

So then Oswald began to see, and he said, 'Break away for all you're worth, it's all right.' And Denny said, drawing relief's deepest breath, 'Well then, Oswald and I have got a pistol – shares – and I had it last night. And when I couldn't sleep last night because of the toothache I got up and went out early this morning. And I took the pistol. And I loaded it just for fun. And down in the wood I heard a whining like a dog, and I went, and there was the poor fox caught in an iron trap with teeth. And I went to let it out and it bit me – look, here's the place – and the pistol went off and the fox died, and I am so sorry.'

'But why didn't you tell the others?'

'They weren't awake when I went to the dentist's.'

'But why didn't you tell your uncle if you've been with him all the morning?'

'It was the oath,' H. O. said –

> *'May I be called a beastly sneak*
> *If this great secret I ever repeat.'*

White Whiskers actually grinned.

'Well,' he said, 'I see it was an accident, my boy.' Then he turned to us and said –

'I owe you an apology for doubting your word – all of you. I hope it's accepted.'

We said it was all right and he was to never mind.

But all the same we hated him for it. He tried to make up for his unbelievingness afterwards by asking Albert's uncle to shoot rabbits; but we did not really forgive him till the day when he sent the fox's brush to Alice, mounted in silver with a note about her plucky conduct in standing by her brothers.

We got a lecture about not playing with firearms, but no punishment, because our conduct had not been exactly sinful, Albert's uncle said, but merely silly.

The pistol and the cartridges were confiscated.

I hope the house will never be attacked by burglars. When it is, Albert's uncle will only have himself to thank if we are rapidly overpowered, because it will be his fault that we shall have to meet them totally unarmed, and be their almost unresisting prey.

THE SALE OF ANTIQUITIES

IT began one morning at breakfast. It was the fifteenth of August – the birthday of Napoleon the Great, Oswald Bastable, and another very nice writer. Oswald was to keep his birthday on the Saturday, so that his Father could be there. A birthday when there are only many happy returns is a little like Sunday or Christmas Eve. Oswald had a birthday-card or two – that was all; but he did not repine, because he knew they always make it up to you for putting off keeping your birthday, and he looked forward to Saturday.

Albert's uncle had a whole stack of letters as usual, and presently he tossed one over to Dora, and said, 'What do you say, little lady? Shall we let them come?'

But Dora, butter-fingered as ever, missed the catch, and Dick and Noël both had a try for it, so that the letter went into the place where the bacon had been, and where now only a frozen-looking lake of bacon fat was slowly hardening, and then somehow it got into the marmalade, and then H. O. got it, and Dora said –

'I don't want the nasty thing now – all grease and stickiness.' So H. O. read it aloud –

'MAIDSTONE SOCIETY OF ANTIQUITIES AND
FIELD CLUB

Aug. 14, 1900

'DEAR SIR, – At a meeting of the – '

392

H. O. stuck fast here, and the writing was really very bad, like a spider that has been in the ink-pot crawling in a hurry over the paper without stopping to rub its feet properly on the mat. So Oswald took the letter. He is above minding a little marmalade or bacon. He began to read. It ran thus:

'It's not Antiquities, you little silly,' he said; 'it's *Antiquaries*.'

'The other's a very good word,' said Albert's uncle, 'and I never call names at breakfast myself – it upsets the digestion, my egregious Oswald.'

'That's a name though,' said Alice, 'and you got it out of "Stalky", too. Go on, Oswald.'

So Oswald went on where he had been interrupted:

'MAIDSTONE SOCIETY OF "ANTIQUARIES"
AND FIELD CLUB

Aug. 14, 1900.

'DEAR SIR, – At a meeting of the Committee of this Society it was agreed that a field day should be held on Aug. 20, when the Society proposes to visit the interesting church of Ivybridge and also the Roman remains in the vicinity. Our president, Mr Longchamps, F.R.S., has obtained permission to open a barrow in the Three Trees pasture. We venture to ask whether you would allow the members of the Society to walk through your grounds and to inspect – from without, of course – your beautiful house, which is, as you are doubtless aware, of great historic interest, having been for some years the residence of the celebrated Sir Thomas Wyatt. – I am, dear Sir, yours faithfully,

EDWARD K. TURNBULL (*Hon. Sec.*).'

'Just so,' said Albert's uncle; 'well, shall we permit the eye of the Maidstone Antiquities to profane these sacred solitudes, and the foot of the Field Club to kick up a dust on our gravel?'

'Our gravel is all grass,' H. O. said. And the girls said, 'Oh, do let them come!' It was Alice who said –

'Why not ask them to tea? They'll be very tired coming all the way from Maidstone.'

'Would you really like it?' Albert's uncle asked. 'I'm afraid they'll be but dull dogs, the Antiquities, stuffy old gentlemen with amphorae in their buttonholes instead of orchids, and pedigrees poking out of all their pockets.'

We laughed – because we knew what an amphorae is. If you don't you might look it up in the dicker. It's not a flower, though it sounds like one out of the gardening book, the kind you never hear of anyone growing.

Dora said she thought it would be splendid.

'And we could have out the best china,' she said, 'and decorate the table with flowers. We could have tea in the garden. We've never had a party since we've been here.'

'I warn you that your guests may be boresome; however, have it your own way,' Albert's uncle said; and he went off to write the invitation to tea to the Maidstone Antiquities. I know that is the wrong word – but somehow we all used it whenever we spoke of them, which was often.

In a day or two Albert's uncle came in to tea with a lightly-clouded brow.

'You've let me in for a nice thing,' he said. 'I asked the Antiquities to tea, and I asked casually how many we might expect. I thought we might need at least the full dozen of the best teacups. Now the secretary writes accepting my kind invitation – '

'Oh, good!' we cried. 'And how many are coming?'

'Oh, only about sixty,' was the groaning rejoinder. 'Perhaps more, should the weather be exceptionally favourable.'

Though stunned at first, we presently decided that we were pleased. We had never, never given such a big party.

The girls were allowed to help in the kitchen, where Mrs Pettigrew made cakes all day long without stopping. They did not let us boys be there, though I cannot see any harm in putting your finger in a cake before it is baked, and then licking your finger, if you are careful to put a different finger in the cake next time. Cake before it is baked is delicious – like a sort of cream.

Albert's uncle said he was the prey of despair. He drove in to Maidstone one day. When we asked him where he was going, he said –

'To get my hair cut: if I keep it this length I shall certainly tear it out by double handfuls in the extremity of my anguish every time I think of those innumerable Antiquities.'

But we found out afterwards that he really went to borrow china and things to give the Antiquities their tea out of; though he did have his hair cut too, because he is the soul of truth and honour.

Oswald had a very good sort of birthday, with bows and arrows as well as other presents. I think these were meant to make up for the pistol that was taken away after the adventure of the fox-hunting. These gave us boys something to do between the birthday-keeping, which was on the Saturday, and the Wednesday when the Antiquities were to come.

We did not allow the girls to play with the bows and arrows, because they had the cakes that we were cut off from: there was little or no unpleasantness over this.

On the Tuesday we went down to look at the Roman

place where the Antiquities were going to dig. We sat on the Roman wall and ate nuts. And as we sat there, we saw coming through the beet-field two labourers with picks and shovels, and a very young man with thin legs and a bicycle. It turned out afterwards to be a free-wheel, the first we had ever seen.

They stopped at a mound inside the Roman wall, and the men took their coats off and spat on their hands.

We went down at once, of course. The thin-legged bicyclist explained his machine to us very fully and carefully when we asked him, and then we saw the men were cutting turfs and turning them over and rolling them up and putting them in a heap. So we asked the gentleman with the thin legs what they were doing. He said –

'They are beginning the preliminary excavation in readiness for to-morrow.'

'What's up to-morrow?' H. O. asked.

'To-morrow we propose to open this barrow and examine it.'

'Then *you're* the Antiquities?' said H. O.

'I'm the secretary,' said the gentleman, smiling, but narrowly.

'Oh, you're all coming to tea with us,' Dora said, and added anxiously, 'how many of you do you think there'll be?'

'Oh, not more than eighty or ninety, I should think,' replied the gentleman.

This took our breath away and we went home. As we went, Oswald, who notices many things that would pass unobserved by the light and careless, saw Denny frowning hard.

So he said, 'What's up?'

'I've got an idea,' the Dentist said. 'Let's call a council.' The Dentist had grown quite used to our ways now. We had called him Dentist ever since the fox-hunt day. He called a council as if he had been used to calling such things all his life, and having them come, too; whereas we all know that his former existing was that of a white mouse in a trap, with that cat of a Murdstone aunt watching him through the bars.

(That is what is called a figure of speech. Albert's uncle told me.)

Councils are held in the straw-loft. As soon as we were all there, and the straw had stopped rustling after our sitting down, Dicky said – 'I hope it's nothing to do with the Wouldbegoods?'

'No,' said Denny in a hurry: 'quite the opposite.'

'I hope it's nothing wrong,' said Dora and Daisy together.

'It's – it's "Hail to thee, blithe spirit – bird thou never wert",' said Denny. 'I mean, I think it's what is called a lark.'

'You never know your luck. Go on, Dentist,' said Dicky.

'Well, then, do you know a book called *The Daisy Chain*?'

We didn't.

'It's by Miss Charlotte M. Yonge,' Daisy interrupted, 'and it's about a family of poor motherless children who tried so hard to be good, and they were confirmed, and had a bazaar, and went to church at the Minster, and one of them got married and wore black watered silk and silver ornaments. So her baby died, and then she was sorry she had not been a good mother to it. And –'

Here Dicky got up and said he'd got some snares to attend to, and he'd receive a report of the Council after it was over. But he only got as far as the trap-door, and then Oswald, the fleet of foot, closed with him, and they rolled together on the floor, while all the others called out 'Come back! Come back!' like guinea-hens on a fence.

Through the rustle and bustle and hustle of the struggle with Dicky, Oswald heard the voice of Denny murmuring one of his everlasting quotations –

> ' "*Come back, come back!*" *he cried in Greek,*
> "*Across the stormy water,*
> *And I'll forgive your Highland cheek,*
> *My daughter, O my daughter!*" '

When quiet was restored and Dicky had agreed to go through with the Council, Denny said –

'*The Daisy Chain* is not a bit like that really. It's a ripping book. One of the boys dresses up like a lady and comes to call, and another tries to hit his little sister with a hoe. It's jolly fine, I tell you.'

Denny is learning to say what he thinks, just like other boys. He would never have learnt such words as 'ripping' and 'jolly fine' while under the auntal tyranny.

Since then I have read *The Daisy Chain*. It is a first-rate book for girls and little boys.

But we did not want to talk about *The Daisy Chain* just then, so Oswald said –

'But what's your lark?'

Denny got pale pink and said –

'Don't hurry me. I'll tell you directly. Let me think a minute.'

Then he shut his pale pink eyelids a moment in thought, and then opened them and stood up on the straw and said very fast –

'Friends, Romans, countrymen, lend me your ears, or if not ears, pots. You know Albert's uncle said they were going to open the barrow, to look for Roman remains to-morrow. Don't you think it seems a pity they shouldn't find any?'

'Perhaps they will,' Dora said. But Oswald *saw*, and he said 'Primus! Go ahead, old man.'

The Dentist went ahead.

'In *The Daisy Chain*,' he said, 'they dug in a Roman encampment and the children went first and put some pottery there they'd made themselves, and Harry's old medal of the Duke of Wellington. The doctor helped them to some stuff to partly efface the inscription, and all the grown-ups were sold. I thought we might –

> '*You may break, you may shatter*
> *The vase if you will;*
> *But the scent of the Romans*
> *Will cling round it still.*'

Denny sat down amid applause. It really was a great idea, at least for *him*. It seemed to add just what was wanted to the visit of the Maidstone Antiquities. To sell the Antiquities thoroughly would be indeed splendiferous. Of course Dora made haste to point out that we had not got an old medal of the Duke of Wellington, and that we hadn't any doctor who would 'help us to stuff to efface', and etcetera; but we sternly bade her stow it. We weren't going to do *exactly* like those *Daisy Chain* kids.

The pottery was easy. We had made a lot of it by the stream – which was the Nile when we discovered its source – and dried it in the sun, and then baked it under a bonfire, like in *Foul Play*. And most of the things were such queer shapes that they should have done for almost anything – Roman or Greek, or even Egyptian or antediluvian, or household milk-jugs of the cavemen, Albert's uncle said. The pots were, fortunately, quite ready and dirty, because we had already buried them in mixed sand and river mud to improve the colour, and not remembered to wash it off.

So the Council at once collected it all – and some rusty hinges and some brass buttons and a file without a handle; and the girl Councillors carried it all concealed in their pinafores, while the men members carried digging tools. H. O. and Daisy were sent on ahead as scouts to see if the coast was clear. We have learned the true usefulness of scouts from reading about the Transvaal War. But all was still in the hush of evening sunset on the Roman ruin.

We posted sentries, who were to lie on their stomachs on the walls and give a long, low, signifying whistle if aught approached.

Then we dug a tunnel, like the one we once did after treasure, when we happened to bury a boy. It took some time; but never shall it be said that a Bastable grudged time or trouble when a lark was at stake. We put the things in as naturally as we could, and shoved the dirt back, till everything looked just as before. Then we went home, late for tea. But it was in a good cause; and there was no hot toast, only bread-and-butter, which does not get cold with waiting.

That night Alice whispered to Oswald on the stairs, as we went up to bed –

'Meet me outside your door when the others are asleep. Hist! Not a word.'

Oswald said, 'No kid?'

And she replied in the affirmation.

So he kept awake by biting his tongue and pulling his hair – for he shrinks from no pain if it is needful and right.

And when the others all slept the sleep of innocent youth, he got up and went out, and there was Alice dressed.

She said, 'I've found some broken things that look

ever so much more Roman – they were on top of the cupboard in the library. If you'll come with me, we'll bury them – just to see how surprised the others will be.'

It was a wild and daring act, but Oswald did not mind.

He said –

'Wait half a shake.' And he put on his knickerbockers and jacket, and slipped a few peppermints into his pocket in case of catching cold. It is these thoughtful expedients which mark the born explorer and adventurer.

It *was* a little cold; but the white moonlight was very fair to see, and we decided we'd do some other daring moonlight act some other day. We got out of the front door, which is never locked till Albert's uncle goes to bed at twelve or one, and we ran swiftly and silently across the bridge and through the fields to the Roman ruin.

Alice told me afterwards she should have been afraid if it had been dark. But the moonlight made it as bright as day is in your dreams.

Oswald had taken the spade and a sheet of newspaper.

We did not take all the pots Alice had found – but just the two that weren't broken – two crooked jugs, made of stuff like flower-pots are made of. We made two long cuts with the spade and lifted the turf up and scratched the earth under, and took it out very carefully in handfuls on to the newspaper, till the hole was deepish. Then we put in the jugs, and filled it up with earth and flattened the turf over. Turf stretches like elastic. This we did a couple of yards from the place where the mound was dug into by the men, and we had been so careful with the newspaper that there was no loose earth about.

Then we went home in the wet moonlight – at least,

It was a wild and daring act

the grass was very wet – chuckling through the peppermint, and got up to bed without anyone knowing a
single thing about it.

The next day the Antiquities came. It was a jolly hot day, and the tables were spread under the trees on the lawn, like a large and very grand Sunday-school treat. There were dozens of different kinds of cake, and bread-and-butter, both white and brown, and gooseberries and plums and jam sandwiches. And the girls decorated the tables with flowers – blue larkspur and white canterbury bells. And at about three there was a noise of people walking in the road, and presently the Antiquities began to come in at the front gate, and stood about on the lawn by twos and threes and sixes and sevens, looking shy and uncomfy, exactly like a Sunday-school treat. Presently some gentlemen came, who looked like the teachers; they were not shy, and they came right up to the door. So Albert's uncle, who had not been too proud to be up in our room with us watching the people on the lawn through the netting of our short blinds, said –

'I suppose that's the Committee. Come on!'

So we all went down – we were in our Sunday things – and Albert's uncle received the Committee like a feudal system baron, and we were his retainers.

He talked about dates, and king posts and gables, and mullions, and foundations, and records, and Sir Thomas Wyatt, and poetry, and Julius Caesar, and Roman remains, and lych gates and churches, and dog's-tooth moulding till the brain of Oswald reeled. I suppose that Albert's uncle remarked that all our mouths were open, which is a sign of reels in the brain, for he whispered –

'Go hence, and mingle unsuspected with the crowd!'

So we went out on to the lawn, which was now crowded with men and women and one child. This was a girl; she was fat, and we tried to talk to her, though we did not like her. (She was covered in red velvet like an arm-chair.) But she wouldn't. We thought at first she was from a deaf-and-dumb asylum, where her kind teachers had only managed to teach the afflicted to say 'Yes' and 'No'. But afterwards we knew better, for Noël heard her say to her mother, 'I wish you hadn't brought me, mamma. I didn't have a pretty teacup, and I haven't enjoyed my tea one bit.' And she had had five pieces of cake, besides little cakes and nearly a whole plate of plums, and there were only twelve pretty teacups altogether.

Several grown-ups talked to us in a most uninterested way, and then the President read a paper about the Moat House, which we couldn't understand, and other people made speeches we couldn't understand either, except the part about kind hospitality, which made us not know where to look.

Then Dora and Alice and Daisy and Mrs Pettigrew poured out the tea, and we handed cups and plates.

Albert's uncle took me behind a bush to see him tear what was left of his hair when he found there were one hundred and twenty-three Antiquities present, and I heard the President say to the Secretary that 'tea always fetched them'.

Then it was time for the Roman ruin, and our hearts beat high as we took our hats – it was exactly like Sunday – and joined the crowded procession of eager Antiquities. Many of them had umbrellas and overcoats, though the weather was fiery and without a cloud. That is the sort of people they were. The ladies all wore stiff bonnets, and no one took their gloves off, though, of course, it was quite in the country, and it is not wrong to take your gloves off there.

We had planned to be quite close when the digging went on; but Albert's uncle made us a mystic sign and drew us apart.

Then he said: 'The stalls and dress circle are for the guests. The hosts and hostesses retire to the gallery, whence, I am credibly informed, an excellent view may be obtained.'

So we all went up on the Roman walls, and thus missed the cream of the lark; for we could not exactly see what was happening. But we saw that things were being taken from the ground as the men dug, and passed round for the Antiquities to look at. And we knew they must be our Roman remains; but the Antiquities did not seem to care for them much, though we heard sounds of pleased laughter. And at last Alice and I exchanged meaning glances when the spot was reached where we had put in the extras. Then the crowd closed up thick, and we heard excited talk and we knew we really *had* sold the Antiquities this time.

Presently the bonnets and coats began to spread out and trickle towards the house and we were aware that all would soon be over. So we cut home the back way, just in time to hear the President saying to Albert's uncle –

'A genuine find – most interesting. Oh, really, you ought to have *one*. Well, if you insist – '

And so, by slow and dull degrees, the thick sprinkling of Antiquities melted off the lawn; the party was over, and only the dirty teacups and plates, and the trampled grass and the pleasures of memory were left.

We had a very beautiful supper – out of doors, too – with jam sandwiches and cakes and things that were over; and as we watched the setting monarch of the skies – I mean the sun – Alice said –

'Let's tell.'

We let the Dentist tell, because it was he who hatched the lark, but we helped him a little in the narrating of

405

the fell plot, because he has yet to learn how to tell a story straight from the beginning.

When he had done, and we had done, Albert's uncle said, 'Well, it amused you; and you'll be glad to learn that it amused your friends the Antiquities.'

'Didn't they think they were Roman?' Daisy said; 'they did in *The Daisy Chain*.'

'Not in the least,' said Albert's uncle; 'but the Treasurer and Secretary were charmed by your ingenious preparations for their reception.'

'We didn't want them to be disappointed,' said Dora.

'They weren't,' said Albert's uncle. 'Steady on with those plums, H.O. A little way beyond the treasure you had prepared for them they found two specimens of *real* Roman pottery which sent every man-jack of them home thanking his stars he had been born a happy little Antiquary child.'

'Those were *our* jugs,' said Alice, 'and we really *have* sold the Antiquities. She unfolded the tale about our getting the jugs and burying them in the moonlight, and the mound; and the others listened with deeply respectful interest. 'We really have done it this time, haven't we?' she added in tones of well-deserved triumph.

But Oswald had noticed a queer look about Albert's uncle from almost the beginning of Alice's recital; and he now had the sensation of something being up, which has on other occasions frozen his noble blood. The silence of Albert's uncle now froze it yet more Arcticly.

'Haven't we?' repeated Alice, unconscious of what her sensitive's brother's delicate feelings had already got hold of. 'We have done it this time, haven't we?'

'Since you ask me thus pointedly,' answered Albert's uncle at last, 'I cannot but confess that I think you have indeed done it. Those pots on the top of the library cupboard *are* Roman pottery. The amphorae which you hid in the mound are probably – I can't say for certain, mind – priceless. They are the property of the owner of this house. You have taken them out and buried them. The President of the Maidstone Antiquarian Society has taken them away in his bag. Now what are you going to do?'

Alice and I did not know what to say, or where to look. The others added to our pained position by some ungenerous murmurs about our not being so jolly clever as we thought ourselves.

There was a very far from pleasing silence. Then Oswald got up. He said –

'Alice, come here a sec., I want to speak to you.'

As Albert's uncle had offered no advice, Oswald disdained to ask him for any.

Alice got up too, and she and Oswald went into the garden, and sat down on the bench under the quince tree, and wished they had never tried to have a private lark of their very own with the Antiquities – 'A Private Sale', Albert's uncle called it afterwards. But regrets, as nearly always happens, were vain. Something had to be done.

But what?

Oswald and Alice sat in silent desperateness, and the voices of the gay and careless others came to them from the lawn, where, heartless in their youngness, they were playing tag. I don't know how they could. Oswald would not like to play tag when his brother and sister were in a hole, but Oswald is an exception to some boys. But Dicky told me afterwards he thought it was only a joke of Albert's uncle's.

The dusk grew dusker, till you could hardly tell the quinces from the leaves, and Alice and Oswald still sat exhausted with hard thinking, but they could not think of anything. And it grew so dark that the moonlight began to show.

Then Alice jumped up – just as Oswald was opening his mouth to say the same thing – and said, 'Of course – how silly! I know. Come on in, Oswald.'

And they went on in.

Oswald was still far too proud to consult anyone else. But he just asked carelessly if Alice and he might go into Maidstone the next day to buy some wire-netting for a rabbit-hutch, and to see after one or two things.

Albert's uncle said certainly. And they went by train with the bailiff from the farm, who was going in about some sheep-dip and to buy pigs. At any other time Oswald would not have been able to bear to leave the bailiff without seeing the pigs bought. But now it was different. For he and Alice had the weight on their bosoms of being thieves without having meant it – and nothing, not even pigs, had power to charm the young but honourable Oswald till that stain had been wiped away.

So he took Alice to the Secretary of the Maidstone Antiquities' house, and Mr Turnbull was out, but the maid-servant kindly told us where the President lived, and ere long the trembling feet of the unfortunate brother and sister vibrated on the spotless gravel of Camperdown Villa.

When they asked, they were told that Mr Longchamps was at home. Then they waited, paralysed with un-described emotions, in a large room with books and swords and glass bookcases with rotten-looking odds and ends in them. Mr Longchamps was a collector. That means he stuck to anything, no matter how ugly and silly, if only it was old.

He came in rubbing his hands, and very kind. He

remembered us very well, he said, and asked what he could do for us.

Oswald for once was dumb. He could not find words in which to own himself the ass he had been. But Alice was less delicately moulded. She said –

'Oh, if you please, we are most awfully sorry, and we hope you'll forgive us, but we thought it would be such a pity for you and all the other poor dear Antiquities to come all that way and then find nothing Roman – so we put some pots and things in the barrow for you to find.'

'So I perceived,' said the President, stroking his white beard and smiling most agreeably at us; 'a harmless joke, my dear! Youth's the season for jesting. There's no harm done – pray think no more about it. It's very honourable of you to come and apologize, I'm sure.'

His brow began to wear the furrowed, anxious look of one who would fain be rid of his guests and get back to what he was doing before they interrupted him.

Alice said, 'We didn't come for that. It's *much* worse. Those were two *real* true Roman jugs you took away; we put them there; they aren't ours. We didn't know they were real Roman. We wanted to sell the Antiquities – I mean Antiquaries – and we were sold ourselves.'

'This is serious,' said the gentleman. 'I suppose you'd know the – the "jugs" if you saw them again?'

'Anywhere,' said Oswald, with the confidential rashness of one who does not know what he is talking about.

Mr Longchamps opened the door of a little room leading out of the one we were in, and beckoned us to follow. We found ourselves amid shelves and shelves of pottery of all sorts; and two whole shelves – small ones – were filled with the sort of jug we wanted.

'Well,' said the President, with a veiled menacing sort of smile, like a wicked cardinal, 'which is it?'

Oswald said, 'I don't know.'

Alice said, 'I should know if I had it in my hand.'

The President patiently took the jugs down one after another, and Alice tried to look inside them. And one after another she shook her head and gave them back.

At last she said, 'You didn't *wash* them?'

Mr Longchamps shuddered and said 'No'.

'Then,' said Alice, 'there is something written with lead-pencil inside both the jugs. I wish I hadn't. I would rather you didn't read it. I didn't know it would be a nice old gentleman like you would find it. I thought it would be the younger gentleman with the thin legs and the narrow smile.'

'Mr Turnbull.' The President seemed to recognize the description unerringly. 'Well, well – boys will be boys – girls, I mean. I won't be angry. Look at all the "jugs" and see if you can find yours.'

Alice did – and the next one she looked at she said, 'This is one' – and two jugs further on she said, 'This is the other.'

'Well,' the President said, 'these are certainly the specimens which I obtained yesterday. If your uncle will call on me I will return them to him. But it's a disappointment. Yes, I think you must let me look inside.'

He did. And at the first one he said nothing. At the second he laughed.

'Well, well,' he said, 'we can't expect old heads on young shoulders. You're not the first who went forth to shear and returned shorn. Nor, it appears, am I. Next time you have a Sale of Antiquities, take care that you yourself are not "sold". Good-day to you, my dear. Don't let the incident prey on your mind,' he said to

Alice. 'Bless your heart, I was a boy once myself, unlikely as you may think it. Good-bye.'

We were in time to see the pigs bought after all.

I asked Alice what on earth it was she'd scribbled inside the beastly jugs, and she owned that just to make the lark complete she had written 'Sucks' in one of the jugs, and 'Sold again, silly', in the other.

But we know well enough who it was that was sold. And if ever we have any Antiquities to tea again, they shan't find so much as a Greek waistcoat button if we can help it.

Unless it's the President, for he did not behave at all badly. For a man of his age I think he behaved exceedingly well. Oswald can picture a very different scene having been enacted over those rotten pots if the President had been an otherwise sort of man.

But that picture is not pleasing, so Oswald will not distress you by drawing it for you. You can most likely do it easily for yourself.

THE BENEVOLENT BAR

THE tramp was very dusty about the feet and legs, and his clothes were very ragged and dirty, but he had cheerful twinkly grey eyes, and he touched his cap to the girls when he spoke to us, though a little as though he would rather not.

We were on the top of the big wall of the Roman ruin in the Three Tree pasture. We had just concluded a severe siege with bows and arrows – the ones that were given us to make up for the pistol that was confiscated after the sad but not sinful occasion when it shot a fox.

To avoid accidents that you would be sorry for afterwards, Oswald, in his thoughtfulness, had decreed that everyone was to wear wire masks.

Luckily there were plenty of these, because a man who lived in the Moat House once went to Rome, where they throw hundreds and thousands at each other in play, and call it a Comfit Battle or Battaglia di Confetti (that's real Italian). And he wanted to get up that sort of thing among the village people – but they were too beastly slack, so he chucked it.

And in the attic were the wire masks he brought home with him from Rome, which people wear to prevent the nasty comfits getting in their mouths and eyes.

So we were all armed to the teeth with masks and arrows, but in attacking or defending a fort your real strength is not in your equipment, but in your power of Shove. Oswald, Alice, Noël and Denny defended the fort. We were much the strongest side, but that was how Dicky and Oswald picked up.

The others got in, it is true, but that was only because an arrow hit Dicky on the nose, and it bled quarts as usual, though hit only through the wire mask. Then he put into dock for repairs, and while the defending party weren't looking he sneaked up the wall at the back and shoved Oswald off, and fell on top of him, so that the fort, now that it had lost its gallant young leader, the life and soul of the besieged party, was of course soon overpowered, and had to surrender.

Then we sat on the top and ate some peppermints Albert's uncle brought us a bag of from Maidstone when he went to fetch away the Roman pottery we tried to sell the Antiquities with.

The battle was over, and peace raged among us as we sat in the sun on the big wall and looked at the fields, all blue and swimming in the heat.

We saw the tramp coming through the beetfield. He made a dusty blot on the fair scene.

When he saw us he came close to the wall, and touched his cap, as I have said, and remarked –

'Excuse me interrupting of your sports, young gentlemen and ladies, but if you could so far oblige as to tell a labouring man the way to the nearest pub. It's a dry day and no error.'

'The "Rose and Crown" is the best pub,' said Dicky, 'and the landlady is a friend of ours. It's about a mile if you go by the field path.'

'Lor' love a duck!' said the tramp, 'a mile's a long way, and walking's a dry job this ere weather.'

We said we agreed with him.

'Upon my sacred,' said the tramp, 'if there was a pump handy I believe I'd take a turn at it – I would indeed, so help me if I wouldn't! Though water always upsets me and makes my 'and shaky.'

We had not cared much about tramps since the adventure of the villainous sailor-man and the Tower of Mystery, but we had the dogs on the wall with us (Lady was awfully difficult to get up, on account of her long deer-hound legs), and the position was a strong one, and easy to defend. Besides the tramp did not look like that bad sailor, nor talk like it. And we considerably outnumbered the tramp, anyway.

Alice nudged Oswald and said something about Sir Philip Sidney and the tramp's need being greater than his, so Oswald was obliged to go to the hole in the top of the wall where we store provisions during sieges and get out the bottle of ginger-beer which he had gone without when the others had theirs so as to drink it when he got really thirsty.

Meanwhile Alice said –

'We've got some ginger-beer; my brother's getting it. I hope you won't mind drinking out of our glass. We can't wash it, you know – unless we rinse it out with a little ginger-beer.'

'Don't ye do it, miss,' he said eagerly; 'never waste good liquor on washing.'

The glass was beside us on the wall. Oswald filled it with ginger-beer and handed down the foaming tankard to the tramp. He had to lie on his young stomach to do this.

The tramp was really quite polite – one of Nature's gentlemen, and a man as well, we found out afterwards. He said –

'Here's to you!' before he drank. Then he drained the glass till the rim rested on his nose.

'Swelp me, but I *was* dry,' he said. 'Don't seem to matter much what it is, this weather, do it? – so long as it's suthink wet. Well, here's thanking you.'

'You're very welcome,' said Dora; 'I'm glad you liked it.'

'Like it?' – said he. 'I don't suppose you know what it's like to have a thirst on you. Talk of free schools and free libraries, and free baths and wash-houses and such! Why don't someone start free *drinks*? He'd be a 'ero, he would. I'd vote for him any day of the week and one over. Ef yer don't objec I'll set down a bit and put on a pipe.'

He sat down on the grass and began to smoke. We asked him questions about himself, and he told us many of his secret sorrows – especially about there being no work nowadays for an honest man. At last he dropped asleep in the middle of a story about a vestry he worked for that hadn't acted fair and square by him like he had by them, or it (I don't know if vestry is singular or plural), and we went home. But before we went we held a hurried council and collected what money we could from the little we had with us (it was ninepence-halfpenny), and wrapped it in an old envelope Dicky had in his pocket and put it gently on the billowing middle of the poor tramp's sleeping waistcoat, so that he would find it when he woke. None of the dogs said a single syllable while we were doing this, so we knew they believed him to be poor but honest, and we always find it safe to take their word for things like that.

As we went home a brooding silence fell upon us; we found out afterwards that those words of the poor tramp's about free drinks had sunk deep in all our hearts, and rankled there.

After dinner we went out and sat with our feet in the stream. People tell you it makes your grub disagree with you to do this just after meals, but it never hurts us. There is a fallen willow across the stream that just seats the eight of us, only the ones at the end can't get their feet into the water properly because of the bushes, so we keep changing places. We had got some liquorice root to chew. This helps thought. Dora broke a peaceful silence with this speech –

'Free drinks.'

The words awoke a response in every breast.

'I wonder someone doesn't,' H. O. said, leaning back till he nearly toppled in, and was only saved by Oswald and Alice at their own deadly peril.

'Do for goodness sake sit still, H. O.,' observed Alice. 'It would be a glorious act! I wish *we* could.'

'What, sit still?' asked H. O.

'No, my child,' replied Oswald, 'most of us can do that when we try. Your angel sister was only wishing to set up free drinks for the poor and thirsty.'

'Not for all of them,' Alice said, 'just a few. Change places now, Dicky. My feet aren't properly wet at all.'

It is very difficult to change places safely on the willow. The changers have to crawl over the laps of the others, while the rest sit tight and hold on for all they're worth. But the hard task was accomplished and then Alice went on –

'And we couldn't do it for always, only a day or two – just while our money held out. Eiffel Tower lemonade's the best, and you get a jolly lot of it for your money too. There must be a great many sincerely thirsty persons go along the Dover Road every day.'

'It wouldn't be bad. We've got a little chink between us,' said Oswald.

'And then think how the poor grateful creatures would linger and tell us about their inmost sorrows. It would be most frightfully interesting. We could write all their agonied life histories down afterwards like *All the Year Round* Christmas numbers. Oh, do let's!'

Alice was wriggling so with earnestness that Dicky thumped her to make her calm.

'We might do it, just for one day,' Oswald said, 'but it wouldn't be much – only a drop in the ocean compared with the enormous dryness of all the people in the whole world. Still, every little helps, as the mermaid said when she cried into the sea.'

'I know a piece of poetry about that,' Denny said.

> *'Small things are best.*
> *Care and unrest*
> *To wealth and rank are given,*
> *But little things*
> *On little wings –*

do something or other, I forget what, but it means the same as Oswald was saying about the mermaid.'

'What are you going to call it?' asked Noël, coming out of a dream.

'Call what?'

'The Free Drinks game.'

> *'It's a horrid shame*
> *If the Free Drinks game*
> *Doesn't have a name.*
> *You would be to blame*
> *If anyone came*
> *And –'*

'Oh, shut up!' remarked Dicky. 'You've been making that rot up all the time we've been talking instead of listening properly.' Dicky hates poetry. I don't mind it so very much myself, especially Macaulay's and Kipling's and Noël's.

'There was a lot more – "lame" and "dame" and "name" and "game" and things – and now I've forgotten it,' Noël said in gloom.

'Never mind,' Alice answered, 'it'll come back to you in the silent watches of the night; you see if it doesn't. But really, Noël's right, it *ought* to have a name.'

'Free Drinks Company.'

'Thirsty Travellers' Rest.'

'The Travellers' Joy.'

These names were suggested, but not cared for extra. Then someone said – I think it was Oswald –

'Why not "The House Beautiful"?'

'It can't be a house, it must be in the road. It'll only be a stall.'

'The "Stall Beautiful" is simply silly,' Oswald said.

'The "Bar Beautiful" then,' said Dicky, who knows what the 'Rose and Crown' bar is like inside, which of course is hidden from girls.

'Oh, wait a minute,' cried the Dentist, snapping his fingers like he always does when he is trying to remember things. 'I thought of something, only Daisy tickled me and it's gone – I know – let's call it the Benevolent Bar!'

It was exactly right, and told the whole truth in two words. 'Benevolent' showed it was free and 'Bar' showed what was free; e.g. things to drink. The 'Benevolent Bar' it was.

We went home at once to prepare for the morrow, for of course we meant to do it the very next day. Procrastination is you know what – and delays are dangerous. If we had waited long we might have happened to spend our money on something else.

The utmost secrecy had to be observed, because Mrs Pettigrew hates tramps. Most people do who keep fowls. Albert's uncle was in London till the next evening, so we could not consult him, but we know he is always chock full of intelligent sympathy with the poor and needy.

Acting with the deepest disguise, we made an awning to cover the Benevolent Bar keepers from the searching rays of the monarch of the skies. We found some old striped sun-blinds in the attic, and the girls sewed them together. They were not very big when they were done, so we added the girls' striped petticoats. I am sorry their petticoats turn up so constantly in my narrative, but they really are very useful, especially when the band is cut off. The girls borrowed Mrs Pettigrew's sewing-machine; they could not ask her leave without explanations, which we did not wish to give just then, and she had lent it to them before. They took it into the cellar to work it, so that she should not hear the noise and ask bothering questions. They had to balance it on one end of the beer-stand. It was not easy. While they were doing the sewing we boys went out and got willow poles and chopped the twigs off, and got ready as well as we could to put up the awning.

When we returned a detachment of us went down to the shop in the village for Eiffel Tower lemonade. We bought seven-and-sixpence worth; then we made a great label to say what the bar was for. Then there was nothing else to do except to make rosettes out of a blue sash of Daisy's to show we belonged to the Benevolent Bar.

The next day was as hot as ever. We rose early from our innocent slumbers, and went out to the Dover Road to the spot we had marked down the day before. It was at a cross-roads, so as to be able to give drinks to as many people as possible.

We hid the awning and poles behind the hedge and went home to brekker.

After break we got the big zinc bath they wash clothes in, and after filling it with clean water we just had to empty it again because it was too heavy to lift. So we carried it vacant to the trysting-spot and left H. O. and Noël to guard it while we went and fetched separate pails of water; very heavy work, and no one who wasn't really benevolent would have bothered about it for an instant. Oswald alone carried three pails. So did Dicky and the Dentist. Then we rolled down some empty barrels and stood up three of them by the roadside, and put planks on them. This made a very first-class table, and we covered it with the best tablecloth we could find in the linen cupboard. We brought out several glasses and some teacups – not the best ones, Oswald was firm about that – and the kettle and spirit-lamp and the tea-pot, in case any weary tramp-woman fancied a cup of tea instead of Eiffel Tower. H. O. and Noël had to go down to the shop for tea; they need not have grumbled; they had not carried any of the water. And their having to go the second time was only because we forgot to tell them to get some real lemons to put on the bar to show what the drink would be like when you got it. The man at the shop kindly gave us tick for the lemons, and we cashed up out of our next week's pocket-money.

Two or three people passed while we were getting things ready, but no one said anything except the man who said, 'Bloomin' Sunday-school treat', and as it was too early in the day for anyone to be thirsty we did not stop the wayfarers to tell them their thirst could be slaked without cost at our Benevolent Bar.

But when everything was quite ready, and our blue rosettes fastened on our breasts over our benevolent hearts, we stuck up the great placard we had made with 'Benevolent Bar. Free Drinks to all Weary

Travellers', in white wadding on red calico, like Christmas decorations in church. We had meant to fasten this to the edge of the awning, but we had to pin it to the front of the tablecloth, because I am sorry to say the awning went wrong from the first. We could not drive the willow poles into the road; it was much too hard. And in the ditch it was too soft, besides being no use. So we had just to cover our benevolent heads with our hats, and take it in turns to go into the shadow of the tree on the other side of the road. For we had pitched our table on the sunny side of the way, of course, relying on our broken-reed-like awning, and wishing to give it a fair chance.

Everything looked very nice, and we longed to see somebody really miserable come along so as to be able to allieve their distress.

A man and woman were the first; they stopped and stared, but when Alice said, 'Free drinks! Free drinks! Aren't you thirsty?' they said, 'No thank you,' and went on. Then came a person from the village; he didn't even say 'Thank you' when we asked him, and Oswald began to fear it might be like the awful time when we wandered about on Christmas Day trying to find poor persons and persuade them to eat our Conscience pudding.

But a man in a blue jersey and a red bundle eased Oswald's fears by being willing to drink a glass of lemonade, and even to say, 'Thank you, I'm sure,' quite nicely.

After that it was better. As we had foreseen, there were plenty of thirsty people walking along the Dover Road, and even some from the cross-road.

We had had the pleasure of seeing nineteen tumblers drained to the dregs ere we tasted any ourselves. Nobody asked for tea.

More people went by than we gave lemonade to. Some wouldn't have it because they were too grand. One man told us he could pay for his own liquor when he was dry, which, praise be, he wasn't over and above, at present; and others asked if we hadn't any beer, and when we said 'No', they said it showed what sort we were – as if the sort was not a good one, which it is.

And another man said, 'Slops again! You never get nothing for nothing, not this side of heaven you don't. Look at the bloomin' blue ribbon on em! Oh, Lor'!' and went on quite sadly without having a drink.

Our Pig-man who helped us on the Tower of Mystery day went by and we hailed him, and explained it all to him and gave him a drink, and asked him to call as he came back. He liked it all, and said we were a real good sort. How different from the man who wanted the beer. Then he went on.

One thing I didn't like, and that was the way boys began to gather. Of course we could not refuse to give drinks to any traveller who was old enough to ask for it, but when one boy had had three glasses of lemonade and asked for another, Oswald said –

'I think you've had jolly well enough. You can't be really thirsty after all that lot.'

The boy said, 'Oh, can't I? You'll just see if I can't,' and went away. Presently he came back with four other boys, all bigger than Oswald; and they all asked for lemonade. Oswald gave it to the four new ones, but he was determined in his behaviour to the other one, and wouldn't give him a drop. Then the five of them went and sat on a gate a little way off and kept laughing in a nasty way, and whenever a boy went by they called out –

'I say, 'ere's a go,' and as often as not the new boy would hang about with them. It was disquieting, for though they had nearly all had lemonade we could see it had not made them friendly.

A great glorious glow of goodness gladdened (those go all together and are called alliteration) our hearts when we saw our own tramp coming down the road. The dogs did not growl at him as they had at the boys or the beer-man. (I did not say before that we had the dogs with us, but of course we had, because we had promised never to go out without them.)

Oswald said, 'Hullo,' and the tramp said, 'Hullo.'

Then Alice said, 'You see we've taken your advice; we're giving free drinks. Doesn't it all look nice?'

'It does that,' said the tramp. 'I don't mind if I do.'

So we gave him two glasses of lemonade succeedingly, and thanked him for giving us the idea. He said we were very welcome, and if we'd no objection he'd sit down a bit and put on a pipe. He did, and after talking a little more he fell asleep. Drinking anything seemed to end in sleep with him. I always thought it was only beer and things made people sleepy, but he was not so. When he was asleep he rolled into the ditch, but it did not wake him up.

The boys were getting very noisy, and they began to shout things, and to make silly noises with their mouths, and when Oswald and Dicky went over to them and told them to just chuck it, they were worse than ever. I think perhaps Oswald and Dicky might have fought and settled them – though there were eleven, yet back to back you can always do it against overwhelming numbers in a book – only Alice called out –

'Oswald, here's some more, come back!'

We went. Three big men were coming down the road, very red and hot, and not amiable-looking. They stopped in front of the Benevolent Bar and slowly read the wadding and red-stuff label.

Then one of them said he was blessed, or something like that, and another said he was too. The third one said, 'Blessed or not, a drink's a drink. Blue ribbon, though, by — ' (a word you ought not to say, though it is in the Bible and the catechism as well). 'Let's have a liquor, little missy.'

The dogs were growling, but Oswald thought it best not to take any notice of what the dogs said, but to give these men each a drink. So he did. They drank, but not as if they cared about it very much, and then they set their glasses down on the table, a liberty no one else had entered into, and began to try and chaff Oswald. Oswald said in an undervoice to H. O. –

'Just take charge. I want to speak to the girls a sec. Call if you want anything.' And then he drew the others away, to say he thought there'd been enough of it, and considering the boys and new three men, perhaps we'd better chuck it and go home. We'd been benevolent nearly four hours anyway.

While this conversation and the objections of the others were going on, H. O. perpetuated an act which nearly wrecked the Benevolent Bar.

Of course Oswald was not an eye or ear witness of what happened, but from what H. O. said in the calmer moments of later life, I think this was about what happened.

One of the big disagreeable men said to H. O. –

'Ain't got such a thing as a drop o' spirit, 'ave yer?'

H. O. said no, we hadn't, only lemonade and tea.

'Lemonade and tea! blank' (bad word I told you about) 'and blazes,' replied the bad character, for such he afterwards proved to be. 'What's *that* then?'

He pointed to a bottle labelled Dewar's whisky, which stood on the table near the spirit-kettle.

'Oh, is *that* what you want?' said H. O. kindly.

The man is understood to have said he should bloomin' well think so, but H. O. is not sure about the bloomin'.

He held out his glass with about half the lemonade in it, and H. O. generously filled up the tumbler out of the bottle, labelled Dewar's whisky. The man took a great drink, and then suddenly he spat out what happened to be left in his mouth just then, and began to swear. It was then that Oswald and Dicky rushed upon the scene. The man was shaking his fist in H. O.'s face, and H. O. was still holding on to the bottle we had brought out the methylated spirit in for the lamp, in case of anyone wanting tea, which they hadn't.

'If I was Jim,' said the second ruffian, for such indeed they were, when he had snatched the bottle from H. O. and smelt it, 'I'd chuck the whole show over the hedge, so I would, and you young gutter-snipes after it, so I wouldn't.'

Oswald saw in a moment that in point of strength, if not numbers, he and his party were out-matched, and the unfriendly boys were drawing gladly near. It is no shame to signal for help when in distress – the best ships do it every day. Oswald shouted 'Help, help!' Before the words were out of his brave yet trembling lips our own tramp leapt like an antelope from the ditch and said –

'Now then, what's up?'

The biggest of the three men immediately knocked him down. He lay still.

The biggest then said, 'Come on – any more of you? Come on!'

Oswald was so enraged at this cowardly attack that

he actually hit out at the big man – and he really got one in just above the belt. Then he shut his eyes, because he felt that now all was indeed up. There was a shout and a scuffle, and Oswald opened his eyes in astonishment at finding himself still whole and un-impaired. Our own tramp had artfully simulated insensibleness, to get the men off their guard, and then had suddenly got his arms round a leg each of two of the men, and pulled them to the ground, helped by Dicky, who saw his game and rushed in at the same time, exactly like Oswald would have done if he had not had his eyes shut ready to meet his doom.

The unpleasant boys shouted, and the third man tried to help his unrespectable friends, now on their backs involved in a desperate struggle with our own tramp, who was on top of them, accompanied by Dicky. It all happened in a minute, and it was all mixed up. The dogs were growling and barking – Martha had one of the men by the trouser leg and Pincher had another; the girls were screaming like mad and the strange boys shouted and laughed (little beasts!), and then suddenly our Pig-man came round the corner, and two friends of his with him. He had gone and fetched them to take care of us if anything unpleasant occurred. It was a very thoughtful, and just like him.

'Fetch the police!' cried the Pig-man in noble tones, and H. O. started running to do it. But the scoundrels struggled from under Dicky and our tramp, shook off the dogs and some bits of trouser, and fled heavily down the road.

Our Pig-man said, 'Get along home!' to the dis-agreeable boys, and 'Shoo'd' them as if they were hens, and they went. H. O. ran back when they began to go up the road, and there we were, all standing breathless

'Fetch the police,' cried our Pig-man in noble tones

and in tears on the scene of the late desperate engage-
ment. Oswald gives you his word of honour that his
and Dicky's tears were tears of pure rage. There are
such things as tears of pure rage. Anyone who knows
will tell you so.

We picked up our own tramp and bathed the lump
on his forehead with lemonade. The water in the zinc
bath had been upset in the struggle. Then he and the
Pig-man and his kind friends helped us carry our
things home.

The Pig-man advised us on the way not to try these
sort of kind actions without getting a grown-up to help
us. We've been advised this before, but now I really
think we shall never try to be benevolent to the poor
and needy again. At any rate not unless we know them
very well first.

We have seen our own tramp often since. The
Pig-man gave him a job. He has got work to do at last.
The Pig-man says he is not such a very bad chap, only
he will fall asleep after the least drop of drink. We
know that is his failing. We saw it at once. But it was
lucky for us he fell asleep that day near our benevolent
bar.

I will not go into what my father said about it all.
There was a good deal in it about minding your own
business – there generally is in most of the talkings-to
we get. But he gave our tramp a sovereign, and the
Pig-man says he went to sleep on it for a solid week.

THE CANTERBURY PILGRIMS

THE author of these few lines really does hope to goodness that no one will be such an owl as to think from the number of things we did when we were in the country, that we were wretched, neglected little children, whose grown-up relations sparkled in the bright haunts of pleasure, and whirled in the giddy what's-its-name of fashion, while we were left to weep forsaken at home. It was nothing of the kind, and I wish you to know that my father was with us a good deal – and Albert's uncle (who is really no uncle of ours, but only of Albert next door when we lived in Lewisham) gave up a good many of his valuable hours to us. And the father of Denny and Daisy came now and then, and other people, quite as many as we wished to see. And we had some very decent times with them; and enjoyed ourselves very much indeed, thank you. In some ways the good times you have with grown-ups are better than the ones you have by yourselves. At any rate they are safer. It is almost impossible, then, to do anything fatal without being pulled up short by a grown-up ere yet the deed is done. And, if you are careful, anything that goes wrong can be looked on as the grown-up's fault. But these secure pleasures are not so interesting to tell about as the things you do when there is no one to stop you on the edge of the rash act.

It is curious, too, that many of our most interesting

games happened when grown-ups were far away. For instance when we were pilgrims.

It was just after the business of the Benevolent Bar, and it was a wet day. It is not easy to amuse yourself indoors on a wet day as older people seem to think, especially when you are far removed from your own home, and haven't got all your own books and things. The girls were playing Halma – which is a beastly game – Noël was writing poetry, H. O. was singing 'I don't know what to do' to the tune of 'Canaan's happy shore'. It goes like this, and is very tiresome to listen to –

> *'I don't know what to do – oo – oo – oo!*
> *I don't know what to do – oo – oo!*
> *It is a beastly rainy day*
> *And I don't know what to do.'*

The rest of us were trying to make him shut up. We put a carpet bag over his head, but he went on inside it; and then we sat on him, but he sang under us; we held him upside down and made him crawl head first under the sofa, but when, even there, he kept it up, we saw that nothing short of violence would induce him to silence, so we let him go. And then he said we had hurt him, and we said we were only in fun, and he said if we were he wasn't, and ill feeling might have grown up even out of a playful brotherly act like ours had been, only Alice chucked the Halma and said –

'Let dogs delight. Come on – let's play something.'

Then Dora said, 'Yes, but look here. Now we're together I do want to say something. What about the Wouldbegoods Society?'

Many of us groaned, and one said, 'Hear! hear!' I will not say which one, but it was not Oswald.

'No, but really,' Dora said, 'I don't want to be

preachy – but you know we *did* say we'd try to be good. And it says in a book I was reading only yesterday that *not* being naughty is not enough. You must *be* good. And we've hardly done anything. The Golden Deed book's almost empty.'

'Couldn't we have a book of leaden deeds?' said Noël, coming out of his poetry, 'then there'd be plenty for Alice to write about if she wants to, or brass or zinc or aluminium deeds? We shan't ever fill the book with golden ones.'

H. O. had rolled himself in the red tablecloth and said Noël was only advising us to be naughty, and again peace waved in the balance. But Alice said, 'Oh, H. O., *don't* – he didn't mean that; but really and truly, I wish wrong things weren't so interesting. You begin to do a noble act, and then it gets so exciting, and before you know where you are you are doing something wrong as hard as you can lick.'

'And enjoying it too,' Dick said.

'It's very curious,' Denny said, 'but you don't seem to be able to be certain inside yourself whether what you're doing is right if you happen to like doing it, but if you don't like doing it you know quite well. I only thought of that just now. I wish Noël would make a poem about it.'

'I am,' Noël said; 'it began about a crocodile but it is finishing itself up quite different from what I meant it to at first. Just wait a minute.'

He wrote very hard while his kind brothers and sisters and his little friends waited the minute he had said, and then he read:

> '*The crocodile is very wise,*
> *He lives in the Nile with little eyes,*
> *He eats the hippopotamus too,*
> *And if he could he would eat up you.*

> *'The lovely woods and starry skies*
> *He looks upon with glad surprise!*
> *He sees the riches of the east,*
> *And the tiger and lion, kings of beast.*

> *'So let all be good and beware*
> *Of saying shan't and won't and don't care;*
> *For doing wrong is easier far*
> *Than any of the right things I know about are.*

And I couldn't make it king of beasts because of it not rhyming with east, so I put the *s* off beasts on to king. It comes even in the end.'

We all said it was a very nice piece of poetry. Noël gets really ill if you don't like what he writes, and then he said, 'If it's trying that's wanted, I don't care how hard we *try* to be good, but we may as well do it some nice way. Let's be Pilgrim's Progress, like I wanted to at first.'

And we were all beginning to say we didn't want to, when suddenly Dora said, 'Oh, look here! I know. We'll be the Canterbury Pilgrims. People used to go pilgrimages to make themselves good.'

'With peas in their shoes,' the Dentist said. 'It's in a piece of poetry – only the man boiled his peas – which is quite unfair.'

'Oh, yes,' said H. O., 'and cocked hats.'

'Not cocked – cockled' – it was Alice who said this. 'And they had staffs and scrips, and they told each other tales. We might as well.'

Oswald and Dora had been reading about the Canterbury Pilgrims in a book called *A Short History of the English People.* It is not at all short really – three fat volumes – but it has jolly good pictures. It was written by a gentleman named Green. So Oswald said –

'All right. I'll be the Knight.'

'I'll be the wife of Bath,' Dora said. 'What will you be, Dicky?'

'Oh, I don't care, I'll be Mr Bath if you like.'

'We don't know much about the people,' Alice said. 'How many were there?'

'Thirty,' Oswald replied, 'but we needn't be all of them. There's a Nun-Priest.'

'Is that a man or a woman?'

Oswald said he could not be sure by the picture, but Alice and Noël could be it between them. So that was settled. Then we got the book and looked at the dresses to see if we could make up dresses for the parts. At first we thought we would, because it would be something to do, and it was a very wet day; but they looked difficult, especially the Miller's. Denny wanted to be the Miller, but in the end he was the Doctor, because it was next door to Dentist, which is what we call him for short. Daisy was to be the Prioress – because she is good, and has 'a soft little red mouth', and H. O. *would* be the Manciple (I don't know what that is), because the picture of him is bigger than most of the others, and he said Manciple was a nice portmanteau word – half mandarin and half disciple.

'Let's get the easiest parts of the dresses ready first,' Alice said – 'the pilgrims' staffs and hats and the cockles.'

So Oswald and Dicky braved the fury of the elements and went into the wood beyond the orchard to cut ash-sticks. We got eight jolly good long ones. Then we took them home, and the girls bothered till we changed our clothes, which were indeed sopping with the elements we had faced.

Then we peeled the sticks. They were nice and white at first, but they soon got dirty when we carried them. It is a curious thing: however often you wash your hands they always seem to come off on anything white. And we nailed paper rosettes to the tops of them. That was the nearest we could get to cockle-shells.

'And we may as well have them there as on our hats,' Alice said. 'And let's call each other by our right names to-day, just to get into it. Don't you think so, Knight?'

'Yea, Nun-Priest,' Oswald was replying, but Noel said she was only half the Nun-Priest, and again a threat of unpleasantness darkened the air. But Alice said –

'Don't be a piggy-wiggy, Noël, dear; you can have it all, I don't want it. I'll just be a plain pilgrim, or Henry who killed Becket.'

So she was called the Plain Pilgrim, and she did not mind.

We thought of cocked hats, but they are warm to wear, and the big garden hats that make you look like pictures on the covers of plantation songs did beautifully. We put cockle-shells on them. Sandals we did try, with pieces of oil-cloth cut the shape of soles and fastened with tape, but the dust gets into your toes so, and we decided boots were better for such a long walk. Some of the pilgrims who were very earnest decided to tie their boots with white tape crossed outside to pretend sandals. Denny was one of these earnest palmers. As for dresses, there was no time to make them properly, and at first we thought of nightgowns; but we decided not to, in case people in Canterbury were not used to that sort of pilgrim nowadays. We made up our minds to go as we were – or as we might happen to be next day.

You will be ready to believe we hoped next day would be fine. It was.

Fair was the morn when the pilgrims arose and went down to breakfast. Albert's uncle had had brekker early and was hard at work in his study. We heard his quill pen squeaking when we listened at the door. It is not wrong to listen at doors when there is only one person inside, because nobody would tell itself secrets aloud when it was alone.

We got lunch from the housekeeper, Mrs Pettigrew. She seems almost to *like* us all to go out and take our lunch with us. Though I should think it must be very dull for her all alone. I remember, though, that Eliza, our late general at Lewisham, was just the same. We took the dear dogs of course. Since the Tower of Mystery happened we are not allowed to go anywhere without the escort of these faithful friends of man. We did not take Martha, because bull-dogs do not like long walks. Remember this if you ever have one of those valuable animals.

When we were all ready, with our big hats and cockle-shells, and our staves and our tape sandals, the pilgrims looked very nice.

'Only we haven't any scrips,' Dora said.

'What is a scrip?'

'I think it's something to read. A roll of parchment or something.'

So we had old newspapers rolled up, and carried them in our hands. We took the *Globe* and the *Westminster Gazette* because they are pink and green. The Dentist wore his white sandshoes, sandalled with black tape, and bare legs. They really looked almost as good as bare feet.

'We *ought* to have peas in our shoes,' he said. But we did not think so. We knew what a very little stone in your boot will do, let alone peas.

Of course we knew the way to go to Canterbury, because the old Pilgrims' Road runs just above our house. It is a very pretty road, narrow, and often shady.

It is nice for walking, but carts do not like it because it is rough and rutty; so there is grass growing in patches on it.

I have said that it was a fine day, which means that it was not raining, but the sun did not shine all the time.

"Tis well, O Knight,' said Alice, 'that the orb of day shines not in undi – what's-its-name? – splendour.'

'Thou sayest sooth, Plain Pilgrim,' replied Oswald. "Tis jolly warm even as it is.'

'I wish I wasn't two people,' Noël said, 'it seems to make me hotter. I think I'll be a Reeve or something.'

But we would not let him, and we explained that if he hadn't been so beastly particular Alice would have been half of him, and he had only himself to thank if being all of a Nun-Priest made him hot.

But it *was* warm certainly, and it was some time since we'd gone so far in boots. Yet when H. O. complained we did our duty as pilgrims and made him shut up. He did as soon as Alice said that about whining and grizzling being below the dignity of a Manciple.

It was so warm that the Prioress and the wife of Bath gave up walking with their arms round each other in their usual silly way (Albert's uncle calls it Laura Matildaing), and the Doctor and Mr Bath had to take their jackets off and carry them.

I am sure if an artist or a photographer, or any person who liked pilgrims, had seen us he would have been very pleased. The paper cockle-shells were first-rate, but it was awkward having them on the top of the staffs, because they got in your way when you wanted the staff to use as a walking-stick.

We stepped out like a man all of us, and kept it up as well as we could in book-talk, and at first all was merry as a dinner-bell; but presently Oswald, who was the 'very perfect gentle knight', could not help noticing that one of us was growing very silent and rather pale, like people are when they have eaten something that disagrees with them before they are quite sure of the fell truth.

So he said, 'What's up, Dentist, old man?' quite kindly and like a perfect knight, though, of course, he was annoyed with Denny. It is sickening when people turn pale in the middle of a game and everything is spoiled, and you have to go home, and tell the spoiler how sorry you are that he is knocked up, and pretend not to mind about the game being spoiled.

Denny said, 'Nothing', but Oswald knew better.

Then Alice said, 'Let's rest a bit, Oswald, it *is* hot.'

'Sir Oswald, if you please, Plain Pilgrim,' returned her brother dignifiedly. 'Remember I'm a knight.'

So then we sat down and had lunch, and Denny looked better. We played adverbs, and twenty questions, and apprenticing your son, for a bit in the shade, and then Dicky said it was time to set sail if we meant to make the port of Canterbury that night. Of course, pilgrims reck not of ports, but Dicky never does play the game thoughtfully.

We went on. I believe we should have got to Canterbury all right and quite early, only Denny got paler and paler, and presently Oswald saw, beyond any doubt, that he was beginning to walk lame.

'Shoes hurt you, Dentist?' he said, still with kind striving cheerfulness.

'Not much – it's all right,' returned the other.

So on we went – but we were all a bit tired now – and the sun was hotter and hotter; the clouds had gone away. We had to begin to sing to keep up our spirits. We sang 'The British Grenadiers' and 'John Brown's

Body', which is grand to march to, and a lot of others. We were just starting on 'Tramp, tramp, tramp, the boys are marching', when Denny stopped short. He stood first on one foot and then on the other, and suddenly screwed up his face and put his knuckles in his eyes and sat down on a heap of stones by the roadside.

When we pulled his hands down he was actually crying. The author does not wish to say it is babyish to cry.

'Whatever is up?' we all asked, and Daisy and Dora petted him to get him to say, but he only went on howling, and said it was nothing, only would we go on and leave him, and call for him as we came back.

Oswald thought very likely something had given Denny the stomach-ache, and he did not like to say so before all of us, so he sent the others away and told them to walk on a bit.

Then he said, 'Now, Denny, don't be a young ass. What is it? *Is* it stomach-ache?'

And Denny stopped crying to say 'No!' as loud as he could.

'Well, then,' Oswald said, 'look here, you're spoiling the whole thing. Don't be a jackape, Denny. What is it?'

'You won't tell the others if I tell you?'

'Not if you say not,' Oswald answered in kindly tones.

'Well, it's my shoes.'

'Take them off, man.'

'You won't laugh?'

'NO!' cried Oswald, so impatiently that the others looked back to see why he was shouting. He waved them away, and with humble gentleness began to undo the black-tape sandals. Denny let him, crying hard all the time.

When Oswald had got off the first shoe the mystery was made plain to him.

'Well! Of all the – ' he said in proper indignation.

Denny quailed – though he said he did not – but then he doesn't know what quailing is, and if Denny did not quail then Oswald does not know what quailing is either.

For when Oswald took the shoe off he naturally chucked it down and gave it a kick, and a lot of little pinky yellow things rolled out. And Oswald look closer at the interesting sight. And the little things were *split peas*.

'Perhaps you'll tell me,' said the gentle knight, with the politeness of despair, 'why on earth you've played the goat like this?'

'Oh, don't be angry,' Denny said; and now his shoes were off, he curled and uncurled his toes and stopped crying. 'I *knew* pilgrims put peas in their shoes – and – oh, I wish you wouldn't laugh!'

'I'm not,' said Oswald, still with bitter politeness.

'I didn't want to tell you I was going to, because I wanted to be better than all of you, and I thought if you knew I was going to you'd want to too, and you wouldn't when I said it first. So I just put some peas in my pocket and dropped one or two at a time into my shoes when you weren't looking.'

In his secret heart Oswald said, 'Greedy young ass'. For it *is* greedy to want to have more of anything than other people, even goodness.

Outwardly Oswald said nothing.

'You see' – Denny went on – 'I do want to be good. And if pilgriming is to do you good, you ought to do it properly. I shouldn't mind being hurt in my feet if it would make me good for ever and ever. And besides, I wanted to play the game thoroughly. You always say I don't.'

The breast of the kind Oswald was touched by these last words.

'I think you're quite good enough,' he said. 'I'll fetch back the others – no, they won't laugh.'

And we all went back to Denny, and the girls made a fuss with him. But Oswald and Dicky were grave and stood aloof. They were old enough to see that being good was all very well, but after all you had to get the boy home somehow.

When they said this, as agreeably as they could, Denny said –

'It's all right – someone will give me a lift.'

'You think everything in the world can be put right with a lift,' Dicky said, and he did not speak lovingly.

'So it can,' said Denny, 'when it's your feet. I shall easily get a lift home.'

'Not here you won't,' said Alice. 'No one goes down this road; but the high road's just round the corner, where you see the telegraph wires.'

Dickie and Oswald made a sedan chair and carried Denny to the high road, and we sat down in a ditch to wait. For a long time nothing went by but a brewer's dray. We hailed it, of course, but the man was so sound asleep that our hails were vain, and none of us thought soon enough about springing like a flash to the horses' heads, though we all thought of it directly the dray was out of sight.

So we had to keep on sitting there by the dusty road, and more than one pilgrim was heard to say it wished we had never come. Oswald was not one of those who uttered this useless wish.

At last, just when despair was beginning to eat into the vital parts of even Oswald, there was a quick tap-tapping of horses' feet on the road, and a dog-cart came in sight with a lady in it all alone.

We hailed her like the desperate shipwrecked mariners in the long-boat hail the passing sail.

She pulled up. She was not a very old lady – twenty-five we found out afterwards her age was – and she looked jolly.

'Well,' she said, 'what's the matter?'

'It's this poor little boy,' Dora said, pointing to the Dentist, who had gone to sleep in the dry ditch, with his mouth open as usual. 'His feet hurt him so, and will you give him a lift?'

'But why are you all rigged out like this?' asked the lady, looking at our cockle-shells and sandals and things.

We told her.

'And how has he hurt his feet?' she asked.

And we told her that.

She looked very kind. 'Poor little chap,' she said. 'Where do you want to go?'

We told her that too. We had no concealments from this lady.

'Well,' she said, 'I have to go on to – what is its name?'

'Canterbury,' said H. O.

'Well, yes, Canterbury,' she said; 'it's only about half a mile. I'll take the poor little pilgrim – and, yes, the three girls. You boys must walk. Then we'll have tea and see the sights, and I'll drive you home – at least some of you. How will that do?'

We thanked her very much indeed, and said it would do very nicely.

Then we helped Denny into the cart, and the girls got up, and the red wheels of the cart spun away through the dust.

We hailed her like desperate,

'I wish it had been an omnibus the lady was driving,' said H. O., 'then we could all have had a ride.'

'Don't you be so discontented,' Dicky said.

And Noël said –

'You ought to be jolly thankful you haven't got to carry Denny all the way home on your back. You'd have had to if you'd been out alone with him.'

When we got to Canterbury it was much smaller than we expected, and the cathedral not much bigger than the Church that is next to the Moat House. There seemed to be only one big street, but we supposed the rest of the city was hidden away somewhere.

There was a large inn, with a green before it, and the red-wheeled dogcart was standing in the stable-

shipwrecked mariners

yard, and the lady, with Denny and the others, sitting on the benches in the porch, looking out for us. The inn was called the 'George and Dragon', and it made me think of the days when there were coaches and highwaymen and foot-pads and jolly landlords, and adventures at country inns, like you read about.

'We've ordered tea,' said the lady. 'Would you like to wash your hands?' We saw that she wished us to, so we said yes, we would. The girls and Denny were already much cleaner than when we parted from them.

There was a courtyard to the inn and a wooden staircase outside the house. We were taken up this, and washed our hands in a big room with a fourpost wooden bed and dark red hangings – just the sort of hangings that would not show the stains of gore in the dear old adventurous times.

Then we had tea in a great big room with wooden chairs and tables, very polished and old.

It was a very nice tea, with lettuces, and cold meat, and three kinds of jam, as well as cake, and new bread, which we are not allowed at home.

While tea was being had, the lady talked to us. She was very kind. There are two sorts of people in the world, besides others; one sort understand what you're driving at, and the other don't. This lady was the one sort.

After everyone had had as much to eat as they could possibly want, the lady said, 'What was it you particularly wanted to see at Canterbury?'

'The cathedral,' Alice said, 'and the place where Thomas à Becket was murdered.'

'And the Danejohn,' said Dicky.

Oswald wanted to see the walls, because he likes the Story of St Alphege and the Danes.

'Well, well,' said the lady, and she put on her hat; it was a really sensible one – not a blob of fluffy stuff and feathers put on sideways and stuck on with long pins, and no shade to your face, but almost as big as ours, with a big brim and red flowers, and black strings to tie under your chin to keep it from blowing off.

Then we went out all together to see Canterbury. Dicky and Oswald took it in turns to carry Denny on their backs. The lady called him 'The Wounded Comrade'.

We went first to the church. Oswald, whose quick brain was easily aroused to suspicions, was afraid the lady might begin talking in the church, but she did not. The church door was open. I remember mother telling us once it was right and good for churches to be left open all day, so that tired people could go in and be quiet, and say their prayers, if they wanted to. But it does not seem respectful to talk out loud in church. (*See* Note A.)

When we got outside the lady said, 'You can imagine how on the chancel steps began the mad struggle in which Becket, after hurling one of his assailants, armour and all, to the ground –'

'It would have been much cleverer,' H. O. interrupted, 'to hurl him without his armour, and leave that standing up.'

'Go on,' said Alice and Oswald, when they had given H. O. a withering glance. And the lady did go on. She told us all about Becket, and then about St Alphege, who had bones thrown at him till he died, because he wouldn't tax his poor people to please the beastly rotten Danes.

And Denny recited a piece of poetry he knows called 'The Ballad of Canterbury'.

It begins about Danish warships snake-shaped, and ends about doing as you'd be done by. It is long, but it has all the beef-bones in it, and all about St Alphege.

Then the lady showed us the Danejohn, and it was like an oast-house. And Canterbury walls that Alphege defied the Danes from looked down on a quite common farmyard. The hospital was like a barn, and other things were like other things, but we went all about and enjoyed it very much. The lady was quite amusing, besides sometimes talking like a real cathedral guide I met afterwards. (*See* Note B.) When at last we said we thought Canterbury was very small considering, the lady said –

'Well, it seemed a pity to come so far and not at least *hear* something about Canterbury.'

And then at once we knew the worst, and Alice said –

'What a horrid sell!'

But Oswald, with immediate courteousness, said –

'I don't care. You did it awfully well.'

And he did not say, though he owns he thought of it –

'I knew it all the time,' though it was a great temptation. Because really it was more than half true. He had felt from the first that this was too small for Canterbury. (*See* Note C.)

The real name of the place was Hazelbridge, and not Canterbury at all. We went to Canterbury another time. (*See* Note D.)

We were not angry with the lady for selling us about it being Canterbury, because she had really kept it up first-rate. And she asked us if we minded, very handsomely, and we said we liked it. But now we did not care how soon we got home. The lady saw this, and said –

'Come, our chariots are ready, and our horses caparisoned.'

That is a first-rate word out of a book. It cheered Oswald up, and he liked her for using it, though he wondered why she said chariots. When we got back to the inn I saw her dogcart was there, and a grocer's cart too, with B. Munn, grocer, Hazelbridge, on it. She took the girls in her cart, and the boys went with the grocer. His horse was a very good one to go, only you had to hit it with the wrong end of the whip. But the cart was very bumpety.

The evening dews were falling – at least, I suppose so, but you do not feel dew in a grocer's cart – when we reached home. We all thanked the lady very much, and said we hoped we should see her again some day. She said she hoped so.

The grocer drove off, and when we had all shaken hands with the lady and kissed her, according as we were boys or girls, or little boys, she touched up her horse and drove away.

She turned at the corner to wave to us, and just as we had done waving, and were turning into the house, Albert's uncle came into our midst like a whirling wind. He was in flannels, and his shirt had no stud in at the neck, and his hair was all rumpled up and his hands were inky, and we knew he had left off in the middle of a chapter by the wildness of his eye.

'Who was that lady?' he said. 'Where did you meet her?'

Mindful, as ever, of what he was told, Oswald began to tell the story from the beginning.

'The other day, protector of the poor,' he began, 'Dora and I were reading about the Canterbury pilgrims. . . .'

Oswald thought Albert's uncle would be pleased to find his instructions about beginning at the beginning had borne fruit, but instead he interrupted.

'Stow it, you young duffer! Where did you meet her?'

Oswald answered briefly, in wounded accents, 'Hazelbridge.'

Then Albert's uncle rushed upstairs three at a time, and as he went he called out to Oswald –

'Get out my bike, old man, and blow up the back tyre.'

I am sure Oswald was as quick as anyone could have been, but long ere the tyre was thoroughly blowed Albert's uncle appeared, with a collar-stud and tie and blazer, and his hair tidy, and wrenching the unoffending machine from Oswald's surprised fingers.

Albert's uncle finished pumping up the tyre, and then flinging himself into the saddle he set off, scorching down the road at a pace not surpassed by any highwayman, however black and high-mettled his steed.

We were left looking at each other.

'He must have recognized her,' Dicky said.

'Perhaps,' Noël said, 'she is the old nurse who alone knows the dark secret of his highborn birth.'

'Not old enough, by chalks,' Oswald said.

'I shouldn't wonder,' said Alice, 'if she holds the secret of the will that will make him rolling in long-lost wealth.'

'I wonder if he'll catch her,' Noël said. 'I'm quite certain all his future depends on it. Perhaps she's his long-lost sister, and the estate was left to them equally, only she couldn't be found, so it couldn't be shared up.'

'Perhaps he's only in love with her,' Dora said; 'parted by cruel Fate at an early age, he has ranged the wide world ever since trying to find her.'

'I hope to goodness he hasn't – anyway, he's not ranged since we knew him – never further than Hastings,' Oswald said. 'We don't want any of that rot.'

'What rot?' Daisy asked.

And Oswald said –

'Getting married, and all that sort of rubbish.'

And Daisy and Dora were the only ones that didn't agree with him. Even Alice owned that being bridesmaids must be fairly good fun. It's no good. You may treat girls as well as you like, and give them every comfort and luxury, and play fair just as if they were boys, but there is something unmanly about the best of girls. They go silly, like milk goes sour, without any warning.

When Albert's uncle returned he was very hot, with a beaded brow, but pale as the Dentist when the peas were at their worst.

'Did you catch her?' H. O. asked.

Albert's uncle's brow looked black as the cloud that thunder will presently break from.

'No,' he said.

'Is she your long-lost nurse?' H. O. went on, before we could stop him.

'Long-lost grandmother! I knew the lady long ago in India,' said Albert's uncle, as he left the room, slamming the door in a way we should be forbidden to.

And that was the end of the Canterbury Pilgrimage.

As for the lady, we did not then know whether she was his long-lost grandmother that he had known in India or not, though we thought she seemed youngish for the part. We found out afterwards whether she was or not, but that comes in another part. His manner was not the one that makes you go on asking questions.

The Canterbury Pilgriming did not exactly make us good, but then, as Dora said, we had not done anything wrong that day. So we were twenty-four hours to the good.

Note A. – Afterwards we went and saw real Canterbury. It is very large. A disagreeable man showed us round the cathedral, and jawed all the time quite loud as if it wasn't a church. I remember one thing he said. It was this:

'This is the Dean's Chapel; it·was the Lady Chapel in the wicked days when people used to worship the Virgin Mary.'

And H. O. said, 'I suppose they worship the Dean now?'

Some strange people who were there laughed out loud. I think this is worse in church than not taking your cap off when you come in, as H. O. forgot to do, because the cathedral was so big he didn't think it was a church.

Note B. (See *Note C.*)
Note C. (See *Note D.*)
Note D. (See *Note E.*)
Note E. (See *Note A.*)

This ends the Canterbury Pilgrims.

THE DRAGON'S TEETH; OR, ARMY-SEED

ALBERT'S uncle was out on his bicycle as usual. After the day when we became Canterbury Pilgrims and were brought home in the dog-cart with red wheels by the lady he told us was his long-lost grandmother he had known years ago in India, he spent not nearly so much of his time in writing, and he used to shave every morning instead of only when requisite, as in earlier days. And he was always going out on his bicycle in his new Norfolk suit. We are not so unobserving as grown-up people make out. We knew well enough he was looking for the long-lost. And we jolly well wished he might find her. Oswald, always full of sympathy with misfortune, however undeserved, had himself tried several times to find the lady. So had the others. But all this is what they call a digression; it has nothing to do with the dragon's teeth I am now narrating.

It began with the pig dying - it was the one we had for the circus, but it having behaved so badly that day had nothing to do with its illness and death, though the girls said they felt remorse, and perhaps if we hadn't made it run so that day it might have been spared to us. But Oswald cannot pretend that people were right just because they happen to be dead, and as long as that pig was alive we all knew well enough that it was it that made us run - and not us it.

The pig was buried in the kitchen garden. Bill, that

we made the tombstone for, dug the grave, and while he was away at his dinner we took a turn at digging, because we like to be useful, and besides, when you dig you never know what you may turn up. I knew a man once that found a gold ring on the point of his fork when he was digging potatoes, and you know how we found two half-crowns ourselves once when we were digging for treasure.

Oswald was taking his turn with the spade, and the others were sitting on the gravel and telling him how to do it.

'Work with a will,' Dicky said, yawning.

Alice said, 'I wish we were in a book. People in books never dig without finding something. I think I'd rather it was a secret passage than anything.'

Oswald stopped to wipe his honest brow ere replying.

'A secret's nothing when you've found it out. Look at the secret staircase. It's no good, not even for hide-and-seek, because of its squeaking. I'd rather have the pot of gold we used to dig for when we were little.' It was really only last year, but you seem to grow old very quickly after you have once passed the prime of your youth, which is at ten, I believe.

'How would you like to find the mouldering bones of Royalist soldiers foully done to death by nasty Iron-sides?' Noël asked, with his mouth full of plum.

'If they were really dead it wouldn't matter,' Dora said. 'What I'm afraid of is a skeleton that can walk about and catch at your legs when you're going upstairs to bed.'

'Skeletons can't walk,' Alice said in a hurry; 'you know they can't, Dora.'

And she glared at Dora till she made her sorry she had said what she had. The things you are frightened of, or even those you would rather not meet in the dark, should never be mentioned before the little ones, or else they cry when it comes to bed-time, and say it was because of what you said.

'We shan't find anything. No jolly fear,' said Dicky.

And just then my spade I was digging with struck on something hard, and it felt hollow. I did really think for one joyful space that we had found that pot of gold. But the thing, whatever it was, seemed to be longish; longer, that is, than a pot of gold would naturally be. And as I uncovered it I saw that it was not at all pot-of-gold-colour, but like a bone Pincher has buried. So Oswald said –

'It *is* the skeleton.'

The girls all drew back, and Alice said, 'Oswald, I wish you wouldn't.'

A moment later the discovery was unearthed, and Oswald lifted it up, with both hands.

'It's a dragon's head,' Noël said, and it certainly looked like it. It was long and narrowish and bony, and with great yellow teeth sticking in the jaw.

Bill came back just then and said it was a horse's head, but H. O. and Noël would not believe it, and Oswald owns that no horse he has ever seen had a head at all that shape.

But Oswald did not stop to argue, because he saw a keeper who showed me how to set snares going by, and he wanted to talk to him about ferrets, so he went off and Dicky and Denny and Alice with him. Also Daisy and Dora went off to finish reading *Ministering Children*. So H. O. and Noël were left with the bony head. They took it away.

The incident had quite faded from the mind of Oswald next day. But just before breakfast Noël and H. O. came in, looking hot and anxious. They had got up early and had not washed at all – not even their hands and faces. Noël made Oswald a secret signal. All the others saw it, and with proper delicate feeling pretended not to have.

When Oswald had gone out with Noël and H. O. in obedience to the secret signal, Noël said –

'You know that dragon's head yesterday?'

'Well?' Oswald said quickly, but not crossly the two things are quite different.

'Well, you know what happened in Greek history when some chap sowed dragon's teeth?'

'They came up armed men,' said H. O., but Noël sternly bade him shut up, and Oswald said 'Well,' again. If he spoke impatiently it was because he smelt the bacon being taken in to breakfast.

'Well,' Noël went on, 'what do you suppose would have come up if we'd sowed those dragon's teeth we found yesterday?'

'Why, nothing, you young duffer,' said Oswald, who could now smell the coffee. 'All that isn't History – it's Humbug. Come on in to brekker.'

'It's *not* humbug,' H. O. cried, 'it *is* history. We *did* sow – '

'Shut up,' said Noël again. 'Look here, Oswald. We did sow those dragon's teeth in Randall's ten-acre meadow, and what do you think has come up?'

'Toadstools I should think,' was Oswald's contemptible rejoinder.

'They have come up a camp of soldiers,' said Noël – '*armed men*. So you see it *was* history. We have sowed army-seed, just like Cadmus, and it has come up. It was a very wet night. I daresay that helped it along.'

Oswald could not decide which to disbelieve – his brother or his ears. So, disguising his doubtful emotions without a word, he led the way to the bacon and the banqueting hall.

He said nothing about the army-seed then, neither did Noël and H. O. But after the bacon we went into the garden, and then the good elder brother said –

'Why don't you tell the others your cock-and-bull story?'

So they did, and their story was received with warm expressions of doubt. It was Dicky who observed –

'Let's go and have a squint at Randall's ten-acre, anyhow. I saw a hare there the other day.'

We went. It is some little way, and as we went, disbelief reigned superb in every breast except Noël's and H. O.'s, so you will see that even the ready pen of the present author cannot be expected to describe to you his variable sensations when he got to the top of the hill and suddenly saw that his little brothers had spoken the truth. I do not mean that they generally tell lies, but people make mistakes sometimes, and the effect is the same as lies if you believe them.

There *was* a camp there with real tents and soldiers in grey and red tunics. I daresay the girls would have said coats. We stood in ambush, too astonished even to think of lying in it, though of course we know that this is customary. The ambush was the wood on top of the little hill, between Randall's ten-acre meadow and Sugden's Waste Wake pasture.

'There would be cover here for a couple of regiments,' whispered Oswald, who was, I think, gifted by Fate with the far-seeingness of a born general.

Alice merely said 'Hist', and we went down to mingle with the troops as though by accident, and seek for information.

The first man we came to at the edge of the camp was cleaning a sort of cauldron thing like witches brew bats in.

We went up to him and said, 'Who are you? Are you English, or are you the enemy?'

'We're the enemy,' he said, and he did not seem ashamed of being what he was. And he spoke English with quite a good accent for a foreigner.

'The enemy!' Oswald echoed in shocked tones. It is a terrible thing to a loyal and patriotic youth to see an enemy cleaning a pot in an English field, with English sand, and looking as much at home as if he was in his foreign fastnesses.

The enemy seemed to read Oswald's thoughts with deadly unerringness. He said –

'The English are somewhere over on the other side of the hill. They are trying to keep us out of Maidstone.'

After this our plan of mingling with the troops did not seem worth going on with. This soldier, in spite of his unerringness in reading Oswald's innermost heart, seemed not so very sharp in other things, or he would never have given away his secret plans like this, for he must have known from our accents that we were Britons to the backbone. Or perhaps (Oswald thought this, and it made his blood at once boil and freeze, which our uncle had told us was possible, but only in India), perhaps he thought that Maidstone was already as good as taken and it didn't matter what he said. While Oswald was debating within his intellect what to say next, and how to say it so as to discover as many as possible of the enemy's dark secrets, Noël said –

'How did you get here? You weren't here yesterday at tea-time.'

The soldier gave the pot another sandy rub, and said –

'I daresay it does seem quick work – the camp seems as if it had sprung up in the night, doesn't it? – like a mushroom.'

Alice and Oswald looked at each other, and then at

He spoke English with quite a good accent for a foreigner

the rest of us. The words '*sprung up in the night*' seemed to touch a string in every heart.

'You see,' whispered Noël, 'he won't tell us how he came here. *Now*, is it humbug or history?'

Oswald, after whisperedly requesting his young brother to dry up and not bother, remarked, 'Then you're an invading army?'

'Well,' said the soldier, 'we're a skeleton battalion, as a matter of fact, but we're invading all right enough.'

And now indeed the blood of the stupidest of us froze, just as the quick-witted Oswald's had done earlier in the interview. Even H. O. opened his mouth and went the colour of mottled soap; he is so fat that this is the nearest he can go to turning pale.

Denny said, 'But you don't look like skeletons.'

The soldier stared, then he laughed and said, 'Ah, that's the padding in our tunics. You should see us in the grey dawn taking our morning bath in a bucket.'

It was a dreadful picture for the imagination. A skeleton, with its bones all loose most likely, bathing anyhow in a pail. There was a silence while we thought it over.

Now, ever since the cleaning-cauldron soldier had said that about taking Maidstone, Alice had kept on pulling at Oswald's jacket behind, and he had kept on not taking any notice. But now he could not stand it any longer, so he said –

'Well, what is it?'

Alice drew him aside, or rather, she pulled at his jacket so that he nearly fell over backwards, and then she whispered, 'Come along, don't stay parleying with the foe. He's only talking to you to gain time.'

'What for?' said Oswald.

'Why, so that we shouldn't warn the other army, you silly,' Alice said, and Oswald was so upset by what she said, that he forgot to be properly angry with her for the wrong word she used.

'But we ought to warn them at home,' she said; 'suppose the Moat House was burned down, and all the supplies commandeered for the foe?'

Alice turned boldly to the soldier. '*Do* you burn down farms?' she asked.

'Well, not as a rule,' he said, and he had the cheek to wink at Oswald, but Oswald would not look at him. 'We've not burned a farm since – oh, not for years.'

'A farm in Greek history it was, I expect,' Denny murmured.

'Civilized warriors do not burn farms nowadays,' Alice said sternly, 'whatever they did in Greek times. You ought to know that.'

The soldier said things had changed a good deal since Greek times. So we said good morning as quickly as we could: it is proper to be polite even to your enemy, except just at the moments when it has really come to rifles and bayonets or other weapons.

The soldier said 'So long!' in quite a modern voice, and we retraced our footsteps in silence to the ambush – I mean the wood. Oswald did think of lying in the ambush then, but it was rather wet, because of the rain the night before, that H. O. said had brought the army-seed up. And Alice walked very fast, saying nothing but 'Hurry up, can't you!' and dragging H. O. by one hand and Noël by the other. So we got into the road.

Then Alice faced round and said, 'This is all our fault. If we hadn't sowed those dragon's teeth there wouldn't have been any invading army.'

I am sorry to say Daisy said, 'Never mind, Alice, dear. *We* didn't sow the nasty things, did we, Dora?'

But Denny told her it was just the same. It was *we* had done it, so long as it was any of us, especially if it got any of us into trouble. Oswald was very pleased to see that the Dentist was beginning to understand the meaning of true manliness, and about the honour of the house of Bastable, though of course he is only a Foulkes. Yet it is something to know he does his best to learn.

If you are very grown-up, or very clever, I daresay you will now have thought of a great many things. If you have you need not say anything, especially if you're reading this aloud to anybody. It's no good putting in what you think in this part, because none of us thought anything of the kind at the time.

We simply stood in the road without any of your clever thoughts, filled with shame and distress to think of what might happen owing to the dragon's teeth being sown. It was a lesson to us never to sow seed without being quite sure what sort it is. This is particularly true of the penny packets, which sometimes do not come up at all, quite unlike dragon's teeth.

Of course H. O. and Noël were more unhappy than the rest of us. This was only fair.

'How can we possibly prevent their getting to Maidstone?' Dickie said. 'Did you notice the red cuffs on their uniforms? Taken from the bodies of dead English soldiers, I shouldn't wonder.'

'If they're the old Greek kind of dragon's-teeth soldiers, they ought to fight each other to death,' Noël said; 'at least, if we had a helmet to throw among them.'

But none of us had, and it was decided that it would be of no use for H. O. to go back and throw his straw hat at them, though he wanted to.

Denny said suddenly –

'Couldn't we alter the sign-posts, so that they wouldn't know the way to Maidstone?'

Oswald saw that this was the time for true generalship to be shown. He said –

'Fetch all the tools out of your chest – Dicky go too, there's a good chap, and don't let him cut his legs with the saw.' He did once, tumbling over it. 'Meet us at the cross-roads, you know, where we had the Benevolent Bar. Courage and dispatch, and look sharp about it.'

When they had gone we hastened to the crossroads, and there a great idea occurred to Oswald. He used the forces at his command so ably that in a very short time the board in the field which says 'No thoroughfare. Trespassers will be prosecuted' was set up in the middle of the road to Maidstone. We put stones, from a heap by the road, behind it to make is stand up.

Then Dicky and Denny came back, and Dicky shinned up the sign-post and sawed off the two arms, and we nailed them up wrong, so that it said 'To Maidstone' on the Dover Road, and 'To Dover' on the road to Maidstone. We decided to leave the Trespassers board on the real Maidstone road, as an extra guard.

Then we settled to start at once to warn Maidstone.

Some of us did not want the girls to go, but it would have been unkind to say so. However, there was at least one breast that felt a pang of joy when Dora and Daisy gave out that they would rather stay where they were and tell anybody who came by which was the real road.

'Because it would be so dreadful if someone was going to buy pigs or fetch a doctor or anything in a hurry and then found they had got to Dover instead of where they wanted to go to,' Dora said. But when it came to dinner-time they went home, so that they were entirely out of it. This often happens to them by some strange fatalism.

We left Martha to take care of the two girls, and Lady and Pincher went with us. It was getting late in the day, but I am bound to remember no one said anything about their dinners, whatever they may have 'ght. We cannot always help our thoughts. We happened to know it was roast rabbits and currant jelly that day.

We walked two and two, and sang the 'British Grenadiers' and 'Soldiers of the Queen' so as to be as much part of the British Army as possible. The Cauldron-Man had said the English were the other side of the hill. But we could not see any scarlet anywhere, though we looked for it as carefully as if we had been fierce bulls.

But suddenly we went round a turn in the road and came plump into a lot of soldiers. Only they were not red-coats. They were dressed in grey and silver. And it was a sort of furzy-common place, and three roads branching out. The men were lying about, with some of their belts undone, smoking pipes and cigarettes.

'It's not British soldiers,' Alice said. 'Oh dear, oh dear, I'm afraid it's more enemy. You didn't sow the army-seed anywhere else, did you, H. O. dear?'

H. O. was positive he hadn't. 'But perhaps lots more came up where we did sow them,' he said; 'they're all over England by now very likely. *I* don't know how many men can grow out of one dragon's tooth.'

Then Noël said, 'It was my doing anyhow, and I'm not afraid,' and he walked straight up to the nearest soldier, who was cleaning his pipe with a piece of grass, and said –

'Please, are you the enemy?' The man said –

'No, young Commander-in-Chief, we're the English.'
Then Oswald took command.

'Where is the General?' he said.

'We're out of generals just now, Field-Marshal,' the man said, and his voice was a gentleman's voice. 'Not a single one in stock. We might suit you in majors now – and captains are quite cheap. Competent corporals going for a song. And we have a very nice colonel, too – quiet to ride or drive.'

Oswald does not mind chaff at proper times. But this was not one.

'You seem to be taking it very easy,' he said with disdainful expression.

'This *is* an easy,' said the grey soldier, sucking at his pipe to see if it would draw.

'I suppose *you* don't care if the enemy gets into Maidstone or not!' exclaimed Oswald bitterly. 'If I were a soldier I'd rather die than be beaten.'

The soldier saluted. 'Good old patriotic sentiment,' he said, smiling at the heart-felt boy. But Oswald could bear no more.

'Which is the Colonel?' he asked.

'Over there – near the grey horse.'

'The one lighting a cigarette?' H. O. asked.

'Yes – but I say, kiddie, he won't stand any jaw. There's not an ounce of vice about him, but he's peppery. He might kick out. You'd better bunk.'

'Better what?' asked H. O.

'Bunk, bottle, scoot, skip, vanish, exit,' said the soldier.

'That's what you'd do when the fighting begins,' said H. O. He is often rude like that – but it was what we all thought, all the same. The soldier only laughed.

A spirited but hasty altercation among ourselves in whispers ended in our allowing Alice to be the one to speak to the Colonel. It was she who wanted to. 'However peppery he is he won't kick a girl,' she said, and perhaps this was true.

But of course we all went with her. So there were six of us to stand in front of the Colonel. And as we went along we agreed that we would salute him on the word three. So when we got near, Dick said, 'One, two, three', and we all saluted very well – except H. O., who chose that minute to trip over a rifle a soldier had left lying about, and was only saved from falling by a man in a cocked hat who caught him deftly by the back of his jacket and stood him on his legs.

'Let go, can't you,' said H. O. 'Are you the General?'

Before the Cocked Hat had time to frame a reply, Alice spoke to the Colonel. I knew what she meant to say, because she had told me as we threaded our way among the resting soldiery. What she really said was –

'Oh, how *can* you!'

'How can I *what*?' said the Colonel, rather crossly.

'Why, *smoke*?' said Alice.

'My good children, if you're an infant Band of Hope, let me recommend you to play in some other backyard,' said the Cock-Hatted Man.

H. O. said, 'Band of Hope yourself' – but no one noticed it.

'We're *not* a Band of Hope,' said Noël. 'We're British, and the man over there told us you are. And Maidstone's in danger, and the enemy not a mile off, and you stand *smoking*.' Noël was standing crying, himself, or something very like it.

'It's quite true,' Alice said.

The Colonel said, 'Fiddle-de-dee.'

But the Cocked-Hatted Man said, 'What was the enemy like?'

We told him exactly. And even the Colonel then owned there might be something in it.

'Can you show me the place where they are on the map?' he asked.

'Not on the map, we can't,' said Dicky; 'at least, I don't think so, but on the ground we could. We could take you there in a quarter of an hour.'

The Cocked-Hatted One looked at the Colonel, who returned his scrutiny, then he shrugged his shoulders.

'Well, we've got to do something,' he said, as if to himself. 'Lead on, Macduff!'

The Colonel roused his soldiery from their stupor of pipes by words of command which the present author is sorry he can't remember.

Then he bade us boys lead the way. I tell you it felt fine, marching at the head of a regiment. Alice got a lift on the Cocked-Hatted One's horse. It was a red-roan steed of might, exactly as if it had been in a ballad. They call a grey-roan a 'blue' in South Africa, the Cocked-Hatted One said.

We led the British Army by unfrequented lanes till we got to the gate of Sugden's Waste Wake pasture. Then the Colonel called a whispered halt, and choosing two of us to guide him, the dauntless and discerning commander went on, on foot, with an orderly. He chose Dicky and Oswald as guides. So we led him to the ambush, and we went through it as quietly as we could. But twigs do crackle and snap so when you are reconnoitring, or anxious to escape detection for whatever reason.

Our Colonel's orderly crackled most. If you're not near enough to tell a colonel by the crown and stars on his shoulder-strap, you can tell him by the orderly behind him, like 'follow my leader'.

'Look out!' said Oswald in a low but commanding

whisper, 'the camp's down in that field. You can see if you take a squint through this gap.'

The speaker took a squint himself as he spoke, and drew back, baffled beyond the power of speech. While he was struggling with his baffledness the British Colonel had his squint. He also drew back, and said a word that he must have known was not right – at least when he was a boy.

'I don't care,' said Oswald, 'they were there this morning. White tents like mushrooms, and an enemy cleaning a cauldron.'

'With sand,' said Dicky.

'That's most convincing,' said the Colonel, and I did not like the way he said it.

'I say,' Oswald said, 'let's get to the top corner of the ambush – the wood, I mean. You can see the cross-roads from there.'

We did, and quickly, for the crackling of branches no longer dismayed our almost despairing spirits.

We came to the edge of the wood, and Oswald's patriotic heart really did give a jump, and he cried, 'There they are, on the Dover Road.'

Our miscellaneous signboard had done its work.

'By Jove, young un, you're right! And in quarter column, too! We've got em on toast – on toast – egad!'

I never heard anyone not in a book say 'egad' before, so I saw something really out of the way was indeed up.

The Colonel was a man of prompt and decisive action. He sent the orderly to tell the Major to advance two companies on the left flank and take cover. Then we led him back through the wood the nearest way, because he said he must rejoin the main body at once. We found the main body very friendly with Noël and H. O. and the others, and Alice was talking to the Cocked-Hatted One as if she had known him all her life. 'I think he's a general in disguise,' Noël said. 'He's been giving us chocolate out of a pocket in his saddle.' Oswald thought about the roast rabbit then – and he is not ashamed to own it – yet he did not say a word. But Alice is really not a bad sort. She had saved two bars of chocolate for him and Dicky. Even in war girls can sometimes be useful in their humble way.

The Colonel fussed about and said, 'Take cover there!' and everybody hid in the ditch, and the horses and the Cocked Hat, with Alice, retreated down the road out of sight. We were in the ditch too. It was muddy – but nobody thought of their boots in that perilous moment. It seemed a long time we were crouching there. Oswald began to feel the water squelching in his boots, so we held our breath and listened. Oswald laid his ear to the road like a Red Indian. You would not do this in time of peace, but when your country is in danger you care but little about keeping your ears clean. His backwoods' strategy was successful. He rose and dusted himself and said –

'They're coming!'

It was true. The footsteps of the approaching foe were now to be heard quite audibly, even by ears in their natural position. The wicked enemy approached. They were marching with a careless swaggeringness that showed how little they suspected the horrible doom which was about to teach them England's might and supremeness. Just as the enemy turned the corner so that we could see them, the Colonel shouted –

'Right section, fire!' and there was a deafening banging.

The enemy's officer said something, and then the enemy got confused and tried to get into the fields through the hedges. But all was vain. There was firing now from our men, on the left as well as the right. And then our Colonel strode nobly up to the enemy's Colonel and demanded surrender. He told me so afterwards. His exact words are only known to himself and the other Colonel. But the enemy's Colonel said, 'I would rather die than surrender,' or words to that effect.

Our Colonel returned to his men and gave the order to fix bayonets, and even Oswald felt his manly cheek turn pale at the thought of the amount of blood to be shed. What would have happened can never now be revealed. For at this moment a man on a piebald horse came clattering over a hedge – as carelessly as if the air was not full of lead and steel at all. Another man rode behind him with a lance and a red pennon on it. I think he must have been the enemy's General coming to tell his men not to throw away their lives on a forlorn hope, for directly he said they were captured the enemy gave in and owned that they were. The enemy's Colonel saluted and ordered his men to form quarter column again. I should have thought he would have had about enough of that myself.

He had now given up all thought of sullen resistance to the bitter end. He rolled a cigarette for himself, and had the foreign cheek to say to our Colonel –

'By Jove, old man, you got me clean that time! Your scouts seem to have marked us down uncommonly neatly.'

It was a proud moment when our Colonel laid his military hand on Oswald's shoulder and said –

'This is my chief scout,' which were high words, but not undeserved, and Oswald owns he felt red with gratifying pride when he heard them.

'So you are the traitor, young man,' said the wicked Colonel, going on with his cheek.

Oswald bore it because our Colonel had, and you

should be generous to a fallen foe, but it is hard to be called a traitor when you haven't.

He did not treat the wicked Colonel with silent scorn as he might have done, but he said –

'We aren't traitors. We are the Bastables and one of us is a Foulkes. We only mingled unsuspected with the enemy's soldiery and learned the secrets of their acts, which is what Baden-Powell always does when the natives rebel in South Africa; and Denis Foulkes thought of altering the sign-posts to lead the foe astray. And if we did cause all this fighting, and get Maidstone threatened with capture and all that, it was only because we didn't believe Greek things could happen in Great Britain and Ireland, even if you sow dragon's teeth, and besides, some of us were not asked about sowing them.'

Then the Cocked-Hatted One led his horse and walked with us and made us tell him all about it, and so did the Colonel. The wicked Colonel listened too, which was only another proof of his cheek.

And Oswald told the tale in the modest yet manly way that some people think he has, and gave the others all the credit they deserved. His narration was interrupted no less than four times by shouts of 'Bravo!' in which the enemy's Colonel once more showed his cheek by joining. By the time the story was told we were in sight of another camp. It was the British one this time. The Colonel asked us to have tea in his tent, and it only shows the magnanimosity of English chivalry in the field of battle that he asked the enemy's Colonel too. With his usual cheek he accepted. We were jolly hungry.

When everyone had had as much tea as they possibly could, the Colonel shook hands with us all, and to Oswald he said –

'Well, good-bye, my brave scout. I must mention your name in my dispatches to the War Office.'

H. O. interrupted him to say, 'His name's Oswald Cecil Bastable, and mine is Horace Octavius.' I wish H. O. would learn to hold his tongue. No one ever knows Oswald was christened Cecil as well, if he can possibly help it. *You* didn't know it till now.

'Mr Oswald Bastable,' the Colonel went on – he had the decency not to take any notice of the 'Cecil' – 'you would be a credit to any regiment. No doubt the War Office will reward you properly for what you have done for your country. But meantime, perhaps, you'll accept five shillings from a grateful comrade-in-arms.'

Oswald felt heart-felt sorry to wound the good Colonel's feelings, but he had to remark that he had only done his duty, and he was sure no British scout would take five bob for doing that. 'And besides,' he said, with that feeling of justice which is part of his young character, 'it was the others just as much as me.'

'Your sentiments, sir,' said the Colonel, who was one of the politest and most discerning colonels I ever saw, 'your sentiments do you honour. But, Bastables all, and – and non-Bastables' (he couldn't remember Foulkes; it's not such an interesting name as Bastable, of course) – 'at least you'll accept a soldier's pay?'

'Lucky to touch it, a shilling a day!' Alice and Denny said together. And the Cocked-Hatted Man said something about knowing your own mind and knowing your own Kipling.

'A soldier,' said the Colonel, 'would certainly be lucky to touch it. You see there are deductions for rations. Five shillings is exactly right, deducting twopence each for six teas.'

This seemed cheap for the three cups of tea and the

three eggs and all the strawberry jam and bread-and-butter Oswald had had, as well as what the others ate, and Lady's and Pincher's teas, but I suppose soldiers get things cheaper than civilians, which is only right.

Oswald took the five shillings then, there being no longer any scruples why he should not.

Just as we had parted from the brave Colonel and the rest we saw a bicycle coming. It was Albert's uncle. He got off and said –

'What on earth have you been up to? What were you doing with those volunteers?'

We told him the wild adventures of the day, and he listened, and then he said he would withdraw the word volunteers if we liked.

But the seeds of doubt were sown in the breast of Oswald. He was now almost sure that we had made jolly fools of ourselves without a moment's pause throughout the whole of this eventful day. He said nothing at the time, but after supper he had it out with Albert's uncle about the word which had been withdrawn.

Albert's uncle said, of course, no one could be sure that the dragon's teeth hadn't come up in the good old-fashioned way, but that, on the other hand, it was barely possible that both the British and the enemy were only volunteers having a field-day or sham fight, and he rather thought the Cocked-Hatted Man was not a general, but a doctor. And the man with a red pennon carried behind him *might* have been the umpire.

Oswald never told the others a word of this. Their young breasts were all panting with joy because they had saved their country; and it would have been but heartless unkindness to show them how silly they had been. Besides, Oswald felt he was much too old to have been so taken in – if he *had* been. Besides, Albert's uncle did say that no one could be sure about the dragon's teeth.

The thing that makes Oswald feel most that, perhaps, the whole thing was a beastly sell, was that we didn't see any wounded. But he tries not to think of this. And if he goes into the army when he grows up, he will not go quite green. He has had experience of the arts of war and the tented field. And a real colonel has called him 'Comrade-in-Arms', which is exactly what Lord Roberts called his own soldiers when he wrote home about them.

ALBERT'S UNCLE'S GRANDMOTHER;
OR, THE LONG-LOST

THE shadow of the termination now descended in sable thunder-clouds upon our devoted nobs. As Albert's uncle said, 'School now gaped for its prey'. In a very short space of time we should be wending our way back to Blackheath, and all the variegated delightfulness of the country would soon be only preserved in memory's faded flowers. (I don't care for that way of writing very much. It would be an awful swot to keep it up – looking out the words and all that.)

To speak in the language of everyday life, our holiday was jolly nearly up. We had had a ripping time, but it was all but over. We really did feel sorry – though, of course, it was rather decent to think of getting back to Father and being able to tell the other chaps about our raft, and the dam, and the Tower of Mystery, and things like that.

When but a brief time was left to us, Oswald and Dicky met by chance in an apple-tree. (That sounds like 'consequences', but it is mere truthfulness.) Dicky said –

'Only four more days.' Oswald said, 'Yes.'

'There's one thing,' Dickie said, 'that beastly society. We don't want that swarming all over everything when we get home. We ought to dissolve it before we leave here.'

The following dialogue now took place:

473

Oswald – 'Right you are. I always said it was piffling hot.'

Dicky – 'So did I.'

Oswald – 'Let's call a council. But don't forget we've jolly well got to put our foot down.'

Dicky assented, and the dialogue concluded with apples.

The council, when called, was in but low spirits. This made Oswald's and Dicky's task easier. When people are sunk in gloomy despair about one thing, they will agree to almost anything about something else. (Remarks like this are called philosophic generalizations, Albert's uncle says.) Oswald began by saying –

'We've tried the society for being good in, and perhaps it's done us good. But now the time has come for each of us to be good or bad on his own, without hanging on to the others.'

> '*The race is run by one and one,*
> *But never by two and two,*'

the Dentist said. The others said nothing. Oswald went on: 'I move that we chuck – I mean dissolve – the Wouldbegoods Society; its appointed task is done. If it's not well done, that's *its* fault and not ours.'

Dicky said, 'Hear! hear! I second this prop.'

The unexpected Dentist said, 'I third it. At first I thought it would help, but afterwards I saw it only made you want to be naughty, just because you were a Wouldbegood.'

Oswald owns he was surprised. We put it to the vote at once, so as not to let Denny cool. H. O. and Noël and Alice voted with us, so Daisy and Dora were what is called a hopeless minority. We tried to cheer their hopelessness by letting them read the things out of the Golden Deed book aloud. Noël hid his face in the straw so that we should not see the faces he made while he made poetry instead of listening, and when the Wouldbegoods was by vote dissolved for ever he sat up, straws in his hair, and said –

'THE EPITAPH

> The Wouldbegoods are dead and gone
> But not the golden deeds they have done
> These will remain upon Glory's page
> To be an example to every age,
> And by this we have got to know
> How to be good upon our ow – N.

N is for Noël, that makes the rhyme and the sense both right. O, W, N, own; do you see?'

We saw it, and said so, and the gentle poet was satisfied. And the council broke up. Oswald felt that a weight had been lifted from his expanding chest, and it is curious that he never felt so inclined to be good and a model youth as he did then.

As he went down the ladder out of the loft he said –

'There's one thing we ought to do, though, before we go home. We ought to find Albert's uncle's long-lost grandmother for him.'

Alice's heart beat true and steadfast. She said, 'That's just exactly what Noël and I were saying this morning. Look out, Oswald, you wretch, you're kicking chaff into my eyes.' She was going down the ladder just under me.

Oswald's younger sister's thoughtful remark ended in another council. But not in the straw loft. We decided to have a quite new place, and disregarded H. O.'s idea of the dairy and Noël's of the cellars. We had the new council on the secret staircase, and there we settled exactly what we ought to do. This is the same thing, if you really wish to be good, as what you are going to do. It was a very interesting council, and when it was over Oswald was so pleased to think that the Would-begoods was unrecoverishly dead that he gave Denny and Noël, who were sitting on the step below him, a good-humoured, playful, gentle, loving, brotherly shove, and said, 'Get along down, it's tea-time!'

No reader who understands justice and the real rightness of things, and who is to blame for what, will ever think it could have been Oswald's fault that the two other boys got along down by rolling over and over each other, and bursting the door at the bottom of the stairs open by their revolving bodies. And I should like to know whose fault it was that Mrs Pettigrew was just on the other side of that door at that very minute? The door burst open, and the im-petuous bodies of Noël and Denny rolled out of it into Mrs Pettigrew, and upset her and the tea-tray. Both revolving boys were soaked with tea and milk, and there were one or two cups and things smashed. Mrs Pettigrew was knocked over, but none of her bones were broken. Noël and Denny were going to be sent to bed, but Oswald said it was all his fault. He really did this to give the others a chance of doing a refined golden deed by speaking the truth and saying it was *not* his fault. But you cannot really count on anyone. They did not say anything, but only rubbed the lumps on their late-revolving heads. So it was bed for Oswald, and he felt the injustice hard.

But he sat up in bed and read *The Last of the Mohicans*, and then he began to think. When Oswald really thinks he almost always thinks of something. He thought of something now, and it was miles better than the idea we had decided on in the secret staircase, of advertising in the *Kentish Mercury* and saying if Albert's uncle's long-lost grandmother would call at the Moat

House she might hear of something much to her advantage.

What Oswald thought of was that if we went to Hazelbridge and asked Mr B. Munn, Grocer, that drove us home in the cart with the horse that liked the wrong end of the whip best, he would know who the lady was in the red hat and red wheels that paid him to drive us home that Canterbury night. He must have been paid, of course, for even grocers are not generous enough to drive perfect strangers, and five of them too, about the country for nothing.

Thus we may learn that even unjustness and sending the wrong people to bed may bear useful fruit, which ought to be a great comfort to everyone when they are unfairly treated. Only it most likely won't be. For if Oswald's brothers and sisters had nobly stood by him as he expected, he would not have had the solitudy reflections that led to the great scheme for finding the grandmother.

Of course when the others came up to roost they all came and squatted on Oswald's bed and said how sorry they were. He waived their apologies with noble dignity, because there wasn't much time, and said he had an idea that would knock the council's plan into a cocked hat. But he would not tell them what it was. He made them wait till next morning. This was not sulks, but kind feeling. He wanted them to have something else to think of besides the way they hadn't stood by him in the bursting of the secret staircase door and the tea-tray and the milk.

Next morning Oswald kindly explained, and asked who would volunteer for a forced march to Hazel-bridge. The word volunteer cost the young Oswald a pang as soon as he had said it, but I hope he can bear pangs with any man living. 'And mind,' he added, hiding the pang under a general-like severeness, 'I won't have anyone in the expedition who has anything in his shoes except his feet.'

This could not have been put more delicately and decently. But Oswald is often misunderstood. Even Alice said it was unkind to throw the peas up at Denny. When this little unpleasantness had passed away (it took some time because Daisy cried, and Dora said, 'There now, Oswald!') there were seven volunteers, which, with Oswald, made eight, and was, indeed, all of us. There were no cockle-shells, or tape-sandals, or staves, or scrips, or anything romantic and pious about the eight persons who set out for Hazelbridge that morning, more earnestly wishful to be good and deedful – at least Oswald, I know, was – than ever they had been in the days of the beastly Wouldbegood Society. It was a fine day. Either it was fine nearly all last summer, which is how Oswald remembers it, or else nearly all the interesting things we did came on fine days.

With hearts light and gay, and no peas in anyone's shoes, the walk to Hazelbridge was perseveringly conducted. We took our lunch with us, and the dear dogs. Afterwards we wished for a time that we had left one of them at home. But they did so want to come, all of them, and Hazelbridge is not nearly as far as Canterbury, really, so even Martha was allowed to put on her things – I mean her collar – and come with us. She walks slowly, but we had the day before us so there was no extra hurry.

At Hazelbridge we went into B. Munn's grocer's shop and asked for ginger-beer to drink. They gave it us, but they seemed surprised at us wanting to drink it there, and the glass was warm – it had just been washed. We only did it, really, so as to get into conversation with B. Munn, grocer, and extract information without rousing suspicion. You cannot be too careful.'

However, when we had said it was first-class ginger-beer, and paid for it, we found it not so easy to extract anything more from B. Munn, grocer; and there was an anxious silence while he fiddled about behind the counter among the tinned meats and sauce bottles, with a fringe of hob-nailed boots hanging over his head.

H. O. spoke suddenly. He is like the sort of person who rushes in where angels fear to tread, as Denny says (say what sort of person that is). He said –

'I say, you remember driving us home that day. Who paid for the cart?'

Of course B. Munn, grocer, was not such a nincompoop (I like that word, it means so many people I know) as to say right off. He said –

'I was paid all right, young gentleman. Don't you terrify yourself.'

People in Kent say terrify when they mean worry.

So Dora shoved in a gentle oar. She said –

'We want to know the kind lady's name and address, so that we can write and thank her for being so jolly that day.'

B. Munn, grocer, muttered something about the lady's address being goods he was often asked for. Alice said, 'But do tell us. We forgot to ask her. She's a relation of a second-hand uncle of ours, and I do so want to thank her properly. And if you've got any extra-strong peppermints at a penny an ounce, we should like a quarter of a pound.'

This was a master-stroke. While he was weighing out the peppermints his heart got soft, and just as he was twisting up the corner of the paper bag, Dora said, 'What lovely fat peppermints! Do tell us.'

479

And B. Munn's heart was now quite melted, he said –

'It's Miss Ashleigh, and she lives at The Cedars – about a mile down the Maidstone Road.'

We thanked him, and Alice paid for the peppermints. Oswald was a little anxious when she ordered such a lot, but she and Noël had got the money all right, and when we were outside on Hazelbridge Green (a good deal of it is gravel, really), we stood and looked at each other.

Then Dora said –

'Let's go home and write a beautiful letter and all sign it.'

Oswald looked at the others. Writing is all very well, but it's such a beastly long time to wait for anything to happen afterwards.

The intelligent Alice divined his thoughts, and the Dentist divined hers – he is not clever enough yet to divine Oswald's – and the two said together –

'Why not go and see her?'

'She *did* say she would like to see us again some day,' Dora replied. So after we had argued a little about it we went.

And before we had gone a hundred yards down the dusty road Martha began to make us wish with all our hearts we had not let her come. She began to limp, just as a pilgrim, who I will not name, did when he had the split peas in his silly palmering shoes.

So we called a halt and looked at her feet. One of them was quite swollen and red. Bulldogs almost always have something the matter with their feet, and it always comes on when least required. They are not the right breed for emergencies.

There was nothing for it but to take it in turns to carry her. She is very stout, and you have no idea how heavy she is. A half-hearted unadventurous person (I name no names, but Oswald, Alice, Noël, H. O., Dicky, Daisy, and Denny will understand me) said, why not go straight home and come another day without Martha? But the rest agreed with Oswald when he said it was only a mile, and perhaps we might get a lift home with the poor invalid. Martha was very grateful to us for our kindness. She put her fat white arms round the person's neck who happened to be carrying her. She is very affectionate, but by holding her very close to you you can keep her from kissing your face all the time. As Alice said, 'Bulldogs do give you such large, wet, pink kisses.'

A mile is a good way when you have to take your turn at carrying Martha.

At last we came to a hedge with a ditch in front of it, and chains swinging from posts to keep people off the grass and out of the ditch, and a gate with 'The Cedars' on it in gold letters. All very neat and tidy, and showing plainly that more than one gardener was kept. There we stopped. Alice put Martha down, grunting with exhaustedness, and said –

'Look here, Dora and Daisy, I don't believe a bit that it's his grandmother. I'm sure Dora was right, and it's only his horrid sweetheart. I feel it in my bones. Now, don't you really think we'd better chuck it; we're sure to catch it for interfering. We always do.'

'The cross of true love never did come smooth,' said the Dentist. 'We ought to help him to bear his cross.'

'But if we find her for him, and she's not his grandmother, he'll *marry* her,' Dicky said in tones of gloominess and despair.

Oswald felt the same, but he said, 'Never mind. We should all hate it, but perhaps Albert's uncle *might* like it. You can never tell. If you want to do a really un-selfish action and no kid, now's your time, my late Wouldbegoods.'

No one had the face to say right out that they didn't want to be unselfish.

But it was with sad hearts that the unselfish seekers opened the long gate and went up the gravel drive between the rhododendrons and other shrubberies towards the house.

I think I have explained to you before that the eldest son of anybody is called the representative of the family if his father isn't there. This was why Oswald now took the lead. When we got to the last turn of the drive it was settled that the others were to noiselessly ambush in the rhododendrons, and Oswald was to go on alone and ask at the house for the grandmother from India – I mean Miss Ashleigh.

So he did, but when he got to the front of the house and saw how neat the flower-beds were with red geraniums, and the windows all bright and speckless with muslin blinds and brass rods, and a green parrot in a cage in the porch, and the doorstep newly whited, lying clean and untrodden in the sunshine, he stood still and thought of his boots and how dusty the roads were, and wished he had not gone into the farmyard after eggs before starting that morning. As he stood there in anxious uncertainness he heard a low voice among the bushes. It said, 'Hist! Oswald here!' and it was the voice of Alice.

So he went back to the others among the shrubs and they all crowded round their leader full of impartable news.

'She's not in the house; she's *here*,' Alice said in a low whisper that seemed nearly all S's. 'Close by – she went by just this minute with a gentleman.'

'And they're sitting on a seat under a tree on a little lawn, and she's got her head on his shoulder, and he's holding her hand. I never saw anyone look so silly in all my born,' Dicky said.

'It's sickening,' Denny said, trying to look very manly with his legs wide apart.

'I don't know,' Oswald whispered. 'I suppose it wasn't Albert's uncle?'

'Not much,' Dicky briefly replied.

'Then don't you see it's all right. If she's going on like that with this fellow she'll want to marry him, and Albert's uncle is safe. And we've really done an unselfish action without having to suffer for it afterwards.' With a stealthy movement Oswald rubbed his hands as he spoke in real joyfulness. We decided that we had better bunk unnoticed. But we had reckoned without Martha. She had strolled off limping to look about her a bit in the shrubbery. 'Where's Martha?' Dora suddenly said.

'She went that way,' pointingly remarked H. O.

'Then fetch her back, you young duffer! What did you let her go for?' Oswald said. 'And look sharp. Don't make a row.'

He went. A minute later we heard a hoarse squeak from Martha – the one she always gives when suddenly collared from behind – and a little squeal in a lady-like voice, and man say 'Hallo!' and then we knew that H. O. had once more rushed in where angels might have thought twice about it. We hurried to the fatal spot, but it was too late. We were just in time to hear H. O. say –

'I'm sorry if she frightened you. But we've been looking for you. Are you Albert's uncle's long-lost grandmother?'

'*No*,' said our lady unhesitatingly.

483

It seemed vain to add seven more agitated actors to the scene now going on. We stood still. The man was standing up. He was a clergyman, and I found out afterwards he was the nicest we ever knew except our own Mr Briston at Lewisham, who is now a canon or a dean, or something grand that no one ever sees. At present I did not like him. He said, 'No, this lady is nobody's grandmother. May I ask in return how long it is since you escaped from the lunatic asylum, my poor child, and whence your keeper is?'

H. O. took no notice of this at all, except to say, 'I think you are very rude, and not at all funny, if you think you are.'

The lady said, 'My dear, I remember you now perfectly. How are all the others, and are you pilgrims again to-day?'

H. O. does not always answer questions. He turned to the man and said –

'Are you going to marry the lady?'

'Margaret,' said the clergyman, 'I never thought it would come to this: he asks me my intentions.'

'If you *are*,' said H. O., 'it's all right, because if you do Albert's uncle can't – at least, not till you're dead. And we don't want him to.'

'Flattering, upon my word,' said the clergyman, putting on a deep frown. 'Shall I call him out, Margaret, for his poor opinion of you, or shall I send for the police?'

Alice now saw that H. O., though firm, was getting muddled and rather scared. She broke cover and sprang into the middle of the scene.

'Don't let him rag H. O. any more,' she said, 'it's all our faults. You see, Albert's uncle was so anxious to find you, we thought perhaps you were his long-lost heiress sister or his old nurse who alone knew the secret of his birth, or something, and we asked him, and he said you were his long-lost grandmother he had known in India. And we thought that must be a mistake and that really you were his long-lost sweetheart. And we tried to do a really unselfish act and find you for him. Because we don't want him to be married at all.'

'It isn't because we don't like *you*,' Oswald cut in, now emerging from the bushes, 'and if he must marry, we'd sooner it was you than anyone. Really we would.'

'A generous concession, Margaret,' the strange clergyman uttered, 'most generous, but the plot thickens. It's almost pea-soup-like now. One or two points clamour for explanation. Who are these visitors of yours? Why this Red Indian method of paying morning calls? Why the lurking attitude of the rest of the tribe which I now discern among the undergrowth? Won't you ask the rest of the tribe to come out and join the glad throng?'

Then I liked him better. I always like people who know the same songs we do, and books and tunes and things.

The others came out. The lady looked very uncomfy, and partly as if she was going to cry. But she couldn't help laughing too, as more and more of us came out.

'And who,' the clergyman went on, 'who in fortune's name is Albert? And who is his uncle? And what have they or you to do in this *galère* – I mean garden?'

We all felt rather silly, and I don't think I ever felt more than then what an awful lot there were of us.

'Three years' absence in Calcutta or elsewhere may explain my ignorance of these details, but still – '

'I think we'd better go,' said Dora. 'I'm sorry if we've done anything rude or wrong. We didn't mean to. Good-bye. I hope you'll be happy with the gentleman, I'm sure.'

'I *hope* so too,' said Noël, and I know he was thinking

how much nicer Albert's uncle was. We turned to go. The lady had been very silent compared with what she was when she pretended to show us Canterbury. But now she seemed to shake off some dreamy silliness, and caught hold of Dora by the shoulder.

'No, dear, no,' she said, 'it's all right, and you must have some tea we'll have it on the lawn. John, don't tease them any more. Albert's uncle is the gentleman I told you about. And, my dear children, this is my brother that I haven't seen for three years.'

'Then he's a long-lost too,' said H. O.

The lady said 'Not now' and smiled at him.

And the rest of us were dumb with confounding emotions. Oswald was particularly dumb. He might have known it was her brother, because in rotten grown-up books if a girl kisses a man in a shrubbery that is not the man you think she's in love with; it always turns out to be a brother, though generally the disgrace of the family and not a respectable chaplain from Calcutta.

The lady now turned to her reverend and surprising brother and said, 'John, go and tell them we'll have tea on the lawn.'

When he was gone she stood quite still a minute. Then she said, 'I'm going to tell you something, but I want to put you on your honour not to talk about it to other people. You see it isn't everyone I would tell about it. He, Albert's uncle, I mean, has told me a lot about you, and I know I can trust you.'

We said 'Yes', Oswald with a brooding sentiment of knowing all too well what was coming next.

The lady then said, 'Though I am not Albert's uncle's grandmother I did know him in India once, and we were going to be married, but we had a – a – misunderstanding.'

486

'Quarrel?' 'Row?' said Noël and H. O. at once.

'Well, yes, a quarrel, and he went away. He was in the Navy then. And then ... well, we were both sorry, but well, anyway, when his ship came back we'd gone to Constantinople, then to England, and he couldn't find us. And he says he's been looking for me ever since.'

'Not you for him?' said Noël.

'Well, perhaps,' said the lady.

And the girls said 'Ah!' with deep interest. The lady went on more quickly, 'And then I found you, and then he found me, and now I must break it to you. Try to bear up ... '

She stopped. The branches crackled, and Albert's uncle was in our midst. He took off his hat. 'Excuse my tearing my hair,' he said to the lady, 'but has the pack really hunted you down?'

'It's all right,' she said, and when she looked at him she got miles prettier quite suddenly. 'I was just breaking to them ... '

'Don't take that proud privilege from me,' he said. 'Kiddies, allow me to present you to the future Mrs Albert's uncle, or shall we say Albert's new aunt?'

There was a good deal of explaining done before tea – about how we got there, I mean, and why. But after the first bitterness of disappointment we felt not nearly so sorry as we had expected to. For Albert's uncle's lady was very jolly to us, and her brother was awfully decent, and showed us a lot of first-class native curiosities and things, unpacking them on purpose; skins of beasts, and beads, and brass things, and shells from different savage lands besides India. And the lady told the girls that she hoped they would like her as much as she liked them, and if they wanted a new aunt

'It's all right,' she said

she would do her best to give satisfaction in the new situation. And Alice thought of the Murdstone aunt belonging to Daisy and Denny, and how awful it would have been if Albert's uncle had married *her*. And she decided, she told me afterwards, that we might think ourselves jolly lucky it was no worse.

Then the lady led Oswald aside, pretending to show him the parrot which he had explored thoroughly before, and told him she was not like some people in books. When she was married she would never try to separate her husband from his bachelor friends, she only wanted them to be her friends as well.

Then there was tea, and thus all ended in amicableness, and the reverend and friendly drove us home in a wagonette. But for Martha we shouldn't have had tea, or explanations, or lift or anything. So we honoured her, and did not mind her being so heavy and walking up and down constantly on our laps as we drove home.

And that is all the story of the long-lost grandmother and Albert's uncle. I am afraid it is rather dull, but it was very important (to him), so I felt it ought to be narrated. Stories about lovers and getting married are generally slow. I like a love-story where the hero parts with the girl at the garden-gate in the gloaming and goes off and has adventures, and you don't see her any more till he comes home to marry her at the end of the book. And I suppose people have to marry. Albert's uncle is awfully old – more than thirty, and the lady is advanced in years – twenty-six next Christmas. They are to be married then. The girls are to be bridesmaids in white frocks with fur. This quite consoles them. If Oswald repines sometimes, he hides it. What's the use? We all have to meet our fell destiny, and Albert's uncle is not extirpated from this awful law.

Now the finding of the long-lost was the very last thing we did for the sake of its being a noble act, so that is the end of the Wouldbegoods, and there are no more chapters after this. But Oswald hates books that finish up without telling you the things you might want to know about the people in the book. So here goes. We went home to the beautiful Blackheath house. It seemed very stately and mansion-like after the Moat

House, and everyone was most frightfully pleased to see us.

Mrs Pettigrew *cried* when we went away. I never was so astonished in my life. She made each of the girls a fat red pincushion like a heart, and each of us boys had a knife bought out of the housekeeping (I mean housekeeper's own) money.

Bill Simpkins is happy as sub-under-gardener to Albert's uncle's lady's mother. They do keep three gardeners – I knew they did. And our tramp still earns enough to sleep well on from our dear old Pig-man.

Our last three days were entirely filled up with visits of farewell sympathy to all our many friends who were so sorry to lose us. We promised to come and see them next year. I hope we shall.

Denny and Daisy went back to live with their father at Forest Hill. I don't think they'll ever be again the victims of the Murdstone aunt – who is really a great-aunt and about twice as much in the autumn of her days as our new Albert's-uncle aunt. I think they plucked up spirit enough to tell their father they didn't like her – which they'd never thought of doing before. Our own robber says their holidays in the country did them both a great deal of good. And he says us Bastables have certainly taught Daisy and Denny the rudiments of the art of making home happy. I believe they have thought of several quite new naughty things entirely on their own – and done them too – since they came back from the Moat House.

I wish you didn't grow up so quickly. Oswald can see that ere long he will be too old for the kind of games we can all play, and he feels grown-upness creeping inordiously upon him. But enough of this.

And now, gentle reader, farewell. If anything in these chronicles of the Wouldbegoods should make you try to be good yourself, the author will be very glad, of course. But take my advice and don't make a society for trying in. It is much easier without.

And do try to forget that Oswald has another name besides Bastable. The one beginning with C., I mean. Perhaps you have not noticed what it was. If so, don't look back for it. It is a name no manly boy would like to be called by – if he spoke the truth. Oswald is said to be a very manly boy, and he despises that name, and will never give it to his own son when he has one. Not if a rich relative offered to leave him an immense fortune if he did. Oswald would still be firm. He would, on the honour of the House of Bastable.

NEW
TREASURE
SEEKERS

To
ARTHUR WATTS
[Oswald in Paris]
From
E. NESBIT

CONTENTS

THE ROAD TO ROME; OR,
THE SILLY STOWAWAY

WE Bastables have only two uncles, and neither of them are our own natural-born relatives. One is a great-uncle, and the other is the uncle from his birth of Albert, who used to live next door to us in the Lewisham Road. When we first got to know him (it was over some baked potatoes, and is quite another story) we called him Albert-next-door's-Uncle, and then Albert's uncle for short. But Albert's uncle and my father joined in taking a jolly house in the country, called the Moat House, and we stayed there for our summer holidays; and it was there, through an accident to a pilgrim with peas in his shoes – that's another story too – that we found Albert's uncle's long-lost love; and as she was very old indeed – twenty-six next birthday – and he was ever so much older in the vale of years, he had to get married almost directly, and it was fixed for about Christmastime. And when our holidays came the whole six of us went down to the Moat House with Father and Albert's uncle. We never had a Christmas in the country before. It was simply ripping. And the long-lost love – her name was Miss Ashleigh, but we were allowed to call her Aunt Margaret even before the wedding made it really legal for us to do so – she and her jolly clergyman brother used to come over, and sometimes we went to the Cedars, where they live, and we had games and charades, and hide-and-seek, and Devil in the Dark, which is a game girls pretend to like, and very few do really, and crackers and a Christmas-tree for the village children, and everything you can jolly well think of.

And all the time, whenever we went to the Cedars, there was all sorts of silly fuss going on about the beastly wedding; boxes coming from London with hats and jackets in, and wedding presents – all glassy and silvery, or else brooches and chains – and clothes sent down from London to choose from. I can't think how a lady can want so many petticoats and boots and things just because she's going to be married. No man would think of getting twenty-four shirts and twenty-four waistcoats, and so on, just to be married in.

'It's because they're going to Rome, I think,' Alice said, when we talked it over before the fire in the kitchen the day Mrs Pettigrew went to see her aunt, and we were allowed to make toffee. 'You see, in Rome you can only buy Roman clothes, and I think they're all stupid bright colours – at least I know the sashes are. You stir now, Oswald. My face is all burnt black.'

Oswald took the spoon, though it was really not his turn by three; but he is one whose nature is so that he cannot make a fuss about little things – and he knows he can make toffee.

'Lucky hounds,' H.O. said, 'to be going to Rome. I wish I was.'

'Hounds isn't polite, H.O., dear,' Dora said; and H.O. said –

'Well, lucky bargees, then.'

'It's the dream of my life to go to Rome,' Noël said. Noël is our poet brother. 'Just think of what the man says in the "Roman Road". I wish they'd take me.'

'They won't,' Dicky said. 'It costs a most awful lot. I heard Father saying so only yesterday.'

'It would only be the fare,' Noël answered; 'and I'd go third, or even in a cattle-truck, or a luggage van. And when I got there I could easily earn my own living. I'd make ballads and sing them in the streets. The Italians would give me lyres – that's the Italian kind of shilling, they spell it with an *i*. It shows how poetical they are out there, their calling it that.'

'But you couldn't make Italian poetry,' H.O. said, staring at Noël with his mouth open.

'Oh, I don't know so much about that,' Noël said. 'I could jolly soon learn anyway, and just to begin with I'd do it in English. There are sure to be some people who would understand. And if they didn't, don't you think their warm Southern hearts would be touched to see a pale, slender, foreign figure singing plaintive ballads in an unknown tongue? I do. Oh! they'd chuck along the lyres fast enough – they're not hard and cold like North people. Why, every one here is a brewer, or a baker, or a banker, or a butcher, or something dull. Over there they're all bandits, or vineyardiners, or play the guitar, or something, and they crush the red grapes and dance and laugh in the sun – you know jolly well they do.'

'This toffee's about done,' said Oswald suddenly. 'H.O., shut your silly mouth and get a cupful of cold water.' And then, what with dropping a little of the toffee into the water to see if it was ready, and pouring some on a plate that wasn't buttered and not being able to get it off again when it was cold without breaking the plate, and the warm row there was about its being one of the best dinner-service ones, the wild romances of Noël's poetical intellect went out of our heads altogether; and it was not till later, and when deep in the waters of affliction, that they were brought back to us.

Next day H.O. said to Dora, 'I want to speak to you all by yourself and me.' So they went into the secret staircase that creaks and hasn't been secret now for countless years; and after that Dora did some white sewing she wouldn't let us look at, and H.O. helped her.

'It's another wedding present, you may depend,' Dicky

said – 'a beastly surprise, I shouldn't wonder.' And no more was said. The rest of us were busy skating on the moat, for it was now freezing hard. Dora never did care for skating; she says it hurts her feet.

And now Christmas and Boxing Day passed like a radiating dream, and it was the wedding-day. We all had to go to the bride's mother's house before the wedding, so as to go to church with the wedding party. The girls had always wanted to be somebody's bridesmaids, and now they were – in white cloth coats like coachmen, with lots of little capes, and white beaver bonnets. They didn't look so bad, though rather as if they were in a Christmas card; and their dresses were white silk like pocket-handkerchiefs under the long coats. And their shoes had real silver buckles our great Indian uncle gave them. H.O. went back just as the waggonette was starting, and came out with a big brown-paper parcel. We thought it was the secret surprise present Dora had been making, and, indeed, when I asked her she nodded. We little recked what it really was, or how our young brother was going to shove himself forward once again. He *will* do it. Nothing you say is of any lasting use.

There were a great many people at the wedding – quite crowds. There was lots to eat and drink, and though it was all cold, it did not matter, because there were blazing fires in every fireplace in the house, and the place all decorated with holly and mistletoe and things. Every one seemed to enjoy themselves very much, except Albert's uncle and his blushing bride; and they looked desperate. Every one said how sweet she looked, but Oswald thought she looked as if she didn't like being married as much as she expected. She was not at all a blushing bride really; only the tip of her nose got pink, because it was rather cold in the church. But she is very jolly.

Her reverend but nice brother read the marriage service.

He reads better than any one I know, but he is not a bit of a prig really, when you come to know him.

When the rash act was done Albert's uncle and his bride went home in a carriage all by themselves, and then we had the lunch and drank the health of the bride in real champagne, though Father said we kids must only have just a taste. I'm sure Oswald, for one, did not want any more; one taste was quite enough. Champagne is like soda-water with medicine in it. The sherry we put sugar in once was much more decent.

Then Miss Ashleigh – I mean Mrs Albert's uncle – went away and took off her white dress and came back looking much warmer. Dora heard the housemaid say afterwards that the cook had stopped the bride on the stairs with 'a basin of hot soup, that would take no denial, because the bride, poor dear young thing, not a bite or sup had passed her lips that day'. We understood then why she had looked so unhappy. But Albert's uncle had had a jolly good breakfast – fish and eggs and bacon and three goes of marmalade. So it was not hunger made him sad. Perhaps he was thinking what a lot of money it cost to be married and go to Rome.

A little before the bride went to change, H.O. got up and reached his brown-paper parcel from under the sideboard and sneaked out. We thought he might have let us see it given, whatever it was. And Dora said she had understood he meant to; but it was his secret.

The bride went away looking quite comfy in a furry cloak, and Albert's uncle cheered up at the last and threw off the burden of his cares and made a joke. I forget what it was; it wasn't a very good one, but it showed he was trying to make the best of things.

Then the Bridal Sufferers drove away, with the luggage on a cart – heaps and heaps of it, and we all cheered and threw rice and slippers. Mrs Ashleigh and some other old ladies cried.

And then every one said, 'What a pretty wedding!' and began to go. And when our waggonette came round we all began to get in. And suddenly Father said –

'Where's H.O.?' And we looked round. He was in absence.

'Fetch him along sharp – some of you,' Father said; 'I don't want to keep the horses standing here in the cold all day.'

So Oswald and Dicky went to fetch him along. We thought he might have wandered back to what was left of the lunch – for he is young and he does not always know better. But he was not there, and Oswald did not even take a crystallized fruit in passing. He might easily have done this, and no one would have minded, so it would not have been wrong. But it would have been ungentlemanly. Dicky did not either. H.O. was not there.

We went into the other rooms, even the one the old ladies were crying in, but of course we begged their pardons. And at last into the kitchen, where the servants were smart with white bows and just sitting down to their dinner, and Dicky said –

'I say, cookie love, have you seen H.O.?'

'Don't come here with your imperence!' the cook said, but she was pleased with Dicky's unmeaning compliment all the same.

'*I* see him,' said the housemaid. 'He was colloguing with the butcher in the yard a bit since. He'd got a brown-paper parcel. Perhaps he got a lift home.'

So we went and told Father, and about the white present in the parcel.

'I expect he was ashamed to give it after all,' Oswald said, 'so he hooked off home with it.'

And we got into the waggonette.

'It wasn't a present, though,' Dora said; 'it was a different kind of surprise – but it really is a secret.'

Our good Father did not command her to betray her young brother.

But when we got home H.O. wasn't there. Mrs Pettigrew hadn't seen him, and he was nowhere about. Father biked back to the Cedars to see if he'd turned up. No. Then all the gentlemen turned out to look for him through the length and breadth of the land.

'He's too old to be stolen by gipsies,' Alice said.

'And too ugly,' said Dicky.

'Oh *don't*!' said both the girls; 'and now when he's lost, too!'

We had looked for a long time before Mrs Pettigrew came in with a parcel she said the butcher had left. It was not addressed, but we knew it was H.O.'s, because of the label on the paper from the shop where Father gets his shirts. Father opened it at once.

Inside the parcel we found H.O.'s boots and braces, his best hat and his chest-protector. And Oswald felt as if we had found his skeleton.

'Any row with any of you?' Father asked. But there hadn't been any.

'Was he worried about anything? Done anything wrong, and afraid to own up?'

We turned cold, for we knew what he meant. That parcel was so horribly like the lady's hat and gloves that she takes off on the seashore and leaves with a letter saying it has come to this.

'*No, no*, NO, NO!' we all said. 'He was perfectly jolly all the morning.'

Then suddenly Dicky leaned on the table and one of H.O.'s boots toppled over, and there was something white inside. It was a letter. H.O. must have written it before we left home. It said –

DEAR FATHER AND EVERY ONE, – I am going to be a Clown. When I am rich and reveared I will come back rolling.

Your affectionate son,
HORACE OCTAVIUS BASTABLE.

'Rolling?' Father said.

'He means rolling in money,' Alice said. Owsald noticed that every one round the table where H.O.'s boots were dignifiedly respected as they lay, was a horrid pale colour, like when the salt is thrown into snapdragons.

'Oh dear!' Dora cried, 'that was it. He asked me to make him a clown's dress and keep it deeply secret. He said he wanted to surprise Aunt Margaret and Albert's uncle. And I didn't think it was wrong,' said Dora, screwing up her face; she then added, 'Oh dear, oh dear, oh oh!' and with these concluding remarks she began to howl.

Father thumped her on the back in an absent yet kind way.

'But where's he gone?' he said, not to any one in particular. 'I saw the butcher; he said H.O. asked him to take a parcel home and went back round the Cedars.'

Here Dicky coughed and said –

'I didn't think he meant anything, but the day after Noël was talking about singing ballads in Rome, and getting poet's lyres given him, H.O. did say if Noël had been really keen on the Roman lyres and things he could easily have been a stowaway, and gone unknown.'

'A stowaway!' said my father, sitting down suddenly and hard.

'In Aunt Margaret's big dress basket – the one she let him hide in when we had hide-and-seek there. He talked a lot about it after Noël had said that about the lyres – and the Italians being so poetical, you know. You remember that day we had toffee.'

My father is prompt and decisive in action, so is his eldest son.

'I'm off to the Cedars,' he said.

'Do let me come, Father,' said the decisive son. 'You may want to send a message.'

So in a moment Father was on his bike and Oswald on the step – a dangerous but delightful spot – and off to the Cedars.

'Have your teas; and *don't* any more of you get lost, and don't sit up if we're late,' Father howled to them as we rushed away. How glad then the thoughtful Oswald was that he was the eldest. It was very cold in the dusk on the bicycle, but Oswald did not complain.

At the Cedars my father explained in a few manly but well-chosen words, and the apartment of the dear departed bride was searched.

'Because,' said my father, 'if H.O. really was little ass enough to get into that basket, he must have turned out something to make room for himself.'

Sure enough, when they came to look, there was a great bundle rolled in a sheet under the bed – all lace things and petticoats and ribbons and dressing-gowns and ladies' flummery.

'If you will put the things in something else, I'll catch the express to Dover and take it with me,' Father said to Mrs Ashleigh; and while she packed the things he explained to some of the crying old ladies who had been unable to leave off, how sorry he was that a son of his – but you know the sort of thing.

Oswald said: 'Father, I wish you'd let me come too. I won't be a bit of trouble.'

Perhaps it was partly because my father didn't want to let me walk home in the dark, and he didn't want to worry the Ashleighs any more by asking them to send me home. He said this was why, but I hope it was his loving wish to have his prompt son, so like himself in his decisiveness, with him.

We went.

It was an anxious journey. We know how far from pleased the bride would be to find no dressing-gowns and ribbons, but only H.O. crying and cross and dirty, as likely as not, when she opened the basket at the hotel at Dover.

Father smoked to pass the time, but Oswald had not so much as a peppermint or a bit of Spanish liquorice to help him through the journey. Yet he bore up.

When we got out at Dover there were Mr and Mrs Albert's uncle on the platform.

'Hullo,' said Albert's uncle. 'What's up? Nothing wrong at home, I hope.'

'We've only lost H.O.,' said my father. 'You don't happen to have him with you?'

'No; but you're joking,' said the bride. 'We've lost a dress-basket.'

Lost a dress-basket! The words struck us dumb, but my father recovered speech and explained. The bride was very glad when we said we had brought her ribbons and things, but we stood in anxious gloom, for now H.O. was indeed lost. The dress-basket might be on its way to Liverpool, or rocking on the Channel, and H.O. might never be found again. Oswald did not say these things. It is best to hold your jaw when you want to see a thing out, and are liable to be sent to bed at a strange hotel if any one happens to remember you.

Then suddenly the station master came with a telegram.

It said: 'A dress-basket without label at Cannon Street detained for identification suspicious sounds from inside detain inquirers dynamite machine suspected.'

He did not show us this till my father had told him about H.O., which it took some time for him to believe, and then he did and laughed, and said he would wire them to get the dynamite machine to speak, and if so, to take it out and keep it till its father called for it.

So back we went to London, with hearts a little lighter, but not gay, for we were a very long time from the last things we had had to eat. And Oswald was almost sorry he had not taken those crystallized fruits.

It was quite late when we got to Cannon Street, and we went straight into the cloak-room, and there was the man in charge, a very jolly chap, sitting on a stool. And there was H.O., the guilty stowaway, dressed in a red-and-white clown's dress, very dusty, and his face as dirty as I have ever seen it, sitting on some one else's tin box, with his feet on some body's else's portmanteau, eating bread and cheese, and drinking ale out of a can.

My father claimed him at once, and Oswald identified the basket. It was very large. There was a tray on the top with hats in it, and H.O. had this on top of him. We all went to bed in Cannon Street Hotel. My father said nothing to H.O. that night. When we were in bed I tried to get H.O. to tell me all about it, but he was too sleepy and cross. It was the beer and the knocking about in the basket, I suppose. Next day we went back to the Moat House, where the raving anxiousness of the others had been cooled the night before by a telegram from Dover.

My father said he would speak to H.O. in the evening. It is very horrid not to be spoken to at once and get it over. But H.O. certainly deserved something.

It is hard to tell this tale, because so much of it happened all at once but at different places. But this is what H.O. said to us about it. He said –

'Don't bother – let me alone.'

But we were all kind and gentle, and at last we got it out of him what had happened. He doesn't tell a story right from the beginning like Oswald and some of the others do,

but from his disjunctured words the author has made the
following narration. This is called editing, I believe.

'It was all Noël's fault,' H.O. said; 'what did he want to
go jawing about Rome for? – and a clown's as good as a
beastly poet, anyhow! You remember that day we made
toffee? Well, I thought of it then.'

'You didn't tell us.'

'Yes, I did. I half told Dicky. He never said don't, or
you'd better not, or gave me any good advice or anything.
It's his fault as much as mine. Father ought to speak to him
to-night the same as me – and Noël, too.'

We bore with him just then because we wanted to hear
the story. And we made him go on.

'Well – so I thought if Noël's a cowardy custard I'm not –
and I wasn't afraid of being in the basket, though it was
quite dark till I cut the air-holes with my knife in the
railway van. I think I cut the string off the label. It fell off
afterwards, and I saw it through the hole, but of course I
couldn't say anything. I thought they'd look after their silly
luggage better than that. It was all their fault I was
lost.'

'Tell us how you did it, H.O. dear,' Dora said; 'never
mind about it being everybody else's fault.'

'It's yours as much as any one's, if you come to that,'
H.O. said. 'You made me the clown dress when I asked
you. You never said a word about not. So there!'

'Oh, H.O., you *are* unkind!' Dora said. 'You know you
said it was for a surprise for the bridal pair.'

'So it would have been, if they'd found me at Rome, and
I'd popped up like what I meant to – like a jack-in-the-box –
and said, "Here we are again!" in my clown's clothes, at
them. But it's all spoiled, and Father's going to speak to me
this evening.' H.O. sniffed every time he stopped speaking.
But we did not correct him then. We wanted to hear about
everything.

'Why didn't you tell me straight out what you were going to do?' Dicky asked.

'Because you'd jolly well have shut me up. You always do if I want to do anything you haven't thought of yourself.'

'What did you take with you, H.O.?' asked Alice in a hurry, for H.O. was now sniffing far beyond a whisper.

'Oh, I'd saved a lot of grub, only I forgot it at the last. It's under the chest of drawers in our room. And I had my knife – and I changed into the clown's dress in the cupboard at the Ashleighs – over my own things because I thought it would be cold. And then I emptied the rotten girl's clothes out and hid them – and the top-hatted tray I just put it on a chair near, and I got into the basket, and I lifted the tray up over my head and sat down and fitted it down over me – it's got webbing bars, you know, across it. And none of you would ever have thought of it, let alone doing it.'

'I should hope not,' Dora said, but H.O. went on unhearing.

'I began to think perhaps I wished I hadn't directly they strapped up the basket. It was beastly hot and stuffy – I had to cut an airhole in the cart, and I cut my thumb; it was so bumpety. And they threw me about as if I was coals – and wrong way up as often as not. And the train was awful wobbly, and I felt so sick, and if I'd had the grub I couldn't have eaten it. I had a bottle of water. And that was all right till I dropped the cork, and I couldn't find it in the dark till the water got upset, and then I found the cork that minute.

'And when they dumped the basket on to the platform I was so glad to sit still a minute without being jogged I nearly went to sleep. And then I looked out, and the label was off, and lying close by. And then some one gave the basket a kick – big brute, I'd like to kick him! – and said, "What's this here?" And I daresay I did squeak – like a rabbit-noise, you know – and then some one said, "Sounds like live-stock, don't it? No label." And he was standing on the label all the time. I saw the string sticking out under his nasty boot. And then they trundled me off somewhere, on a wheelbarrow it felt like, and dumped me down again in a dark place – and I couldn't see anything more.'

'I wonder,' said the thoughtful Oswald, 'what made them think you were a dynamite machine?'

'Oh, that was awful!' H.O. said. 'It was my watch. I wound it up, just for something to do. You know the row it makes since it was broken, and I heard some one say, "Shish! what's that?" and then, "Sounds like an infernal machine" – don't go shoving me, Dora, it was him said it, not me – and then, "If I was the inspector I'd dump it down in the river, so I would. Any way, let's shift it." But the other said, "Let well alone," so I wasn't dumped any more. And they fetched another man, and there was a heap of jaw, and I heard them say "Police", so I let them have it.'

'What *did* you do?'

'Oh, I just kicked about in the basket, and I heard them all start off, and I shouted, "Hi, here! let me out, can't you!"'

'And did they?'

'Yes, but not for ever so long, I had to jaw at them through the cracks of the basket. And when they opened it there was quite a crowd, and they laughed ever so, and gave me bread and cheese, and said I was a plucky youngster – and I am, and I do wish Father wouldn't put things off so. He might just as well have spoken to me this morning. And I can't see I've done anything so awful – and it's all your faults for not looking after me. Aren't I your little brother? and it's your duty to see I do what's right. You've told me so often enough.'

These last words checked the severe reprimand trembling on the hitherto patient Oswald's lips. And then H.O. began to cry, and Dora nursed him, though generally he is much too big for this and knows it. And he went to sleep on her lap, and said he didn't want any dinner.

When it came to Father's speaking to H.O. that evening it never came off, because H.O. was ill in bed, not sham, you know, but real, send-for-the-doctor ill. The doctor said it was fever from chill and excitement, but I think myself it was very likely the things he ate at lunch, and the shaking up, and then the bread and cheese, and the beer out of a can.

He was ill a week. When he was better, not much was said. My father, who is the justest man in England, said the boy had been punished enough – and so he had, for he missed going to the pantomime, and to 'Shock-Headed Peter' at the Garrick Theatre, which is far and away the best play that ever was done, and quite different from any other acting I ever saw. They are exactly like real boys; I think they must have been reading about us. And he had to take a lot of the filthiest medicine I ever tasted. I wonder if Father told the doctor to make it nasty on purpose? A woman would have directly, but gentlemen are not generally so sly. Any way, you live and learn. None of us would now ever consent to be a stowaway, no matter who wanted us to, and I don't think H.O.'s very likely to do it again.

The only *meant* punishment he had was seeing the clown's dress burnt before his eyes by Father. He had bought it all with his own saved-up money, red trimmings and all.

Of course, when he got well we soon taught him not to say again that it was any of our faults. As he owned himself, he *is* our little brother, and we are not going to stand that kind of cheek from *him*.

THE CONSCIENCE PUDDING

It was Christmas, nearly a year after Mother died. I cannot write about Mother – but I will just say one thing. If she had only been away for a little while, and not for always, we shouldn't have been so keen on having a Christmas. I didn't understand this then, but I am much older now, and I think it was just because everything was so different and horrid we felt we *must* do something; and perhaps we were not particular enough *what*. Things make you much more unhappy when you loaf about than when you are doing events.

Father had to go away just about Christmas. He had heard that his wicked partner, who ran away with his money, was in France, and he thought he could catch him, but really he was in Spain, where catching criminals is never practised. We did not know this till afterwards.

Before Father went away he took Dora and Oswald into his study, and said –

'I'm awfully sorry I've got to go away, but it is very serious business, and I must go. You'll be good while I'm away, kiddies, won't you?'

We promised faithfully. Then he said –

'There are reasons – you wouldn't understand if I tried to tell you – but you can't have much of a Christmas this year. But I've told Matilda to make you a good plain pudding. Perhaps next Christmas will be brighter.'

(It was; for the next Christmas saw us the affluent nephews and nieces of an Indian uncle – but that is quite another story, as good old Kipling says.)

When Father had been seen off at Lewisham Station with

his bags, and a plaid rug in a strap, we came home again, and it was horrid. There were papers and things littered all over his room where he had packed. We tidied the room up – it was the only thing we could do for him. It was Dicky who accidentally broke his shaving-glass, and H.O. made a paper boat out of a letter we found out afterwards Father particularly wanted to keep. This took us some time, and when we went into the nursery the fire was black out, and we could not get it alight again, even with the whole *Daily Chronicle*. Matilda, who was our general then, was out, as well as the fire, so we went and sat in the kitchen. There is always a good fire in kitchens. The kitchen hearthrug was not nice to sit on, so we spread newspapers on it.

It was sitting in the kitchen, I think, that brought to our minds my father's parting words – about the pudding, I mean.

Oswald said, 'Father said we couldn't have much of a Christmas for secret reasons, and he said he had told Matilda to make us a plain pudding.'

The plain pudding instantly cast its shadow over the deepening gloom of our young minds.

'I wonder *how* plain she'll make it?' Dicky said.

'As plain as plain, you may depend,' said Oswald. 'A here-am-I-where-are-you pudding – that's her sort.'

The others groaned, and we gathered closer round the fire till the newspapers rustled madly.

'I believe I could make a pudding that *wasn't* plain, if I tried,' Alice said. 'Why shouldn't we?'

'No chink,' said Oswald, with brief sadness.

'How much would it cost?' Noël asked, and added that Dora had twopence and H.O. had a French halfpenny.

Dora got the cookery-book out of the dresser drawer, where it lay doubled up among clothes-pegs, dirty dusters, scallop shells, string, penny novelettes, and the dining-room corkscrew. The general we had then – it seemed as if she did all the cooking on the cookery-book instead of on the baking-board, there were traces of so many bygone meals upon its pages.

'It doesn't say Christmas pudding at all,' said Dora.

'Try plum,' the resourceful Oswald instantly counselled. Dora turned the greasy pages anxiously.

'"Plum-pudding, 518.

'"A rich, with flour, 517.

'"Christmas, 517.

'"Cold brandy sauce for, 241.

'We shouldn't care about that, so it's no use looking.

'"Good without eggs, 518.

'"Plain, 518."

'We don't want *that* anyhow. "Christmas 517" – that's the one.'

It took her a long time to find the page. Oswald got a shovel of coals and made up the fire. It blazed up like the devouring elephant the *Daily Telegraph* always calls it. Then Dora read –

'"Christmas plum-pudding. Time six hours."'

'To eat it in?' said H.O.

'No, silly! to make it.'

'Forge ahead, Dora,' Dicky replied.

Dora went on –

'"2072. One pound and a half of raisins; half a pound of currants; three quarters of a pound of breadcrumbs; half a pound of flour; three-quarters of a pound of beef suet; nine eggs; one wine glassful of brandy; half a pound of citron and orange peel; half a nutmeg; and a little ground ginger." I wonder *how* little ground ginger.'

'A teacupful would be enough, I think,' Alice said; 'we must not be extravagant.'

'We haven't got anything yet to be extravagant *with*,' said Oswald, who had toothache that day. 'What would you do with the things if you'd got them?'

'You'd "chop the suet as fine as possible" – I wonder how fine that is?' replied Dora and the book together – '"and mix it with the breadcrumbs and flour; add the currants washed and dried."'

'Not starched, then,' said Alice.

'"The citron and orange peel cut into thin slices" – I wonder what they call thin? Matilda's thin bread-and-butter is quite different from what I mean by it – "and the raisins stoned and divided." How many heaps would you divide them into?'

'Seven, I suppose,' said Alice; 'one for each person and one for the pot – I mean pudding.'

'"Mix it all well together with the grated nutmeg and ginger. Then stir in nine eggs well beaten, and the brandy" – we'll leave that out, I think – "and again mix it thoroughly together that every ingredient may be moistened; put it into a buttered mould, tie over tightly, and boil for six hours. Serve it ornamented with holly and brandy poured over it."'

'I should think holly and brandy poured over it would be simply beastly,' said Dicky.

'I expect the book knows. I daresay holly and water would do as well though. "This pudding may be made a month before" – it's no use reading about that though, because we've only got four days to Christmas.'

'It's no use reading about any of it,' said Oswald, with thoughtful repeatedness, 'because we haven't got the things, and we haven't got the coin to get them.'

'We might get the tin somehow,' said Dicky.

'There must be lots of kind people who would subscribe to a Christmas pudding for poor children who hadn't any,' Noël said.

'Well, I'm going skating at Penn's,' said Oswald. 'It's no use thinking about puddings. We must put up with it plain.'

So he went, and Dicky went with him.

When they returned to their home in the evening the fire had been lighted again in the nursery, and the others were just having tea. We toasted our bread-and-butter on the bare side, and it gets a little warm among the butter. This is called French toast. 'I like English better, but it is more expensive,' Alice said –

'Matilda is in a frightful rage about your putting those coals on the kitchen fire, Oswald. She says we shan't have enough to last over Christmas as it is. And Father gave her a talking to before he went about them – asked her if she ate them, she says – but I don't believe he did. Anyway, she's locked the coal-cellar door, and she's got the key in her pocket. I don't see how we can boil the pudding.'

'What pudding?' said Oswald dreamily. He was thinking of a chap he had seen at Penn's who had cut the date 1899 on the ice with four strokes.

'*The* pudding,' Alice said. 'Oh, we've had such a time, Oswald! First Dora and I went to the shops to find out exactly what the pudding would cost – it's only two and elevenpence halfpenny, counting in the holly.'

'It's no good,' Oswald repeated; he is very patient and will say the same thing any number of times. 'It's no good. You know we've got no tin.'

'Ah,' said Alice, 'but Noël and I went out, and we called at some of the houses in Granville Park and Dartmouth Hill – and we got a lot of sixpences and shillings, besides pennies, and one old gentleman gave us half-a-crown. He was so nice. Quite bald, with a knitted red and blue waistcoat. We've got eight-and-sevenpence.'

Oswald did not feel quite sure Father would like us to go asking for shillings and sixpences, or even half-crowns from strangers, but he did not say so. The money had been asked for and got, and it couldn't be helped – and perhaps he wanted the pudding – I am not able to remember exactly why he did not speak up and say, 'This is wrong', but anyway he didn't.

Alice and Dora went out and bought the things next morning. They bought double quantities, so that it came to five shillings and elevenpence, and was enough to make a noble pudding. There was a lot of holly left over for decorations. We used very little for the sauce. The money that was left we spent very anxiously in other things to eat, such as dates and figs and toffee.

We did not tell Matilda about it. She was a red-haired girl, and apt to turn shirty at the least thing.

Concealed under our jackets and overcoats, we carried the parcels up to the nursery, and hid them in the treasure-chest we had there. It was the bureau drawer. It was locked up afterwards because the treacle got all over the green baize and the little drawers inside it while we were waiting to begin to make the pudding. It was the grocer told us we ought to put treacle in the pudding, and also about not so much ginger as a teacupful.

When Matilda had begun to pretend to scrub the floor (she pretended this three times a week so as to have an excuse not to let us in the kitchen, but I know she used to read novelettes most of the time, because Alice and I had a squint through the window more than once), we barricaded the nursery door and set to work. We were very careful to be quite clean. We washed our hands as well as the currants. I have sometimes thought we did not get all the soap off the currants. The pudding smelt like a washing-day when the time came to cut it open. And we washed a corner of the table to chop the suet on. Chopping suet looks easy till you try.

Father's machine he weighs letters with did to weigh out the things. We did this very carefully, in case the grocer had not done so. Everything was right except the raisins. H.O. had carried them home. He was very young then, and there was a hole in the corner of the paper bag and his mouth was sticky.

Lots of people have been hanged to a gibbet in chains on evidence no worse than that, and we told H.O. so till he cried. This was good for him, It was not unkindness to H.O., but part of our duty.

Chopping suet as fine as possible is much harder than any one would think, as I said before. So is crumbling bread – especially if your loaf is new, like ours was. When we had done them the breadcrumbs and the suet were both very large and lumpy, and of a dingy grey colour, something like pale slate pencil.

They looked a better colour when we had mixed them with the flour. The girls had washed the currants with Brown Windsor soap and the sponge. Some of the currants got inside the sponge and kept coming out in the bath for days afterwards. I see now that this was not quite nice. We cut the candied peel as thin as we wish people would cut our bread-and-butter. We tried to take the stones out of the raisins, but they were too sticky, so we just divided them up in seven lots. Then we mixed the other things in the wash-hand basin from the spare bedroom that was always spare. We each put in our own lot of raisins and turned it all into a pudding-basin, and tied it up in one of Alice's pinafores, which was the nearest thing to a proper pudding-cloth we could find – at any rate clean. What was left sticking to the wash-hand basin did not taste so bad.

'It's a little bit soapy,' Alice said, 'but perhaps that will boil out; like stains in table-cloths.'

It was a difficult question how to boil the pudding. Matilda proved furious when asked to let us, just because some one had happened to knock her hat off the scullery door and Pincher had got it and done for it. However, part of the embassy nicked a saucepan while the others were being told what Matilda thought about the hat, and we got hot water out of the bath-room and made it boil over our nursery fire. We put the pudding in – it was now getting on towards the hour of tea – and let it boil. With some exceptions – owing to the fire going down, and Matilda not hurrying up with coals – it boiled for an hour and a quarter. Then Matilda came suddenly in and said, 'I'm not going to have you messing about in here with my saucepans'; and she tried to take it off the fire. You will see that we couldn't stand this; it was not likely. I do not remember who it was that told her to mind her own business, and I think I have forgotten who caught hold of her first to make her chuck it. I am sure no needless violence was used. Anyway, while the struggle progressed, Alice and Dora took the saucepan away and put it in the boot-cupboard under the stairs and put the key in their pocket.

This sharp encounter made every one very hot and cross. We got over it before Matilda did, but we brought her round before bedtime. Quarrels should always be made up before bedtime. It says so in the Bible. If this simple rule was followed there would not be so many wars and martyrs and law suits and inquisitions and bloody deaths at the stake.

All the house was still. The gas was out all over the house except on the first landing, when several darkly shrouded figures might have been observed creeping downstairs to the kitchen.

On the way, with superior precaution, we got out our saucepan. The kitchen fire was red, but low; the coal-cellar was locked, and there was nothing in the scuttle but a little coal-dust and the piece of brown paper that is put in to keep the coals from tumbling out through the bottom where the hole is. We put the saucepan on the fire and plied it with fuel – two *Chronicles*, a *Telegraph*, and two *Family Herald* novelettes were burned in vain. I am almost sure the pudding did not boil at all that night.

'Never mind,' Alice said. 'We can each nick a piece of coal every time we go into the kitchen to-morrow.'

This daring scheme was faithfully performed, and by night we had nearly half a waste-paper basket of coal, coke, and cinders. And in the depth of night once more we might have been observed, this time with our collier-like waste-paper basket in our guarded hands.

There was more fire left in the grate that night, and we fed it with the fuel we had collected. This time the fire blazed up, and the pudding boiled like mad. This was the time it boiled two hours – at least I think it was about that, but we dropped asleep on the kitchen tables and dresser. You dare not be lowly in the night in the kitchen, because of the beetles. We were aroused by a horrible smell. It was the pudding-cloth burning. All the water had secretly boiled itself away. We filled it up at once with cold, and the saucepan cracked. So we cleaned it and put it back on the shelf and took another and went to bed. You see what a lot of trouble we had over the pudding. Every evening till Christmas, which had now become only the day after to-morrow, we sneaked down in the inky midnight and boiled that pudding for as long as it would.

On Christmas morning we chopped the holly for the sauce, but we put hot water (instead of brandy) and moist sugar. Some of them said it was not so bad. Oswald was not one of these.

Then came the moment when the plain pudding Father had ordered smoked upon the board. Matilda brought it in and went away at once. She had a cousin out of Woolwich Arsenal to see her that day, I remember. Those far-off days are quite distinct in memory's recollection still.

Then we got out our own pudding from its hiding-place and gave it one last hurried boil – only seven minutes, because of the general impatience which Oswald and Dora could not cope with.

We had found means to secrete a dish, and we now tried to dish the pudding up, but it stuck to the basin, and had to be dislodged with the chisel. The pudding was horribly pale. We poured the holly sauce over it, and Dora took up the knife and was just cutting it when a few simple words from H.O. turned us from happy and triumphing cookery artists to persons in despair.

He said: 'How pleased all those kind ladies and gentlemen would be if they knew *we* were the poor children they gave the shillings and sixpences and things for!'

We all said, '*What?*' It was no moment for politeness.

'I say,' H.O. said, 'they'd be glad if they knew it was us was enjoying the pudding, and not dirty little, really poor children.'

'You should say "you were", not "you was",' said Dora, but it was as in a dream and only from habit.

'Do you mean to say' – Oswald spoke firmly, yet not angrily – 'that you and Alice went and begged for money for poor children, and then *kept* it?'

'We didn't keep it,' said H.O., 'we spent it.'

'We've kept the *things*, you little duffer!' said Dicky, looking at the pudding sitting alone and uncared for on its dish. 'You begged for money for poor children, and then *kept* it. It's stealing, that's what it is. I don't say so much about you – you're only a silly kid – but Alice knew better. Why did you do it?'

He turned to Alice, but she was now too deep in tears to get a word out.

H.O. looked a bit frightened, but he answered the question. We have taught him this. He said –

'I thought they'd give us more if I said poor children than if I said just us.'

'*That*'s cheating,' said Dicky – 'downright beastly, mean, low cheating.'

'I'm not,' said H.O.; 'and you're another.' Then he

began to cry too. I do not know how the others felt, but I understand from Oswald that he felt that now the honour of the house of Bastable had been stamped on in the dust, and it didn't matter what happened. He looked at the beastly holly that had been left over from the sauce and was stuck up over the pictures. It now appeared hollow and disgusting, though it had got quite a lot of berries, and some of it was the varied kind – green and white. The figs and dates and toffee were set out in the doll's dinner service. The very sight of it all made Oswald blush sickly. He owns he would have liked to cuff H.O., and, if he did for a moment wish to shake Alice, the author, for one, can make allowances.

Now Alice choked and spluttered, and wiped her eyes fiercely, and said, 'It's no use ragging H.O. It's my fault. I'm older than he is.'

H.O. said, 'It couldn't be Alice's fault. I don't see as it was wrong.'

'That, not as,' murmured Dora, putting her arm round the sinner who had brought this degrading blight upon our family tree, but such is girls' undetermined and affectionate silliness. 'Tell sister all about it, H.O. dear. Why couldn't it be Alice's fault?'

H.O. cuddled up to Dora and said snufflingly in his nose –

'Because she hadn't got nothing to do with it. I collected it all. She never went into one of the houses. She didn't want to.'

'And then took all the credit of getting the money,' said Dicky savagely.

Oswald said, 'Not much *credit*,' in scornful tones.

'Oh, you are *beastly*, the whole lot of you, except Dora!' Alice said, stamping her foot in rage and despair. 'I tore my frock on a nail going out, and I didn't want to go back, and I got H.O. to go to the houses alone, and I waited for him outside. And I asked him not to say anything because I didn't want Dora to know about the frock – it's my best. And *I* don't know what he said inside. He never told me. But I'll bet anything he didn't *mean* to cheat.'

'You *said* lots of kind people would be ready to give money to get pudding for poor children. So I asked them to.'

Oswald, with his strong right hand, waved a wave of passing things over.

'We'll talk about that another time,' he said; 'just now we've got weightier things to deal with.'

He pointed to the pudding, which had grown cold during the conversation to which I have alluded. H.O. stopped crying, but Alice went on with it. Oswald now said –

'We're a base and outcast family. Until that pudding's out of the house we shan't be able to look any one in the face. We must see that that pudding goes to poor children – not grisling, grumpy, whiney-piney, pretending poor children – but real poor ones, just as poor as they can stick.'

'And the figs too – and the dates,' said Noël, with regretting tones.

'Every fig,' said Dicky sternly. 'Oswald is quite right.'

This honourable resolution made us feel a bit better. We hastily put on our best things, and washed ourselves a bit, and hurried out to find some really poor people to give the pudding to. We cut it in slices ready, and put it in a basket with the figs and dates and toffee. We would not let H.O. come with us at first because he wanted to. And Alice would not come because of him. So at last we had to let him. The excitement of tearing into your best things heals the hurt that wounded honour feels, as the poetry writer said – or at any rate it makes the hurt feel better.

We went out into the streets. They were pretty quiet – nearly everybody was eating its Christmas dessert. But presently we met a woman in an apron. Oswald said very politely –

'Please, are you a poor person?' And she told us to get along with us.

The next we met was a shabby man with a hole in his left boot.

Again Oswald said, 'Please, are you a poor person, and have you any poor little children?'

The man told us not to come any of our games with him, or we should laugh on the wrong side of our faces. We went on sadly. We had no heart to stop and explain to him that we had no games to come.

The next was a young man near the Obelisk. Dora tried this time.

She said, 'Oh, if you please we've got some Christmas pudding in this basket, and if you're a poor person you can have some.'

'Poor as Job,' said the young man in a hoarse voice, and he had to come up out of a red comforter to say it.

We gave him a slice of the pudding, and he bit into it without thanks or delay. The next minute he had thrown the pudding slap in Dora's face, and was clutching Dicky by the collar.

'Blime if I don't chuck ye in the river, the whole bloomin' lot of you!' he exclaimed.

The girls screamed, the boys shouted, and though Oswald threw himself on the insulter of his sister with all his manly vigour, yet but for a friend of Oswald's, who is in the police, passing at that instant, the author shudders to think what might have happened, for he was a strong young man, and Oswald is not yet come to his full strength, and the Quaggy runs all too near.

Our policeman led our assailant aside, and we waited anxiously, as he told us to. After long uncertain moments the young man in the comforter loafed off grumbling, and our policeman turned to us.

'Said you give him a dollop o'pudding, and it tasted of soap and hair-oil.'

I suppose the hair-oil must have been the Brown Windsoriness of the soap coming out. We were sorry, but it was still our duty to get rid of the pudding. The Quaggy was handy, it is true, but when you have collected money to feed poor children and spent it on pudding it is not right to throw that pudding in the river. People do not subscribe shillings and sixpences and half-crowns to feed a hungry flood with Christmas pudding.

Yet we shrank from asking any more people whether they were poor persons, or about their families, and still more from offering the pudding to chance people who might bite into it and taste the soap before we had time to get away.

It was Alice, the most paralysed with disgrace of all of us, who thought of the best idea.

She said, 'Let's take it to the workhouse. At any rate they're all poor there, and they mayn't go out without leave, so they can't run after us to do anything to us after the pudding. No one would give them leave to go out to pursue people who had brought them pudding, and wreck vengeance on them, and at any rate we shall get rid of the conscience-pudding – it's a sort of conscience-money, you know – only it isn't money but pudding.'

The workhouse is a good way, but we stuck to it, though very cold, and hungrier than we thought possible when we started, for we had been so agitated we had not even stayed to eat the plain pudding our good father had so kindly and thoughtfully ordered for our Christmas dinner.

The big bell at the workhouse made a man open the door to us, when we rang it. Oswald said (and he spoke because he is next eldest to Dora, and she had had jolly well enough of saying anything about pudding) – he said –

'Please we've brought some pudding for the poor people.'

527

He looked us up and down, and he looked at our basket, then he said: 'You'd better see the Matron.'

We waited in a hall, feeling more and more uncomfy, and less and less like Christmas. We were very cold indeed, especially our hands and our noses. And we felt less and less able to face the Matron if she was horrid, and one of us at least wished we had chosen the Quaggy for the pudding's long home, and made it up to the robbed poor in some other way afterwards.

Just as Alice was saying earnestly in the burning cold ear of Oswald, 'Let's put down the basket and make a bolt for it. Oh, Oswald, *let's*!' a lady came along the passage. She was very upright, and she had eyes that went through you like blue gimlets. I should not like to be obliged to thwart that lady if she had any design, and mine was opposite. I am glad this is not likely to occur.

She said, 'What's all this about a pudding?'

H.O. said at once, before we could stop him, 'They say I've stolen the pudding, so we've brought it here for the poor people.'

'No, we didn't!' 'That wasn't why!'

'The money was given!' 'It was meant for the poor!' 'Shut up, H.O.!' said the rest of us all at once.

Then there was an awful silence. The lady gimleted us again one by one with her blue eyes.

Then she said: 'Come into my room. You all look frozen.'

She took us into a very jolly room with velvet curtains and a big fire, and the gas lighted, because now it was almost dark, even out of doors. She gave us chairs, and Oswald felt as if his was a dock, he felt so criminal, and the lady looked so Judgular.

Then she took the arm-chair by the fire herself, and said, 'Who's the eldest?'

'I am,' said Dora, looking more like a frightened white rabbit than I've ever seen her.

'Then tell me all about it.'

Dora looked at Alice and began to cry. That slab of pudding in the face had totally unnerved the gentle girl. Alice's eyes were red, and her face was puffy with crying; but she spoke up for Dora and said –

'Oh, please let Oswald tell. Dora can't. She's tired with the long walk. And a young man threw a piece of it in her face, and –'

The lady nodded and Oswald began. He told the story from the very beginning, as he has always been taught to, though he hated to lay bare the family honour's wound before a stranger, however judgelike and gimlet-eyed.

He told all – not concealing the pudding-throwing, nor what the young man said about soap.

'So,' he ended, 'we want to give the conscience-pudding to you. It's like conscience-money – you know what that is, don't you? But if you really think it is soapy and not just the young man's horridness, perhaps you'd better not let them eat it. But the figs and things are all right.'

When he had done the lady said, for most of us were crying more or less –

'Come, cheer up! It's Christmas-time, and he's very little – your brother, I mean. And I think the rest of you seem pretty well able to take care of the honour of the family. I'll take the conscience-pudding off your minds. Where are you going now?'

'Home, I suppose,' Oswald said. And he thought how nasty and dark and dull it would be. The fire out most likely and Father away.

'And your father's not at home, you say,' the blue-gimlet lady went on. 'What do you say to having tea with me, and then seeing the entertainment we have got up for our old people?'

Then the lady smiled and the blue gimlets looked quite merry.

The room was so warm and comfortable and the invitation was the last thing we expected. It was jolly of her, I do think.

No one thought quite at first of saying how pleased we should be to accept her kind invitation. Instead we all just said 'Oh!' but in a tone which must have told her we meant 'Yes, please', very deeply.

Oswald (this has more than once happened) was the first to restore his manners. He made a proper bow like he has been taught, and said –

'Thank you very much. We should like it very much. It is very much nicer than going home. Thank you very much.'

I need not tell the reader that Oswald could have made up a much better speech if he had had more time to make it up in, or if he had not been so filled with mixed flusteredness and furification by the shameful events of the day.

We washed our faces and hands and had a first rate muffin and crumpet tea, with slices of cold meats, and many nice jams and cakes. A lot of other people were there, most of them people who were giving the entertainment to the aged poor.

After tea it was the entertainment. Songs and conjuring and a play called 'Box and Cox', very amusing, and a lot of throwing things about in it – bacon and chops and things – and nigger minstrels. We clapped till our hands were sore.

When it was over we said goodbye. In between the songs and things Oswald had had time to make up a speech of thanks to the lady.

He said –

'We all thank you heartily for your goodness. The entertainment was beautiful. We shall never forget your kindness and hospitableness.'

The lady laughed, and said she had been very pleased to have us. A fat gentleman said –

'And your teas? I hope you enjoyed those – eh?'

Oswald had not had time to make up an answer to that, so he answered straight from the heart, and said –

'Ra – *ther*!'

And every one laughed and slapped us boys on the back and kissed the girls, and the gentleman who played the bones in the nigger minstrels saw us home. We ate the cold pudding that night, and H.O. dreamed that something came to eat him, like it advises you to in the advertisements on the hoardings. The grown-ups said it was the pudding, but I don't think it could have been that, because, as I have said more than once, it was so very plain.

Some of H.O.'s brothers and sisters thought it was a judgement on him for pretending about who the poor children were he was collecting the money for. Oswald does not believe such a little boy as H.O. would have a real judgement made just for him and nobody else, whatever he did.

But it certainly is odd. H.O. was the only one who had bad dreams, and he was also the only one who got any of the things we bought with that ill-gotten money, because, you remember, he picked a hole in the raisin-paper as he was bringing the parcel home. The rest of us had nothing, unless you count the scrapings of the pudding-basin, and those don't really count at all.

ARCHIBALD THE UNPLEASANT

THE house of Bastable was once in poor, but honest, circs. That was when it lived in a semi-detached house in the Lewisham Road, and looked for treasure. There were six scions of the house who looked for it – in fact there were seven, if you count Father. I am sure he looked right enough, but he did not do it the right way. And we did. And so we found a treasure of a great-uncle, and we and Father went to live with him in a very affluent mansion on Blackheath – with gardens and vineries and pineries and everything jolly you can think of. And then, when we were no longer so beastly short of pocket-money, we tried to be good, and sometimes it came out right, and sometimes it didn't. Something like sums.

And then it was the Christmas holidays – and we had a bazaar and raffled the most beautiful goat you ever saw, and we gave the money to the poor and needy.

And then we felt it was time to do something new, because we were as rich as our worthy relative, the uncle, and our father – now also wealthy, at least, compared to what he used to be – thought right for us; and we were as good as we could be without being good for nothing and muffs, which I hope no one calling itself a Bastable will ever stoop to.

So then Oswald, so often the leader in hazardous enterprises, thought long and deeply in his interior self, and he saw that something must be done, because, though there was still the goat left over, unclaimed by its fortunate winner at the Bazaar, somehow no really fine idea seemed to come out of it, and nothing else was happening. Dora was getting a bit domineering, and Alice was too much taken up with trying to learn to knit. Dicky was bored and so was Oswald, and Noël was writing far more poetry than could be healthy for any poet, however young, and H.O. was simply a nuisance. His boots are always much louder when he is not amused, and that gets the rest of us into rows, because there are hardly any grown-up persons who can tell the difference between his boots and mine. Oswald decided to call a council (because even if nothing comes of a council it always means getting Alice to drop knitting, and making Noël chuck the poetical influences, that are no use and only make him silly), and he went into the room that is our room. It is called the common-room, like in colleges, and it is very different from the room that was ours when we were poor, but honest. It is a jolly room, with a big table and a big couch, that is most useful for games, and a thick carpet because of H.O.'s boots.

Alice was knitting by the fire; it was for Father, but I am sure his feet are not at all that shape. He has a high and beautifully formed instep like Oswald's. Noël was writing poetry, of course.

> *My dear sister sits*
> *And knits,*
> *I hope to goodness the stocking fits,*

was as far as he had got.

'It ought to be "my dearest sister" to sound right,' he said, 'but that wouldn't be kind to Dora.'

'Thank you,' said Dora. 'You needn't trouble to be kind to me, if you don't want to.'

'Shut up, Dora!' said Dicky, 'Noël didn't mean anything.'

'He never does,' said H.O., 'nor yet his poetry doesn't neither.'

'*And* his poetry doesn't *either*,' Dora corrected; 'and besides, you oughtn't to say that at all, it's unkind –'

'You're too jolly down on the kid,' said Dicky.

And Alice said, 'Eighty-seven, eighty-eight – oh, do be quiet half a sec.! – eighty-nine, ninety – now I shall have to count the stitches all over again!'

Oswald alone was silent and not cross. I tell you this to show that the sort of worryingness was among us that is catching, like measles. Kipling calls it the cameelious hump, and, as usual, that great and good writer is quite correct.

So Oswald said, 'Look here, let's have a council. It says in Kipling's book when you've got the hump go and dig till you gently perspire. Well, we can't do that, because it's simply pouring, but –'

The others all interrupted him, and said they hadn't got the hump and they didn't know what he meant. So he shrugged his shoulders patiently (it is not his fault that the others hate him to shrug his shoulders patiently) and he said no more.

Then Dora said, 'Oh, don't be so disagreeable, Oswald, for goodness' sake!'

I assure you she did, though he had done simply nothing.

Matters were in this cryptical state when the door opened and Father came in.

'Hullo, kiddies!' he remarked kindly. 'Beastly wet day, isn't it? And dark too, I can't think why the rain can't always come in term time. It seems a poor arrangement to have it in "vac.", doesn't it?'

I think every one instantly felt better. I know one of us did, and it was me.

Father lit the gas, and sat down in the armchair and took Alice on his knee.

'First,' he said, 'here is a box of chocs.' It was an extra big and beautiful one and Fuller's best. 'And besides the chocs., a piece of good news! You're all asked to a party at Mrs Leslie's. She's going to have all sorts of games and things, with prizes for every one, and a conjurer and a magic lantern.'

The shadow of doom seemed to be lifted from each young brow, and we felt how much fonder we were of each other than any one would have thought. At least Oswald felt this, and Dicky told me afterwards he felt Dora wasn't such a bad sort after all.

'It's on Tuesday week,' said Father. 'I see the prospect pleases. Number three is that your cousin Archibald has come here to stay a week or two. His little sister has taken it into her head to have whooping-cough. And he's downstairs now, talking to your uncle.'

We asked what the young stranger was like, but Father did not know, because he and cousin Archibald's father had not seen much of each other for some years. Father said this, but we knew it was because Archibald's father hadn't bothered to see ours when he was poor and honest, but now he was the wealthy sharer of the red-brick, beautiful Blackheath house it was different. This made us not like Uncle Archibald very much, but we were too just to blame it on to young Archibald. All the same we should have liked him better if his father's previous career had not been of such a worldly and stuck-up sort. Besides, I do think Archibald is quite the most rotten sort of name. We should have called him Archie, of course, if he had been at all decent.

'You'll be as jolly to him as you can, I know,' Father said; 'he's a bit older than you, Oswald. He's not a bad-looking chap.'

Then Father went down and Oswald had to go with him, and there was Archibald sitting upright in a chair and talking to our Indian uncle as if he was some beastly grown-up. Our cousin proved to be dark and rather tall, and though he was only fourteen he was always stroking his lip to see if his moustache had begun to come.

Father introduced us to each other, and we said, 'How do

you do?' and looked at each other, and neither of us could think of anything else to say. At least Oswald couldn't. So then we went upstairs. Archibald shook hands with the others, and every one was silent except Dora, and she only whispered to H.O. to keep his feet still.

You cannot keep for ever in melancholy silence however few things you have to say, and presently some one said it was a wet day, and this well-chosen remark made us able to begin to talk.

I do not wish to be injurious to anybody, especially one who was a Bastable, by birth at least if not according to the nobler attributes, but I must say that Oswald never did dislike a boy so much as he did that young Archibald. He was as cocky as though he'd done something to speak of – been captain of his eleven, or passed a beastly exam., or something – but we never could find that he had done anything. He was always bragging about the things he had at home, and the things he was allowed to do, and all the things he knew all about, but he was a most untruthful chap. He laughed at Noël's being a poet – a thing we never do, because it makes him cry and crying makes him ill – and of course Oswald and Dicky could not punch his head in their own house because of the laws of hospitableness, and Alice stopped it at last by saying she didn't care if it was being a sneak, she would tell Father the very next time. I don't think she would have, because we made a rule, when we were poor and honest, not to bother Father if we could possibly help it. And we keep it up still. But Archibald didn't know that. Then this cousin, who is, I fear, the black sheep of the Bastables, and hardly worthy to be called one, used to pull the girls' hair, and pinch them at prayers when they could not call out or do anything to him back.

And he was awfully rude to the servants, ordering them about, and playing tricks on them, not amusing tricks like other Bastables might have done – such as booby-traps and mice under dish-covers, which seldom leaves any lasting ill-feeling – but things no decent boy would do – like hiding their letters and not giving them to them for days, and then it was too late to meet the young man the letter was from, and squirting ink on their aprons when they were just going to open the door, and once he put a fish-hook in the cook's pocket when she wasn't looking. He did not do anything to Oswald at that time. I suppose he was afraid. I just tell you this to show you that Oswald didn't cotton to him for no selfish reason, but because Oswald has been taught to feel for others.

He called us all kids – and he was that kind of boy we knew at once it was no good trying to start anything new and jolly – so Oswald, ever discreet and wary, shut up entirely about the council. We played games with him sometimes, not really good ones, but Snap and Beggar my Neighbour, and even then he used to cheat. I hate to say it of one of our blood, but I can hardly believe he was. I think he must have been changed at nurse like the heirs to monarchies and dukeries.

Well, the days passed slowly. There was Mrs Leslie's party shining starrishly in the mysteries of the future. Also we had another thing to look forward to, and that was when Archibald would have to go back to school. But we could not enjoy that foreshadowing so much because of us having to go back at nearly the same time.

Oswald always tries to be just, no matter how far from easy, and so I will say that I am not quite sure that it was Archibald that set the pipes leaking, but we were all up in the loft the day before, snatching a golden opportunity to play a brief game of robbers in a cave, while Archibald had gone down to the village to get his silly hair cut. Another thing about him that was not natural was his being always looking in the glass and wanting to talk about whether people were handsome or not; and he made as much fuss about his ties as though he had been a girl. So when he was gone Alice said –

'Hist! The golden moment. Let's be robbers in the loft, and when he comes back he won't know where we are.

'He'll hear us,' said Noël, biting his pencil.

'No, he won't. We'll be the Whispering Band of Weird Bandits. Come on, Noël; you can finish the poetry up here.'

'It's about *him*,' said Noël gloomily, 'when he's gone back to –' (Oswald will not give the name of Archibald's school for the sake of the other boys there, as they might not like everybody who reads this to know about there being a chap like him in their midst.) 'I shall do it up in an envelope and put a stamp on it and post it to him, and –'

'Haste!' cried Alice. 'Bard of the Bandits, haste while yet there's time.'

So we tore upstairs and put on our slippers and socks over them, and we got the high-backed chair out of the girls' bedroom, and the others held it steady while Oswald agilitively mounted upon its high back and opened the trap-door and got up into the place between the roof and the ceiling (the boys in *Stalky & Co.* found this out by accident, and they were surprised and pleased, but we have known all about it ever since we can remember).

Then the others put the chair back, and Oswald let down the rope ladder that we made out of bamboo and clothes-line after uncle told us the story of the missionary lady who was shut up in a rajah's palace, and some one shot an arrow to her with a string tied to it, and it might have killed her I should have thought, but it didn't, and she hauled in the string and there was a rope and a bamboo ladder, and so she escaped, and we made one like it on purpose for the loft. No one had ever told us not to make ladders.

The others came up by the rope-ladder (it was partly bamboo, but rope-ladder does for short) and we shut the trap-door down. It is jolly up there. There are two big cisterns, and one little window in a gable that gives you just enough light. The floor is plaster with wooden things going across, beams and joists they are called. There are some planks laid on top of these here and there. Of course if you walk on the plaster you will go through with your foot into the room below.

We had a very jolly game, in whispers, and Noël sat by the little window, and was quite happy, being the bandit bard. The cisterns are rocks you hide behind. But the jolliest part was when we heard Archibald shouting out, 'Hullo! kids, where are you?' and we all stayed as still as mice, and heard Jane say she thought we must have gone out. Jane was the one that hadn't got her letter, as well as having her apron inked all over.

Then we heard Archibald going all over the house looking for us. Father was at business and uncle was at his club. And we were *there*. And so Archibald was all alone. And we might have gone on for hours enjoying the spectacle of his confusion and perplexedness, but Noël happened to sneeze – the least thing gives him cold and he sneezes louder for his age than any·one I know – just when Archibald was on the landing underneath. Then he stood there and said –

'I know where you are. Let me come up.'

We cautiously did not reply. Then he said:

'All right. I'll go and get the step-ladder.'

We did not wish this. We had not been told not to make rope-ladders, nor yet about not playing in the loft; but if he fetched the step-ladder Jane would know, and there are some secrets you like to keep to yourself.

So Oswald opened the trap-door and squinted down, and there was that Archibald with his beastly hair cut. Oswald said –

'We'll let you up if you promise not to tell you've been up here.'

So he promised, and we let down the rope-ladder. And it will show you the kind of boy he was that the instant he had got up by it he began to find fault with the way it was made.

Then he wanted to play with the ball-cock. But Oswald knows it is better not to do this.

'I daresay *you're* forbidden,' Archibald said, 'little kids like you. But *I* know all about plumbing.'

And Oswald could not prevent his fiddling with the pipes and the ball-cock a little. Then we went down. All chance of further banditry was at an end. Next day was Sunday. The leak was noticed then. It was slow, but steady, and the plumber was sent for on Monday morning.

Oswald does not know whether it was Archibald who made the leak, but he does know about what came after.

I think our displeasing cousin found that piece of poetry that Noël was beginning about him, and read it, because he is a sneak. Instead of having it out with Noël he sucked up to him and gave him a sixpenny fountain-pen which Noël liked, although it is really no good for him to try to write poetry with anything but a pencil, because he always sucks whatever he writes with, and ink is poisonous, I believe.

Then in the afternoon he and Noël got quite thick, and went off together. And afterwards Noël seemed very peacocky about something, but he would not say what, and Archibald was grinning in a way Oswald would have liked to pound his head for.

Then, quite suddenly, the peaceable quietness of that happy Blackheath home was brought to a close by screams. Servants ran about with brooms and pails, and the water was coming through the ceiling of uncle's room like mad, and Noël turned white and looked at our unattractive cousin and said: 'Send him away.'

Alice put her arm round Noël and said: 'Do go, Archibald.'

But he wouldn't.

So then Noël said he wished he had never been born, and whatever would Father say.

'Why, what is it, Noël?' Alice asked that. 'Just tell us, we'll all stand by you. What's he been doing?'

'You won't let him do anything to me if I tell?'

'Tell tale tit,' said Archibald.

'He got me to go up into the loft and he said it was a secret, and would I promise not to tell, and I won't tell; only I've done it, and now the water's coming in.'

'You've done it? You young ass, I was only kidding you!' said our detestable cousin. And he laughed.

'I don't understand,' said Oswald. 'What did you tell Noël?'

'He can't tell you because he promised – and I won't – unless you vow by the honour of the house you talk so much about that you'll never tell I had anything to do with it.'

That will show you what he was. We had never mentioned the honour of the house except once quite at the beginning, before we knew how discapable he was of understanding anything, and how far we were from wanting to call him Archie.

We had to promise, for Noël was getting greener and more gurgly every minute, and at any moment Father or uncle might burst in foaming for an explanation, and none of us would have one except Noël, and him in this state of all-anyhow.

So Dicky said –

'We promise, you beast, you!' And we all said the same.

Then Archibald said, drawling his words and feeling for the moustache that wasn't there, and I hope he'll be quite old before he gets one –

'It's just what comes of trying to amuse silly little kids. I told the foolish little animal about people having arteries cut, and your having to cut the whole thing to stop the bleeding. And he said, "Was that what the plumber would do to the leaky pipe?" And how pleased your governor would be to find it mended. And then he went and did it.'

'You told me to,' said Noël, turning greener and greener.

'Go along with Alice,' said Oswald. 'We'll stand by you. And Noël, old chap, you must keep your word and not sneak about that sneaking hound.'

Alice took him away, and we were left with the horrid Archibald.

'Now,' said Oswald, 'I won't break my word, no more will the rest of us. But we won't speak another word to you as long as we live.'

'Oh, Oswald,' said Dora, 'what about the sun going down?'

'Let it jolly well go,' said Dicky in furiousness. 'Oswald didn't say we'd go on being angry for ever, but I'm with Oswald all the way. I won't talk to cads – no, not even before grown-ups. They can jolly well think what they like.'

After this no one spoke to Archibald.

Oswald rushed for a plumber, and such was his fiery eloquence he really caught one and brought him home. Then he and Dicky waited for Father when he came in, and they got him into the study, and Oswald said what they had all agreed on. It was this:

'Father, we are all most awfully sorry, but one of us has cut the pipe in the loft, and if you make us tell you any more it will not be honourable, and we are very sorry. Please, please don't ask who it was did it.'

Father bit his moustache and looked worried, and Dicky went on –

'Oswald has got a plumber and he is doing it now.'

Then Father said, 'How on earth did you get into the loft?'

And then of course the treasured secret of the rope-ladder had to be revealed. We had never been told not to make rope-ladders and go into the loft, but we did not try to soften the anger of our father by saying this. It would not have been any good either. We just had to stick it. And the punishment of our crime was most awful. It was that we weren't to go to Mrs Leslie's party. And Archibald was to go, because when Father asked him if he was in it with the rest of us, he said 'No.' I cannot think of any really gentle, manly, and proper words to say what I think about my unnatural cousin.

We kept our word about not speaking to him, and I think Father thought we were jealous because he was going to that conjuring, magic lantern party and we were not. Noël was the most unhappy, because he knew we were all being punished for what he had done. He was very affectionate and tried to write pieces of poetry to us all, but he was so unhappy he couldn't even write, and he went into the kitchen and sat on Jane's knee and said his head ached.

Next day it was the day of the party and we were plunged in gloom. Archibald got out his Etons and put his clean shirt ready, and a pair of flashy silk socks with red spots, and then he went into the bath-room.

Noël and Jane were whispering on the stairs. Jane came up and Noël went down. Jane knocked at the bath-room door and said –

'Here's the soap, Master Archerbald. I didn't put none in to-day.'

He opened the door and put out his hand.

'Half a moment,' said Jane, 'I've got something else in my hand.'

As she spoke the gas all over the house went down blue, and then went out. We held our breaths heavily.

'Here it is,' she said; 'I'll put it in your hand. I'll go down and turn off the burners and see about the gas. You'll be late, sir. If I was you I should get on a bit with the washing of myself in the dark. I daresay the gas'll be five or ten minutes, and it's five o'clock now.'

It wasn't, and of course she ought not to have said it, but it was useful all the same.

Noël came stumping up the stairs in the dark. He fumbled about and then whispered, 'I've turned the little white china knob that locks the bath-room door on the outside.'

The water was bubbling and hissing in the pipes inside, and the darkness went on. Father and uncle had not come in yet, which was a fortunate blessing.

'Do be quiet!' said Noël. 'Just you wait.'

We all sat on the stairs and waited. Noël said –

'Don't ask me yet – you'll see – you wait.'

And we waited, and the gas did not come back.

At last Archibald tried to come out – he thought he had washed himself clean, I suppose – and of course the door was fastened. He kicked and he hammered and he shouted, and we were glad.

At last Noël banged on the door and screamed through the keyhole –

'If we let you out will you let us off our promise not to tell about you and the pipes? We won't tell till you've gone back to school.'

He wouldn't for a long time, but at last he had to.

'I shan't ever come to your beastly house again,' he bellowed through the keyhole, 'so I don't mind.'

'Turn off the gas-burners then,' said Oswald, ever thoughtful, though he was still in ignorance of the beautiful truth.

Then Noël sang out over the stairs, 'Light up!' and Jane went round with a taper, and when the landing gas was lighted Noël turned the knob of the bath-room, and Archibald exited in his Indian red and yellow dressing-gown that he thought so much of. Of course we expected his face to be red with rage, or white with passion, or purple with mixed emotions, but you cannot think what our feelings were –

indeed, we hardly knew what they were ourselves – when we saw that he was not red or white or purple, but *black*. He looked like an uneven sort of bluish nigger. His face and hands were all black and blue in streaks, and so were the bits of his feet that showed between his Indian dressing-gown and his Turkish slippers.

The word 'Crikey' fell from more than one lip.

'What are you staring at?' he asked.

We did not answer even then, though I think it was less from keep-your-wordishness than amazement. But Jane did.

'Nyang, Nyang!' she uttered tauntingly. 'You thought it was soap I was giving you, and all the time it was Maple's dark bright navy-blue indelible dye – won't wash out.' She flashed a looking-glass in his face, and he looked and saw the depth of his dark bright navy-blueness.

Now, you may think that we shouted with laughing to see him done brown and dyed blue like this, but we did not. There was a spellbound silence. Oswald, I know, felt a quite uncomfortable feeling inside him.

When Archibald had had one good look at himself he did not want any more. He ran to his room and bolted himself in.

'*He* won't go to no parties,' said Jane, and she flounced downstairs.

We never knew how much Noël had told her. He is very young, and not so strong as we are, and we thought it better not to ask.

Oswald and Dicky and H.O. – particularly H.O. – told each other it served him right, but after a bit Dora asked Noël if he would mind her trying to get some of it off our unloved cousin, and he said 'No.'

But nothing would get it off him; and when Father came home there was an awful row. And he said we had disgraced ourselves and forgotten the duties of hospitality. We got it pretty straight, I can tell you. And we bore it all. I do not say we were martyrs to the honour of our house and to our plighted word, but I do say that we got it very straight indeed, and we did not tell the provocativeness we had had from our guest that drove the poet Noël to this wild and desperate revenge.

But some one told, and I have always thought it was Jane, and that is why we did not ask too many questions about what Noël had told her, because late that night Father came and said he now understood that we had meant to do right, except perhaps the one who cut the pipe with a chisel, and that must have been more silliness than naughtiness; and perhaps the being dyed blue served our cousin rather right. And he gave Archibald a few remarks in private, and when the dye began to come off – it was not a fast dye, though it said so on the paper it was wrapped in – Archibald, now a light streaky blue, really did seem to be making an effort to be something like decent. And when, now merely a pale grey, he had returned to school, he sent us a letter. It said:

My dear Cousins,

I think that I was beastlier than I meant to be, but I am not accustomed to young kids. And I think uncle was right, and the way you stand up for the honour of our house is not all nonsense, like I said it was. If we ever meet in the future life I hope you will not keep a down on me about things. I don't think you can expect me to say more. From your affectionate cousin,

Archibald Bastable.

So I suppose rays of remorse penetrated that cold heart, and now perhaps he will be a reformed Bastable. I am sure I hope so, but I believe it is difficult, if not impossible, for a leopard to change his skin.

Still, I remember how indelibly black he looked when he came out of the fatal bathroom; and it nearly all wore off. And perhaps spots on the honourable inside parts of your soul come off with time. I hope so. The dye never came off the inside of the bath though. I think that was what annoyed our good great-uncle the most.

OVER THE WATER TO CHINA

OSWALD is a very modest boy, I believe, but even he would not deny that he has an active brain. The author has heard both his father and Albert's uncle say so. And the most far-reaching ideas often come to him quite naturally – just as silly notions that aren't any good might come to you. And he had an idea which he meant to hold a council about with his brothers and sisters; but just as he was going to unroll his idea to them our father occurred suddenly in our midst and said a strange cousin was coming, and he came, and he was strange indeed! And when Fate had woven the threads of his dark destiny and he had been dyed a dark bright navy-blue, and had gone from our midst, Oswald went back to the idea that he had not forgotten. The words 'tenacious of purpose' mean sticking to things, and these words always make me think of the character of the young hero of these pages. At least I suppose his brothers Dicky and Noël and H.O. are heroes too, in a way, but somehow the author of these lines knows more about Oswald's inside realness than he does about the others. But I am getting too deep for words.

So Oswald went into the common-room. Every one was busy. Noël and H.O. were playing Halma. Dora was covering boxes with silver paper to put sweets in for a school treat, and Dicky was making a cardboard model of a new screw he has invented for ocean steamers. But Oswald did not mind interrupting, because Dora ought not to work too hard, and Halma always ends in a row, and I would rather not say what I think of Dicky's screw. So Oswald said –

'I want a council. Where's Alice?'

Every one said they didn't know, and they made haste to say that we couldn't have a council without her. But Oswald's determined nature made him tell H.O. to chuck that rotten game and go and look for her. H.O. is our youngest brother, and it is right that he should remember this and do as he was told. But he happened to be winning the beastly Halma game, and Oswald saw that there was going to be trouble – 'big trouble', as Mr Kipling says. And he was just bracing his young nerves for the conflict with H.O., because he was not going to stand any nonsense from his young brother about his not fetching Alice when he was jolly well told to, when the missing maiden bounced into the room bearing upon her brow the marks of ravaging agitatedness.

'Have any of you seen Pincher?' she cried, in haste.

We all said, 'No, not since last night.'

'Well, then, he's lost,' Alice said, making the ugly face that means you are going to blub in half a minute.

Every one had sprung to their feet. Even Noël and H.O. saw at once what a doddering game Halma is, and Dora and Dicky, whatever their faults, care more for Pincher than for boxes and screws. Because Pincher is our fox-terrier. He is of noble race, and he was ours when we were poor, lonely treasure-seekers and lived in humble hardupness in the Lewisham Road.

To the faithful heart of young Oswald the Blackheath affluent mansion and all it contains, even the stuffed fox eating a duck in the glass case in the hall that he is so fond of, and even the council he wanted to have, seemed to matter much less than old Pincher.

'I want you all to let's go out and look for him,' said Alice, carrying out the meaning of the faces she had made and beginning to howl. 'Oh, Pincher, suppose something happens to him; you might get my hat and coat, Dora. Oh, oh, oh!'

We all got our coats and hats, and by the time we were ready Alice had conquered it to only sniffing, or else, as Oswald told her kindly, she wouldn't have been allowed to come.

'Let's go on the Heath,' Noël said. 'The dear departed dog used to like digging there.'

So we went. And we said to every single person we met –

'Please have you seen a thoroughbred fox-terrier dog with a black patch over one eye, and another over his tail, and a tan patch on his right shoulder?' And every one said, 'No, they hadn't', only some had more polite ways of saying it than others. But after a bit we met a policeman, and he said, 'I see one when I was on duty last night, like what you describe, but it was at the end of a string. There was a young lad at the other end. The dog didn't seem to go exactly willing.'

He also told us the lad and the dog had gone over Greenwich way. So we went down, not quite so wretched in our insides, because now it seemed that there was some chance, though we wondered the policeman *could* have let Pincher go when he saw he didn't want to, but he said it wasn't his business. And now we asked every one if they'd seen a lad and a thoroughbred fox-terrier with a black patch, and cetera.

And one or two people said they had, and we thought it must be the same the policeman had seen, because they said, too, that the dog didn't seem to care about going where he was going.

So we went on and through the Park and past the Naval College, and we didn't even stop to look at that life-sized firm ship in the playground that the Naval Collegians have to learn about ropes and spars on, and Oswald would willingly give a year of his young life to have that ship for his very own.

And we didn't go into the Painted Hall either, because

our fond hearts were with Pincher, and we could not really have enjoyed looking at Nelson's remains, of the shipwrecks where the drowning people all look so dry, or even the pictures where young heroes are boarding pirates from Spain, just as Oswald would do if he had half a chance, with the pirates fighting in attitudes more twisted and Spanish than the pirates of any nation could manage even if they were not above it. It is an odd thing, but all those pictures are awfully bad weather – even the ones that are not shipwrecks. And yet in books the skies are usually a stainless blue and the sea is a liquid gem when you are engaged in the avocation of pirate-boarding.

The author is sorry to see that he is not going on with the story.

We walked through Greenwich Hospital and asked there if they have seen Pincher, because I heard Father say once that dogs are sometimes stolen and taken to hospitals and never seen again. It is wrong to steal, but I suppose the hospital doctors forget this because they are so sorry for the poor ill people and like to give them dogs to play with them and amuse them on their beds of anguish. But no one had seen our Pincher, who seemed to be becoming more dear to our hearts every moment.

When we got through the Hospital grounds – they are big and the buildings are big, and I like it all because there's so much room everywhere and nothing niggling – we got down to the terrace over the river, next to the Trafalgar Hotel. And there was a sailor leaning on the railings, and we asked him the usual question. It seems that he was asleep, but of course we did not know, or we would not have disturbed him. He was very angry, and he swore, and Oswald told the girls to come away; but Alice pulled away from Oswald and said,

'Oh, don't be so cross. Do tell us if you've seen our dog? He is –' and she recited Pincher's qualifications.

'Ho yes,' said the sailor – he had a red and angry face. 'I see 'im a hour ago 'long of a Chinaman. 'E crossed the river in a open boat. You'd best look slippy arter 'im.' He grinned and spat; he was a detestable character, I think. 'Chinamen puts puppy-dogs in pies. If 'e catches you three young chaps 'e'll 'ave a pie as'll need a big crust to cover it. Get along with your cheek!'

So we got along. Of course, we knew that the Chinese are not cannibals, so we were not frightened by that rot; but we knew, too, that the Chinese do really eat dogs, as well as rats and birds' nests and other disgraceful forms of eating.

H.O. was very tired, and he said his boots hurt him; and Noël was beginning to look like a young throstle – all eyes and beak. He always does when he is tired. The others were tired too, but their proud spirits would never have owned it. So we went round to the Trafalgar Hotel's boathouse, and there was a man in slippers, and we said could we have a boat, and he said he would send a boatman, and would we walk in?

We did, and we went through a dark room piled up to the ceiling with boats and out on to a sort of thing half like a balcony and half like a pier. And there were boats there too, far more than you would think any one could want; and then a boy came. We said we wanted to go across the river, and he said, 'Where to?'

'To where the Chinamen live,' said Alice.

'You can go to Millwall if you want to,' he said, beginning to put oars into the boat.

'Are there any Chinese people there?' Alice asked.

And the boy replied, 'I dunno.' He added that he supposed we could pay for the boat.

By a fortunate accident – I think Father had rather wanted to make up to us for our martyr-like enduring when our cousin was with us – we were fairly flush of chink. Oswald and Dicky were proudly able to produce handfuls of money; it was mostly copper, but it did not fail of its effect.

The boy seemed not to dislike us quite so much as before, and he helped the girls into the boat, which was now in the water at the edge of a sort of floating, unsteady raft, with openings in it that you could see the water through. The water was very rough, just like real sea, and not like a river at all. And the boy rowed; he wouldn't let us, although I can, quite well. The boat tumbled and tossed just like a sea-boat. When we were about half-way over, Noël pulled Alice's sleeve and said –

'Do I look very green?'

'You do rather, dear,' she said kindly.

'I feel much greener than I look,' said Noël. And later on he was not at all well.

The boy laughed, but we pretended not to notice. I wish I could tell you half the things we saw as our boat was pulled along through the swishing, lumpy water that turned into great waves after every steamer that went by. Oswald was quite fit, but some of the others were very silent. Dicky says he saw everything that Oswald saw, but I am not sure. There were wharves and engines, and great rusty cranes swinging giant's handfuls of iron rails about in the air, and once we passed a ship that was being broken up. All the wood was gone, and they were taking away her plates, and the red rust was running from her and colouring the water all round; it looked as though she was bleeding to death. I suppose it was silly to feel sorry for her, but I did. I thought how beastly it was that she would never go to sea again, where the waves are clean and green, even if no rougher than the black waves now raging around our staunch little bark. I never knew before what lots of kinds of ships there can be, and I think I could have gone on and on for ever and ever looking at the shapes of things and the colours they were, and dreaming about being a pirate, and things like that, but we had come some way; and now Alice said –

'Oswald, I think Noël will die if we don't make land soon.'

And indeed he had been rather bad for some time, only I thought it was kinder to take no notice.

So our ship was steered among other pirate craft, and moored at a landing-place where there were steps up

Noël was now so ill that we felt we could not take him on a Chinese hunt, and H.O. had sneaked his boots off in the boat, and he said they hurt him too much to put them on again; so it was arranged that those two should sit on a dry corner of the steps and wait, and Dora said she would stay with them.

'I think we ought to go home,' she said. 'I'm quite sure Father wouldn't like us being in these wild, savage places. The police ought to find Pincher.'

But the others weren't going to surrender like that, especially as Dora had actually had the sense to bring a bag of biscuits, which all, except Noël, were now eating.

'Perhaps they ought, but they *won't*,' said Dicky. 'I'm boiling hot. I'll leave you my overcoat in case you're cold.'

Oswald had been just about to make the same manly proposal, though he was not extra warm. So they left their coats, and, with Alice, who would come though told not to, they climbed the steps, and went along a narrow passage and started boldly on the Chinese hunt. It was a strange sort of place over the river; all the streets were narrow, and the houses and the pavements and the people's clothes and the mud in the road all seemed the same sort of dull colour – a sort of brown-grey it was.

All the house doors were open, and you could see that the insides of the houses were the same colour as the outsides. Some of the women had blue, or violet or red shawls, and they sat on the doorsteps and combed their children's hair, and shouted things to each other across the street. They seemed very much struck by the appearance of the three travellers, and some of the things they said were not pretty.

That was the day when Oswald found out a thing that has often been of use to him in after-life. However rudely poor people stare at you they become all right instantly if you ask them something. I think they don't hate you so much when they've done something for you, if it's only to tell you the time or the way.

So we got on very well, but it does not make me comfortable to see people so poor and we have such a jolly house. People in books feel this, and I know it is right to feel it, but I hate the feeling all the same. And it is worse when the people are nice to you.

And we asked and asked and asked, but nobody had seen a dog or a Chinaman, and I began to think all was indeed lost, and you can't go on biscuits all day, when we went round a corner rather fast, and came slap into the largest woman I have ever seen. She must have been yards and yards round, and before she had time to be in the rage that we saw she was getting into, Alice said –

'Oh, I beg your pardon! I *am* so sorry, but we really didn't mean to! I *do* so hope we didn't hurt you!'

We saw the growing rage fade away, and she said, as soon as she got her fat breath –

'No 'arm done, my little dear. An' w'ere are you off to in such a 'urry?'

So we told her all about it. She was quite friendly, although so stout, and she said we oughtn't to be gallivanting about all on our own. We told her we were all right, though I own Oswald was glad that in the hurry of departing Alice hadn't had time to find anything smarter-looking to wear than her garden coat and grey Tam, which had been regretted by some earlier in the day.

'Well,' said the woman, 'if you go along this 'ere turning as far as ever you can go, and then take the first to the right and bear round to the left, and take the second to the right again, and go down the alley between the stumps, you'll come to Rose Gardens. There's often Chinamen about there. And if you come along this way as you come back, keep your eye open for me, and I'll arks some young chaps as I know as is interested like in dogs, and perhaps I'll have news for you.'

'Thank you very much,' Alice said, and the woman asked her to give her a kiss. Everybody is always wanting to kiss Alice. I can't think why. And we got her to tell us the way again, and we noticed the name of the street, and it was Nightingale Street, and the stairs where we had left the others was Bullamy's Causeway, because we have the true explorer's instincts, and when you can't blaze your way on trees with your axe, or lay crossed twigs like the gipsies do, it is best to remember the names of streets.

So we said goodbye, and went on through the grey-brown streets with hardly any shops, and those only very small and common, and we got to the alley all right. It was a narrow place between high blank brown-grey walls. I think by the smell it was gasworks and tanneries. There was hardly any one there, but when we got into it we heard feet running ahead of us, and Oswald said –

'Hullo, suppose that's some one with Pincher, and they've recognized his long-lost masters and they're making a bolt for it?'

And we all started running as hard as ever we could. There was a turn in the passage, and when we got round it we saw that the running was stopping. There were four or five boys in a little crowd round some one in blue – blue looked such a change after the muddy colour of everything in that dead Eastern domain – and when we got up, the person the blue was on was a very wrinkled old man, with a yellow wrinkled face and a soft felt hat and blue blouse-like coat, and I see that I ought not to conceal any longer from the discerning reader that it was exactly what we had been looking for. It was indeed a Celestial Chinaman in deep difficulties with these boys who were, as Alice said afterwards, truly fiends in mortal shape. They were laughing at the old Chinaman, and shouting to each other, and their language was of that kind I was sorry we had got Alice with us. But she told Oswald afterwards that she was so angry she did not know what they were saying.

'Pull his bloomin' pigtail,' said one of these outcasts from decent conduct.

The old man was trying to keep them off with both hands, but the hands were very wrinkled and trembly.

Oswald is grateful to his good father who taught him and Dicky the proper way to put their hands up. If it had not been for that, Oswald does not know what on earth would have happened, for the outcasts were five to our two, because no one could have expected Alice to do what she did.

Before Oswald had even got his hands into the position required by the noble art of self-defence, she had slapped the largest boy on the face as hard as ever she could – and she can slap pretty hard, as Oswald knows but too well – and she had taken the second-sized boy and was shaking him before Dicky could get his left in on the eye of the slapped assailant of the aged denizen of the Flowery East. The other three went for Oswald, but three to one is nothing to one who has hopes of being a pirate in his spare time when he grows up.

In an instant the five were on us. Dicky and I got in some good ones, and though Oswald cannot approve of my sister being in a street fight, he must own she was very quick and useful in pulling ears and twisting arms and slapping and pinching. But she had quite forgotten how to hit out from the shoulder like I have often shown her.

The battle raged, and Alice often turned the tide of it by a well-timed shove or nip. The aged Eastern leaned against the wall, panting and holding his blue heart with his yellow hand. Oswald had got a boy down, and was kneeling on him, and Alice was trying to pull off two other boys who had fallen on top of the fray, while Dicky was letting the fifth have it, when there was a flash of blue and another China-man dashed into the tournament. Fortunately this one was not old, and with a few well-directed, if foreign looking, blows he finished the work so ably begun by the brave Bastables, and next moment the five loathsome and youthful aggressors were bolting down the passage. Oswald and Dicky were trying to get their breath and find out exactly where they were hurt and how much, and Alice had burst out crying and was howling as though she would never stop. That is the worst of girls – they never can keep anything up. Any brave act they may suddenly do, when for a moment they forget that they have not the honour to be boys, is almost instantly made into contemptibility by a sudden attack of crybabyishness. But I will say no more: for she did strike the first blow, after all, and it did turn out that the boys had scratched her wrist and kicked her shins. These things make girls cry.

The venerable stranger from distance shores said a good deal to the other in what I suppose was the language used in China. It all sounded like 'hung' and 'li' and 'chi', and then the other turned to us and said –

'Nicee lilly girlee, same piecee flowelee, you takee my head to walkee on. This is alle samee my father first chop ancestor. Dirty white devils makee him hurt. You come alongee fightee ploper. Me likee you welly muchee.'

Alice was crying too much to answer, especially as she could not find her handkerchief. I gave her mine, and then she was able to say that she did not want to walk on anybody's head, and she wanted to go home.

'This not nicee place for lillee whitee girlee,' said the young Chinaman. His pigtail was thicker than his father's and black right up to the top. The old man's was grey at the beginning, but lower down it was black, because that part of it was not hair at all, but black threads and ribbons and odds and ends of trimmings, and towards the end both pigtails were greenish.

'Me lun backee takee him safee,' the younger of the Eastern adventurers went on, pointing to his father. 'Then me makee walkee all alonk you, takee you back same placee you comee from. Little white devils waitee for you on ce load. You comee with? Not? Lillee girlee not cly. John givee her one piecee pletty-pletty. Come makee talkee with the House Lady.'

I believe this is about what he said, and we understood that he wanted us to come and see his mother, and that he would give Alice something pretty, and then see us safe out of the horrible brown-grey country.

So we agreed to go with them, for we knew those five boys would be waiting for us on the way back, most likely with strong reinforcements. Alice stopped crying the minute she could – I must say she is better than Dora in that way – and we followed the Chinamen, who walked in single file like Indians, so we did the same, and talked to each other over our shoulders. Our grateful Oriental friends led us through a good many streets, and suddenly opened a door with a key, pulled us in, and shut the door. Dick thought of the kidnapping of Florence Dombey and good Mrs Brown, but Oswald had no such unnoble thoughts.

The room was small, and very, very odd. It was very dirty too, but perhaps it is not polite to say that. There was a sort of sideboard at one end of the room, with an embroidered dirty cloth on it, and on the cloth a bluey-white crockery image over a foot high. It was very fat and army and leggy, and I think it was an idol. The minute we got inside the young man lighted little brown sticks, and set them to burn in front of it. I suppose it was incense. There was a sort of long, wide, low sofa, without any arms or legs, and a table that was like a box, with another box in front of it for you to sit down on when you worked, and on the table were all sorts of tiny little tools – awls and brads they looked like – and pipe-stems and broken bowls of pipes and mouthpieces, for our rescued Chinaman was a pipe-mender by trade. There wasn't much else in the room except the smell, and that seemed to fill it choke-full. The smell seemed to have all sorts of things in it – glue and gunpowder, and white garden lilies and burnt fat, and it was not so easy to breathe as plain air.

Then a Chinese lady came in. She had green-grey trousers, shiny like varnish, and a blue gown, and her hair was pulled back very tight, and twisted into a little knob at the back.

She wanted to go down on the floor before Alice, but we wouldn't let her. Then she said a great many things that we feel sure were very nice, only they were in Chinese, so we could not tell what they were.

And the Chinaman said that his mother also wanted Alice to walk on her head – not Alice's own, of course, but the mother's.

I wished we had stayed longer, and tried harder to understand what they said, because it was an adventure, take it how you like, that we're not likely to look upon the like of again. Only we were too flustered to see this.

We said, 'Don't mention it', and things like that; and when Dicky said, 'I think we ought to be going', Oswald said so too.

Then they all began talking Chinese like mad, and the Chinese lady came back and suddenly gave Alice a parrot.

It was red and green, with a very long tail, and as tame as any pet fawn I ever read about. It walked up her arm and round her neck, and stroked her face with its beak. And it did not bite Oswald or Alice, or even Dicky, though they could not be sure at first that it was not going to.

We said all the polite things we could, and the old lady made thousands of hurried Chinese replies, and repeated many times, 'All litey, John', which seemed to be all the English she knew.

We never had so much fuss made over us in all our lives. I think it was that that upset our calmness, and seemed to put us into a sort of silly dream that made us not see what idiots we were to hurry off from scenes we should never again behold. So we went. And the youthful Celestial saw us safely to the top of Bullamy's Stairs, and left us there with the parrot and floods of words that seemed all to end in double 'e'.

We wanted to show him to the others, but he would not come, so we rejoined our anxious relations without him.

The scene of rejoinder was painful, at first because they were most frightfully sick at us having been such an age away; but when we let them look at the parrot, and told them about the fight, they agreed that it was not our fault, and we really had been unavoidably detained.

But Dora said, 'Well, you may say I'm always preaching, but I *don't* think Father would like Alice to be fighting street boys in Millwall.'

'I suppose *you'd* have run away and let the old man be killed,' said Dicky, and peace was not restored till we were nearly at Greenwich again.

We took the tram to Greenwich Station, and then we took a cab home (and well worth the money, which was all we now had got, except fourpence-halfpenny), for we were all dog-tired.

And dog-tired reminds me that we hadn't found Pincher, in spite of all our trouble.

Miss Blake, who is our housekeeper, was angrier than I have ever seen her. She had been so anxious that she had sent the police to look for us. But, of course, they had not found us. You ought to make allowances for what people do when they are anxious, so I forgive her everything, even what she said about Oswald being a disgrace to a respectable house. He owns we were rather muddy, owing to the fight.

And when the jaw was over and we were having tea – and there was meat to it, because we were as near starving as I ever wish to be – we all ate lots. Even the thought of Pincher could not thwart our bold appetites, though we kept saying, 'Poor old Pincher!' 'I do wish we'd found him', and things like that. The parrot walked about among the tea-things as tame as tame. And just as Alice was saying how we'd go out again to-morrow and have another try for our faithful hound there was a scratching at the door, and we rushed – and there was Pincher, perfectly well and mad with joy to see us.

H.O. turned an abrupt beetroot colour.

'Oh!' he said.

We said, 'What? Out with it.'

And though he would much rather have kept it a secret buried in his breast, we made him own that he had shut Pincher up yesterday in the empty rabbit-hutch when he was playing Zoological Gardens and forgotten all about it in the pleasures of our cousin having left us.

So we need not have gone over the water at all. But though Oswald pities all dumb animals, especially those helplessly shut in rabbit-hutches at the bottoms of gardens, he cannot be sorry that we had such a Celestial adventure and got hold of such a parrot. For Alice says that Oswald and Dicky and she shall have the parrot between them.

She is tremendously straight. I often wonder why she was made a girl. She's a jolly sight more of a gentleman than half the boys at our school.

THE YOUNG ANTIQUARIES

THIS really happened before Christmas, but many authors go back to bygone years for whole chapters, and I don't see why I shouldn't.

It was one Sunday – the Somethingth Sunday in Advent, I think – and Denny and Daisy and their father and Albert's uncle came to dinner, which is in the middle of the day on that day of rest and the same things to eat for grown-ups and us. It is nearly always roast beef and Yorkshire, but the puddings and vegetables are brightly variegated and never the same two Sundays running.

At dinner some one said something about the coat-of-arms that is on the silver tankards which once, when we were poor and honest, used to stay at the shop having the dents slowly taken out of them for months and months. But now they are always at home and are put at the four corners of the table every day, and any grown-up who likes can drink beer out of them.

After some talk of the sort you don't listen to, in which bends and lioncels and gules and things played a promising part, Albert's uncle said that Mr Turnbull had told him something about that coat-of-arms being carved on a bridge somewhere in Cambridgeshire, and again the conversation wandered into things like Albert's uncle had talked about to the Maidstone Antiquarian Society the day they came over to see his old house in the country and we arranged the time-honoured Roman remains for them to dig up. So, hearing the words king-post and mullion and moulding and underpin, Oswald said might we go; and we went, and took our dessert with us and had it in our own common-room, where you can roast chestnuts with a free heart and never mind what your fingers get like.

When first we knew Daisy we used to call her the White Mouse, and her brother had all the appearance of being one too, but you know how untruthful appearances are, or else it was that we taught him happier things, for he certainly turned out quite different in the end; and she was not a bad sort of kid, though we never could quite cure her of wanting to be 'ladylike' – that is the beastliest word there is, I think, and Albert's uncle says so, too. He says if a girl can't be a lady it's not worth while to be only like one – she'd better let it alone and be a free and happy bounder.

But all this is not what I was going to say, only the author does think of so many things besides the story, and sometimes he puts them in. This is the case with Thackeray and the Religious Tract Society and other authors, as well as Mrs Humphrey Ward. Only I don't suppose you have ever heard of her, though she writes books that some people like very much. But perhaps they are her friends. I did not like the one I read about the Baronet. It was on a wet Sunday at the seaside, and nothing else in the house but Bradshaw and 'Elsie; or like a –' or I shouldn't have. But what really happened to us before Christmas is strictly the following narrative.

'I say,' remarked Denny, when he had burned his fingers with a chestnut that turned out a bad one after all – and such is life – and he had finished sucking his fingers and getting rid of the chestnut, 'about these antiquaries?'

'Well, what about them?' said Oswald. He always tries to be gentle and kind to Denny, because he knows he helped to make a man of the young Mouse.

'I shouldn't think,' said Denny, 'that it was so very difficult to be one.'

'I don't know,' said Dicky. 'You have to read very dull

books and an awful lot of them, and remember what you read, what's more.'

'I don't think so,' said Alice. 'That girl who came with the antiquities – the one Albert's uncle said was up-holstered in red plush like furniture – *she* hadn't read anything, you bet.'

Dora said, 'You ought not to bet, especially on Sunday,' and Alice altered it to 'You may be sure.'

'Well, but what then?' Oswald asked Denny. 'Out with it,' for he saw that his youthful friend had got an idea and couldn't get it out. You should always listen patiently to the ideas of others, no matter how silly you expect them to be.

'I do wish you wouldn't hurry me so,' said Denny, snapping his fingers anxiously. And we tried to be patient.

'Why shouldn't we *be* them?' Denny said at last.

'He means antiquaries,' said Oswald to the bewildered others. 'But there's nowhere to go and nothing to do when we get there.'

The Dentist (so-called for short, his real name being Denis) got red and white, and drew Oswald aside to the window for a secret discussion. Oswald listened as carefully as he could, but Denny always buzzes so when he whispers.

'Right oh,' he remarked, when the confidings of the Dentist had got so that you could understand what he was driving at. 'Though you're being shy with us now, after all we went through together in the summer, is simply skittles.'

Then he turned to the polite and attentive others and said –

'You remember that day we went to Bexley Heath with Albert's uncle? Well, there was a house, and Albert's uncle said a clever writer lived there, and in more ancient years that chap in history – Sir Thomas What's his name; and Denny thinks he might let us be antiquaries there. It looks a ripping place from the railway.'

It really does. It's a fine big house, and splendid gardens, and a lawn with a sundial, and the tallest trees anywhere about here.

'But what could we *do*?' said Dicky. 'I don't suppose *he'd* give *us* tea,' though such, indeed, had been our hospitable conduct to the antiquaries who came to see Albert's uncle.

'Oh, I don't know,' said Alice. 'We might dress up for it, and wear spectacles, and we could all read papers. It would be lovely – something to fill up the Christmas holidays – the part before the wedding, I mean. Do let's.'

'All right, I don't mind. I suppose it would be improving,' said Dora. 'We should have to read a lot of history. You can settle it. I'm going to show Daisy our bridesmaids' dresses.'

It was, alas! too true. Albert's uncle was to be married but shortly after, and it was partly our faults, though that does not come into this story.

So the two D.'s went to look at the clothes – girls like this – but Alice, who wishes she had never consented to be born a girl, stayed with us, and we had a long and earnest council about it.

'One thing,' said Oswald, 'it can't possibly be wrong – so perhaps it won't be amusing.'

'Oh, Oswald!' said Alice, and she spoke rather like Dora.

'I don't mean what you mean,' said Oswald in lofty scorn. 'What I mean to say is that when a thing is quite sure to be right, it's not so – well – I mean to say there it is, don't you know; and if it might be wrong, and isn't, it's a score to you; and if it might be wrong, and is – as so often happens – well, you know yourself, adventures sometimes turn out wrong that you didn't think were going to, but seldom, or never, the uninteresting kind, and –'

Dicky told Oswald to dry up – which, of course, no one stands from a younger brother, but though Oswald explained this at the time, he felt in his heart that he has sometimes said what he meant with more clearness. When

Oswald and Dicky had finished, we went on and arranged everything.

Every one was to write a paper – and read it.

'If the papers are too long to read while we're there,' said Noël, 'we can read them in the long winter evenings when we are grouped along the household hearthrug. I shall do my paper in poetry – about Agincourt.'

Some of us thought Agincourt wasn't fair, because no one could be sure about any knight who took part in that well-known conflict having lived in the Red House; but Alice got us to agree, because she said it would be precious dull if we all wrote about nothing but Sir Thomas What-doyoucallhim – whose real name in history Oswald said he would find out, and then write his paper on that world-renowned person, who is a household word in all families. Denny said he would write about Charles the First, because they were just doing that part at his school.

'I shall write about what happened in 1066,' said H.O. 'I know that.'

Alice said, 'If I write a paper it will be about Mary Queen of Scots.'

Dora and Daisy came in just as she said this, and it transpired that this ill-fated but good-looking lady was the only one they either of them wanted to write about. So Alice gave it up to them and settled to do Magna Charta, and they could settle something between themselves for the one who would have to give up Mary Queen of Scots in the end. We all agreed that the story of that lamented wearer of pearls and black velvet would not make enough for two papers.

Everything was beautifully arranged, when suddenly H.O. said –

'Supposing he doesn't let us?'

'Who doesn't let us what?'

'The Red House man – read papers at his Red House.'

This was, indeed, what nobody had thought of – and even now we did not think any one could be so lost to proper hospitableness as to say no. Yet none of us liked to write and ask. So we tossed up for it, only Dora had feelings about tossing up on Sunday, so we did it with a hymn-book instead of a penny.

We all won except Noël, who lost, so he said he would do it on Albert's uncle's typewriter, which was on a visit to us at the time, waiting for Mr Remington to fetch it away to mend the 'M'. We think it was broken through Albert's uncle writing 'Margaret' so often, because it is the name of the lady he was doomed to be married by.

The girls had got the letter the Maidstone Antiquarian Society and Field Clubs Secretary had sent to Albert's uncle – H.O. said they kept it for a momentum of the day – and we altered the dates and names in blue chalk and put in a piece about might we skate on the moat, and gave it to Noël, who had already begun to make up his poetry about Agincourt, and so had to be shaken before he would attend. And that evening, when Father and our Indian uncle and Albert's uncle were seeing the others on the way to Forest Hill, Noël's poetry and pencil were taken away from him and he was shut up in Father's room with the Remington typewriter, which we had never been forbidden to touch. And I don't think he hurt it much, except quite at the beginning, when he jammed the 'S' and the 'J' and the thing that means per cent so that they stuck – and Dicky soon put that right with a screwdriver.

He did not get on very well, but kept on writing MOR7E HOAS5 or MORD6M HOVCE on new pieces of paper and then beginning again, till the floor was strewn with his remains; so we left him at it, and went and played Celebrated Painters – a game even Dora cannot say anything about on Sunday, considering the Bible kind of pictures most of them painted. And much later, the library door having banged once and the front door twice, Noël came in and said he had posted it, and already he was deep in poetry again, and had to be roused when requisite for bed.

It was not till next day that he owned that the typewriter had been a fiend in disguise, and that the letter had come out so odd that he could hardly read it himself.

'The hateful engine of destruction wouldn't answer to the bit in the least,' he said, 'and I'd used nearly a wastepaper basket of Father's best paper, and I thought he might come in and say something, so I just finished it as well as I could, and I corrected it with the blue chalk – because you'd bagged that B.B. of mine – and I didn't notice what name I'd signed till after I'd licked the stamp.'

The hearts of his kind brothers and sisters sank low. But they kept them up as well as they could, and said –

'What name *did* you sign?'

And Noël said, 'Why, Edward Turnbull, of course – like at the end of the real letter. You never crossed it out like you did his address.'

'No,' said Oswald witheringly. 'You see, I did think, whatever else you didn't know, I did think you knew your own silly name.'

Then Alice said Oswald was unkind, though you see he was not, and she kissed Noël and said she and he would take turns to watch for the postman, so as to get the answer (which of course would be subscribed on the envelope with the name of Turnbull instead of Bastable) before the servant could tell the postman that the name was a stranger to her.

And next evening it came, and it was very polite and grown-up – and said we should be welcome, and that we might read our papers and skate on the moat. The Red House has a moat, like the Moat House in the country, but not so wild and dangerous. Only we never skated on it because the frost gave out the minute we had got leave to.

Such is life, as the sparks fly upwards. (The last above is called a moral reflection.)

So now, having got leave from Mr Red House (I won't give his name because he is a writer of worldly fame and he might not like it), we set about writing our papers. It was not bad fun, only rather difficult because Dora said she never knew which Encyclo. volume she might be wanting, as she was using Edinburgh, Mary, Scotland, Bothwell, Holywell, and France, and many others, and Oswald never knew which he might want, owing to his not being able exactly to remember the distinguished and deathless other appellation of Sir Thomas Thingummy, who had lived in the Red House.

Noël was up to the ears in Agincourt, yet that made but little difference to our destiny. He is always plunged in poetry of one sort or another, and if it hadn't been that, it would have been something else. This, at least, we insisted on having kept a secret, so he could not read it to us.

H.O. got very inky the first half-holiday, and then he got some sealing-wax and a big envelope from Father, and put something in and fastened it up, and said he had done his.

Dicky would not tell us what his paper was going to be about, but he said it would not be like ours, and he let H.O. help him by looking on while he invented more patent screws for ships.

The spectacles were difficult. We got three pairs of the uncle's, and one that had belonged to the housekeeper's grandfather, but nine pairs were needed, because Albert-next-door mouched in one half-holiday and wanted to join, and said if we'd let him he'd write a paper on the Constitutions of Clarendon, and we thought he couldn't do it, so we let him. And then, after all, he did.

So at last Alice went down to Bennett's in the village, that we are such good customers of, because when our watches stop we take them there, and he lent us a lot of empty frames on the instinctive understanding that we would pay for them if we broke them or let them get rusty.

And so all was ready. And the fatal day approached; and it was the holidays. For us, that is, but not for Father, for his business never seems to rest by day and night, except at Christmas and times like that. So we did not need to ask him if we might go. Oswald thought it would be more amusing for Father if we told it all to him in the form of an entertaining anecdote, afterwards.

Denny and Daisy and Albert came to spend the day.

We told Mrs Blake Mr Red House had asked us, and she let us, and she let the girls put on their second-best things, which are coats with capes and red Tam-o'shanters. These capacious coats are very good for playing highwaymen in.

We made ourselves quite clean and tidy. At the very last we found that H.O. had been making marks on his face with burnt matches, to imitate wrinkles, but really it only imitated dirt, so we made him wash it off. Then he wanted to paint himself red like a clown, but we had decided that the spectacles were to be our only disguise, and even those were not to be assumed till Oswald gave the word.

No casuist observer could have thought that the nine apparently light-headed and careless party who now wended their way to Blackheath Station, looking as if they were not up to anything in particular, were really an Antiquarian Society of the deepest dye. We got an empty carriage to ourselves, and halfway between Blackheath and the other station Oswald gave the word, and we all put on the spectacles. We had our antiquarian papers of lore and researched history in exercise-books, rolled up and tied with string.

The stationmaster and porter, of each of which the station boasted but one specimen, looked respectfully at us as we got out of the train, and we went straight out of the station, under the railway arch, and down to the green gate of the Red House. It has a lodge, but there is no one in it. We peeped in at the window, and there was nothing in the room but an old beehive and a broken leather strap.

We waited in the front for a bit, so that Mr Red House could come out and welcome us like Albert's uncle did the other antiquaries, but no one came, so we went round the garden. It was very brown and wet, but full of things you didn't see every day. Furze summer-houses, for instance, and a red wall all round it, with holes in it that you might have walled heretics up in in the olden times. Some of the holes were quite big enough to have taken a very small heretic. There was a broken swing, a fish-pond – but we were on business, and Oswald insisted on reading the papers.

He said, 'Let's go to the sundial. It looks dryer there, my feet are like ice-houses.'

It was dryer because there was a soaking wet green lawn round it, and round that a sloping path made of little squares of red and white marble. This was quite waterless, and the sun shone on it, so that it was warm to the hands, though not to the feet, because of boots. Oswald called on Albert to read first. Albert is not a clever boy. He is not one of us, and Oswald wanted to get over the Constitutions. For Albert is hardly ever amusing, even in fun, and when he tries to show off it is sometimes hard to bear. He read –

'THE CONSTITUTIONS OF CLARENDON.

'Clarendon (sometimes called Clarence) had only one constitution. It must have been a very bad one, because he was killed by a butt of Malmsey. If he had had more constitutions or better ones he would have lived to be very old. This is a warning to everybody.'

To this day none of us know how he could, and whether his uncle helped him.

We clapped, of course, but not with our hearts, which

were hissing inside us, and then Oswald began to read his paper. He had not had a chance to ask Albert's uncle what the other name of the world-famous Sir Thomas was, so he had to put him in as Sir Thomas Blank, and make it up by being very strong on scenes that could be better imagined than described, and, as we knew that the garden was five hundred years old, of course he could bring in any eventful things since the year 1400.

He was just reading the part about the sundial, which he had noticed from the train when we went to Bexley Heath. It was rather a nice piece, I think.

'Most likely this sundial told the time when Charles the First was beheaded, and recorded the death-devouring progress of the Great Plague and the Fire of London. There is no doubt that the sun often shone even in these devastating occasions, so that we may picture Sir Thomas Blank telling the time here and remarking – O crikey!'

These last words are what Oswald himself remarked. Of course a person in history would never have said them.

The reader of the paper had suddenly heard a fierce, woodeny sound, like giant singlesticks, terrifyingly close behind him, and looking hastily round, he saw a most angry lady, in a bright blue dress with fur on it, like a picture, and very large wooden shoes, which had made the singlestick noise. Her eyes were very fierce, and her mouth tight shut. She did not look hideous, but more like an avenging sprite or angel, though of course we knew she was only mortal, so we took off our caps. A gentleman also bounded towards us over some vegetables, and acted as reserve support to the lady.

Her voice when she told us we were trespassing and it was a private garden was not so furious as Oswald had expected from her face, but it *was* angry. H.O. at once said it wasn't her garden, was it? But, of course, we could see it *was*, because of her not having any hat or jacket or gloves, and wearing those wooden shoes to keep her feet dry, which no one would do in the street.

So then Oswald said we had leave, and showed her Mr Red House's letter.

'But that was written to Mr Turnbull,' said she, 'and how did *you* get it?'

Then Mr Red House wearily begged us to explain, so Oswald did, in that clear, straightforward way some people think he has, and that no one can suspect for an instant. And he ended by saying how far from comfortable it would be to have Mr Turnbull coming with his thin mouth and his tight legs, and that we were Bastables, and much nicer than the tight-legged one, whatever she might think.

And she listened, and then she quite suddenly gave a most jolly grin and asked us to go on reading our papers.

It was plain that all disagreeableness was at an end, and, to show this even to the stupidest, she instantly asked us to lunch. Before we could politely accept H.O. shoved his oar in as usual and said *he* would stop no matter how little there was for lunch because he liked her very much.

So she laughed, and Mr Red House laughed, and she said they wouldn't interfere with the papers, and they went away and left us.

Of course Oswald and Dicky insisted on going on with the papers; though the girls wanted to talk about Mrs Red House, and how nice she was, and the way her dress was made. Oswald finished his paper, but later he was sorry he had been in such a hurry, because after a bit Mrs Red House came out, and said she wanted to play too. She pretended to be a very ancient antiquary, and was most jolly, so that the others read their papers to her, and Oswald knows she would have liked his paper best, because it *was* the best, though I say it.

Dicky's turned out to be all about the patent screw, and

how Nelson would not have been killed if his ship had been built with one.

Daisy's paper was about Lady Jane Grey, and hers and Dora's were exactly alike, the dullest by far, because they had got theirs out of books.

Alice had not written hers because she had been helping Noël to copy his.

Denny's was about King Charles, and he was very grown-up and fervent about this ill-fated monarch and white roses.

Mrs Red House took us into the summer-houses, where it was warmer, and such is the wonderful architecture of the Red House gardens that there was a fresh summer-house for each paper, except Noël's and H.O.'s, which were read in the stable. There were no horses there.

Noël's was very long, and it began –

> *This is the story of Agincourt.*
> *If you don't know it you jolly well ought.*
> *It was a famous battle fair,*
> *And all your ancestors fought there*
> *That is if you come of a family old.*
> *The Bastables do; they were always very bold.*
> > *And at Agincourt*
> > > *They fought*
> > *As they ought;*
> > *So we have been taught.*

And so on and so on, till some of us wondered why poetry was ever invented. But Mrs Red House said she liked it awfully, so Noël said –

'You may have it to keep. I've got another one of it at home.'

'I'll put it next my heart, Noël,' she said. And she did, under the blue stuff and fur.

H.O.'s was last, but when we let him read it he wouldn't,

so Dora opened his envelope and it was thick inside with blotting-paper, and in the middle there was a page with

1066 WILLIAM THE CONQUEROR,

and nothing else.

'Well,' he said, 'I said I'd write all I knew about 1066, and that's it. I can't write more than I know, can I?' The girls said he couldn't, but Oswald thought he might have tried.

'It wasn't worth blacking your face all over just for that,' he said. But Mrs Red House laughed very much and said it was a lovely paper, and told *her* all she wanted to know about 1066.

Then we went into the garden again and ran races, and Mrs Red House held all our spectacles for us and cheered us on. She said she was the Patent Automatic Cheering Winning-post. We do like her.

Lunch was the glorious end of the Morden House Antiquarian Society and Field Club's Field Day. But after lunch was the beginning of a real adventure such as real antiquarians hardly ever get. This will be unrolled later. I will finish with some French out of a newspaper. Albert's uncle told it me, so I know it is right. Any of your own grown-ups will tell you what it means.

Au prochain numéro je vous promets des émotions.

P.S. – In case your grown-ups can't be bothered, '*émotions*' means sensation, I believe.

THE INTREPID EXPLORER AND
HIS LIEUTENANT

WE had spectacles to play antiquaries in, and the rims were vaselined to prevent rust, and it came off on our faces with other kinds of dirt, and when the antiquary game was over, Mrs Red House helped us to wash it off with all the thoroughness of aunts, and far more gentleness.

Then, clean and with our hairs brushed, we were led from the bath-room to the banqueting hall or dining-room.

It is a very beautiful house. The girls thought it was bare, but Oswald likes bareness because it leaves more room for games. All the furniture was of agreeable shapes and colours, and so were all the things on the table – glasses and dishes and everything. Oswald politely said how nice everything was.

The lunch was a blissful dream of perfect A.1.-ness. Tongue, and nuts, and apples, and oranges, and candied fruits, and ginger-wine and tiny glasses that Noël said were fairy goblets. Everybody drank everybody else's health – and Noël told Mrs Red House just how lovely she was, and he would have paper and pencil and write her a poem for her very own. I will not put it in here, because Mr Red House is an author himself, and he might want to use it in some of his books. And the writer of these pages has been taught to think of others, and besides I expect you are jolly well sick of Noël's poetry.

There was no restrainingness about that lunch. As far as a married lady can possibly be a regular brick, Mrs Red House is one. And Mr Red House is not half bad, and knows how to talk about interesting things like sieges, and cricket, and foreign postage stamps.

Even poets think of things sometimes, and it was Noël who said directly he had finished his poetry,

'Have you got a secret staircase? And have you explored your house properly?'

'Yes – we have,' said that well-behaved and unusual lady – Mrs Red House, 'but *you* haven't. You may if you like. Go anywhere,' she added with the unexpected magnificence of a really noble heart. 'Look at everything – only don't make hay. Off with you!' or words to that effect.

And the whole of us, with proper thanks, offed with us instantly, in case she should change her mind.

I will not describe the Red House to you – because perhaps you do not care about a house having three staircases and more cupboards and odd corners than we'd ever seen before, and great attics with beams, and enormous drawers on rollers, let into the wall – and half the rooms not furnished, and those that were all with old-looking, interesting furniture. There was something about that furniture that even the present author can't describe – as though any of it might have secret drawers or panels – even the chairs. It was all beautiful, and mysterious in the deepest degree.

When we had been all over the house several times, we thought about the cellars. There was only one servant in the kitchen (so we saw Mr and Mrs Red House must be poor but honest, like we used to be), and we said to her –

'How do you do? We've got leave to go wherever we like, and please where are the cellars, and may we go in?'

She was quite nice, though she seemed to think there was an awful lot of us. People often think this. She said:

'Lor, love a duck – yes, I suppose so,' in not ungentle tones, and showed us.

I don't think we should ever have found the way from the

house into the cellar by ourselves. There was a wide shelf in the scullery with a row of gentlemanly boots on it that had been cleaned, and on the floor in front a piece of wood. The general servant for such indeed she proved to be – lifted up the wood and opened a little door under the shelf. And there was the beginning of steps, and the entrance to them was half trap-door, and half the upright kind a thing none of us had seen before.

She gave us a candle-end, and we pressed forward to the dark unknown. The stair was of stone, arched overhead like churches – and it twisted most unlike other cellar stairs. And when we got down it was all arched like vaults, very cobwebby.

'Just the place for crimes,' said Dicky. There was a beer cellar, and a wine cellar with bins, and a keeping cellar with hooks in the ceiling and stone shelves – just right for venison pasties and haunches of the same swift animal.

Then we opened a door and there was a cellar with a well in it.

'To throw bodies down, no doubt,' Oswald explained.

They were cellars full of glory, and passages leading from one to the other like the Inquisition, and I wish ours at home were like them.

There was a pile of beer barrels in the largest cellar, and it was H.O. who said, 'Why not play "King of the Castle"?'

So we did. We had a most refreshing game. It was exactly like Denny to be the one who slipped down behind the barrels, and did not break a single one of all his legs or arms.

'No,' he cried, in answer to our anxious inquiries. 'I'm not hurt a bit, but the wall here feels soft – at least not soft – but it doesn't scratch your nails like stone does, so perhaps it's the door of a secret dungeon or something like that.'

'Good old Dentist!' replied Oswald, who always likes Denny to have ideas of his own, because it was us who taught him the folly of white-mousishness.

'It might be,' he went on, 'but these barrels are as heavy as lead, and much more awkward to collar hold of.'

'Couldn't we get in some other way?' Alice said. 'There ought to be a subterranean passage. I expect there is if we only knew.'

Oswald has an enormous geographical bump in his head. He said –

'Look here! That far cellar, where the wall doesn't go quite up to the roof – that space we made out was under the dining-room – I could creep under there. I believe it leads into behind this door.'

'Get me out! Oh do, do get me out, and let me come!' shouted the barrel-imprisoned Dentist from the unseen regions near the door.

So we got him out by Oswald lying flat on his front on the top barrel, and the Dentist clawed himself up by Oswald's hands while the others kept hold of the boots of the representative of the house of Bastable, which, of course, Oswald is, whenever Father is not there.

'Come on,' cried Oswald, when Denny was at last able to appear, very cobwebby and black. 'Give us what's left of the matches!'

The others agreed to stand by the barrels and answer our knocking on the door if we ever got there.

'But I daresay we shall perish on the way,' said Oswald hopefully.

So we started. The other cellar was easily found by the ingenious and geography-bump-headed Oswald. It opened straight on to the moat, and we think it was a boathouse in middle-aged times.

Denny made a back for Oswald, who led the way, and then he turned round and hauled up his inexperienced, but rapidly improving, follower on to the top of the wall that did not go quite up to the roof.

'It is like coal mines,' he said, beginning to crawl on hands and knees over what felt like very prickly beach, 'only we've no picks or shovels.'

'And no Sir Humphry Davy safety lamps,' said Denny in sadness.

'They wouldn't be any good,' said Oswald; 'they're only to protect the hard-working mining men against fire-damp and choke-damp. And there's none of those kinds here.'

'No,' said Denny, 'the damp here is only just the common kind.'

'Well, then,' said Oswald, and they crawled a bit further still on their furtive and unassuming stomachs.

'This is a very glorious adventure. It is, isn't it?' inquired the Dentist in breathlessness, when the young stomachs of the young explorers had bitten the dust for some yards further.

'Yes,' said Oswald, encouraging the boy, 'and it's *your* find, too,' he added, with admirable fairness and justice, unusual in one so young. 'I only hope we shan't find a mouldering skeleton buried alive behind that door when we get to it. Come on. What are you stopping for now?' he added kindly.

'It's – it's only cobwebs in my throat,' Denny remarked, and he came on, though slower than before.

Oswald, with his customary intrepid caution, was leading the way, and he paused every now and then to strike a match because it was pitch dark, and at any moment the courageous leader might have tumbled into a well or a dungeon, or knocked his dauntless nose against something in the dark.

'It's all right for you,' he said to Denny, when he had happened to kick his follower in the eye. 'You've nothing to fear except my boots, and whatever they do is accidental, and so it doesn't count, but *I* may be going straight into some trap that has been yawning for me for countless ages.'

'I won't come on so fast, thank you,' said the Dentist. 'I don't think you've kicked my eye out yet.'

So they went on and on, crampedly crawling on what I have mentioned before, and at last Oswald did not strike the next match carefully enough, and with the suddenness of a falling star his hands, which, with his knees, he was crawling on, went over the edge into infinite space, and his chest alone, catching sharply on the edge of the precipice, saved him from being hurled to the bottom of it.

'Halt!' he cried, as soon as he had any breath again. But, alas! it was too late! The Dentist's nose had been too rapid, and had caught up the boot-heel of the daring leader. This was very annoying to Oswald, and was not in the least his fault.

'Do keep your nose off my boots half a sec.,' he remarked, but not crossly. 'I'll strike a match.'

And he did, and by its weird and unscrutatious light looked down into the precipice.

Its bottom transpired to be not much more than six feet below, so Oswald turned the other end of himself first, hung by his hands, and dropped with fearless promptness, uninjured, in another cellar. He then helped Denny down. The cornery thing Denny happened to fall on could not have hurt him so much as he said.

The light of the torch, I mean match, now revealed to the two bold and youthful youths another cellar, with *things* in it – very dirty indeed, but of thrilling interest and unusual shapes, but the match went out before we could see exactly what the things were.

The next match was the last but one, but Oswald was undismayed, whatever Denny may have been. He lighted it and looked hastily round. There was a door.

'Bang on that door – over there, silly!' he cried, in cheering accents, to his trusty lieutenant; 'behind that thing that looks like a *chevaux de frize.*'

Denny had never been to Woolwich, and while Oswald was explaining what a *chevaux de frize* is, the match burnt his fingers almost to the bone, and he had to feel his way to the door and hammer on it himself.

The blows of the others from the other side were deafening.

All was saved.

It was the right door.

'Go and ask for candles and matches,' shouted the brave Oswald. 'Tell them there are all sorts of things in here – a *chevaux de frize* of chair-legs, and –'

'A shovel of *what?*' asked Dicky's voice hollowly from the other side of the door.

'Freeze,' shouted Denny. 'I don't know what it means, but do get a candle and make them unbarricade the door. I don't want to go back the way we came.' He said something about Oswald's boots that he was sorry for afterwards, so I will not repeat it, and I don't think the others heard, because of the noise the barrels made while they were being climbed over.

This noise, however, was like balmy zephyrs compared to the noise the barrels insisted on making when Dicky had collected some grown-ups and the barrels were being rolled away. During this thunder-like interval Denny and Oswald were all the time in the pitch dark. They had lighted their last match, and by its flickering gleam we saw a long, large mangle.

'It's like a double coffin,' said Oswald, as the match went out. 'You can take my arm if you like, Dentist.'

The Dentist did – and then afterwards he said he only did it because he thought Oswald was frightened of the dark.

'It's only for a little while,' said Oswald in the pauses of the barrel-thunder, 'and I once read about two brothers confined for life in a cage so constructed that the unfortunate prisoners could neither sit, lie, nor stand in comfort. We can do all those things.'

'Yes,' said Denny; 'but I'd rather keep on standing if it's the same to you, Oswald. I don't like spiders – not much, that is.'

'You are right,' said Oswald with affable gentleness; 'and there might be toads perhaps in a vault like this – or serpents guarding the treasure like in the Cold Lairs. But of course they couldn't have cobras in England. They'd have to put up with vipers, I suppose.'

Denny shivered, and Oswald could feel him stand first on one leg and then on the other.

'I wish I could stand on neither of my legs for a bit,' he said, but Oswald answered firmly that this could not be.

And then the door opened with a crack-crash, and we saw lights and faces through it, and something fell from the top of the door that Oswald really did think for one awful instant was a hideous mass of writhing serpents put there to guard the entrance.

'Like a sort of live booby-trap,' he explained; 'just the sort of thing a magician or a witch would have thought of doing.'

But it was only dust and cobwebs – a thick, damp mat of them.

Then the others surged in, in light-hearted misunderstanding of the perils Oswald had led Denny into – I mean through, with Mr Red House and another gentleman, and loud voices and candles that dripped all over everybody's hands, as well as their clothes, and the solitary confinement of the gallant Oswald was at an end. Denny's solitary confinement was at an end, too – and he was now able to stand on both legs and to let go the arm of his leader who was so full of fortitude.

'This *is* a find,' said the pleased voice of Mr Red House. 'Do you know, we've been in this house six whole months and a bit, and *we* never thought of there being a door here.'

'Perhaps you don't often play "King of the Castle",' said Dora politely; 'it *is* rather a rough game, I always think.'

'Well, curiously enough, we never have,' said Mr Red House, beginning to lift out the chairs, in which avocation we all helped, of course.

'Nansen is nothing to you! You ought to have a medal for daring explorations,' said the other gentleman, but nobody gave us one, and, of course, we did not want any reward for doing our duty, however tight and cobwebby.

The cellars proved to be well stocked with spiders and old furniture, but no toads or snakes, which few, if any, regretted. Snakes are outcasts from human affection. Oswald pities them, of course.

There was a great lumpish thing in four parts that Mr Red House said was a press, and a ripping settle – besides the chairs, and some carved wood that Mr Red House and his friend made out to be part of an old four-post bed. There was also a wooden thing like a box with another box on it at one end, and H.O. said –

'You could make a ripping rabbit-hutch out of that.'

Oswald thought so himself. But Mr Red House said he had other uses for it, and would bring it up later.

It took us all that was left of the afternoon to get the things up the stairs into the kitchen. It was hard work, but we know all about the dignity of labour. The general hated the things we had so enterprisingly discovered. I suppose she knew who would have to clean them, but Mrs Red House was awfully pleased and said we were dears.

We were not very clean dears by the time our work was done, and when the other gentleman said, 'Won't you all take a dish of tea under my humble roof?' the words 'Like this?' were formed by more than one youthful voice.

'Well, if you would be happier in a partially cleansed state?' said Mr Red House. And Mrs Red House, who is my idea of a feudal lady in a castle, said, 'Oh, come along, let's go and partially clean ourselves. I'm dirtier than anybody, though I haven't explored a bit. I've often noticed that the more you admire things the more they come off on you!'

So we all washed as much as we cared to, and went to tea at the gentleman's house, which was only a cottage, but very beautiful. He had been a war correspondent, and he knew a great many things, besides having books and books of pictures.

It was a splendid party.

We thanked Mrs R.H. and everybody when it was time to go, and she kissed the girls and the little boys, and then she put her head on one side and looked at Oswald and said, 'I suppose you're too old?'

Oswald did not like to say he was not. If kissed at all he would prefer it being for some other reason than his being not too old for it. So he did not know what to say. But Noël chipped in with –

'*You'll* never be too old for it,' to Mrs Red House – which seemed to Oswald most silly and unmeaning, because she was already much too old to be kissed by people unless she chose to begin it. But every one seemed to think Noël had said something clever. And Oswald felt like a young ass. But Mrs R. H. looked at him so kindly and held out her hand so queenily that, before he knew he meant to, he had kissed it like you do the Queen's. Then, of course, Denny and Dicky went and did the same. Oswald wishes that the word 'kiss' might never be spoken again in this world. Not that he minded kissing Mrs Red House's hand in the least, especially as she seemed to think it was nice of him to – but the whole thing is such contemptible piffle.

We were seen home by the gentleman who wasn't Mr

587

Red House, and he stood a glorious cab with a white horse who had a rolling eye, from Blackheath Station, and so ended one of the most adventuring times we ever got out of a play-beginning

The *time* ended as the author has pointed out, but not its resultingness. Thus we ever find it in life – the most unharmful things, thoroughly approved even by grownups, but too often lead to something quite different, and that no one can possibly approve of, not even yourself when you come to think it over afterwards, like Noël and H.O. had to.

It was but natural that the hearts of the young explorers should have dwelt fondly on everything underground, even drains, which was what made us read a book by Mr Hugo, all the next day. It is called 'The Miserables', in French, and the man in it, who is a splendid hero, though a convict and a robber and various other professions, escapes into a drain with great rats in it, and is miraculously restored to the light of day, unharmed by the kindly rodents. (N.B. – Rodents mean rats.)

When we had finished all the part about drains it was nearly dinner-time, and Noël said quite suddenly in the middle of a bite of mutton –

'The Red House isn't nearly so red as ours is outside. Why should the cellars be so much cellarier? Shut up H.O.!' For H.O. was trying to speak.

Dora explained to him how we don't all have exactly the same blessings, but he didn't seem to see it.

'It doesn't seem like the way things happen in books,' he said. 'In Walter Scott it wouldn't be like that, nor yet in Anthony Hope. I should think the rule would be the redder the cellarier. If I was putting it into poetry I should make our cellars have something much wonderfuller in them than just wooden things. H.O., if you don't shut up I'll never let you be in anything again.'

'There's that door you go down steps to,' said Dicky; 'we've never been in there. If Dora and I weren't going with Miss Blake to be fitted for boots we might try that.'

'That's just what I was coming to. (Stow it, H.O.!) I felt just like cellars to-day, while you other chaps were washing your hands for din. – and it was very cold; but I made H.O. feel the same, and we went down, and – that door *isn't shut now.*'

The intelligible reader may easily guess that we finished our dinner as quickly as we could, and we put on our outers, sympathizing with Dicky and Dora, who, owing to boots, were out of it, and we went into the garden. There are five steps down to that door. They were red brick when they began, but now they are green with age and mysteriousness and not being walked on. And at the bottom of them the door was, as Noël said, not fastened. We went in.

'It isn't beery, winey cellars at all,' Alice said; 'it's more like a robber's store-house. Look there.'

We had got to the inner cellar, and there were heaps of carrots and other vegetables.

'Halt, my men!' cried Oswald, 'advance not an inch further! The bandits may lurk not a yard from you!'

'Suppose they jump out on us?' said H.O.

'They will not rashly leap into the light,' said the discerning Oswald. And he went to fetch a new dark-lantern of his that he had not had any chance of really using before. But some one had taken Oswald's secret matches, and then the beastly lantern wouldn't light for ever so long. But he thought it didn't matter his being rather a long time gone, because the others could pass the time in wondering whether anything would jump out on them, and if so, what and when.

So when he got back to the red steps and the open door and flashed his glorious bull's-eye round it was rather an annoying thing for there not to be a single other eye for it to flash into. Every one had vanished.

'Hallo!' cried Oswald, and if his gallant voice trembled he is not ashamed of it, because he knows about wells in cellars, and, for an instant, even he did not know what had happened.

But an answering hullo came from beyond, and he hastened after the others.

'Look out,' said Alice; 'don't tumble over that heap of bones.'

Oswald did look out – of course, he would not wish to walk on any one's bones. But he did not jump back with a scream, whatever Noël may say when he is in a temper.

The heap really did look very like bones, partly covered with earth. Oswald was glad to learn that they were only parsnips.

'We waited as long as we could,' said Alice, 'but we thought perhaps you'd been collared for some little thing you'd forgotten all about doing, and wouldn't be able to come back, but we found Noël had, fortunately, got your matches. I'm so glad you weren't collared, Oswald dear.'

Some boys would have let Noël know about the matches, but Oswald didn't. The heaps of carrots and turnips and parsnips and things were not very interesting when you knew that they were not bleeding warriors' or pilgrims' bones, and it was too cold to pretend for long with any comfort to the young Pretenders. So Oswald said –

'Let's go out on the Heath and play something warm. You can't warm yourself with matches, even if they're not your own.'

That was all he said. A great hero would not stoop to argue about matches.

And Alice said, 'All right', and she and Oswald went out and played pretending golf with some walking-sticks of

Father's. But Noël and H.O. preferred to sit stuffily over the common-room fire. So that Oswald and Alice, as well as Dora and Dicky, who were being measured for boots, were entirely out of the rest of what happened, and the author can only imagine the events that now occurred.

When Noël and H.O. had roasted their legs by the fire till they were so hot that their stockings quite hurt them, one of them must have said to the other – I never knew which:

'Let's go and have another look at that cellar.'

The other – whoever it was – foolishly consented. So they went, and they took Oswald's dark-lantern in his absence and without his leave.

They found a hitherto unnoticed door behind the other one, and Noël says he said, 'We'd better not go in.' H.O. says he said so too. But any way, they *did* go in.

They found themselves in a small vaulted place that we found out afterwards had been used for mushrooms. But it was long since any fair bud of a mushroom had blossomed in that dark retreat. The place had been cleaned and new shelves put up, and when Noël and H.O. saw what was on these shelves the author is sure they turned pale, though they say not.

For what they saw was coils, and pots, and wires; and one of them said, in a voice that must have trembled –

'It is dynamite, I am certain of it; what shall we do?'

I am certain the other said, 'This is to blow up Father because he took part in the Lewisham Election, and his side won.'

The reply no doubt was, 'There is no time for delay; we must act. We must cut the fuse – all the fuses; there are dozens.'

Oswald thinks it was not half bad business, those two kids – for Noël is little more than one, owing to his poetry and his bronchitis – standing in the abode of dynamite and not screeching, or running off to tell Miss Blake, or the servants, or any one – but just doing *the right thing* without any fuss.

I need hardly say it did not prove to be the right thing – but they thought it was. And Oswald cannot think that you are really doing wrong if you really think you are doing right. I hope you will understand this.

I believe the kids tried cutting the fuses with Dick's pocket-knife that was in the pocket of his other clothes. But the fuses would not – no matter how little you trembled when you touched them.

But at last, with scissors and the gas pliers, they cut every fuse. The fuses were long, twisty, wire things covered with green wool, like blind-cords.

Then Noël and H.O. (and Oswald for one thinks it showed a goodish bit of pluck, and policemen have been made heroes for less) got cans and cans of water from the tap by the greenhouse and poured sluicing showers of the icy fluid in among the internal machinery of the dynamite arrangement – for so they believed it to be.

Then, very wet, but feeling that they had saved their father and the house, they went and changed their clothes. I think they were a little stuck-up about it, believing it to be an act unrivalled in devotedness, and they were most tiresome all the afternoon, talking about their secret, and not letting us know what it was.

But when Father came home, early, as it happened, those swollen-headed, but, in Oswald's opinion, quite-to-be-excused, kiddies learned the terrible truth.

Of course Oswald and Dicky would have known at once; if Noël and H.O. hadn't been so cocky about not telling us, we could have exposed the truth to them in all its un-interesting nature.

I hope the reader will now prepare himself for a shock. In a wild whirl of darkness, and the gas being cut off, and not being able to get any light, and Father saying all sorts of things, it all came out.

Those coils and jars and wires in that cellar were not an infernal machine at all. It was – I know you will be very much surprised – it was the electric lights and bells that Father had had put in while we were at the Red House the day before.

H.O. and Noël caught it very fully; and Oswald thinks this was one of the few occasions when my father was not as just as he meant to be. My uncle was not just either, but then it is much longer since he was a boy, so we must make excuses for him.

We sent Mrs Red House a Christmas card each. In spite of the trouble that her cellars had lured him into, Noël sent her a home-made one with an endless piece of his everlasting poetry on it, and next May she wrote and asked us to come and see her. *We* try to be just, and we saw that it was not really her fault that Noël and H.O. had cut those electric wires, so we all went; but we did not take Albert Morrison, because he was fortunately away with an aged god-parent of his mother's who writes tracts at Tunbridge Wells.

The garden was all flowery and green, and Mr and Mrs Red House were nice and jolly, and we had a distinguished and first-class time.

But would you believe it? – that boxish thing in the cellar, that H.O. wanted them to make a rabbit-hutch of – well, Mr Red House had cleaned it and mended it, and Mrs Red House took us up to the room where it was, to let us look at it again. And, unbelievable to relate, it turned out to have rockers, and some one in dark, bygone ages seems, for reasons unknown to the present writer, to have wasted no end of carpentry and carving on it, just to make it into a *Cradle*. And what is more, since we were there last Mr and

Mrs Red House had succeeded in obtaining a small but quite alive baby to put in it.

I suppose they thought it was wilful waste to have a cradle and no baby to use it. But it could so easily have been used for something else. It would have made a ripping rabbit-hutch, and babies are far more trouble than rabbits to keep, and not nearly so profitable, I believe.

THE TURK IN CHAINS; OR,
RICHARD'S REVENGE

THE morning dawned in cloudless splendour. The sky was a pale cobalt colour, as in pictures of Swiss scenery. The sun shone brightly, and all the green things in the garden sparkled in the bewitching rays of the monarch of the skies.

The author of this does not like to read much about the weather in books, but he is obliged to put this piece in because it is true; and it is a thing that does not very often happen in the middle of January. In fact, I never remember the weather being at all like that in the winter except on that one day.

Of course we all went into the garden directly after brekker. (PS. – I have said green things: perhaps you think that is a *lapsus lazuli*, or slip of the tongue, and that there are not any green things in the winter. But there are. And not just evergreens either. Wallflowers and pansies and snapdragons and primroses, and lots of things, keep green all the year unless it's too frosty. Live and learn.)

And it was so warm we were able to sit in the summerhouse. The birds were singing like mad. Perhaps they thought it was springtime. Or perhaps they always sing when they see the sun, without paying attention to dates.

And now, when all his brothers and sisters were sitting on the rustic seats in the summer-house, the far-sighted Oswald suddenly saw that now was the moment for him to hold that council he had been wanting to hold for some time.

So he stood in the door of the summer-house, in case any

of the others should suddenly remember that they wanted to be in some other place. And he said –

'I say. About that council I want to hold.'

And Dicky replied; 'Well, what about it?'

So then Oswald explained all over again that we had been Treasure Seekers, and we had been Would-be-Goods, and he thought it was time we were something else.

'Being something else makes you think of things,' he said at the end of all the other things he said.

'Yes,' said H.O., yawning, without putting up his hand, which is not manners, and we told him so. 'But *I* can think of things without being other things. Look how I thought about being a clown, and going to Rome.'

'I shouldn't think you would want us to remember *that*,' said Dora. And indeed Father had not been pleased with H.O. about that affair. But Oswald never encourages Dora to nag, so he said patiently –

'Yes, you think of things you'd much better not have thought of. Now my idea is let's each say what sort of a society we shall make ourselves into – like we did when we were Treasure Seekers – about the different ways to look for it, I mean. Let's hold our tongues (no, not with your dirty fingers, H.O., old chap; hold it with your teeth if you must hold it with something) – let's hold our tongues for a bit, and then all say what we've thought of – in ages,' the thoughtful boy added hastily, so that every one should not speak at once when we had done holding our tongues.

So we were all silent, and the birds sang industriously among the leafless trees of our large sunny garden in beautiful Blackheath. (The author is sorry to see he is getting poetical. It shall not happen again, and it *was* an extra fine day, really, and the birds did sing, a fair treat.)

When three long minutes had elapsed themselves by the hands of Oswald's watch, which always keeps perfect time

for three or four days after he has had it mended, he closed
the watch and observed –

'Time! Go ahead, Dora.'

Dora went ahead in the following remarks:

'I've thought as hard as I can, and nothing will come into
my head except –

> *Be good, sweet maid, and let who will be clever.*

Don't you think we might try to find some new ways to be
good in?'

'No, you don't!' 'I bar that!' came at once from the
mouths of Dicky and Oswald.

'You don't come that over us twice,' Dicky added. And
Oswald eloquently said, 'No more Would-be-Goods, thank
you, Dora.'

Dora said, well, she couldn't think of anything else. And
she didn't expect Oswald had thought of anything better.

'Yes, I have,' replied her brother. 'What I think is that we
don't *know* half enough.'

'If you mean extra swat,' said Alice; 'I've more homers
than I care for already, thank you.'

'I do not mean swat,' rejoined the experienced Oswald. 'I
want to know all about real things, not booky things. If you
kids had known about electric bells you wouldn't have –'
Oswald stopped, and then said, 'I won't say any more,
because Father says a gentleman does not support his
arguments with personal illusions to other people's faults
and follies.'

'Faults and follies yourself,' said H.O. The girls restored
peace, and Oswald went on –

'Let us seek to grow wiser, and to teach each other.'

'*I* bar that,' said H.O. 'I don't want Oswald and Dicky
always on to me and call it teaching.'

'We might call the society the Would-be-Wisers,' said
Oswald hastily.

'It's not so dusty,' said Dicky; 'let's go on to the others before we decide.'

'You're next yourself,' said Alice.

'Oh, so I am,' remarked Dicky, trying to look surprised. 'Well, my idea is let's be a sort of Industrious Society of Beavers, and make a solemn vow and covenant to make something every day. We might call it the Would-be-Clevers.'

'It would be the Too-clever-by-half's before we'd done with it,' said Oswald.

And Alice said, 'We couldn't always make things that would be any good, and then we should have to do something that wasn't any good, and that would be rot. Yes, I know it's my turn – H.O., you'll kick the table to pieces if you go on like that. Do, for goodness' sake, keep your feet still. The only thing I can think of is a society called the Would-be-Boys.'

'With you and Dora for members.'

'And Noël – poets aren't boys exactly,' said H.O.

'If you don't shut up you shan't be in it at all,' said Alice, putting her arm round Noël. 'No; I meant us all to be in it – only you boys are not to keep saying we're only girls, and let us do everything the same as you boys do.'

'I don't want to be a boy, thank you,' said Dora, 'not when I see how they behave. H.O., *do* stop sniffing and use your handkerchief. Well, take mine, then.'

It was now Noël's turn to disclose his idea, which proved most awful.

'Let's be Would-be-Poets,' he said, 'and solemnly vow and convenient to write one piece of poetry a day as long as we live.'

Most of us were dumb at the dreadful thought. But Alice said –

'That would never do, Noël dear, because you're the only one of us who's clever enough to do it.'

So Noël's detestable and degrading idea was shelved without Oswald having to say anything that would have made the youthful poet weep.

'I suppose you don't mean me to say what I thought of,' said H.O., 'but I shall. I think you ought all to be in a Would-be-Kind Society, and vow solemn convents and things not to be down on your younger brother.'

We explained to him at once that *he* couldn't be in that, because he hadn't got a younger brother.

'And you may think yourself lucky you haven't,' Dicky added.

The ingenious and felicitous Oswald was just going to begin about the council all over again, when the portable form of our Indian uncle came stoutly stumping down the garden path under the cedars.

'Hi, brigands!' he cried in his cheerful unclish manner. 'Who's on for the Hippodrome this bright day?'

And instantly we all were. Even Oswald – because after all you can have a council any day, but Hippodromes are not like that.

We got ready like the whirlwind of the desert for quickness, and started off with our kind uncle, who has lived so long in India that he is much more warm-hearted than you would think to look at him.

Half-way to the station Dicky remembered his patent screw for working ships with. He had been messing with it in the bath while he was waiting for Oswald to have done plunging cleanly in the basin. And in the desert-whirlwinding he had forgotten to take it out. So now he ran back, because he knew how its cardboardiness would turn to pulp if it was left.

'I'll catch you up,' he cried.

The uncle took the tickets and the train came in and still Dicky had not caught us up.

'Tiresome boy!' said the uncle; 'you don't want to miss

the beginning – eh, what? Ah, here he comes!' The uncle got in, and so did we, but Dicky did not see the uncle's newspaper which Oswald waved, and he went running up and down the train looking for us instead of just getting in any where sensibly, as Oswald would have done. When the train began to move he did try to open a carriage door but it stuck, and the train went faster, and just as he got it open a large heavy porter caught him by the collar and pulled him off the train, saying –

'Now, young shaver, no susansides on this 'ere line, if *you* please.'

Dicky hit the porter, but his fury was vain. Next moment the train had passed away, and us in it. Dicky had no money, and the uncle had all the tickets in the pocket of his fur coat.

I am not going to tell you anything about the Hippodrome because the author feels that it was a trifle beastly of us to have enjoyed it as much as we did considering Dicky. We tried not to talk about it before him when we got home, but it was very difficult – especially the elephants.

I suppose he spent an afternoon of bitter thoughts after he had told that porter what he thought of him, which took some time, and the station-master interfered in the end.

When we got home he was all right with us. He had had time to see it was not our faults, whatever he thought at the time.

He refused to talk about it. Only he said –

'I'm going to take it out of that porter. You leave me alone. I shall think of something presently.'

'Revenge is very wrong,' said Dora; but even Alice asked her kindly to dry up. We all felt that it was simply piffle to talk copy-book to one so disappointed as our unfortunate brother.

'It *is* wrong, though,' said Dora.

'Wrong be blowed!' said Dicky, snorting; 'who began it I should like to know! The station's a beastly awkward place to take it out of any one in. I wish I knew where he lived.'

'*I* know *that*,' said Noël. 'I've known it a long time – before Christmas, when we were going to the Moat House.'

'Well, what is it, then?' asked Dicky savagely.

'Don't bite his head off,' remarked Alice. 'Tell us about it, Noël. How do you know?'

'It was when you were weighing yourselves on the weighing machine. I didn't because my weight isn't worth being weighed for. And there was a heap of hampers and turkeys and hares and things, and there was a label on a turkey and brown-paper parcel; and that porter that you hate so said to the other porter –'

'Oh, hurry up, do!' said Dicky.

'I won't tell you at all if you bully me,' said Noël, and Alice had to coax him before he would go on.

'Well, he looked at the label and said, "Little mistake here, Bill – wrong address; ought to be 3, Abel Place, eh?"

'And the other one looked, and he said, "Yes; it's got your name right enough. Fine turkey, too, and his chains in the parcel. Pity they ain't more careful about addressing things, eh?" So when they had done laughing about it I looked at the label and it said, "James Johnson, 8, Granville Park." So I knew it was 3, Abel Place, he lived at, and his name was James Johnson.'

'Good old Sherlock Holmes!' said Oswald.

'You won't really *hurt* him,' said Noël, 'will you? Not Corsican revenge with knives, or poisoned bowls? I wouldn't do more than a good booby-trap, if I was you.'

When Noël said the word 'booby-trap', we all saw a strange, happy look come over Dicky's face. It is called a far-away look, I believe, and you can see it in the picture of a woman cuddling a photograph-album with her hair down, that is in all the shops, and they call it 'The Soul's Awakening'.

Directly Dicky's soul had finished waking up he shut his teeth together with a click. Then he said, 'I've got it.'

Of course we all knew that.

'Any one who thinks revenge is wrong is asked to leave *now*.'

Dora said he was very unkind, and did he really want to turn her out?

'There's a jolly good fire in Father's study,' he said. 'No, I'm not waxy with you, but I'm going to have my revenge, and I don't want you to do anything you thought wrong. You'd only make no end of a fuss afterwards.'

'Well, it *is* wrong, so I'll go,' said Dora. 'Don't say I didn't warn you, that's all!'

And she went.

Then Dicky said, 'Now, any more conscious objectors?'

And when no one replied he went on: 'It was you saying "Booby-trap" gave me the idea. His name's James Johnson, is it? And he said the things were addressed wrong, did he? Well, *I'll* send him a Turkey-and-chains.'

'A Turk in chains,' said Noël, growing owley-eyed at the thought – 'a *live* Turk – or – no, not a dead one, Dicky?'

'The Turk I'm going to send won't be a live one nor yet a dead one.'

'How horrible! *Half* dead. That's worse than anything,' and Noël became so green in the face that Alice told Dicky to stop playing the goat, and tell us what his idea really was.

'Don't you see *yet*?' he cried; '*I* saw it directly.'

'I daresay,' said Oswald; 'it's easy to see your own idea. Drive ahead.'

'Well, I'm going to get a hamper and pack it full of parcels and put a list of them on the top – beginning Turk-and-chains, and send it to Mister James Johnson, and when he opens the parcels there'll be nothing inside.'

'There must be something, you know,' said H.O., 'or the parcels won't be any shape except flatness.'

'Oh, there'll be *something* right enough,' was the bitter reply of the one who had not been to the Hippodrome, 'but it won't be the sort of something he'll expect it to be. Let's do it now. I'll get a hamper.'

He got a big one out of the cellar and four empty bottles with their straw cases. We filled the bottles with black ink and water, and red ink and water, and soapy water, and water plain. And we put them down on the list –

1 bottle of port wine.
1 bottle of sherry wine.
1 bottle of sparkling champagne.
1 bottle of rum.

The rest of the things we put on the list were –

1 turkey-and-chains.
2 pounds of chains.
1 plum pudding.
4 pounds of mince-pies.
2 pounds of almonds and raisins.
1 box of figs.
1 bottle of French plums.
1 large cake.

And we made up parcels to look outside as if their inside was full of the delicious attributes described in the list. It was rather difficult to get anything the shape of a turkey but with coals and crushed newspapers and firewood we did it, and when it was done up with lots of string and the paper artfully squeezed tight to the firewood to look like the Turk's legs it really was almost lifelike in its deceivingness. The chains, or sausages, we did with dusters – and not clean ones – rolled tight, and the paper moulded gently to their forms. The plum-pudding was a newspaper ball. The mince-pies were newspapers too, and so were the almonds and raisins. The box of figs was a real fig-box with cinders and ashes in it damped to keep them from rattling about. The French-plum bottle was real too. It had newspaper soaked in ink in it, and the cake was half a muff-box of Dora's done up very carefully and put at the bottom of the hamper. Inside the muff-box we put a paper with –

'Revenge is not wrong when the other people begin. It was you began, and now you are jolly well served out.'

We packed all the bottles and parcels into the hamper, and put the list on the very top, pinned to the paper that covered the false breast of the imitation Turk.

Dicky wanted to write –'From an unknown friend', but we did not think that was fair, considering how Dicky felt.

So at last we put –'From one who does not wish to sign his name'.

And that was true, at any rate.

Dicky and Oswald lugged the hamper down to the shop that has Carter Paterson's board outside.

'I vote we don't pay the carriage,' said Dicky, but that was perhaps because he was still so very angry about being pulled off the train. Oswald had not had it done to him, so he said that we ought to pay the carriage. And he was jolly glad afterwards that this honourable feeling had arisen in his young bosom, and that he had jolly well made Dicky let it rise in his.

We paid the carriage. It was one-and-five-pence, but Dicky said it was cheap for a high-class revenge like this, and after all it was his money the carriage was paid with.

So then we went home and had another go in of grub – because tea had been rather upset by Dicky's revenge.

The people where we left the hamper told us that it would be delivered next day. So next morning we gloated over the thought of the sell that porter was in for, and Dicky was more deeply gloating than any one.

'I expect it's got there by now,' he said at dinner-time; 'it's a first class booby-trap; what a sell for him! He'll read the list and then he'll take out one parcel after another till he comes to the cake. It *was* a ripping idea! I'm glad I thought of it!'

'I'm not,' said Noël suddenly. 'I wish you hadn't – I wish we hadn't. I know just exactly what he feels like now. He feels as if he'd like to *kill* you for it, and I daresay he would if you hadn't been a craven, white-feathered skulker and not signed your name.'

It was a thunderbolt in our midst Noël behaving like this. It made Oswald feel a sick inside feeling that perhaps Dora had been right. She sometimes is – and Oswald hates this feeling.

Dicky was so surprised at the unheard-of cheek of his young brother that for a moment he was speechless, and before he got over his speechlessness Noël was crying and wouldn't have any more dinner. Alice spoke in the eloquent language of the human eye and begged Dicky to look over it this once. And he replied by means of the same useful organ that he didn't care what a silly kid thought. So no more was said. When Noël had done crying he began to write a piece of poetry and kept at it all the afternoon. Oswald only saw just the beginning. It was called

THE DISAPPOINTED PORTER'S FURY
Supposed to be by the Porter himself,

and it began:

> When first I opened the hamper fair
> And saw the parcel inside there
> My heart rejoiced like dry gardens when
> It rains – but soon I changed and then
> I seized my trusty knife and bowl
> Of poison, and said 'Upon the whole

I will have the life of the man
Or woman who thought of this wicked plan
To deceive a trusting porter so.
No noble heart would have thought of it. No.'

There were pages and pages of it. Of course it was all nonsense – the poetry, I mean. And yet . . . (I have seen that put in books when the author does not want to let out all he thought at the time.)

That evening at tea-time Jane came and said –

'Master Dicky, there's an old aged man at the door inquiring if you live here.'

So Dicky thought it was the bootmaker perhaps; so he went out, and Oswald went with him, because he wanted to ask for a bit of cobbler's wax.

But it was not the shoemaker. It was an old man, pale in the face and white in the hair, and he was so old that we asked him into Father's study by the fire, as soon as we had found out it was really Dicky he wanted to see.

When we got him there he said –

'Might I trouble you to shut the door?'

This is the way a burglar or a murderer might behave, but we did not think he was one. He looked too old for these professions.

When the door was shut, he said –

'I ain't got much to say, young gemmen. It's only to ask was it you sent this?'

He pulled a piece of paper out of his pocket, and it was our list. Oswald and Dicky looked at each other.

'Did you send it?' said the old man again.

So then Dicky shrugged his shoulders and said, 'Yes.'

Oswald said, 'How did you know and who are you?'

The old man got whiter than ever. He pulled out a piece of paper – it was the greenish-grey piece we'd wrapped the Turk and chains in. And it had a label on it that we hadn't noticed, with Dicky's name and address on it. The new bat he got at Christmas had come in it.

'That's how I know,' said the old man. 'Ah, be sure your sin will find you out.'

'But who are you, anyway!' asked Oswald again.

'Oh, *I* ain't nobody in particular,' he said. 'I'm only the father of the pore gell as you took in with your cruel, deceitful, lying tricks. Oh, you may look uppish, young sir, but I'm here to speak my mind, and I'll speak it if I die for it. So now!'

'But we didn't send it to a girl,' said Dicky. 'We wouldn't do such a thing. We sent it for a – for a —' I think he tried to say for a joke, but he couldn't with the fiery way the old man looked at him – 'for a sell, to pay a porter out for stopping me getting into a train when it was just starting, and I missed going to the Circus with the others.' Oswald was glad Dicky was not too proud to explain to the old man. He was rather afraid he might be.

'I never sent it to a girl,' he said again.

'Ho,' said the aged one. 'An' who told you that there porter was a single man? It was his wife – my pore gell – as opened your low parcel, and she sees your lying list written out so plain on top, and, sez she to me, "Father," says she, "'ere's a friend in need! All these good things for us, and no name signed, so that we can't even say thank you. I suppose it's some one knows how short we are just now, and hardly enough to eat with coals the price they are," says she to me. "I do call that kind and Christian," says she, "and I won't open not one of them lovely parcels till Jim comes 'ome," she says, "and we'll enjoy the pleasures of it together, all three of us," says she. And when he came home – we opened of them lovely parcels. She's a cryin' her eyes out at home now, and Jim, he only swore once, and I don't blame him for that one – though never an evil speaker myself – and then he set himself down on a chair and puts his elbows on it to hide his face like – and "Emmie," says he, "so help me. I didn't know I'd got an enemy in the world. I always thought we'd got nothing but good friends," says he. An' I says nothing, but I picks up the paper, and comes here to your fine house to tell you what I think of you. It's a mean, low-down, dirty, nasty trick, and no gentleman wouldn't a-done it. So that's all – and it's off my chest, and good-night to you gentlemen both!'

He turned to go out. I shall not tell you what Oswald felt, except that he did hope Dicky felt the same, and would behave accordingly. And Dicky did, and Oswald was both pleased and surprised.

Dicky said –

'Oh, I say, stop a minute. I didn't think of your poor girl.'

'And her youngest but a bare three weeks old,' said the old man angrily.

'I didn't, on my honour I didn't think of anything but paying the porter out.'

'He was only a doing of his duty,' the old man said.

'Well, I beg your pardon and his,' said Dicky; 'it was ungentlemanly, and I'm very sorry. And I'll try to make it up somehow. Please make it up. I can't do more than own I'm sorry. I wish I hadn't – there!'

'Well,' said the old man slowly, 'we'll leave it at that. Next time p'r'aps you'll think a bit who it's going to be as'll get the benefit of your payings out.'

Dicky made him shake hands, and Oswald did the same.

Then we had to go back to the others and tell them. It was hard. But it was ginger-ale and seed-cake compared to having to tell Father, which was what it came to in the end. For we all saw, though Noël happened to be the one to say it first, that the only way we could really make it up to James Johnson and his poor girl and his poor girl's father, and the baby that was only three weeks old, was to send them a hamper with all the things in it – *real* things, that we had put on the list in the revengeful hamper. And as we had only six-and-sevenpence among us we had to tell Father. Besides, you feel better inside when you have. He talked to us about it a bit, but he is a good father and does not jaw unduly. He advanced our pocket-money to buy a real large Turk-and-chains. And he gave us six bottles of port wine, because he thought that would be better for the poor girl who had the baby than rum or sherry or even sparkling champagne.

We were afraid to send the hamper by Carter Pat. for fear they should think it was another Avenging Take-in. And that was one reason why we took it ourselves in a cab. The other reason was that we wanted to see them open the hamper, and another was that we wanted – at least Dicky wanted – to have it out man to man with the porter and his wife, and tell them himself how sorry he was.

So we got our gardener to find out secretly when that porter was off duty, and when we knew the times we went to his house at one of them.

Then Dicky got out of the cab and went in and said what he had to say. And then we took in the hamper.

And the old man and his daughter and the porter were most awfully decent to us, and the porter's wife said, 'Lor! let bygones be bygones is what *I* say! Why, we wouldn't never have had this handsome present but for the other. Say no more about it, sir, and thank you kindly, I'm sure.'

And we have been friends with them ever since.

We were short of pocket-money for some time, but Oswald does not complain, though the Turk was Dicky's idea entirely. Yet Oswald is just, and he owns that he helped as much as he could in packing the Hamper of the Avenger. Dora paid her share, too, though she wasn't in it. The author does not shrink from owning that this was very decent of Dora.

This is all the story of –

THE TURK IN CHAINS; or,
RICHARD'S REVENGE.

(His name is really Richard, the same as Father's. We only call him Dicky for short.)

THE GOLDEN GONDOLA

ALBERT'S uncle is tremendously clever, and he writes books. I have told how he fled to Southern shores with a lady who is rather nice. His having to marry her was partly our fault, but we did not mean to do it, and we were very sorry for what we had done. But afterwards we thought perhaps it was all for the best, because if left alone he might have married widows, or old German governesses, or Murdstone aunts, like Daisy and Denny have, instead of the fortunate lady that we were the cause of his being married by.

The wedding was just before Christmas, and we were all there. And then they went to Rome for a period of time that is spoken of in books as the honeymoon. You know that H.O., my youngest brother, tried to go too, disguised as the contents of a dress-basket – but was betrayed and brought back.

Conversation often takes place about the things you like, and we often spoke of Albert's uncle.

One day we had a ripping game of hide-and-seek-all-over-the-house-and-all-the-lights-out, sometimes called devil-in-the-dark, and never to be played except when your father and uncle are out, because of the screams which the strongest cannot suppress when caught by 'he' in unexpectedness and total darkness. The girls do not like this game so much as we do. But it is only fair for them to play it. We have more than once played doll's tea-parties to please them.

Well, when the game was over we were panting like dogs

on the hearthrug in front of the common-room fire, and H.O. said –

'I wish Albert's uncle had been here; he does enjoy it so.'

Oswald has sometimes thought Albert's uncle only played to please us. But H.O. may be right.

'I wonder if they often play it in Rome,' H.O. went on. 'That post-card he sent us with the Colly-whats-its-name-on – you know, the round place with the arches. They could have ripping games there –'

'It's not much fun with only two,' said Dicky.

'Besides,' Dora said, 'when people are first married they always sit in balconies and look at the moon, or else at each other's eyes.'

'They ought to know what their eyes look like by this time,' said Dicky.

'I believe they sit and write poetry about their eyes all day, and only look at each other when they can't think of the rhymes,' said Noël.

'I don't believe she knows how, but I'm certain they read aloud to each other out of the poetry books we gave them for wedding presents,' Alice said.

'It would be beastly ungrateful if they didn't, especially with their backs all covered with gold like they are,' said H.O.

'About those books,' said Oswald slowly, now for the first time joining in what was being said; 'of course it was jolly decent of Father to get such ripping presents for us to give them. But I've sometimes wished we'd given Albert's uncle a really truly present that we'd chosen ourselves and bought with our own chink.'

'I wish we could have *done* something for him,' Noël said; 'I'd have killed a dragon for him as soon as look at it, and Mrs Albert's uncle could have been the Princess, and I would have let him have her.'

'Yes,' said Dicky; 'and we just gave rotten books. But it's no use grizzling over it now. It's all over, and he won't get married again while she's alive.'

This was true, for we live in England which is a morganatic empire where more than one wife at a time is not allowed. In the glorious East he might have married again and again and we could have made it all right about the wedding present.

'I wish he was a Turk for some things,' said Oswald, and explained why.

'I don't think *she* would like it,' said Dora.

Oswald explained that if he was a Turk, she would be a Turquoise (I think that is the feminine Turk), and so would be used to lots of wives and be lonely without them.

And just then . . . You know what they say about talking of angels, and hearing their wings? (There is another way of saying this, but it is not polite, as the present author knows.)

Well, just then the postman came, and of course we rushed out, and among Father's dull letters we found one addressed to 'The Bastables Junior'. It had an Italian stamp – not at all a rare one, and it was a poor specimen too, and the post-mark was *Roma*.

That is what the Italians have got into the habit of calling Rome. I have been told that they put the 'a' instead of the 'e' because they like to open their mouths as much as possible in that sunny and agreeable climate.

The letter was jolly – it was just like hearing him talk (I mean reading, not hearing, of course, but reading him talk is not grammar, and if you can't be both sensible and grammarical, it is better to be senseless).

'Well, kiddies,' it began, and it went on to tell us about things he had seen, not dull pictures and beastly old buildings, but amusing incidents of comic nature. The

Italians must be extreme Jugginses for the kind of things he described to be of such everyday occurring. Indeed, Oswald could hardly believe about the soda-water label that the Italian translated for the English traveller so that it said, 'To distrust of the Mineral Waters too fountain-like foaming. They spread the shape.'

Near the end of this letter came this:

You remember the chapter of 'The Golden Gondola' that I wrote for the *People's Pageant* just before I had the honour to lead to the altar, &c. I mean the one that ends in the subterranean passage, with Geraldine's hair down, and her last hope gone, and the three villains stealing upon her with Venetian subtlety in their hearts and Toledo daggers (specially imported) in their garters? I didn't care much for it myself, you remember. I think I must have been thinking of other things when I wrote it. But you, I recollect, consoled me by refusing to regard it as other than 'ripping'. 'Clinking' was, as I recall it, Oswald's consolatory epithet. You'll weep with me, I feel confident, when you hear that my Editor does not share your sentiments. He writes me that it is not up to my usual form. He fears that the public, &c., and he trusts that in the next chapter, &c. Let us hope that the public will, in this matter, take your views, and not his. Oh! for a really discerning public, just like you – you amiable critics! Albert's new aunt is leaning over my shoulder. I can't break her of the distracting habit. How on earth am I ever to write another line? Greetings to all from

ALBERT'S UNCLE AND AUNT.

PS. – She insists on having her name put to this, but of course she didn't write it. I am trying to teach her to spell.

PSS. – Italian spelling, of course.

'And now,' cried Oswald, 'I see it all.'
The others didn't. They often don't when Oswald does.
'Why, don't you see!' he patiently explained, for he

knows that it is vain to be angry with people because they are not so clever as – as other people. 'It's the direct aspiration of Fate. He wants it, does he? Well, he shall have it!'

'What?' said everybody.

'We'll be it.'

'*What?*' was the not very polite remark now repeated by all.

'Why, his discerning public.'

And still they all remained quite blind to what was so clear to Oswald, the astute and discernful.

'It will be much more useful than killing dragons,' Oswald went on, 'especially as there aren't any; and it will be a really truly wedding present – just what we were wishing we'd given him.'

The five others now fell on Oswald and rolled him under the table and sat on his head so that he had to speak loudly and plainly.

'All right! I'll tell you – in words of one syllable if you like. Let go, I say!' And when he had rolled out with the others and the tablecloth that caught on H.O.'s boots and the books and Dora's workbox, and the glass of paint-water that came down with it, he said –

'We will *be* the public. We will all write to the editor of the *People's Pageant* and tell him what we think about the Geraldine chapter. Do mop up that water, Dora; it's running all under where I'm sitting.'

'Don't you think,' said Dora, devoting her handkerchief and Alice's in the obedient way she does not always use, 'that six letters, all signed "Bastable", and all coming from the same house, would be rather – rather –'

'A bit too thick? Yes,' said Alice; 'but of course we'd have all different names and addresses.'

'We might as well do it thoroughly,' said Dicky, 'and send three or four different letters each.'

'And have them posted in different parts of London. Right oh!' remarked Oswald.

'*I* shall write a piece of poetry for mine,' said Noël.

'They ought all to be on different kinds of paper,' said Oswald. 'Let's go out and get the paper directly after tea.'

We did, but we could only get fifteen different kinds of paper and envelopes, though we went to every shop in the village.

At the first shop, when we said, 'Please we want a penn'orth of paper and envelopes of each of all the different kinds you keep,' the lady of the shop looked at us thinly over blue-rimmed spectacles and said, 'What for?'

And H.O. said, 'To write unonymous letters.'

'Anonymous letters are very wrong,' the lady said, and she wouldn't sell us any paper at all.

But at the other places we did not say what it was for, and they sold it us. There were bluey and yellowy and grey and white kinds, and some was violetish with violets on it, and some pink, with roses. The girls took the florivorous ones, which Oswald thinks are unmanly for any but girls, but you excuse their using it. It seems natural to them to mess about like that.

We wrote the fifteen letters, disguising our handwritings as much as we could. It was not easy. Oswald tried to write one of them with his left hand, but the consequences were almost totally unreadable. Besides, if any one could have read it, they would only have thought it was written in an asylum for the insane, the writing was so delirious. So he chucked it.

Noël was only allowed to write one poem. It began –

> *Oh, Geraldine! Oh, Geraldine!*
> *You are the loveliest heroine!*
> *I never read about one before*
> *That made me want to write more*
> *Poetry. And your Venetian eyes,*

They must have been an awful size;
And black and blue, and like your hair,
And your nose and chin were a perfect pair.

and so on for ages.

The other letters were all saying what a beautiful chapter 'Beneath the Doge's Home' was, and how we liked it better than the other chapters before, and how we hoped the next would be like it. We found out when all too late that H.O. had called it the 'Dog's Home'. But we hoped this would pass unnoticed among all the others. We read the reviews of books in the old *Spectators* and *Athenaeums*, and put in the words they say there about other people's books. We said we thought that chapter about Geraldine and the garters was 'subtle' and 'masterly' and 'inevitable' – that it had an 'old-world charm', and was 'redolent of the soil'. We said, too, that we had 'read it with breathless interest from cover to cover', and that it had 'poignant pathos and a convincing realism', and the 'fine flower of delicate sentiment', besides much other rot that the author can't remember.

When all the letters were done we addressed them and stamped them and licked them down, and then we got different people to post them. Our under-gardener, who lives in Greenwich, and the other under-gardener, who lives in Lewisham, and the servants on their evenings out, which they spent in distant spots like Plaistow and Grove Park – each had a letter to post. The piano-tuner was a great catch – he lived in Highgate; and the electric-bell man was Lambeth. So we got rid of all the letters, and watched the post for a reply. We watched for a week, but no answer came.

You think, perhaps, that we were duffers to watch for a reply when we had signed all the letters with fancy names like Daisy Dolman, Everard St Maur, and Sir Cholmondely Marjoribanks, and put fancy addresses on them, like Chatsworth House, Loampit Vale, and The Bungalow,

Eaton Square. But we were not such idiots as you think, dear reader, and you are not so extra clever as you think, either. We had written *one* letter (it had the grandest *Spectator* words in it) on our own letter-paper, with the address on the top and the uncle's coat-of-arms outside the envelope. Oswald's real own name was signed to this letter, and this was the one we looked for the answer to. See?

But that answer did not come. And when three long days had passed away we all felt most awfully stale about it. Knowing the great good we had done for Albert's uncle made our interior feelings very little better, if at all.

And on the fourth day Oswald spoke up and said what was in everybody's inside heart. He said –

'This is futile rot. I vote we write and ask that editor why he doesn't answer letters.'

'He wouldn't answer that one any more than he did the other,' said Noël. 'Why should he? He knows you can't do anything to him for not.'

'Why shouldn't we go and ask him?' H.O. said. 'He couldn't not answer us if we was all there, staring him in the face.'

'I don't suppose he'd see you,' said Dora; 'and it's "were", not "was".'

'The other editor did when I got the guinea for my beautiful poems,' Noël reminded us.

'Yes,' said the thoughtful Oswald; 'but then it doesn't matter how young you are when you're just a poetry-seller. But we're the discerning public now, and he'd think we ought to be grown up. I say, Dora, suppose you rigged yourself up in old Blakie's things. You'd look quite twenty or thirty.'

Dora looked frightened, and said she thought we'd better not.

But Alice said, 'Well, I will, then. I don't care. I'm as tall as Dora. But I won't go alone. Oswald, you'll have to dress up old and come too. Its not much to do for Albert's uncle's sake.'

'You know you'll enjoy it,' said Dora, and she may have wished that she did not so often think that we had better not. However, the dye was now cast, and the remainder of this adventure was doomed to be coloured by the dye we now prepared. (This is an allegory. It means we had burned our boats. And that is another.)

We decided to do the deed next day, and during the evening Dicky and Oswald went out and bought a grey beard and moustache, which was the only thing we could think of to disguise the manly and youthful form of the bold Oswald into the mature shape of a grown-up and discerning public character.

Meanwhile, the girls made tiptoe and brigand-like excursions into Miss Blake's room (she is the housekeeper) and got several things. Among others, a sort of undecided thing like part of a wig, which Miss Blake wears on Sundays. Jane, our housemaid, says it is called a 'transformation', and that duchesses wear them.

We had to be very secret about the dressing-up that night, and to put Blakie's things all back when they had been tried on.

Dora did Alice's hair. She twisted up what little hair Alice has got by natural means, and tied on a long tail of hair that was Miss Blake's too. Then she twisted that up, bun-like, with many hairpins. Then the wiglet, or transformation, was plastered over the front part, and Miss Blake's Sunday hat, which is of a very brisk character, with half a blue bird in it, was placed on top of everything. There were several petticoats used, and a brown dress and some stockings and hankies to stuff it out where it was too big. A black jacket and crimson tie completed the picture. We thought Alice would do.

Then Oswald went out of the room and secretly assumed

his dark disguise. But when he came in with the beard on, and a hat of Father's, the others were not struck with admiration and respect, like he meant them to be. They rolled about, roaring with laughter, and when he crept into Miss Blake's room and turned up the gas a bit, and looked in her long glass, he owned that they were right and that it was no go. He is tall for his age, but that beard made him look like some horrible dwarf; and his hair being so short added to everything. Any idiot could have seen that the beard had not originally flourished where it now was, but had been transplanted from some other place of growth.

And when he laughed, which now became necessary, he really did look most awful. He has read of beards wagging, but he never saw it before.

While he was looking at himself the girls had thought of a new idea.

But Oswald had an inside presentiment that made it some time before he could even consent to listen to it. But at last, when the others reminded him that it was a noble act, and for the good of Albert's uncle, he let them explain the horrid scheme in all its lurid parts.

It was this: That Oswald should consent to be disguised in women's raiments and go with Alice to see the Editor.

No man ever wants to be a woman, and it was a bitter thing for Oswald's pride, but at last he consented. He is glad he is not a girl. You have no idea what it is like to wear petticoats, especially long ones. I wonder that ladies continue to endure their miserable existences. The top parts of the clothes, too, seemed to be too tight and too loose in the wrong places. Oswald's head, also, was terribly in the way. He had no wandering hairs to fasten transformations on to, even if Miss Blake had had another one, which was not the case. But the girls remembered a governess they had once witnessed whose hair was brief as any boy's, so they put a large hat, with a very tight elastic behind, on to Oswald's head, just as it was, and then with a tickly, pussyish, featherish thing round his neck, hanging wobblily down in long ends, he looked more young-lady-like than he will ever feel.

Some courage was needed for the start next day. Things look so different in the daylight.

'Remember Lord Nithsdale coming out of the Tower,' said Alice. 'Think of the great cause and be brave,' and she tied his neck up.

'I'm brave all right,' said Oswald, 'only I do feel such an ass.'

'I feel rather an ape myself,' Alice owned, 'but I've got three-penn'orth of peppermints to inspire us with bravery. It is called Dutch courage, I believe.'

Owing to our telling Jane we managed to get out unseen by Blakie.

All the others would come, too, in their natural appearance, except that we made them wash their hands and faces. We happened to be flush of chink, so we let them come.

'But if you do,' Oswald said, 'you must surround us in a hollow square of four.'

So they did. And we got down to the station all right. But in the train there were two ladies who stared, and porters and people like that came round the window far more than there could be any need for. Oswald's boots must have shown as he got in. He had forgotten to borrow a pair of Jane's, as he had meant to, and the ones he had on were his largest. His ears got hotter and hotter, and it got more and more difficult to manage his feet and hands. He failed to suck any courage, of any nation, from the peppermints.

Owing to the state Oswald's ears were now in, we agreed to take a cab at Cannon Street. We all crammed in somehow, but Oswald saw the driver wink as he put his boot on the step, and the porter who was opening the cab door

winked back, and I am sorry to say Oswald forgot that he
was a high-born lady, and he told the porter that he had
better jolly well stow his cheek. Then several bystanders
began to try and be funny, and Oswald knew exactly what
particular sort of fool he was being.

But he bravely silenced the fierce warnings of his ears,
and when we got to the Editor's address we sent Dick up
with a large card that we had written on,

MISS DAISY DOLMAN
and
THE RIGHT HONOURABLE MISS
ETHELTRUDA BUSTLER.
On urgent business.

and Oswald kept himself and Alice concealed in the cab till
the return of the messenger.

'All right; you're to go up,' Dicky came back and said;
'but the boy grinned who told me so. You'd better be jolly
careful.'

We bolted like rabbits across the pavement and up the
Editor's stairs.

He was very polite. He asked us to sit down, and Oswald
did. But first he tumbled over the front of his dress because
it would get under his boots, and he was afraid to hold it up,
not having practised doing this.

'I think I have had letters from you?' said the Editor.

Alice, who looked terrible with the transformation leaning right-ear-ward, said yes, and that we had come to say
what a fine, bold conception we thought the Doge's chapter
was. This was what we had settled to say, but she needn't
have burst out with it like that. I suppose she forgot herself.
Oswald, in the agitation of his clothes, could say nothing.
The elastic of the hat seemed to be very slowly slipping up
the back of his head, and he knew that, if it once passed the
bump that backs of heads are made with, the hat would

spring from his head like an arrow from a bow. And all would be frustrated.

'Yes,' said the Editor; 'that chapter seems to have had a great success – a wonderful success. I had no fewer than sixteen letters about it, all praising it in unmeasured terms.' He looked at Oswald's boots, which Oswald had neglected to cover over with his petticoats. He now did this.

'It *is* a nice story, you know,' said Alice timidly.

'So it seems,' the gentleman went on. 'Fourteen of the sixteen letters bear the Blackheath postmark. The enthusiasm for the chapter would seem to be mainly local.'

Oswald would not look at Alice. He could not trust himself, with her looking like she did. He knew at once that only the piano-tuner and the electric man had been faithful to their trust. The others had all posted their letters in the pillar-box just outside our gate. They wanted to get rid of them as quickly as they could, I suppose. Selfishness is a vile quality.

The author cannot deny that Oswald now wished he hadn't. The elastic was certainly moving, slowly, but too surely. Oswald tried to check its career by swelling out the bump on the back of his head, but he could not think of the right way to do this.

'I am very pleased to see you,' the Editor went on slowly, and there was something about the way he spoke that made Oswald think of a cat playing with a mouse. 'Perhaps you can tell me. Are there many spiritualists in Blackheath? Many clairvoyants?'

'Eh?' said Alice, forgetting that that is not the way to behave.

'People who foretell the future?' he said.

'I don't think so,' said Alice. 'Why?'

His eye twinkled. Oswald saw he had wanted her to ask this.

'Because,' said the Editor, more slowly than ever, 'I think

623

there must be. How otherwise can we account for that chapter about the "Doge's Home" being read and admired by sixteen different people before it is even printed. That chapter has not been printed, it has not been published; it will not be published till the May number of the *People's Pageant*. Yet in Blackheath sixteen people already appreciate its subtlety and its realism and all the rest of it. How do you account for this, Miss Daisy Dolman?'

'I am the Right Honourable Etheltruda,' said Alice. 'At least – oh, it's no use going on. We are not what we seem.'

'Oddly enough, I inferred that at the very beginning of our interview,' said the Editor.

Then the elastic finished slipping up Oswald's head at the back, and the hat leapt from his head exactly as he had known it would. He fielded it deftly, however, and it did not touch the ground.

'Concealment,' said Oswald, 'is at an end.'

'So it appears,' said the Editor. 'Well, I hope next time the author of the "Golden Gondola" will choose his instruments more carefully.'

'He didn't! We aren't!' cried Alice, and she instantly told the Editor everything.

Concealment being at an end, Oswald was able to get at his trousers pocket – it did not matter now how many boots he showed – and to get out Albert's uncle's letter.

Alice was quite eloquent, especially when the Editor had made her take off the hat with the blue bird, and the transformation and the tail, so that he could see what she really looked like. He was quite decent when he really understood how Albert's uncle's threatened marriage must have upset his brain while he was writing that chapter, and pondering on the dark future.

He began to laugh then, and kept it up till the hour of parting.

He advised Alice not to put on the transformation and the tail again to go home in, and she didn't.

Then he said to me: 'Are you in a finished state under Miss Daisy Dolman?' and when Oswald said, 'Yes,' the Editor helped him to take off all the womanly accoutrements, and to do them up in brown paper. And he lent him a cap to go home in.

I never saw a man laugh more. He is an excellent sort.

But no slow passage of years, however many, can ever weaken Oswald's memory of what those petticoats were like to walk in, and how ripping it was to get out of them, and have your own natural legs again.

We parted from the Editor without a strain on anybody's character.

He must have written to Albert's uncle, and told him all, for we got a letter next week. It said –

My dear Kiddies, – Art cannot be forced. Nor can Fame. May I beg you for the future to confine your exertions to blowing my trumpet – or Fame's – with your natural voices? Editors may be led, but they won't be druv. The Right Honourable Miss Etheltruda Bustler seems to have aroused a deep pity for me in my Editor's heart. Let that suffice. And for the future permit me, as firmly as affectionately, to reiterate the assurance and the advice which I have so often breathed in your long young ears, '*I am not ungrateful; but I do wish you would mind your own business.*'

'That's just because we were found out,' said Alice. 'If we'd succeeded he'd have been sitting on the top of the pinnacle of Fame, and he would have owed it all to us. That would have been making him something like a wedding present.'

What we had really done was to make something very like – but the author is sure he has said enough.

THE FLYING LODGER

FATHER knows a man called Eustace Sandal. I do not know how to express his inside soul, but I have heard Father say he means well. He is a vegetarian and a Primitive Social Something, and an all-wooler, and things like that, and he is really as good as he can stick, only most awfully dull. I believe he eats bread and milk from choice. Well, he has great magnificent dreams about all the things you can do for other people, and he wants to distil cultivatedness into the sort of people who live in Model Workmen's Dwellings, and teach them to live up to better things. This is what he says. So he gives concerts in Camberwell, and places like that, and curates come from far and near, to sing about Bold Bandaleros and the Song of the Bow, and people who have escaped being curates give comic recitings, and he is sure that it does every one good, and 'gives them glimpses of the Life Beautiful'. He said that. Oswald heard him with his own trustworthy ears. Anyway the people enjoy the concerts no end, and that's the great thing.

Well, he came one night, with a lot of tickets he wanted to sell, and Father bought some for the servants, and Dora happened to go in to get the gum for a kite we were making, and Mr Sandal said, 'Well, my little maiden, would you not like to come on Thursday evening, and share in the task of raising our poor brothers and sisters to the higher levels of culture?' So of course Dora said she would, very much. Then he explained about the concert, calling her 'My little one', and 'dear child', which Alice never would have borne, but Dora is not of a sensitive nature, and hardly minds what she is called, so long as it is not names, which she does not

deem 'dear child' and cetera to be, though Oswald
would.

Dora was quite excited about it, and the stranger so
worked upon her feelings that she accepted the deep responsibility of selling tickets, and for a week there was no
bearing her. I believe she did sell nine, to people in
Lewisham and New Cross who knew no better. And Father
bought tickets for all of us, and when the eventful evening
dawned we went to Camberwell by train and tram *via* Miss
Blake (that means we shouldn't have been allowed to go
without her).

The tram ride was rather jolly, but when we got out and
walked we felt like 'Alone in London', or 'Jessica's First
Prayer', because Camberwell is a devastating region that
makes you think of rickety attics with the wind whistling
through them, or miserable cellars where forsaken children
do wonders by pawning their relations' clothes and looking
after the baby. It was a dampish night, and we walked on
greasy mud. And as we walked along Alice kicked against
something on the pavement, and it chinked, and when she
picked it up it was five bob rolled up in newspaper.

'I expect it's somebody's little all,' said Alice, 'and the
cup was dashed from their lips just when they were going to
joyfully spend it. We ought to give it to the police.'

But Miss Blake said no, and that we were late already, so
we went on, and Alice held the packet in her muff throughout the concert which ensued. I will not tell you anything
about the concert except that it was quite fairly jolly – you
must have been to these Self-Raising Concerts in the course
of your young lives.

When it was over we reasoned with Miss Blake, and she
let us go through the light blue paper door beside the stage
and find Mr Sandal. We thought he might happen to hear
who had lost the five bob, and return it to its sorrowing
family. He was in a great hurry, but he took the chink and

said he'd let us know if anything happened. Then we went home very cheerful, singing bits of the comic songs a bishop's son had done in the concert, and little thinking what we were taking home with us.

It was only a few days after this, or perhaps a week, that we all began to be rather cross. Alice, usually as near a brick as a girl can go, was the worst of the lot, and if you said what you thought of her she instantly began to snivel. And we all had awful colds, and our handkerchiefs gave out, and then our heads ached. Oswald's head was particularly hot, I remember, and he wanted to rest it on the backs of chairs or on tables – or anything steady.

But why prolong the painful narrative? What we had brought home from Camberwell was the measles, and as soon as the grown-ups recognized the Grim Intruder for the fell disease it is we all went to bed, and there was an end of active adventure for some time.

Of course, when you begin to get better there are grapes and other luxuries not of everyday occurrences, but while you're sniffling and fevering in bed, as red as a lobster and blazing hot, you are inclined to think it is a heavy price to pay for any concert, however raising.

Mr Sandal came to see Father the very day we all marched Bedward. He had found the owner of the five shillings. It was a doctor's fee, about to be paid by the parent of a thoroughly measly family. And if we had taken it to the police at once Alice would not have held it in her hand all through the concert – but I will not blame Blakie. She was a jolly good nurse, and read aloud to us with unfatigu-able industry while we were getting better.

Our having fallen victims to this disgusting complaint ended in our being sent to the seaside. Father could not take us himself, so we went to stay with a sister of Mr Sandal's. She was like him, only more so in every way.

The journey was very joyous. Father saw us off at

Cannon Street, and we had a carriage to ourselves all the way, and we passed the station where Oswald would not like to be a porter. Rude boys at this station put their heads out of the window and shout, 'Who's a duffer?' and things like that, and the porters have to shout 'I am!' because Higham is the name of the station, and porters seldom have any H's with which to protect themselves from this cruel joke.

It was a glorious moment when the train swooped out of a tunnel and we looked over the downs and saw the grey-blue line that was the sea. We had not seen the sea since before Mother died. I believe we older ones all thought of that, and it made us quieter than the younger ones were. I do not want to forget anything, but it makes you feel empty and stupid when you remember some things.

There was a good drive in a waggonette after we got to our station. There were primroses under some of the hedges, and lots of dog-violets. And at last we got to Miss Sandal's house. It is before you come to the village, and it is a little square white house. There is a big old windmill at the back of it. It is not used any more for grinding corn, but fishermen keep their nets in it.

Miss Sandal came out of the green gate to meet us. She had a soft, drab dress and a long thin neck, and her hair was drab too, and it was screwed up tight.

She said, 'Welcome, one and all!' in a kind voice, but it was too much like Mr Sandal's for me. And we went in. She showed us the sitting-rooms, and the rooms where we were to sleep, and then she left us to wash our hands and faces. When we were alone we burst open the doors of our rooms with one consent, and met on the landing with a rush like the great rivers of America.

'*Well!*' said Oswald, and the others said the same.

'Of all the rummy cribs!' remarked Dicky.

'It's like a workhouse or a hospital,' said Dora. 'I think I like it.'

'It makes me think of bald-headed gentlemen,' said H.O., 'it is so bare.'

It was. All the walls were white plaster, the furniture was white deal – what there was of it, which was precious little There were no carpets – only white matting. And there was not a single ornament in a single room! There was a clock on the dining-room mantelpiece, but that could not be counted as an ornament because of the useful side of its character. There were only about six pictures – all of a brownish colour. One was the blind girl sitting on an orange with a broken fiddle. It is called Hope.

When we were clean Miss Sandal gave us tea. As we sat down she said, 'The motto of our little household is "Plain living and high thinking".'

And some of us feared for an instant that this might mean not enough to eat. But fortunately this was not the case. There was plenty, but all of a milky, bunny, fruity, vegetable sort. We soon got used to it, and liked it all right.

Miss Sandal was very kind. She offered to read aloud to us after tea, and, exchanging glances of despair, some of us said that we should like it very much.

It was Oswald who found the manly courage to say very politely –

'Would it be all the same to you if we went and looked at the sea first? Because –'

And she said, 'Not at all,' adding something about 'Nature, the dear old nurse, taking somebody on her knee,' and let us go.

We asked her which way, and we tore up the road and through the village and on to the sea-wall, and then with six joyous bounds we leaped down on to the sand.

The author will not bother you with a description of the mighty billows of ocean, which you must have read about, if not seen, but he will just say what perhaps you are not aware of – that seagulls eat clams and mussels and cockles, and crack the shells with their beaks. The author has seen this done.

You also know, I suppose, that you can dig in the sand (if you have a spade) and make sand castles, and stay in them till the tide washes you out.

I will say no more, except that when we gazed upon the sea and the sand we felt we did not care tuppence how highly Miss Sandal might think of us or how plainly she might make us live, so long as we had got the briny deep to go down to.

It was too early in the year and too late in the day to bathe, but we paddled, which comes to much the same thing, and you almost always have to change everything afterwards.

When it got dark we had to go back to the White House, and there was supper, and then we found that Miss Sandal did not keep a servant, so of course we offered to help wash up. H.O. only broke two plates.

Nothing worth telling about happened till we had been over there a week, and had got to know the coastguards and a lot of the village people quite well. I do like coastguards. They seem to know everything you want to hear about. Miss Sandal used to read to us out of poetry books, and about a chap called Thoreau, who could tickle fish, and they liked it, and let him. She was kind, but rather like her house – there was something bare and bald about her inside mind, I believe. She was very, very calm, and said that people who lost their tempers were not living the higher life. But one day a telegram came, and then she was not calm at all. She got quite like other people, and quite shoved H.O. for getting in her way when she was looking for her purse to pay for the answer to the telegram.

Then she said to Dora – and she was pale and her eyes

631

red, just like people who live the lower or ordinary life – 'My dears, it's dreadful! My poor brother! He's had a fall. I must go to him *at once*.' And she sent Oswald to order the fly from the Old Ship Hotel, and the girls to see if Mrs Beale would come and take care of us while she was away. Then she kissed us all and went off very unhappy. We heard afterwards that poor, worthy Mr Sandal had climbed a scaffolding to give a workman a tract about drink, and he didn't know the proper part of the scaffolding to stand on (the workman did, of course) so he fetched down half a dozen planks and the workman, and if a dust-cart hadn't happened to be passing just under so that they fell into it their lives would not have been spared. As it was Mr Sandal broke his arm and his head. The workman escaped unscathed but furious. The workman was a teetotaler.

Mrs Beale came, and the first thing she did was to buy a leg of mutton and cook it. It was the first meat we had had since arriving at Lymchurch.

'I 'spect she can't afford good butcher's meat,' said Mrs Beale; 'but your pa, I expect he pays for you, and I lay he'd like you to have your fill of something as'll lay acrost your chesties.' So she made a Yorkshire pudding as well. It was good.

After dinner we sat on the sea-wall, feeling more like after dinner than we had felt for days, and Dora said –

'Poor Miss Sandal! I never thought about her being hard-up, somehow. I wish we could do something to help her.'

'We might go out street-singing,' Noël said. But that was no good, because there is only one street in the village, and the people there are much too poor for one to be able to ask them for anything. And all round it is fields with only sheep, who have nothing to give except their wool, and when it comes to taking that, they are never asked.

Dora thought we might get Father to give her money, but Oswald knew this would never do.

Then suddenly a thought struck some one – I will not say who – and that some one said –

'She ought to let lodgings, like all the other people do in Lymchurch.'

That was the beginning of it. The end – for that day – was our getting the top of a cardboard box and printing on it the following lines in as many different coloured chalks as we happened to have with us.

LODGINGS TO LET.

INQUIRE INSIDE.

We ruled spaces for the letters to go in, and did it very neatly. When we went to bed we stuck it in our bedroom window with stamp-paper.

In the morning when Oswald drew up his blind there was quite a crowd of kids looking at the card. Mrs Beale came out and shoo-ed them away as if they were hens. And we did not have to explain the card to her at all. She never said anything about it. I never knew such a woman as Mrs Beale for minding her own business. She said afterwards she supposed Miss Sandal had told us to put up the card.

Well, two or three days went by, and nothing happened, only we had a letter from Miss Sandal, telling us how the poor sufferer was groaning, and one from Father telling us to be good children, and not get into scrapes. And people who drove by used to look at the card and laugh.

And then one day a carriage came driving up with a gentleman in it, and he saw the rainbow beauty of our chalked card, and he got out and came up the path. He had a pale face, and white hair and very bright eyes that moved about quickly like a bird's, and he was dressed in a quite new tweed suit that did not fit him very well.

Dora and Alice answered the door before any one had time to knock, and the author has reason to believe their hearts were beating wildly.

'How much?' said the gentleman shortly.

Alice and Dora were so surprised by his suddenness that they could only reply –

'Er – er –'

'Just so,' said the gentleman briskly as Oswald stepped modestly forward and said –

'Won't you come inside?'

'The very thing,' said he, and came in.

We showed him into the dining-room and asked him to excuse us a minute, and then held a breathless council outside the door.

'It depends how many rooms he wants,' said Dora.

'Let's say so much a room,' said Dicky, 'and extra if he wants Mrs Beale to wait on him.'

So we decided to do this. We thought a pound a room seemed fair.

And we went back.

'How many rooms do you want?' Oswald asked.

'All the room there is,' said the gentleman.

'They are a pound each,' said Oswald, 'and extra for Mrs Beale.'

'How much altogether?'

Oswald thought a minute and then said 'Nine rooms is nine pounds, and two pounds a week for Mrs Beale, because she is a widow.'

'Done!' said the gentleman. 'I'll go and fetch my portmanteaus.'

He bounced up and out and got into his carriage and drove away. It was not till he was finally gone quite beyond recall that Alice suddenly said –

'But if he has all the rooms where are *we* to sleep?'

'He must be awfully rich,' said H.O., 'wanting all those rooms.'

'Well, he can't sleep in more than one at once,' said Dicky, 'however rich he is. We might wait till he was bedded down and then sleep in the rooms he didn't want.'

But Oswald was firm. He knew that if the man paid for the rooms he must have them to himself.

'He won't sleep in the kitchen,' said Dora; 'couldn't we sleep there?'

But we all said we couldn't and wouldn't.

Then Alice suddenly said –

'I know! The Mill. There are heaps and heaps of fishing-nets there, and we could each take a blanket like Indians and creep over under cover of the night after the Beale has gone, and get back before she comes in the morning.'

It seemed a sporting thing to do, and we agreed. Only Dora said she thought it would be draughty.

Of course we went over to the Mill at once to lay our plans and prepare for the silent watches of the night.

There are three stories to a windmill, besides the ground-floor. The first floor is pretty empty; the next is nearly full of millstones and machinery, and the one above is where the corn runs down from on to the millstones.

We settled to let the girls have the first floor, which was covered with heaps of nets, and we would pig in with the millstones on the floor above.

We had just secretly got out the last of the six blankets from the house and got it into the Mill disguised in a clothes-basket, when we heard wheels, and there was the gentleman back again. He had only got one portmanteau after all, and that was a very little one.

Mrs Beale was bobbing at him in the doorway when we got up. Of course we had told her he had rented rooms, but we had not said how many, for fear she should ask where we were going to sleep, and we had a feeling that but few grown-ups would like our sleeping in a mill, however much we were living the higher life by sacrificing ourselves to get money for Miss Sandal.

The gentleman ordered sheep's-head and trotters for dinner, and when he found he could not have that he said –

'Gammon and spinach!'

But there was not any spinach in the village, so he had to fall back on eggs and bacon. Mrs Beale cooked it, and when he had fallen back on it she washed up and went home. And we were left. We could hear the gentleman singing to himself, something about woulding he was a bird that he might fly to thee.

Then we got the lanterns that you take when you go 'up street' on a dark night, and we crept over to the Mill. It was much darker than we expected.

We decided to keep our clothes on, partly for warmness and partly in case of any sudden alarm or the fishermen wanting their nets in the middle of the night, which some-times happens if the tide is favourable.

We let the girls keep the lantern, and we went up with a bit of candle Dicky had saved, and tried to get comfortable among the millstones and machinery, but it was not easy, and Oswald, for one, was not sorry when he heard the voice of Dora calling in trembling tones from the floor below.

'Oswald! Dicky!' said the voice, 'I wish one of you would come down a sec.'

Oswald flew to the assistance of his distressed sister.

'It's only that we're a little bit uncomfortable,' she whispered. 'I didn't want to yell it out because of Noël and H.O. I don't want to frighten them, but I can't help feeling that if anything popped out of the dark at us I should die. Can't you all come down here? The nets are quite comfort-able, and I do wish you would.'

Alice said she was not frightened, but suppose there were

rats, which are said to infest old buildings, especially mills?

So we consented to come down, and we told Noël and H.O. to come down because it was more comfy, and it is easier to settle yourself for the night among fishing-nets than among machinery. There *was* a rustling now and then among the heap of broken chairs and jack-planes and baskets and spades and hoes and bits of the spars of ships at the far end of our sleeping apartment, but Dicky and Oswald resolutely said it was the wind or else jackdaws making their nests, though, of course, they knew this is not done at night.

Sleeping in a mill was not nearly the fun we had thought it would be – somehow. For one thing, it was horrid not having a pillow, and the fishing-nets were so stiff you could not bunch them up properly to make one. And unless you have been born and bred a Red Indian you do not know how to manage your blanket so as to make it keep out the draughts. And when we had put out the light Oswald more than once felt as though earwigs and spiders were walking on his face in the dark, but when we struck a match there was nothing there.

And empty mills do creak and rustle and move about in a very odd way. Oswald was not afraid, but he did think we might as well have slept in the kitchen, because the gentleman could not have wanted to use that when he was asleep. You see, we thought then that he would sleep all night like other people.

We got to sleep at last, and in the night the girls edged up to their bold brothers, so that when the morning sun 'shone in bars of dusty gold through the chinks of the aged edifice' and woke us up we were all lying in a snuggly heap like a litter of puppies.

'Oh, I *am* so stiff!' said Alice, stretching. 'I never slept in my clothes before. It makes me feel as if I had been starched and ironed like a boy's collar.'

We all felt pretty much the same. And our faces were tired too, and stiff, which was rum, and the author cannot account for it, unless it really was spiders that walked on us. I believe the ancient Greeks considered them to be venomous, and perhaps that's how their venom influences their victims.

'I think mills are merely beastly,' remarked H.O. when we had woke him up. 'You can't wash yourself or brush your hair or anything.'

'You aren't always so jolly particular about your hair,' said Dicky.

'Don't be so disagreeable,' said Dora.

And Dicky rejoined, 'Disagreeable yourself!'

There is certainly something about sleeping in your clothes that makes you feel not so kind and polite as usual. I expect this is why tramps are so fierce and knock people down in lonely roads and kick them. Oswald knows he felt just like kicking any one if they had happened to cheek him the least little bit. But by a fortunate accident nobody did.

The author believes there is a picture called 'Hopeless Dawn'. We felt exactly like that. Nothing seemed the least bit of good.

It was a pitiful band with hands and faces dirtier than any one would believe who had not slept in a mill or witnessed others who had done so, that crossed the wet, green grass between the Mill and the white house.

'I shan't ever put morning dew into my poetry again,' Noël said; 'it is not nearly so poetical as people make out, and it is as cold as ice, right through your boots.'

We felt rather better when we had had a good splash in the brick-paved back kitchen that Miss Sandal calls the bath-room. And Alice made a fire and boiled a kettle and we had some tea and eggs. Then we looked at the clock and it was half-past five. So we hastened to get into another part of the house before Mrs Beale came.

'I wish we'd tried to live the higher life some less beastly way,' said Dicky as we went along the passage.

'Living the higher life always hurts at the beginning,' Alice said. 'I expect it's like new boots, only when you've got used to it you're glad you bore it at first. Let's listen at the doors till we find out where he isn't sleeping.'

So we listened at all the bedroom doors, but not a snore was heard.

'Perhaps he was a burglar,' said H.O., 'and only pretended to want lodgings so as to get in and bone all the valuables.'

'There aren't any valuables,' said Noël, and this was quite true, for Miss Sandal had no silver or jewellery except a brooch of pewter, and the very teaspoons were of wood – very hard to keep clean and having to be scraped.

'Perhaps he sleeps without snoring,' said Oswald, 'some people do.'

'Not old gentlemen,' said Noël; 'think of our Indian uncle – H.O. used to think it was bears at first.'

'Perhaps he rises with the lark,' said Alice, 'and is wondering why brekker isn't ready.'

So then we listened at the sitting-room doors, and through the keyhole of the parlour we heard a noise of some one moving, and then in a soft whistle the tune of the 'Would I were a bird' song.

So then we went into the dining-room to sit down. But when we opened the door we almost fell in a heap on the matting, and no one had breath for a word – not even for 'Crikey', which was what we all thought.

I have read of people who could not believe their eyes; and I have always thought it such rot of them, but now, as the author gazed on the scene, he really could not be quite sure that he was not in a dream, and that the gentleman and the night in the Mill weren't dreams too.

'Pull back the curtains,' Alice said, and we did. I wish

I could make the reader feel as astonished as we did.

The last time we had seen the room the walls had been bare and white. Now they were covered with the most splendid drawings you can think of, all done in coloured chalk. I don't mean mixed up, like we do with our chalks – but one picture was done in green, and another in brown, and another in red, and so on. And the chalk must have been of some fat radiant kind quite unknown to us, for some of the lines were over an inch thick.

'How perfectly *lovely*!' Alice said; 'he must have sat up all night to do it. He *is* good. I expect he's trying to live the higher life, too – just going about doing secretly, and spending his time making other people's houses pretty.'

'I wonder what he'd have done if the room had had a large pattern of brown roses on it, like Mrs Beale's,' said Noël. 'I say, *look* at that angel! Isn't it poetical? It makes me feel I must write something about it.'

It *was* a good angel – all drawn in grey, that was – with very wide wings going right across the room, and a whole bundle of lilies in his arms. Then there were seagulls and ravens, and butterflies, and ballet girls with butterflies' wings, and a man with artificial wings being fastened on, and you could see he was just going to jump off a rock. And there were fairies, and bats, and flying-foxes, and flying-fish. And one glorious winged horse done in red chalk – and his wings went from one side of the room to the other, and crossed the angel's. There were dozens and dozens of birds – all done in just a few lines – but exactly right. You couldn't make any mistake about what anything was meant for.

And all the things, whatever they were, had wings to them. How Oswald wishes that those pictures had been done in his house!

While we stood gazing, the door of the other room opened, and the gentleman stood before us, more covered with different-coloured chalks than I should have thought he could have got, even with all those drawings, and he had a thing made of wire and paper in his hand, and he said –

'Wouldn't you like to fly?'

'Yes,' said every one.

'Well then,' he said, 'I've got a nice little flying-machine here. I'll fit it on to one of you, and then you jump out of the attic window. You don't know what it's like to fly.'

We said we would rather not.

'But I insist,' said the gentleman. 'I have your real interest at heart, my children – I can't allow you in your ignorance to reject the chance of a lifetime.'

We still said 'No, thank you,' and we began to feel very uncomfy, for the gentleman's eyes were now rolling wildly.

'Then I'll *make* you!' he said, catching hold of Oswald.

'You jolly well won't,' cried Dicky, catching hold of the arm of the gentleman.

Then Dora said very primly and speaking rather slowly, and she was very pale –

'I think it would be lovely to fly. Will you just show me how the flying-machine looks when it is unfolded?'

The gentleman dropped Oswald, and Dora made 'Go! go' with her lips without speaking, while he began to unfold the flying-machine. We others went, Oswald lingering last, and then in an instant Dora had nipped out of the room and banged the door and locked it.

'To the Mill!' she cried, and we ran like mad, and got in and barred the big door, and went up to the first floor, and looked out of the big window to warn off Mrs Beale.

And we thumped Dora on the back, and Dicky called her a Sherlock Holmes, and Noël said she was a heroine.

'It wasn't anything,' Dora said, just before she began to cry, 'only I remember reading that you must pretend to humour them, and then get away, for of course I saw at once he was a lunatic. Oh, how awful it might have been! He could have made us all jump out of the attic window, and there would have been no one left to tell Father. Oh! oh!' and then the crying began.

But we were proud of Dora, and I am sorry we make fun of her sometimes, but it is difficult not to.

We decided to signal the first person that passed, and we got Alice to take off her red flannel petticoat for a signal,

The first people who came were two men in a dog-cart. We waved the signalizing petticoat and they pulled up, and one got out and came up to the Mill.

We explained about the lunatic and the wanting us to jump out of the windows.

'Right oh!' cried the man to the one still in the cart; 'got him.' And the other hitched the horse to the gate and came over, and the other went to the house.

'Come along down, young ladies and gentlemen,' said the second man when he had been told. 'He's as gentle as a lamb. He does not think it hurts to jump out of windows. He thinks it really is flying. He'll be like an angel when he sees the doctor.'

We asked if he had been mad before, because we had thought he might have suddenly gone so.

'Certainly he has!' replied the man; 'he has never been, so to say, himself since tumbling out of a flying-machine he went up in with a friend. He was an artist previous to that – an excellent one, I believe. But now he only draws objects with wings – and now and then he wants to make people fly – perfect strangers sometimes, like yourselves. Yes, miss, I am his attendant, and his pictures often amuse me by the half-hours together, poor gentleman.'

'How did he get away?' Alice asked

'Well, miss, the poor gentleman's brother got hurt and Mr Sidney – that's him inside – seemed wonderfully put out and hung over the body in a way pitiful to see. But really he was extracting the cash from the sufferer's pockets. Then, while all of us were occupied with Mr Eustace, Mr Sidney just packs his portmanteau and out he goes by the back door. When we missed him we sent for Dr Baker, but by the time he came it was too late to get here. Dr Baker said at once he'd revert to his boyhood's home. And the doctor has proved correct.'

We had all come out of the Mill, and with this polite person we went to the gate, and saw the lunatic into the carriage, very gentle and gay.

'But, Doctor,' Oswald said, 'he did say he'd give nine pounds a week for the rooms. Oughtn't he to pay?'

'You might have known he was mad to say that,' said the doctor. 'No. Why should he, when it's his own sister's house? Gee up!'

And he left us.

It was sad to find the gentleman was not a Higher Life after all, but only mad. And I was more sorry than ever for poor Miss Sandal. As Oswald pointed out to the girls they are much more blessed in their brothers than Miss Sandal is, and they ought to be more grateful than they are.

THE SMUGGLER'S REVENGE

THE days went on and Miss Sandal did not return. We went on being very sorry about Miss Sandal being so poor, and it was not our fault that when we tried to let the house in lodgings, the first lodger proved to be a lunatic of the deepest dye. Miss Sandal must have been a fairly decent sort, because she seems not to have written to Father about it. At any rate he didn't give it us in any of our letters, about our good intentions and their ending in a maniac.

Oswald does not like giving up a thing just because it has once been muffed. The muffage of a plan is a thing that often happens at first to heroes – like Bruce and the spider, and other great characters. Besides, grown-ups always say –

> 'If at first you don't succeed,
> Try, try, try again!'

And if this is the rule for Euclid and rule-of-three and all the things you would rather not do, think how much more it must be the rule when what you are after is your own idea, and not just the rotten notion of that beast Euclid, or the unknown but equally unnecessary author who composed the multiplication table. So we often talked about what we could do to make Miss Sandal rich. It gave us something to jaw about when we happened to want to sit down for a bit, in between all the glorious wet sandy games that happen by the sea.

Of course if we wanted real improving conversation we used to go up to the boat-house and talk to the coastguards.

644

I do think coastguards are A1. They are just the same as sailors, having been so in their youth, and you can get at them to talk to, which is not the case with sailors who are at sea (or even in harbours) on ships. Even if you had the luck to get on to a man-of-war, you would very likely not be able to climb to the top-gallants to talk to the man there. Though in books the young hero always seems able to climb to the mast-head the moment he is told to. The coastguards told us tales of Southern ports, and of shipwrecks, and officers they had *not* cottoned to, and the messmates that they *had*, but when we asked them about smuggling they said there wasn't any to speak of nowadays.

'I expect they think they oughtn't to talk about such dark crimes before innocent kids like us,' said Dicky afterwards, and he grinned as he said it.

'Yes,' said Alice; 'they don't know how much we know about smugglers, and bandits, and highwaymen, and burglars, and coiners,' and she sighed, and we all felt sad to think that we had not now any chance to play at being these things.

'We might play smugglers,' said Oswald.

But he did not speak hopefully. The worst of growing up is that you seem to want more and more to have a bit of the real thing in your games. Oswald could not now be content to play at bandits and just capture Albert next door, as once, in happier days, he was pleased and proud to do.

It was not a coastguard that told us about the smugglers. It was a very old man that we met two or three miles along the beach. He was leaning against a boat that was wrong way up on the shingle, and smoking the strongest tobacco Oswald's young nose has ever met. I think it must have been Black Jack. We said, 'How do you do?' and Alice said, 'Do you mind if we sit down near you?'

'Not me,' replied the aged seafarer. We could see directly that he was this by his jersey and his sea-boots.

The girls sat down on the beach, but we boys leaned against the boat like the seafaring one. We hoped he would join in conversation, but at first he seemed too proud. And there was something dignified about him, bearded and like a Viking, that made it hard for us to begin.

At last he took his pipe out of his mouth and said –

'Here's a precious Quakers' meeting! You didn't set down here just for to look at me?'

'I'm sure you look very nice,' Dora said.

'Same to you, miss, I'm sure,' was the polite reply.

'We want to talk to you awfully,' said Alice, 'if you don't mind?'

'Talk away,' said he.

And then, as so often happens, no one could think of anything to say.

Suddenly Noël said, '*I* think you look nice too, but I think you look as though you had a secret history. Have you?'

'Not me,' replied the Viking-looking stranger. 'I ain't got no history, nor joggraphy neither. They didn't give us that much schooling when I was a lad.'

'Oh!' replied Noël; 'but what I really meant was, were you ever a pirate or anything?'

'Never in all my born,' replied the stranger, now thoroughly roused; 'I'd scorn the haction. I was in the navy, I was, till I lost the sight of my eye, looking too close at gunpowder. Pirates is snakes, and they ought to be killed as such.'

We felt rather sorry, for though of course it is very wrong to be a pirate, it is very interesting too. Things are often like this. That is one of the reasons why it is so hard to be truly good.

Dora was the only one who was pleased. She said –

'Yes, pirates *are* very wrong. And so are highwaymen and smugglers.'

646

'I don't know about highwaymen,' the old man replied; 'they went out afore my time, worse luck; but my father's great-uncle by the mother's side, he see one hanged once. A fine upstanding fellow he was, and made a speech while they was a-fitting of the rope. All the women were snivelling and sniffing and throwing bokays at him.'

'Did any of the bouquets reach him?' asked the interested Alice.

'Not likely,' said the old man. 'Women can't never shy straight. But I shouldn't wonder but what them posies heartened the chap up a bit. An afterwards they was all a-fightin' to get a bit of the rope he was hung with, for luck.'

'Do tell us some more about him,' said all of us but Dora.

'I don't know no more about him. He was just hung – that's all. They was precious fond o' hangin' in them old far-away times.'

'Did you ever know a smuggler?' asked H.O. – 'to speak to, I mean?'

'Ah, that's tellings,' said the old man, and he winked at us all.

So then we instantly knew that the coastguards had been mistaken when they said there were no more smugglers now, and that this brave old man would not betray his comrades, even to friendly strangers like us. But of course he could not know exactly how friendly we were. So we told him.

Oswald said –

'We *love* smugglers. We wouldn't even tell a word about it if you would only tell us.'

'There used to be lots of smuggling on these here coasts when my father was a boy,' he said; 'my own father's cousin, his father took to the smuggling, and he was a doin' so well at it, that what does he do, but goes and gets married, and the Preventives they goes and nabs him on his wedding-day, and walks him straight off from the church door, and claps him in Dover Jail.'

'Oh, his poor wife,' said Alice, 'whatever did she do?'

'*She* didn't do nothing,' said the old man. 'It's a woman's place not to do nothing till she's told to. He'd done so well at the smuggling, he'd saved enough by his honest toil to take a little public. So she sets there awaitin' and attendin' to customers – for well she knowed him, as he wasn't the chap to let a bit of a jail stand in the way of his station in life. Well, it was three weeks to a day after the wedding, there comes a dusty chap to the "Peal of Bells" door. That was the sign over the public, you understand.'

We said we did, and breathlessly added, 'Go on!'

'A dusty chap he was; got a beard and a patch over one eye, and he come of a afternoon when there was no one about the place but her.

'"Hullo, missis," says he; "got a room for a quiet chap?"

'"I don't take in no men-folks," says she; "can't be bothered with 'em."

'"You'll be bothered with me, if I'm not mistaken," says he.

'"Bothered if I will," says she.

'"Bothered if you won't," says he, and with that he ups with his hand and off comes the black patch, and he pulls off the beard and gives her a kiss and a smack on the shoulder. She always said she nearly died when she see it was her new-made bridegroom under the beard.

'So she took her own man in as a lodger, and he went to work up at Upton's Farm with his beard on, and of nights he kept up the smuggling business. And for a year or more no one knowd as it was him. But they got him at last.'

'What became of him?' We all asked it.

'He's dead,' said the old man. 'But, Lord love you, so's everybody as lived in them far-off old ancient days – all

648

dead – Preventives too – and smugglers and gentry: all gone under the daisies.'

We felt quite sad. Oswald hastily asked if there wasn't any smuggling now.

'Not hereabouts,' the old man answered, rather quickly for him. 'Don't you go for to think it. But I did know a young chap – quite young he is with blue eyes – up Sunderland way it was. He'd got a goodish bit o' baccy and stuff done up in a ole shirt. And as he was a-goin' up off of the beach a coastguard jumps out at him, and he says to himself, "All u. p. this time," says he. But out loud he says, "Hullo, Jack, that you? I thought you was a tramp," says he.

'"What you got in that bundle?" says the coastguard.

'"My washing," says he, "and a couple of pairs of old boots."

'Then the coastguard he says, "Shall I give you a lift with it?" thinking in himself the other chap wouldn't part if it was anything it oughtn't to be. But that young chap was too sharp. He says to himself, "If I don't he'll nail me, and if I do – well, there's just a chance."

'So he hands over the bundle, and the coastguard he thinks it must be all right, and he carries it all the way up to his mother's for him, feeling sorry for the mean suspicions he'd had about the poor old chap. But that didn't happen near here. No, no.'

I think Dora was going to say, '*Old* chap – but I thought he was young with blue eyes?' but just at that minute a coastguard came along and ordered us quite harshly not to lean on the boat. He was quite disagreeable about it – how different from our own coastguards! He was from a different station to theirs. The old man got off very slowly. And all the time he was arranging his long legs so as to stand on them, the coastguard went on being disagreeable as hard as he could, in a loud voice.

When our old man had told the coastguard that no one

ever lost anything by keeping a civil tongue in his head, we all went away feeling very angry.

Alice took the old man's hand as we went back to the village, and asked him why the coastguard was so horrid.

'They gets notions into their heads,' replied the old man; 'the most innocentest people they comes to think things about. It's along of there being no smuggling in these ere parts now. The coastguards ain't got nothing to do except think things about honest people.'

We parted from the old man very warmly, all shaking hands. He lives at a cottage not quite in the village, and keeps pigs. We did not say goodbye till we had seen all the pigs.

I daresay we should not have gone on disliking that disagreeable coastguard so much if he had not come along one day when we were talking to our own coastguards, and asked why they allowed a pack of young shavers in the boat-house. We went away in silent dignity, but we did not forget, and when we were in bed that night Oswald said –

'Don't you think it would be a good thing if the coastguards had something to do?'

Dicky yawned and said he didn't know.

'I should like to be a smuggler,' said Oswald. 'Oh, yes, go to sleep if you like; but I've got an idea, and if you'd rather be out of it I'll have Alice instead.'

'Fire away!' said Dicky, now full of attention, and leaning on his elbow.

'Well, then,' said Oswald, 'I think we *might* be smugglers.'

'We've played all those things so jolly often,' said Dicky.

'But I don't mean play,' said Oswald. 'I mean the real thing. Of course we should have to begin in quite a small way. But we should get on in time. And we might make quite a lot for poor Miss Sandal.'

'Things that you smuggle are expensive,' said Dicky.

'Well, we've got the chink the Indian uncle sent us on Saturday. I'm certain we could do it. We'd get some one to take us out at night in one of the fishing-boats – just tear across to France and buy a keg or a bale or something, and rush back.'

'Yes, and get nabbed and put in prison. Not me,' said Dicky. 'Besides, who'd take us?'

'That old Viking man would,' said Oswald; 'but of course, if you funk it!'

'I don't funk anything,' said Dicky, 'bar making an ape of myself. Keep your hair on, Oswald. Look here. Suppose we get a keg with nothing in it – or just water. We should have all the fun, and if we *were* collared we should have the laugh of that coastguard brute.'

Oswald agreed, but he made it a condition that we should call it the keg of brandy, whatever was in it, and Dicky consented.

Smuggling is a manly sport, and girls are not fitted for it by nature. At least Dora is not; and if we had told Alice she would have insisted on dressing as a boy and going too, and we knew Father would not like this. And we thought Noël and H.O. were too young to be smugglers with any hope of success. So Dicky and I kept the idea to ourselves.

We went to see the Viking man the next day. It took us some time to make him understand what we wanted, but when he did understand he slapped his leg many times, and very hard, and declared we were chips off the old block.

'But I can't go for to let you,' he said; 'if you was nailed it's the stone jug, bless your hearts.'

So then we explained about the keg really having only water in, and he slapped his leg again harder than ever, so that it would really have been painful to any but the hardened leg of an old sea-dog. But the water made his refusals weaker, and at last he said –

'Well, see here, Benenden, him as owns the *Mary Sarah*,

he's often took out a youngster or two for the night's fishing, when their pa's and ma's hadn't no objection. You write your pa, and ask if you mayn't go for the night's fishing, or you get Mr Charteris to write. He knows it's all right, and often done by visitors' kids, if boys. And if your pa says yes, I'll make it all right with Benenden. But mind, it's just a night's fishing. No need to name no kegs. That's just betwixt ourselves.'

So we did exactly as he said. Mr Charteris is the clergyman. He was quite nice about it, and wrote for us, and Father said 'Yes, but be very careful, and don't take the girls or the little ones.'

We showed the girls the letter, and that removed the trifling ill-feeling that had grown up through Dick and me having so much secret talk about kegs and not telling the others what was up.

Of course we never breathed a word about kegs in public, and only to each other in bated breaths.

What Father said about not taking the girls or the little ones of course settled any wild ideas Alice might have had of going as a cabin-girl.

The old Viking man, now completely interested in our scheme, laid all the plans in the deepest-laid way you can think. He chose a very dark night – fortunately there was one just coming on. He chose the right time of the tide for starting, and just in the greyness of the evening when the sun is gone down, and the sea somehow looks wetter than at any other time, we put on our thick undershirts, and then our thickest suits and football jerseys over everything, because we had been told it would be very cold. Then we said goodbye to our sisters and the little ones, and it was exactly like a picture of the 'Tar's Farewell', because we had bundles, with things to eat tied up in blue checked handkerchiefs, and we said goodbye to them at the gate, and they would kiss us.

Dora said, 'Goodbye, I *know* you'll be drowned. I hope you'll enjoy yourselves, I'm sure!'

Alice said, 'I do think it's perfectly beastly. You might just as well have asked for me to go with you; or you might let us come and see you start.'

'Men must work, and women must weep,' replied Oswald with grim sadness, 'and the Viking said he wouldn't have us at all unless we could get on board in a concealed manner, like stowaways. He said a lot of others would want to go too if they saw us.'

We made our way to the beach, and we tried to conceal ourselves as much as possible, but several people did see us.

When we got to the boat we found she was manned by our Viking and Benenden, and a boy with red hair, and they were running her down to the beach on rollers. Of course Dicky and I lent a hand, shoving at the stern of the boat when the men said, 'Yo, ho! Heave ho, my merry boys all!' It wasn't exactly that that they said, but it meant the same thing, and we heaved like anything.

It was a proud moment when her nose touched the water, and prouder still when only a small part of her stern remained on the beach and Mr Benenden remarked –

'All aboard!'

The red boy gave a 'leg up' to Dicky and me and clambered up himself. Then the two men gave the last shoves to the boat, already cradled almost entirely on the bosom of the deep, and as the very end of the keel grated off the pebbles into the water, they leaped for the gunwale and hung on it with their high sea-boots waving in the evening air.

By the time they had brought their legs on board and coiled a rope or two, we chanced to look back, and already the beach seemed quite a long way off.

We were really afloat. Our smuggling expedition was no longer a dream, but a real realness. Oswald felt almost too excited at first to be able to enjoy himself. I hope you will understand this and not think the author is trying to express, by roundabout means, that the sea did not agree with Oswald. This is not the case. He was perfectly well the whole time. It was Dicky who was not. But he said it was the smell of the cabin, and not the sea, and I am sure he thought what he said was true.

In fact, that cabin was a bit stiff altogether, and was almost the means of upsetting even Oswald.

It was about six feet square, with bunks and an oil stove, and heaps of old coats and tarpaulins and sou'-westers and things, and it smelt of tar, and fish, and paraffin-smoke, and machinery oil, and of rooms where no one ever opens the window.

Oswald just put his nose in, and that was all. He had to go down later, when some fish was cooked and eaten, but by that time he had got what they call your sea-legs; but Oswald felt more as if he had got a sea-waistcoat, rather as if he had got rid of a land-waistcoat that was too heavy and too tight.

I will not weary the reader by telling about how the nets are paid out and dragged in, or about the tumbling, shining heaps of fish that come up all alive over the side of the boat, and it tips up with their weight till you think it is going over. It was a very good catch that night, and Oswald is glad he saw it, for it was very glorious. Dicky was asleep in the cabin at the time and missed it. It was deemed best not to rouse him to fresh sufferings.

It was getting latish, and Oswald, though thrilled in every marrow, was getting rather sleepy, when old Benenden said, 'There she is!'

Oswald could see nothing at first, but presently he saw a dark form on the smooth sea. It turned out to be another boat.

She crept quietly up till she was alongside ours, and then a keg was hastily hoisted from her to us.

A few words in low voices were exchanged. Oswald only heard –

'Sure you ain't give us the wrong un?'

And several people laughed hoarsely.

On first going on board Oswald and Dicky had mentioned kegs, and had been ordered to 'Stow that!' so that Oswald had begun to fear that after all it *was* only a night's fishing, and that his glorious idea had been abandoned.

But now he saw the keg his trembling heart was re-assured.

It got colder and colder. Dicky, in the cabin, was covered with several coats richly scented with fish, and Oswald was glad to accept an oilskin and sou'-wester, and to sit down on some spare nets.

Until you are out on the sea at night you can never have any idea how big the world really is. The sky looks higher up, and the stars look further off, and even if you know it is only the English Channel, yet it is just as good for feeling small on as the most trackless Atlantic or Pacific. Even the fish help to show the largeness of the world, because you think of the deep deepness of the dark sea they come up out of in such rich profusion. The hold was full of fish after the second haul.

Oswald sat leaning against the precious keg, and perhaps the bigness and quietness of everything had really rendered him unconscious. But he did not know he was asleep until the Viking man woke him up by kindly shaking him and saying –

'Here, look alive! Was ye thinking to beach her with that there precious keg of yours all above board, and crying out to be broached?'

So then Oswald roused himself, and the keg was rolled on to the fish where they lay filling the hold, and armfuls of fish thrown over it.

'Is it *really* only water?' asked Oswald. 'There's an

awfully odd smell.' And indeed, in spite of the many different smells that are natural to a fishing-boat, Oswald began to notice a strong scent of railway refreshment-rooms.

'In course it's only water,' said the Viking. 'What else would it be likely to be?' and Oswald thinks he winked in the dark.

Perhaps Oswald fell asleep again after this. It was either that or deep thought. Any way, he was aroused from it by a bump, and a soft grating sound, and he thought at first the boat was being wrecked on a coral reef or something.

But almost directly he knew that the boat had merely come ashore in the proper manner, so he jumped up.

You cannot push a boat out of the water like you push it in. It has to be hauled up by a capstan. If you don't know what that is the author is unable to explain, but there is a picture of one.

When the boat was hauled up we got out, and it was very odd to stretch your legs on land again. It felt shakier than being on sea. The red-haired boy went off to get a cart to take the shining fish to market, and Oswald decided to face the mixed-up smells of that cabin and wake Dicky.

Dicky was not grateful to Oswald for his thoughtful kindness in letting him sleep through the perils of the deep and his own uncomfortableness.

He said, 'I do think you might have waked a chap. I've simply been out of everything.'

Oswald did not answer back. His is a proud and self-restraining nature. He just said –

'Well, hurry up, now, and see them cart the fish away.'

So we hurried up, and as Oswald came out of the cabin he heard strange voices, and his heart leaped up like the persons who 'behold a rainbow in the sky,' for one of the voices was the voice of that inferior and unsailorlike coast-guard from Longbeach, who had gone out of his way to be disagreeable to Oswald and his brothers and sisters on at least two occasions. And now Oswald felt almost sure that his disagreeablenesses, though not exactly curses, were coming home to roost just as though they had been.

'You're missing your beauty sleep, Stokes,' we heard our Viking remark.

'I'm not missing anything else, though,' replied the coastguard.

'Like half a dozen mackerel for your breakfast?' inquired Mr Benenden in kindly accents.

'I've no stomach for fish, thank you all the same,' replied Mr Stokes coldly.

He walked up and down on the beach, clapping his arms to keep himself warm.

'Going to see us unload her?' asked Mr Benenden.

'If it's all the same to you,' answered the disagreeable coastguard.

He had to wait a long time, for the cart did not come, and did not come, and kept on not coming for ages and ages. When it did the men unloaded the boat, carrying the fish by basketfuls to the cart.

Every one played up jolly well. They took the fish from the side of the hold where the keg wasn't till there was quite a deep hole there, and the other side, where the keg really was, looked like a mountain in comparison.

This could be plainly seen by the detested coastguard, and by three of his companions who had now joined him.

It was beginning to be light, not daylight, but a sort of ghost-light that you could hardly believe was the beginning of sunshine, and the sky being blue again instead of black.

The hated coastguard got impatient. He said –

'You'd best own up. It'll be the better for you. It's bound to come out, along of the fish. I know it's there. We've had private information up at the station. The game's up this time, so don't you make no mistake.'

Mr Benenden and the Viking and the boy looked at each other.

'An' what might your precious private information have been about?' asked Mr Benenden.

'Brandy,' replied the coastguard Stokes, and he went and got on to the gunwale. 'And what's more, I can smell it from here.'

Oswald and Dicky drew near, and the refreshment-room smell was stronger than ever. And a brown corner of the keg was peeping out.

'There you are!' cried the Loathed One. 'Let's have that gentleman out, if you please, and then you'll all just come alonger me.'

Remarking, with a shrug of the shoulders, that he supposed it was all up, our Viking scattered the fish that hid the barrel, and hoisted it out from its scaly bed.

'That's about the size of it,' said the coastguard we did not like. 'Where's the rest?'

'That's all,' said Mr Benenden. 'We're poor men, and we has to act according to our means.'

'We'll see the boat clear to her last timber, if you've no objections,' said the Detestable One.

I could see that our gallant crew were prepared to go through with the business. More and more of the coastguards were collecting, and I understood that what the crew wanted was to go up to the coastguard station with that keg of pretending brandy, and involve the whole of the coastguards of Longbeach in one complete and perfect sell.

But Dicky was sick of the entire business. He really has not the proper soul for adventures, and what soul he has had been damped by what he had gone through.

So he said, 'Look here, there's nothing in that keg but water.'

Oswald could have kicked him, though he is his brother.

'Huh!' replied the Unloved One, 'd'you think I haven't

got a nose? Why, it's oozing out of the bunghole now as strong as Samson.'

'Open it and see,' said Dicky, disregarding Oswald's whispered instructions to him to shut up. 'It *is* water.'

'What do you suppose I suppose you want to get water from the other side for, you young duffer!' replied the brutal official. 'There's plenty water and to spare this side.'

'It's – it's *French* water,' replied Dicky madly; 'it's ours, my brother's and mine. We asked these sailors to get it for us.'

'Sailors, indeed!' said the hateful coastguard. 'You come along with me.'

And our Viking said he was something or othered. But Benenden whispered to him in a low voice that it was all right – time was up. No one heard this but me and the Viking.

'I want to go home,' said Dicky. 'I don't want to come along with you.'

'What did you want water for?' was asked. 'To try it?'

'To stand you a drink next time you ordered us off your beastly boat,' said Dicky. And Oswald rejoiced to hear the roar of laughter that responded to this fortunate piece of cheek.

I suppose Dicky's face was so angel-like, innocent-looking, like stowaways in books, that they *had* to believe him. Oswald told him so afterwards, and Dicky hit out.

Any way, the keg was broached, and sure enough it was water, and sea-water at that, as the Unamiable One said when he had tasted it out of a tin cup, for nothing else would convince him. 'But I smell brandy still,' he said, wiping his mouth after the sea-water.

Our Viking slowly drew a good-sized flat labelled bottle out of the front of his jersey.

'From the "Old Ship",' he said gently. 'I may have spilt a drop or two here or there over the keg, my hand not being very steady, as is well known, owing to spells of marsh fever as comes over me every six weeks to the day.'

The coastguard that we never could bear said, 'Marsh fever be something or othered,' and his comrades said the same. But they all blamed *him*, and we were glad.

We went home sleepy, but rejoicing. The whole thing was as complete a sell as ever I wish to see.

Of course we told our own dear and respected Lymchurch coastguards, and I think they may be trusted not to let it down on the Longbeach coastguards for many a good day. If their memories get bad I think there will always be plenty of people along that coast to remind them!

So *that's* all right.

When we had told the girls all, and borne their reproaches for not telling them before, we decided to give the Viking five bob for the game way he had played up.

So we did. He would not take it at first, but when we said, 'Do – you might buy a pig with it, and call it Stokes after that coastguard,' he could no longer resist, and accepted our friendly gift.

We talked with him for a bit, and when we were going we thanked him for being so jolly, and helping us to plant out the repulsive coastguard so thoroughly.

Then he said, 'Don't mention it. Did you tell your little gells what you was up to?'

'No,' said Oswald, 'not till afterwards.'

'Then you *can* hold your tongues. Well, since you've acted so handsome about that there pig, what's to be named for Stokes, I don't mind if I tells you something. Only mum's the word.'

We said we were quite sure it was.

'Well, then,' said he, leaning over the pigstye wall, and rubbing the spotted pig's back with his stick. 'It's an ill wind that blows no good to nobody. You see, that night there was a little bird went an whispered to 'em up at Longbeach about our little bit of a keg. So when we landed they was there.'

'Of course,' said Oswald.

'Well, if they was there they couldn't be somewheres else, could they?'

We owned they could not.

'I shouldn't wonder,' he went on, 'but what a bit of a cargo was run that night further up the beach: something as *wasn't* sea-water. I don't say it was so, mind – and mind you don't go for to say it.'

Then we understood that there is a little smuggling done still, and that we had helped in it, though quite without knowing.

We were jolly glad. Afterwards, when we had had that talk with Father, when he told us that the laws are made by the English people, and it is dishonourable for an Englishman not to stick to them, we saw that smuggling must be wrong.

But we have never been able to feel really sorry. I do not know why this is.

ZAÏDA, THE MYSTERIOUS PROPHETESS OF THE GOLDEN ORIENT

THIS is the story of how we were gipsies and wandering minstrels. And, like everything else we did about that time, it was done to make money for Miss Sandal, whose poorness kept on, making our kind hearts ache.

It is rather difficult to get up any good game in a house like Miss Sandal's, where there is nothing lying about, except your own things, and where everything is so neat and necessary. Your own clothes are seldom interesting, and even if you change hats with your sisters it is not a complete disguise.

The idea of being gipsies was due to Alice. She had not at all liked being entirely out of the smuggling affray, though Oswald explained to her that it was her own fault for having been born a girl. And, of course, after the event, Dicky and I had some things to talk about that the girls hadn't, and we had a couple of wet days.

You have no idea how dull you can be in a house like that, unless you happen to know the sort of house I mean. A house that is meant for plain living and high thinking, like Miss Sandal told us, may be very nice for the high thinkers, but if you are not accustomed to thinking high there is only the plain living left, and it is like boiled rice for every meal to any young mind, however much beef and Yorkshire there may be for the young insides. Mrs Beale saw to our having plenty of nice things to eat, but, alas! it is not always dinner-time, and in between meals the cold rice-pudding feeling is very chilling. Of course we had the splendid drawings of winged things made by our Flying Lodger, but you cannot look at pictures all day long, however many coloured chalks they are drawn with, and however fond you may be of them.

Miss Sandal's was the kind of house that makes you wander all round it and say, 'What shall we do next?' And when it rains the little ones get cross.

It was the second wet day when we were wandering round the house to the sad music of our boots on the clean, bare boards that Alice said –

'Mrs Beale has got a book at her house called *Napoleon's Book of Fate*. You might ask her to let you go and get it, Oswald. She likes you best.'

Oswald is as modest as any one I know, but the truth is the truth.

'We could tell our fortunes, and read the dark future,' Alice went on. 'It would be better than high thinking without anything particular to think about.'

So Oswald went down to Mrs Beale and said –

'I say, Bealie dear, you've got a book up at your place. I wish you'd lend it to us to read.'

'If it's the Holy Book you mean, sir,' replied Mrs Beale, going on with peeling the potatoes that were to be a radiant vision later on, all brown and crisp in company with a leg of mutton – 'if it's the Holy Book you want there's one up on Miss Sandal's chest of drawerses.'

'I know,' said Oswald. He knew every book in the house. The backs of them were beautiful – leather and gold – but inside they were like whited sepulchres, full of poetry and improving reading. 'No – we didn't want that book just now. It is a book called *Napoleon's Book of Fate*. Would you mind if I ran up to your place and got it?'

'There's no one at home,' said Mrs Beale; 'wait a bit till I go along to the bakus with the meat, and I'll fetch it along.'

'You might let me go,' said Oswald, whose high spirit is

663

always ill-attuned to waiting a bit. 'I wouldn't touch anything else, and I know where you keep the key.'

'There's precious little as ye don't know, it seems to me,' said Mrs Beale. 'There, run along do. It's on top of the mantelshelf alongside the picture tea-tin. It's a red book. Don't go taking the *Wesleyan Conference Reports* by mistake, the two is both together on the mantel.'

Oswald in his macker splashed through the mud to Mrs Beale's, found the key under the loose tile behind the water-butt, and got the book without adventure. He had promised not to touch anything else, so he could not make even the gentlest booby-trap as a little surprise for Mrs Beale when she got back.

And most of that day we were telling our fortunes by the ingenious means invented by the great Emperor, or by cards, which it is hard to remember the rules for, or by our dreams. The only blights were that the others all wanted to have the book all the time, and that Noël's dreams were so long and mixed that we got tired of hearing about them before he did. But he said he was quite sure he had dreamed every single bit of every one of them. And the author hopes this was the truth.

We all went to bed hoping we should dream something that we could look up in the dream book, but none of us did.

And in the morning it was still raining and Alice said –

'Look here, if it ever clears up again let's dress up and be gipsies. We can go about in the distant villages telling people's fortunes. If you'll let me have the book all to-day I can learn up quite enough to tell them mysteriously and darkly. And gipsies always get their hands crossed with silver.'

Dicky said that was one way of keeping the book to herself, but Oswald said –

'Let us try. She shall have it for an hour, and then we'll have an exam. to see how much she knows.'

This was done, but while she was swatting the thing up with her fingers in her ears we began to talk about how gipsies should be dressed.

And when we all went out of the room to see if we could find anything in that tidy house to dress up in, she came after us to see what was up. So there was no exam.

We peeped into the cupboards and drawers in Miss Sandal's room, but everything was grey or brown, not at all the sort of thing to dress up for children of the Sunny South in. The plain living was shown in all her clothes; and besides, grey shows every little spot you may happen to get on it.

We were almost in despair. We looked in all the drawers in all the rooms, but found only sheets and tablecloths and more grey and brown clothing.

We tried the attic, with fainting hearts. Servants' clothes are always good for dressing-up with; they have so many different colours. But Miss Sandal had no servant. Still, she might have had one once, and the servant might have left something behind her. Dora suggested this and added –

'If you don't find anything in the attic you'll know it's Fate, and you're not to do it. Besides, I'm almost sure you can be put in prison for telling fortunes.'

'Not if you're a gipsy you can't,' said Noël; 'they have licences to tell fortunes, I believe, and judges can't do anything to them.'

So we went up to the attic. And it was as bare and tidy as the rest of the house. But there were some boxes and we looked in them. The smallest was full of old letters, so we shut it again at once. Another had books in it, and the last had a clean towel spread over what was inside. So we took off the towel, and then every one said 'Oh!'

In right on the top was a scarlet thing, embroidered heavily with gold. It proved, on unfolding, to be a sort of coat, like a Chinaman's. We lifted it out and laid it on the

665

towel on the floor. And then the full glories of that box were revealed. There were cloaks and dresses and skirts and scarves, of all the colours of a well-chosen rainbow, and all made of the most beautiful silks and stuffs, with things worked on them with silk, as well as chains of beads and many lovely ornaments. We think Miss Sandal must have been very fond of pretty things when she was young, or when she was better off.

'Well, there won't be any gipsies near by to come up to *us*,' said Oswald joyously.

'Do you think we ought to take them, without asking?' said Dora.

'Of course not,' said Oswald witheringly; 'we ought to write to her and say, "Please, Miss Sandal, we know how poor you are, and may we borrow your things to be gipsies in so as we got money for you –" All right! You go and write the letter, Dora.'

'I only just asked,' said Dora.

We tried the things on. Some of them were so ladylike that they were no good – evening dresses, and things like that. But there were enough useful things to go round. Oswald, in white shirt and flannel knee-breeches, tied a brick-coloured silk scarf round his middle part, and a green one round his head for a turban. The turban was fastened with a sparkling brooch with pink stones in it. He looked like a Moorish toreador. Dicky had the scarlet and gold coat, which was the right length when Dora had run a tuck in it.

Alice had a blue skirt with embroidery of peacock's feathers on it, and a gold and black jacket very short with no sleeves, and a yellow silk handkerchief on her head like Italian peasants, and another handkie round her neck. Dora's skirt was green and her handkerchiefs purple and pink.

Noël insisted on having his two scarves, one green and

666

one yellow, twisted on his legs like putties, and a red scarf wound round his middle-part, and he stuck a long ostrich feather in his own bicycle cap and said he was a troubadour bard.

H.O. was able to wear a lady's blouse of mouse-coloured silk, embroidered with poppies. It came down to his knees and a jewelled belt kept it in place.

We made up our costumes into bundles, and Alice thoughtfully bought a pennyworth of pins. Of course it was idle to suppose that we could go through the village in our gipsy clothes without exciting *some* remark.

The more we thought of it the more it seemed as if it would be a good thing to get some way from our village before we began our gipsy career.

The woman at the sweet shop where Alice got the pins has a donkey and cart, and for two shillings she consented to lend us this, so that some of us could walk while some of us would always be resting in the cart.

And next morning the weather was bright and blue as ever, and we started. We were beautifully clean, but all our hairs had been arranged with a brush solely, because at the last moment nobody could find its comb. Mrs Beale had packed up a jolly sandwichy and apply lunch for us. We told her we were going to gather bluebells in the woods, and of course we meant to do that too.

The donkey-cart drew up at the door and we started. It was found impossible to get every one into the cart at once, so we agreed to cast lots for who should run behind, and to take it in turns, mile and mile. The lot fell on Dora and H.O., but there was precious little running about. Anything slower than that donkey Oswald has never known, and when it came to passing its own front door the donkey simply would not. It ended in Oswald getting down and going to the animal's head, and having it out with him, man to man. The donkey was small, but of enormous strength.

667

He set all his four feet firm and leant back – and Oswald set his two feet firm and leant back – so that Oswald and the front part of the donkey formed an angry and contentious letter V. And Oswald gazed in the donkey's eyes in a dauntless manner, and the donkey looked at Oswald as though it thought he was hay or thistles.

Alice beat the donkey from the cart with a stick that had been given us for the purpose. The rest shouted. But all was in vain. And four people in a motor car stopped it to see the heroic struggle, and laughed till I thought they would have upset their hateful motor. However, it was all for the best, though Oswald did not see it at the time. When they had had enough of laughing they started their machine again, and the noise it made penetrated the donkey's dull intelligence, and he started off without a word – I mean without any warning, and Oswald had only just time to throw himself clear of the wheels before he fell on the ground and rolled over, biting the dust.

The motor car people behaved as you would expect. But accidents happen even to motor cars, when people laugh too long and too unfeelingly. The driver turned round to laugh, and the motor instantly took the bit between its teeth and bolted into the stone wall of the churchyard. No one was hurt except the motor, but that had to spend the day at the blacksmith's, we heard afterwards. Thus was the outraged Oswald avenged by Fate.

He was not hurt either – though much the motor people would have cared if he had been – and he caught up with the others at the end of the village, for the donkey's pace had been too good to last, and the triumphal progress was resumed.

It was some time before we found a wood sufficiently lurking-looking for our secret purposes. There are no woods close to the village. But at last, up by Bonnington, we found one, and tying our noble steed to the sign-post that says how many miles it is to Ashford, we cast a hasty glance round, and finding no one in sight disappeared in the wood with our bundles.

We went in just ordinary creatures. We came out gipsies of the deepest dye, for we had got a pennorth of walnut stain from Mr Jameson the builder, and mixed with water – the water we had brought in a medicine-bottle – it was a prime disguise. And we knew it would wash off, unlike the Condy's fluid we once stained ourselves with during a never-to-be-forgotten game of Jungle-Book.

We had put on all the glorious things we had bagged from Miss Sandal's attic treasures, but still Alice had a small bundle unopened.

'What's that?' Dora asked.

'I meant to keep it as a reserve force in case the fortune-telling didn't turn out all our fancy painted it,' said Alice; 'but I don't mind telling you now.'

She opened the bundle, and there was a tambourine, some black lace, a packet of cigarette papers, and our missing combs.

'What ever on earth –' Dicky was beginning, but Oswald saw it all. He has a wonderfully keen nose. And he said –

'Bully for you, Alice. I wish I'd thought it myself.'

Alice was much pleased by this handsome speech.

'Yes,' she said; 'perhaps really it would be best to begin with it. It would attract the public's attention, and then we could tell the fortunes. You see,' she kindly explained to Dicky and H.O. and Dora, who had not seen it yet – though Noël had, almost as soon as I did – 'you see, we'll all play on the combs with the veils over our faces, so that no one can see what our instruments are. Why, they might be mouth-organs for anything any one will know, or some costly instruments from the far-off East, like they play to sultans in zenanas. Let's just try a tune or two before we go on, to be sure that all the combs work right. Dora's has such big teeth, I shouldn't wonder if it wouldn't act at all.'

So we all papered our combs and did 'Heroes', but that sounded awful. 'The Girl I Left Behind Me' went better, and so did 'Bonnie Dundee'. But we thought 'See the Conquering' or 'The Death of Nelson' would be the best to begin with.

It was beastly hot doing it under the veils, but when Oswald had done one tune without the veil to see how the others looked he could not help owning that the veils did give a hidden mystery that was a stranger to simple combs.

We were all a bit puffed when we had played for a while, so we decided that as the donkey seemed calm and was eating grass and resting, we might as well follow his example.

'We ought not to be too proud to take pattern by the brute creation,' said Dora.

So we had our lunch in the wood. We lighted a little fire of sticks and fir-cones, so as to be as gipsyish as we could, and we sat round the fire. We made a charming picture in our bright clothes, among what would have been our native surroundings if we had been real gipsies, and we knew how nice we looked, and stayed there though the smoke got in our eyes, and everything we ate tasted of it.

The woods were a little damp, and that was why the fire smoked so. There were the jackets we had cast off when we dressed up, to sit on, and there was a horse-cloth in the cart intended for the donkey's wear, but we decided that our need was greater than its, so we took the blanket to recline on.

It was as jolly a lunch as ever I remember, and we lingered over that and looking romantic till we could not bear the smoke any more.

Then we got a lot of bluebells and we trampled out the fire most carefully, because we know about not setting woods and places alight, rolled up our clothes in bundles, and went out of the shadowy woodland into the bright sunlight, as sparkling looking a crew of gipsies as any one need wish for.

Last time we had seen the road it had been quite white and bare of persons walking on it, but now there were several. And not only walkers, but people in carts. And some carriages passed us too.

Every one stared at us, but they did not seem so astonished as we had every right to expect, and though interested they were not rude, and this is very rare among English people – and not only poor people either – when they see anything at all out of the way.

We asked one man, who was very Sunday-best indeed in black clothes and a blue tie, where every one was going, for every one was going the same way, and every one looked as if it was going to church, which was unlikely, it being but Thursday. He said –

'Same place wot you're going to I expect.'

And when we said where was that we were requested by him to get along with us. Which we did.

An old woman in the heaviest bonnet I have ever seen and the highest – it was like a black church – revealed the secret to us, and we learned that there was a Primrose *fête* going on in Sir Willoughby Blockson's grounds.

We instantly decided to go to the *fête*.

'I've been to a Primrose *fête*, and so have you, Dora,' Oswald remarked, 'and people are so dull at them, they'd gladly give gold to see the dark future. And, besides, the villages will be unpopulated, and no one at home but idiots and babies and their keepers.'

So we went to the *fête*.

The people got thicker and thicker, and when we got to Sir Willoughby's lodge gates, which have sprawling lions on the gate-posts, we were told to take the donkey-cart round to the stable-yard.

This we did, and proud was the moment when a stiff groom had to bend his proud stomach to go to the head of Bates's donkey.

'This is something like,' said Alice, and Noël added:

'The foreign princes are well received at this palace.'

'We aren't princes, we're gipsies,' said Dora, tucking his scarf in. It would keep on getting loose.

'There *are* gipsy princes, though,' said Noël, 'because there are gipsy kings.'

'You aren't always a prince first,' said Dora; 'don't wriggle so or I can't fix you. Sometimes being made a king just happens to some one who isn't any one in particular.'

'I don't think so,' said Noël; 'you have to be a prince before you're a king, just as you have to be a kitten before you're a cat, or a puppy before you're a dog, or a worm before you're a serpent, or –'

'What about the King of Sweden?' Dora was beginning, when a very nice tall, thin man, with white flowers in his buttonhole like for a wedding, came strolling up and said –

'And whose show is this? Eh, what?'

We said it was ours.

'Are you expected?' he asked.

We said we thought not, but we hoped he didn't mind.

'What are you? Acrobats? Tight-rope? That's a ripping Burmese coat you've got there.'

'Yes, it is. No we aren't,' said Alice, with dignity. 'I am Zaïda, the mysterious prophetess of the golden Orient, and the others are mysterious too, but we haven't fixed on their names yet.'

'By Jove!' said the gentleman; 'but who are you really?'

'Our names are our secret,' said Oswald, with dignity, but Alice said, 'Oh, but we don't mind telling *you*, because I'm sure you're nice. We're really the Bastables, and we want to get some money for some one we know that's rather poor – of course I can't tell you *her* name. And we've learnt how to tell fortunes – really we have. Do you think they'll let us tell them at the *fête*. People are often dull at *fêtes*, aren't they?'

'By Jove!' said the gentleman again – 'by Jove, they are!'

He plunged for a moment in deep reflection.

'We've got co— musical instruments,' said Noël; 'shall we play to you a little?'

'Not here,' said the gentleman; 'follow me.'

He led the way by the backs of shrubberies to an old summer-house, and we asked him to wait outside.

Then we put on our veils and tuned up. 'See, see the conquering –'

But he did not let us finish the tune; he burst in upon us, crying –

'Ripping – oh, ripping! And now tell me my fortune.'

Alice took off her veil and looked at his hand.

'You will travel in distant lands,' she said; 'you will have great wealth and honour; you will marry a beautiful lady – a very fine woman, it says in the book, but I think a beautiful lady sounds nicer, don't you?'

'Much; but I shouldn't mention the book when you're telling the fortune.'

'I wouldn't, except to you,' said Alice, 'and she'll have lots of money and a very sweet disposition. Trials and troubles beset your path, but do but be brave and fearless and you will overcome all your enemies. Beware of a dark woman – most likely a widow.'

'I will,' said he, for Alice had stopped for breath. 'Is that all?'

'No. Beware of a dark woman and shun the society of drunkards and gamblers. Be very cautious in your choice of acquaintances, or you will make a false friend who will be your ruin. That's all, except that you will be married very soon and live to a green old age with the beloved wife of your bosom, and have twelve sons and –'

'Stop, stop!' said the gentleman; 'twelve sons are as many as I can bring up handsomely on my present income. Now, look here. You did that jolly well, only go slower, and pretend to look for things in the hand before you say them. Everything's free at the *fête*, so you'll get no money for your fortune-telling.'

Gloom was on each young brow.

'It's like this,' he went on, 'there is a lady fortune-teller in a tent in the park.'

'Then we may as well get along home,' said Dicky.

'Not at all,' said our new friend, for such he was now about to prove himself to be; 'that lady does not want to tell fortunes to-day. She has a headache. Now, if you'll really stick to it, and tell the people's fortunes as well as you told mine, I'll stand you – let's see – two quid for the afternoon. Will that do? What?'

We said we should just jolly well think it would.

'I've got some Eau de Cologne in a medicine-bottle,' Dora said; 'my brother Noël has headaches sometimes, but I think he's going to be all right to-day. Do take it, it will do the lady's head good.'

'I'll take care of her head,' he said, laughing, but he took the bottle and said, 'Thank you.'

Then he told us to stay where we were while he made final arrangements, and we were left with palpitating breasts to look wildly through the Book of Fate, so as to have the things ready. But it turned out to be time thrown away, for when he came back he said to Alice –

'It'll have to be only you and your sister, please, for I see they've stuck up a card with "Esmeralda, the gipsy Princess, reads the hand and foretells the future" on it. So you boys will have to be mum. You can be attendants – mutes, by Jove! – yes that's it. And, I say, kiddies, you will jolly well

play up, won't you? Don't stand any cheek. Stick it on, you
know. I can't tell you how important it is about – about the
lady's headache.'

'I should think this would be a cool place for a headache
to be quiet in,' said Dora; and it was, for it was quite hidden
in the shrubbery and no path to it.

'By Jove!' he remarked yet once again, 'so it would.
You're right!'

He led us out of the shrubbery and across the park. There
were people dotted all about and they stared, but they
touched their hats to the gentleman, and he returned their
salute with stern politeness.

Inside the tent with 'Esmeralda, &c.', outside there was a
lady in a hat and dust-cloak. But we could see her spangles
under the cloak.

'Now,' said the gentleman to Dicky, 'you stand at the
door and let people in, one at a time. You others can just
play a few bars on your instruments for each new person –
only a very little, because you do get out of tune, though
that's barbaric certainly. Now, here's the two quid. And
you stick to the show till five; you'll hear the stable clock
chime.'

The lady was very pale with black marks under her eyes,
and her eyes looked red, Oswald thought. She seemed
about to speak, but the gentleman said –

'Do trust me, Ella. I'll explain everything directly. Just
go to the old summer-house – *you* know – and I'll be there
directly. I'll take a couple of pegs out of the back and you
can slip away among the trees. Hold your cloak close over
your gown. Goodbye, kiddies. Stay, give me your address,
and I'll write and tell you if my fortune comes true.'

So he shook hands with us and went. And we did stick to
it, though it is far less fun than you would think telling
fortunes all the afternoon in a stuffy tent, while outside you
know there are things to eat and people enjoying them-

selves. But there were the two gold quid, and we were determined to earn them. It is very hard to tell a different fortune for each person, and there were a great many. The girls took it in turns, and Oswald wonders why their hairs did not go grey. Though of course it was much better fun for them than for us, because we had just to be mutes when we weren't playing on the combs.

The people we told fortunes to at first laughed rather, and said we were too young to know anything. But Oswald said in a hollow voice that we were as old as the Pyramids, and after that Alice took the tucks out of Dicky's red coat and put it on and turbaned herself, and looked much older.

The stable clock had chimed the quarter to five some little time, when an elderly gentleman with whiskers, who afterwards proved to be Sir Willoughby, burst into the tent.

'Where's Miss Blockson?' he said, and we answered truthfully that we did not know.

'How long have you been here?' he furiously asked.

'Ever since two,' said Alice wearily.

He said a word that I should have thought a baronet would have been above using.

'Who brought you here?'

We described the gentleman who had done this, and again the baronet said things we should never be allowed to say. 'That confounded Carew!' he added, with more words.

'Is anything wrong?' asked Dora – 'can we do anything? We'll stay on longer if you like – if you can't find the lady who was doing Esmeralda before we came.'

'I'm not very likely to find her,' he said ferociously. 'Stay longer indeed! Get away out of my sight before I have you locked up for vagrants and vagabonds.'

He left the scene in bounding and mad fury. We thought it best to do as he said, and went round the back way to the stables so as to avoid exciting his ungoverned rage by meeting him again. We found our cart and went home. We had got two quid and something to talk about.

But none of us – not even Oswald the discerning – understood exactly what we had been mixed up in, till the pink satin box with three large bottles of A1 scent in it, and postmarks of foreign lands, came to Dora. And there was a letter. It said –

MY DEAR GIPSIES, – I beg to return the Eau de Cologne you so kindly lent me. The lady did use a little of it, but I found that foreign travel was what she really wanted to make her quite happy. So we caught the 4.15 to town, and now we are married, and intend to live to a green old age, &c., as you foretold. But for your help my fortune couldn't have come true, because my wife's father, Sir Willoughby, thought I was not rich enough to marry. But you see I was. And my wife and I both thank you heartily for your kind help. I hope it was not an awful swat. I had to say five because of the train. Good luck to you, and thanks awfully.

Yours faithfully,

CARISBROOK CAREW.

If Oswald had known beforehand we should never have made that two quid for Miss Sandal.

For Oswald does not approve of marriages and would never, if he knew it, be the means of assisting one to occur.

THE LADY AND THE LICENCE;
OR, FRIENDSHIP'S GARLAND

MY DEAR KIDDIES, – Miss Sandal's married sister has just come home from Australia, and she feels very tired. No wonder, you will say, after such a long journey. So she is going to Lymchurch to rest. Now I want you all to be very quiet, because when you are in your usual form you aren't exactly restful, are you? If this weather lasts you will be able to be out most of the time, and when you are indoors for goodness' sake control your lungs and your boots, especially H.O.'s. Mrs Bax has travelled about a good deal, and once was nearly eaten by cannibals. But I hope you won't bother her to tell you stories. She is coming on Friday. I am glad to hear from Alice's letter that you enjoyed the Primrose Fête. Tell Noël that 'poetticle' is not the usual way of spelling the word he wants. I send you ten shillings for pocket-money, and again implore you to let Mrs Bax have a little rest and peace.

Your loving
FATHER.

PS.   If you want anything sent down, tell me, and I will get Mrs Bax to bring it. I met your friend Mr Red House the other day at lunch.

When the letter had been read aloud, and we had each read it to ourselves, a sad silence took place.

Dicky was the first to speak.

'It *is* rather beastly, I grant you,' he said, 'but it might be worse.'

'I don't see how,' said H.O. 'I do wish Father would jolly well learn to leave my boots alone.'

'It might be worse, I tell you,' said Dicky. 'Suppose

instead of telling us to keep out of doors it had been the other way?'

'Yes,' said Alice, 'suppose it had been, "Poor Mrs Bax requires to be cheered up. Do not leave her side day or night. Take it in turns to make jokes for her. Let not a moment pass without some merry jest"? Oh yes, it might be much, much worse.'

'Being able to get out all day makes it all right about trying to make that two pounds increase and multiply,' remarked Oswald. 'Now who's going to meet her at the station? Because after all it's her sister's house, and we've got to be polite to visitors even if we're in a house we aren't related to.'

This was seen to be so, but no one was keen on going to the station. At last Oswald, ever ready for forlorn hopes, consented to go.

We told Mrs Beale, and she got the best room ready, scrubbing everything till it smelt deliciously of wet wood and mottled soap. And then we decorated the room as well as we could.

'She'll want some pretty things,' said Alice, 'coming from the land of parrots and opossums and gum-trees and things.'

We did think of borrowing the stuffed wild-cat that is in the bar at the 'Ship', but we decided that our decorations must be very quiet – and the wild-cat, even in its stuffed state, was anything but; so we borrowed a stuffed roach in a glass box and stood it on the chest of drawers. It looked very calm. Sea-shells are quiet things when they are vacant, and Mrs Beale let us have the four big ones off her chiffonnier.

The girls got flowers – bluebells and white wood-anemones. We might have had poppies or buttercups, but we thought the colours might be too loud. We took some books up for Mrs Bax to read in the night. And we took the quietest ones we could find.

Sonnets on Sleep, Confessions of an Opium Eater, Twilight of the Gods, Diary of a Dreamer, and *By Still Walters,* were some of them. The girls covered them with grey paper, because some of the bindings were rather gay.

The girls hemmed grey calico covers for the drawers and the dressing-table, and we drew the blinds half-down, and when all was done the room looked as quiet as a roosting wood-pigeon.

We put in a clock, but we did not wind it up.

'She can do that herself,' said Dora, 'if she feels she can bear to hear it ticking.'

Oswald went to the station to meet her. He rode on the box beside the driver. When the others saw him mount there I think they were sorry they had not been polite and gone to meet her themselves. Oswald had a jolly ride. We got to the station just as the train came in. Only one lady got out of it, so Oswald knew it must be Mrs Bax. If he had not been told how quiet she wanted to be he would have thought she looked rather jolly. She had short hair and gold spectacles. Her skirts were short, and she carried a parrot-cage in her hand. It contained our parrot, and when we wrote to tell Father that it and Pincher were the only things we wanted sent we never thought she would have brought either.

'Mrs Bax, I believe,' was the only break Oswald made in the polite silence that he took the parrot-cage and her bag from her in.

'How do you do?' she said very briskly for a tired lady; and Oswald thought it was noble of her to make the effort to smile. 'Are you Oswald or Dicky?'

Oswald told her in one calm word which he was, and then Pincher rolled madly out of a dog-box almost into his arms. Pincher would not be quiet. Of course he did not understand the need for it. Oswald conversed with Pincher in low, restraining whispers as he led the way to the 'Ship's' fly. He put the parrot-cage on the inside seat of the carriage, held the door open for Mrs Bax with silent politeness, closed it as quietly as possible, and prepared to mount on the box.

'Oh, won't you come inside?' asked Mrs Bax. 'Do!'

'No, thank you,' said Oswald in calm and mouse-like tones; and to avoid any more jaw he got at once on to the box with Pincher.

So that Mrs Bax was perfectly quiet for the whole six miles – unless you count the rattle and shake-up-and-down of the fly. On the box Oswald and Pincher 'tasted the sweets of a blissful re-union', like it says in novels. And the man from the 'Ship' looked on and said how well bred Pincher was. It was a happy drive.

There was something almost awful about the sleek, quiet tidiness of the others, who were all standing in a row outside the cottage to welcome Mrs Bax. They all said, 'How do you do?' in hushed voices, and all looked as if butter would not melt in any of their young mouths. I never saw a more soothing-looking lot of kids.

She went to her room, and we did not see her again till tea-time.

Then, still exquisitely brushed and combed, we sat round the board – in silence. We had left the tea-tray place for Mrs Bax, of course. But she said to Dora –

'Wouldn't you like to pour out?'

And Dora replied in low, soft tones, 'If you wish me to, Mrs Bax. I usually do.' And she did.

We passed each other bread-and-butter and jam and honey with silent courteousness. And of course we saw that she had enough to eat.

'Do you manage to amuse yourself pretty well here?' she asked presently.

We said, 'Yes, thank you,' in hushed tones.

'What do you do?' she asked.

We did not wish to excite her by telling her what we did, so Dicky murmured –

'Nothing in particular,' at the same moment that Alice said –

'All sorts of things.'

'Tell me about them,' said Mrs Bax invitingly.

We replied by a deep silence. She sighed, and passed her cup for more tea.

'Do you ever feel shy,' she asked suddenly. 'I do, dreadfully, with new people.'

We liked her for saying that, and Alice replied that she hoped she would not feel shy with us.

'I hope not,' she said. 'Do you know, there was such a funny woman in the train? She had seventeen different parcels, and she kept counting them, and one of them was a kitten, and it was always under the seat when she began to count, so she always got the number wrong.'

We should have liked to hear about that kitten – especially what colour it was and how old – but Oswald felt that Mrs Bax was only trying to talk for our sakes, so that we shouldn't feel shy, so he simply said, 'Will you have some more cake?' and nothing more was said about the kitten.

Mrs Bax seemed very noble. She kept trying to talk to us about Pincher, and trains and Australia, but we were determined she should be quiet, as she wished it so much, and we restrained our brimming curiosity about opossums up gum-trees, and about emus and kangaroos and wattles, and only said 'Yes' or 'No', or, more often, nothing at all.

When tea was over we melted away, 'like snow-wreaths in Thawjean,' and went out on the beach and had a yelling match. Our throats felt as though they were full of wool, from the hushed tones we had used in talking to Mrs Bax. Oswald won the match. Next day we kept carefully out of the way, except for meals. Mrs Bax tried talking again at breakfast-time, but we checked our wish to listen, and passed the pepper, salt, mustard, bread, toast, butter, marmalade, and even the cayenne, vinegar, and oil, with such politeness that she gave up.

We took it in turns to watch the house and drive away organ-grinders. We told them they must not play in front of that house, because there was an Australian lady who had to be kept quiet. And they went at once. This cost us expense, because an organ-grinder will never consent to fly the spot under twopence a flight.

We went to bed early. We were quite weary with being so calm and still. But we knew it was our duty, and we liked the feel of having done it.

The day after was the day Jake Lee got hurt. Jake is the man who drives about the country in a covered cart, with pins and needles, and combs and frying-pans, and all the sort of things that farmers' wives are likely to want in a hurry, and no shops for miles. I have always thought Jake's was a beautiful life. I should like to do it myself. Well, this particular day he had got his cart all ready to start and had got his foot on the wheel to get up, when a motor-car went by puffing and hooting. I always think motor-cars seem so rude somehow. And the horse was frightened; and no wonder. It shied, and poor Jake was thrown violently to the ground, and hurt so much that they had to send for the doctor. Of course we went and asked Mrs Jake if we could do anything – such as take the cart out and sell the things to the farmers' wives.

But she thought not.

It was after this that Dicky said –

'Why shouldn't we get things of our own and go and sell them – with Bates' donkey?'

Oswald was thinking the same thing, but he wishes to be fair, so he owns that Dicky spoke first. We all saw at once that the idea was a good one.

'Shall we dress up for it?' H.O. asked. We thought not. It

is always good sport to dress up, but I have never heard of people selling things to farmers' wives in really beautiful disguises.

'We ought to go as shabby as we can,' said Alice; 'but somehow that always seems to come natural to your clothes when you've done a few interesting things in them. We have plenty of clothes that look poor but deserving. What shall we buy to sell?'

'Pins and needles, and tape and bodkins,' said Dora.

'Butter,' said Noël; 'it is terrible when there is no butter.'

'Honey is nice,' said H.O., 'and so are sausages.'

'Jake has ready-made shirts and corduroy trousers. I suppose a farmer's shirt and trousers may give at any moment,' said Alice, 'and if he can't get new ones he has to go to bed till they are mended.'

Oswald thought tin-tacks, and glue, and string must often be needed to mend barns and farm tools with if they broke suddenly. And Dicky said –

'I think the pictures of ladies hanging on to crosses in foaming seas are good. Jake told me he sold more of them than anything. I suppose people suddenly break the old ones, and home isn't home without a lady holding on to a cross.'

We went to Munn's shop, and we bought needles and pins, and tapes and bodkins, a pound of butter, a pot of honey and one of marmalade, and tin-tacks, string, and glue. But we could not get any ladies with crosses, and the shirts and trousers were too expensive for us to dare to risk it. Instead, we bought a head-stall for eighteenpence, because how providential we should be to a farmer whose favourite horse had escaped and he had nothing to catch it with; and three tin-openers, in case of a distant farm subsisting entirely on tinned things, and the only opener for miles lost down the well or something. We also bought several other thoughtful and far-sighted things.

That night at supper we told Mrs Bax we wanted to go out for the day. She had hardly said anything that supper-time, and now she said –

'Where are you going? Teaching Sunday school?'

As it was Monday, we felt her poor brain was wandering – most likely for want of quiet. And the room smelt of tobacco smoke, so we thought some one had been to see her and perhaps been too noisy for her. So Oswald said gently –

'No, we are not going to teach Sunday school.'

Mrs Bax sighed. Then she said –

'I am going out myself to-morrow – for the day.'

'I hope it will not tire you too much,' said Dora, with soft-voiced and cautious politeness. 'If you want anything bought we could do it for you, with pleasure, and you could have a nice, quiet day at home.'

'Thank you,' said Mrs Bax shortly; and we saw she would do what she chose, whether it was really for her own good or not.

She started before we did next morning, and we were careful to be mouse-quiet till the 'Ship's' fly which contained her was out of hearing. Then we had another yelling competition, and Noël won with that new shriek of his that is like railway engines in distress; and then we went and fetched Bates' donkey and cart and packed our bales in it and started, some riding and some running behind.

Any faint distant traces of respectableness that were left to our clothes were soon covered up by the dust of the road and by some of the ginger-beer bursting through the violence of the cart, which had no springs.

The first farm we stopped at the woman really did want some pins, for though a very stupid person, she was making a pink blouse, and we said –

'Do have some tape! You never know when you may want it.'

'I believe in buttons,' she said. 'No strings for me, thank you.'

But when Oswald said, 'What about pudding-strings? You can't button up puddings as if they were pillows!' she consented to listen to reason. But it was only twopence altogether.

But at the next place the woman said we were 'mum-mickers', and told us to 'get along, do'. And she set her dog at us; but when Pincher sprang from the inmost recesses of the cart she called her dog off. But too late, for it and Pincher were locked in the barking, scuffling, growling embrace of deadly combat. When we had separated the dogs she went into her house and banged the door, and we went on through the green flat marshes, among the butter-cups and may-bushes.

'I wonder what she meant by "mummickers"?' said H.O.

'She meant she saw our high-born airs through our shabby clothes,' said Alice. 'It's always happening, especi-ally to princes. There's nothing so hard to conceal as a really high-bred air.'

'I've been thinking,' said Dicky, 'whether honesty wouldn't perhaps be the best policy – not always, of course; but just this once. If people knew what we were doing it for they might be glad to help on the good work – What?'

So at the next farm, which was half hidden by trees, like the picture at the beginning of *Sensible Susan*, we tied the pony to the gate-post and knocked at the door. It was opened by a man this time, and Dora said to him –

'We are honest traders. We are trying to sell these things to keep a lady who is poor. If you buy some you will be helping too. Wouldn't you like to do that? It is a good work, and you will be glad of it afterwards, when you come to think over the acts of your life.'

'Upon my word an' 'onner!' said the man, whose red face

686

was surrounded by a frill of white whiskers. 'If ever I see a walkin' Tract 'ere it stands!'

'She doesn't mean to be tractish,' said Oswald quickly; 'it's only her way. But we really are trying to sell things to help a poor person – no humbug, sir – so if we *have* got anything you want we shall be glad. And if not – well, there's no harm in asking, is there, sir?'

The man with the frilly whiskers was very pleased to be called 'sir' – Oswald knew he would be – and he looked at everything we'd got, and bought the head-stall and two tin-openers, and a pot of marmalade, and a ball of string, and a pair of braces. This came to four and twopence, and we were very pleased. It really seemed that our business was establishing itself root and branch.

When it came to its being dinner-time, which was first noticed through H.O. beginning to cry and say he did not want to play any more, it was found that we had forgotten to bring any dinner. So we had to eat some of our stock – the jam, the biscuits, and the cucumber.

'I feel a new man,' said Alice, draining the last of the ginger-beer bottles. 'At that homely village on the brow of yonder hill we shall sell all that remains of the stock, and go home with money in both pockets.'

But our luck had changed. As so often happens, our hearts beat high with hopeful thoughts, and we felt jollier than we had done all day. Merry laughter and snatches of musical song re-echoed from our cart, and from round it as we went up the hill. All Nature was smiling and gay. There was nothing sinister in the look of the trees or the road – or anything.

Dogs are said to have inside instincts that warn them of intending perils, but Pincher was not a bit instinctive that day somehow. He sported gaily up and down the hedge-banks after pretending rats, and once he was so excited that I believe he was playing at weasels and stoats. But of course there was really no trace of these savage denizens of the jungle. It was just Pincher's varied imagination.

We got to the village, and with joyful expectations we knocked at the first door we came to.

Alice had spread out a few choice treasures — needles, pins, tape, a photograph-frame, and the butter, rather soft by now, and the last of the tin-openers – on a basket-lid, like the fish-man does with herrings and whitings and plums and apples (you cannot sell fish in the country unless you sell fruit too. The author does not know why this is).

The sun was shining, the sky was blue. There was no sign at all of the intending thunderbolt, not even when the door was opened. This was done by a woman.

She just looked at our basket-lid of things any one might have been proud to buy, and smiled. I saw her do it. Then she turned her traitorous head and called 'Jim!' into the cottage.

A sleepy grunt rewarded her.

'Jim, I say!' she repeated. 'Come here directly a minute.'

Next moment Jim appeared. He was Jim to her because she was his wife, I suppose, but to us he was the Police, with his hair ruffled – from his hateful sofa-cushions, no doubt – and his tunic unbuttoned.

'What's up?' he said in a husky voice, as if he had been dreaming that he had a cold. 'Can't a chap have a minute to himself to read the paper in?'

'You told me to,' said the woman. 'You said if any folks come to the door with things I was to call you, whether or no.'

Even now we were blind to the disaster that was entangling us in the meshes of its trap. Alice said –

'We've sold a good deal, but we've *some* things left – very nice things. These crochet needles –'

But the Police, who had buttoned up his tunic in a hurry, said quite fiercely –

688

'Let's have a look at your licence.'

'We didn't bring any,' said Noël, 'but if you will give us an order we'll bring you some to-morrow.' He thought a lisen was a thing to sell that we ought to have thought of.

'None of your lip,' was the unexpected reply of the now plainly brutal constable. 'Where's your licence, I say?'

'We have a licence for our dog, but Father's got it,' said Oswald, always quick-witted, but not, this time, quite quick enough.

'Your 'awker's licence is what I want, as well you knows, you young limb. Your pedlar's licence – your licence to sell things. You ain't half so half-witted as you want to make out.'

'We haven't got a pedlar's licence,' said Oswald. If we had been in a book the Police would have been touched to tears by Oswald's simply honesty. He would have said 'Noble boy!' and then gone on to say he had only asked the question to test our honour. But life is not really at all the same as books. I have noticed lots of differences. Instead of behaving like the book-Police, this thick-headed constable said –

'Blowed if I wasn't certain of it! Well, my young blokes, you'll just come along o' me to Sir James. I've got orders to bring up the next case afore him.'

'*Case!*' said Dora. 'Oh, *don't*! We didn't know we oughtn't to. We only wanted –'

'Ho, yes,' said the constable, 'you can tell all that to the magistrate; and anything you say will be used against you.'

'I'm sure it will,' said Oswald. 'Dora, don't lower yourself to speak to him. Come, we'll go home.'

The Police was combing its hair with a half-toothless piece of comb, and we turned to go. But it was vain.

Ere any of our young and eager legs could climb into the cart the Police had seized the donkey's bridle. We could not desert our noble steed – and besides, it wasn't really ours, but Bates's, and this made any hope of flight quite a forlorn one. For better, for worse, we had to go with the donkey.

'Don't cry, for goodness' sake!' said Oswald in stern undertones. 'Bite your lips. Take long breaths. Don't let him see we mind. This beast's only the village police. Sir James will be a gentleman. *He'll* understand. Don't disgrace the house of Bastable. Look here! Fall into line – no, Indian file will be best, there are so few of us. Alice, if you snivel I'll never say you ought to have been a boy again. H.O., shut your mouth; no one's going to hurt you – you're too young.'

'I *am* trying,' said Alice, gasping.

'Noël,' Oswald went on – now, as so often, showing the brilliant qualities of the born leader and general – 'Don't *you* be in a funk. Remember how Byron fought for the Greeks at Missy-what's-its-name. *He* didn't grouse, and he was a poet, like you! Now look here, let's be *game*. Dora, you're the eldest. Strike up – any tune. We'll *march* up, and show this sneak we Bastables aren't afraid, whoever else is.'

You will perhaps find it difficult to believe, but we *did* strike up. We sang 'The British Grenadiers', and when the Police told us to stow it we did not. And Noël said –

'Singing isn't dogs or pedlaring. You don't want a licence for that.'

'I'll soon show you!' said the Police.

But he had to jolly well put up with our melodious song, because he knew that there isn't really any law to prevent you singing if you want to.

We went on singing. It soon got easier than at first, and we followed Bates's donkey and cart through some lodge gates and up a drive with big trees, and we came out in front of a big white house, and there was a lawn. We stopped singing when we came in sight of the house, and got ready to be polite to Sir James. There were some ladies on the lawn in pretty blue and green dresses. This cheered us. Ladies are seldom quite heartless, especially when young.

The Police drew up Bates's donkey opposite the big front door with pillars, and rang the bell. Our hearts were beating desperately. We cast glances of despair at the ladies. Then, quite suddenly, Alice gave a yell that wild Indian war-whoops are simply nothing to, and tore across the lawn and threw her arms round the green waist of one of the ladies.

'Oh, I'm so glad!' she cried; 'oh, save us! We haven't done anything wrong, really and truly we haven't.'

And then we all saw that the lady was our own Mrs Red House, that we liked so much. So we all rushed to her, and before that Police had got the door answered we had told her our tale. The other ladies had turned away when we approached her, and gone politely away into a shrubbery.

'There, there,' she said, patting Alice and Noël and as much of the others as she could get hold of. 'Don't you worry, dears, don't. I'll make it all right with Sir James. Let's all sit down in a comfy heap, and get our breaths again. I am so glad to see you all. My husband met your father at lunch the other day. I meant to come over and see you to-morrow.'

You cannot imagine the feelings of joy and safeness that we felt now we had found someone who knew we were Bastables, and not vagrant outcasts like the Police thought.

The door had now been answered. We saw the base Police talking to the person who answered it. Then he came towards us, very red in the face.

'Leave off bothering the lady,' he said, 'and come along of me. Sir James is in his library, and he's ready to do justice on you, so he is.'

Mrs Red House jumped up, and so did we. She said with smiles, as if nothing was wrong –

'Good morning, Inspector!'

He looked pleased and surprised, as well he might, for it'll be long enough before he's within a mile of being *that*.

'Good morning, miss, I'm sure,' he replied.

'I think there's been a little mistake, Inspector,' she said. 'I expect it's some of your men – led away by zeal for their duties. But I'm sure *you'll* understand. I am staying with Lady Harborough, and these children are very dear friends of mine.'

The Police looked very silly, but he said something about hawking without a licence.

'Oh no, not *hawking*,' said Mrs Red House, 'not *hawking*, surely! They were just *playing* at it, you know. Your subordinates must have been quite mistaken.'

Our honesty bade us say that he was his own only subordinate, and that he hadn't been mistaken; but it is rude to interrupt, especially a lady, so we said nothing.

The Police said firmly, 'You'll excuse me, miss, but Sir James expressly told me to lay on information directly next time I caught any of 'em at it without a licence.'

'But, you see, you didn't catch them at it.' Mrs Red House took some money out of her purse. 'You might just give this to your subordinates to console them for the mistake they've made. And look here, these mistakes do lead to trouble sometimes. So I'll tell you what I'll do. I'll promise not to tell Sir James a word about it. *So* nobody will be blamed.'

We listened breathless for his reply. He put his hands behind him –

'Well, miss,' he said at last, 'you've managed to put the Force in the wrong somehow, which isn't often done, and I'm blest if I know how you make it out. But there's Sir James a-waiting for me to come before him with my complaint. What am I a-goin' to say to him?'

'Oh, anything,' said Mrs Red House; 'surely some one

else has done something wrong that you can tell him about?'

'There was a matter of a couple of snares and some night lines,' he said slowly, drawing nearer to Mrs Red House; 'but I couldn't take no money, of course.'

'Of course not,' she said; 'I beg your pardon for offering it. But I'll give you my name and address, and if ever I can be of any use to you –'

She turned her back on us while she wrote it down with a stumpy pencil he lent her; but Oswald could swear that he heard money chink, and that there was something large and round wrapped up in the paper she gave him.

'Sorry for any little misunderstanding,' the Police now said, feeling the paper with his fingers; 'and my respects to you, miss, and your young friends. I'd best be going.'

And he went – to Sir James, I suppose. He seemed quite tamed. I hope the people who set the snares got off.

'So *that's* all right,' said Mrs Red House. 'Oh, you dear children, you must stay to lunch, and we'll have a splendid time.'

'What a darling Princess you are!' Noël said slowly. 'You are a witch Princess, too, with magic powers over the Police.'

'It's not a very pretty sort of magic,' she said, and she sighed.

'Everything about you is pretty,' said Noël. And I could see him beginning to make the faces that always precur his poetry-fits. But before the fit could break out thoroughly the rest of us awoke from our stupor of grateful safeness and began to dance round Mrs Red House in a ring. And the girls sang –

> *The rose is red, the violet's blue,*
> *Carnation's sweet, and so are you,*

over and over again, so we had to join in; though I think 'She's a jolly good fellow' would have been more manly and less like a poetry book.

Suddenly a known voice broke in on our singing.

'Well!' it said. And we stopped dancing. And there were the other two ladies who had politely walked off when we first discovered Mrs Red House. And one of them was Mrs Bax – of all people in the world! And she was smoking a cigarette. So now we knew where the smell of tobacco came from, in the White House.

We said, 'Oh!' in one breath, and were silent.

'Is it possible,' said Mrs Bax, 'that these are the Sunday-school children I've been living with these three long days?'

'We're sorry,' said Dora, softly; 'we wouldn't have made a noise if we'd known you were here.'

'So I suppose,' said Mrs Bax. 'Chloe, you seem to be a witch. How have you galvanized my six rag dolls into life like this?'

'Rag dolls!' said H.O., before we could stop him. 'I think you're jolly mean and ungrateful; and it was sixpence for making the organs fly.'

'My brain's reeling,' said Mrs Bax, putting her hands to her head.

'H.O. is very rude, and I am sorry,' said Alice, 'but it *is* hard to be called rag dolls, when you've only tried to do as you were told.'

And then, in answer to Mrs Red House's questions, we told how father had begged us to be quiet, and how we had earnestly tried to. When it was told, Mrs Bax began to laugh, and so did Mrs Red House, and at last Mrs Bax said –

'Oh, my dears! you don't know how glad I am that you're really alive! I began to think – oh – I don't know what I thought! And you're not rag dolls. You're heroes and heroines, every man jack of you. And I do thank you. But I never wanted to be quiet like *that*. I just didn't want to be bothered with London and tiresome grown-up people. And now let's enjoy ourselves! Shall it be rounders, or stories about cannibals?'

'Rounders first and stories after,' said H.O. And it was so.

Mrs Bax, now that her true nature was revealed, proved to be A1. The author does not ask for a jollier person to be in the house with. We had rare larks the whole time she stayed with us.

And to think that we might never have known her true character if she hadn't been an old school friend of Mrs Red House's, and if Mrs Red House hadn't been such a friend of ours!

'Friendship,' as Mr William Smith so truly says in his book about Latin, 'is the crown of life.'

'WHAT shall we do to-day, kiddies?' said Mrs Bax. We had discovered her true nature but three days ago, and already she had taken us out in a sailing-boat and in a motor car, had given us sweets every day, and taught us eleven new games that we had not known before; and only four of the new games were rotters. How seldom can as much be said for the games of a grown-up, however gifted!

The day was one of cloudless blue perfectness, and we were all basking on the beach. We had all bathed. Mrs Bax said we might. There are points about having a grown-up with you, if it is the right kind. You can then easily get it to say 'Yes' to what you want, and after that, if anything goes wrong it is their fault, and you are pure from blame. But nothing had gone wrong with the bathe, and, so far, we were all alive, and not cold at all, except our fingers and feet.

'What would you *like* to do?' asked Mrs Bax. We were far away from human sight along the beach, and Mrs Bax was smoking cigarettes as usual.

'I don't know,' we all said politely. But H.O. said –

'What about poor Miss Sandal?'

'Why poor?' asked Mrs Bax.

'Because she is,' said H.O.

'But how? What do you mean?' asked Mrs Bax.

'Why, isn't she?' said H.O.

'Isn't she what?' said Mrs Bax.

'What you said why about,' said H.O.

She put her hands to her head. Her short hair was still

696

damp and rumpled from contact with the foaming billows of ocean.

'Let's have a fresh deal and start fair,' she said; 'why do you think my sister is poor?'

'I forgot she was your sister,' said H.O., 'or I wouldn't have said it – honour bright I wouldn't.'

'Don't mention it,' said Mrs Bax, and began throwing stones at a groin in amiable silence.

We were furious with H.O., first because it is such bad manners to throw people's poverty in their faces, or even in their sisters' faces, like H.O. had just done, and second because it seemed to have put out of Mrs Bax's head what she was beginning to say about what would we like to do.

So Oswald presently remarked, when he had aimed at the stump she was aiming at, and hit it before she did, for though a fair shot for a lady, she takes a long time to get her eye in.

'Mrs Bax, we should like to do whatever *you* like to do.' This was real politeness and true too, as it happened, because by this time we could quite trust her not to want to do anything deeply duffing.

'That's very nice of you,' she replied, 'but don't let me interfere with any plans of yours. My own idea was to pluck a waggonette from the nearest bush. I suppose they grow freely in these parts?'

'There's one at the "Ship",' said Alice; 'it costs seven-and-six to pluck it, just for going to the station.'

'Well, then! And to stuff our waggonette with lunch and drive over to Lynwood Castle, and eat it there.'

'A picnic!' fell in accents of joy from the lips of one and all.

'We'll also boil the billy in the castle courtyard, and eat buns in the shadow of the keep.'

'Tea as well?' said H.O., 'with buns? You can't be poor and needy any way, whatever your –'

We hastily hushed him, stifling his murmurs with sand.

'I always think,' said Mrs Bax dreamily, 'that "the more the merrier" is peculiarly true of picnics. So I have arranged – always subject to your approval, of course – to meet your friends, Mr and Mrs Red House, there, and –'

We drowned her conclusive remarks with a cheer. And Oswald, always willing to be of use, offered to go to the 'Ship' and see about the waggonette. I like horses and stable-yards, and the smell of hay and straw, and talking to ostlers and people like that.

There turned out to be two horses belonging to the best waggonette, or you could have a one-horse one, much smaller, with the blue cloth of the cushions rather frayed, and mended here and there, and green in patches from age and exposition to the weather.

Oswald told Mrs Bax this, not concealing about how shabby the little one was, and she gloriously said –

'The pair by all means! We don't kill a pig every day!'

'No, indeed,' said Dora, but if 'killing a pig' means having a lark, Mrs Bax is as good a pig-killer as any I ever knew.

It was splendid to drive (Oswald, on the box beside the driver, who had his best coat with the bright buttons) along the same roads that we had trodden as muddy pedestrinators, or travelled along behind Bates's donkey.

It was a perfect day, as I said before. We were all clean and had our second-best things on. I think second-bests are much more comfy than first-bests. You feel equivalent to meeting any one, and have 'a heart for any fate', as it says in the poetry-book, and yet you are not starched and booted and stiffened and tightened out of all human feelings.

Lynwood Castle is in a hollow in the hills. It has a moat all round it with water-lily leaves on it. I suppose there are lilies when in season. There is a bridge over the moat – not the draw kind of bridge. And the castle has eight towers – four round and four square ones, and a courtyard in the middle, all green grass, and heaps of stones – stray bits of castle, I suppose they are – and a great white may-tree in the middle that Mrs Bax said was hundreds of years old.

Mrs Red House was sitting under the may-tree when we got there, nursing her baby, in a blue dress and looking exactly like a picture on the top of a chocolate-box.

The girls instantly wanted to nurse the baby so we let them. And we explored the castle. We had never happened to explore one thoroughly before. We did not find the deepest dungeon below the castle moat, though we looked everywhere for it, but we found everything else you can think of belonging to castles – even the holes they used to pour boiling lead through into the eyes of besiegers when they tried to squint up to see how strong the garrison was in the keep – and the little slits they shot arrows through, and the mouldering remains of the portcullis. We went up the eight towers, every single one of them, and some parts were jolly dangerous, I can tell you. Dicky and I would not let H.O. and Noël come up the dangerous parts. There was no lasting ill-feeling about this. By the time we had had a thorough good explore lunch was ready.

It was a glorious lunch – not too many meaty things, but all sorts of cakes and sweets, and grapes and figs and nuts.

We gazed at the feast, and Mrs Bax said –

'There you are, young Copperfield, and a royal spread you've got.'

'*They* had currant wine,' said Noël, who has only just read the book by Mr Charles Dickens.

'Well, so have you,' said Mrs Bax. And we had. Two bottles of it.

'I never knew any one like you,' said Noël to Mrs Red House, dreamily with his mouth full, 'for knowing the things people really like to eat, not the things that are good for them, but what they *like*, and Mrs Bax is just the same.'

'It was one of the things they taught at our school,' said

Mrs Bax. 'Do you remember the Saturday night feasts, Chloe, and how good the cocoanut ice tasted after extra strong peppermints?'

'Fancy you knowing *that*!' said H.O. 'I thought it was us found *that* out.'

'I really know much more about things to eat than *she* does,' said Mrs Bax. 'I was quite an old girl when she was a little thing in pinafores. She was such a nice little girl.'

'I shouldn't wonder if she was always nice,' said Noël, 'even when she was a baby!'

Everybody laughed at this, except the existing baby, and it was asleep on the waggonette cushions, under the white may-tree, and perhaps if it had been awake it wouldn't have laughed, for Oswald himself, though possessing a keen sense of humour, did not see anything to laugh at.

Mr Red House made a speech after dinner, and said drink to the health of everybody, one after the other, in currant wine, which was done, beginning with Mrs Bax and ending with H.O.

Then he said –

'Somnus, avaunt! What shall we play at?' and nobody, as so often happens, had any idea ready. Then suddenly Mrs Red House said –

'Good gracious, look there!' and we looked there, and where we were to look was the lowest piece of the castle wall, just beside the keep that the bridge led over to, and what we were to look at was a strange blobbiness of knobbly bumps along the top, that looked exactly like human heads.

It turned out, when we had talked about cannibals and New Guinea, that human heads were just exactly what they were. Not loose heads, stuck on pikes or things like that, such as there often must have been while the castle stayed in the olden times it was built in and belonged to, but real live heads with their bodies still in attendance on them.

They were, in fact, the village children.

'Poor little Lazaruses!' said Mr Red House.

'There's not such a bad slice of Dives' feast left,' said Mrs Bax. 'Shall we –?'

So Mr Red House went out by the keep and called the heads in (with the bodies they were connected with, of course), and they came and ate up all that was left of the lunch. Not the buns, of course, for those were sacred to tea-time, but all the other things, even the nuts and figs, and we were quite glad that they should have them – really and truly we were, even H.O.!

They did not seem to be very clever children, or just the sort you would choose for your friends, but I suppose you like to play, however little you are other people's sort. So, after they had eaten all there was, when Mrs Red House invited them all to join in games with us we knew we ought to be pleased. But village children are not taught rounders, and though we wondered at first why their teachers had not seen to this, we understood presently. Because it is most awfully difficult to make them understand the very simplest thing.

But they could play all the ring games, and 'Nuts and May' and 'There Came Three Knights' – and another one we had never heard of before. The singing part begins: –

> *Up and down the green grass,*
> *This and that and thus,*
> *Come along, my pretty maid,*
> *And take a walk with us.*
> *You shall have a duck, my dear,*
> *And you shall have a drake,*
> *And you shall have a handsome man*
> *For your father's sake.*

I forget the rest, and if anybody who reads this knows it, and will write and tell me, the author will not have laboured in vain.

The grown-ups played with all their heart and soul – I expect it is but seldom they are able to play, and they enjoy the novel excitement. And when we'd been at it some time we saw there was another head looking over the wall.

'Hullo!' said Mrs Bax, 'here's another of them, run along and ask it to come and join in.'

She spoke to the village children, but nobody ran.

'Here, you go,' she said, pointing at a girl in red plaits tied with dirty sky-blue ribbon.

'Please, miss, I'd leifer not,' replied the red-haired. 'Mother says we ain't to play along of him.'

'Why, what's the matter with him?' asked Mrs Red House.

'His father's in jail, miss, along of snares and night lines, and no one won't give his mother any work, so my mother says we ain't to demean ourselves to speak to him.'

'But it's not the child's fault,' said Mrs Red House, 'is it now?'

'I don't know, miss,' said the red-haired.

'But it's cruel,' said Mrs Bax. 'How would you like it if your father was sent to prison, and nobody would speak to you?'

'Father's always kep' hisself respectable,' said the girl with the dirty blue ribbon. 'You can't be sent to jail, not if you keeps yourself respectable, you can't, miss.'

'And do none of you speak to him?'

The other children put their fingers in their mouths, and looked silly, showing plainly that they didn't.

'Don't you feel sorry for the poor little chap?' said Mrs Bax.

No answer transpired.

'Can't you imagine how you'd feel if it was *your* father?'

'My father always kep' hisself respectable,' the red-haired girl said again.

'Well, I shall ask him to come and play with us,' said Mrs

Red House. 'Little pigs!' she added in low tones only heard by the author and Mr Red House.

But Mr Red House said in a whisper that no one overheard except Mrs R. H. and the present author.

'Don't, Puss-cat; it's no good. The poor little pariah wouldn't like it. And these kids only do what their parents teach them.'

If the author didn't know what a stainless gentleman Mr Red House is he would think he heard him mutter a word that gentlemen wouldn't say.

'Tell off a detachment of consolation,' Mr Red House went on; 'look here, *our* kids – who'll go and talk to the poor little chap?'

We all instantly said, '*I* will!'

The present author was chosen to be the one.

When you think about yourself there is a kind of you that is not what you generally are but that you know you would like to be if only you were good enough. Albert's uncle says this is called your ideal of yourself. I will call it your best I, for short. Oswald's 'best I' was glad to go and talk to that boy whose father was in prison, but the Oswald that generally exists hated being out of the games. Yet the whole Oswald, both the best and the ordinary, was pleased that he was the one chosen to be a detachment of consolation.

He went out under the great archway, and as he went he heard the games beginning again. This made him feel noble, and yet he was ashamed of feeling it. Your feelings are a beastly nuisance, if once you begin to let yourself think about them. Oswald soon saw the broken boots of the boy whose father was in jail so nobody would play with him, standing on the stones near the top of the wall where it was broken to match the boots.

He climbed up and said, 'Hullo!'

To this remark the boy replied, 'Hullo!'

Oswald now did not know what to say. The sorrier you are for people the harder it is to tell them so.

But at last he said –

'I've just heard about your father being where he is. It's beastly rough luck. I hope you don't mind my saying I'm jolly sorry for you.'

The boy had a pale face and watery blue eyes When Oswald said this his eyes got waterier than ever, and he climbed down to the ground before he said –

'I don't care so much, but it do upset mother something crool.'

It is awfully difficult to console those in affliction. Oswald thought this, then he said –

'I say; never mind if those beastly kids won't play with you. It isn't your fault, you know.'

'Nor it ain't father's neither,' the boy said; 'he broke his arm a-falling off of a rick, and he hadn't paid up his club money along of mother's new baby costing what it did when it come, so there warn't nothing – and what's a hare or two, or a partridge? It ain't as if it was pheasants as is as dear to rear as chicks.'

Oswald did not know what to say, so he got out his new pen-and-pencil-combined and said –

'Look here! You can have this to keep if you like.'

The pale-eyed boy took it and looked at it and said –

'You ain't foolin' me?'

And Oswald said no he wasn't, but he felt most awfully rum and uncomfy, and though he wanted most frightfully to do something for the boy he felt as if he wanted to get away more than anything else, and he never was gladder in his life than when he saw Dora coming along, and she said –

'You go back and play, Oswald. I'm tired and I'd like to sit down a bit.'

She got the boy to sit down beside her, and Oswald went back to the others.

Games, however unusually splendid, have to come to an end. And when the games were over and it was tea, and the village children were sent away, and Oswald went to call Dora and the prisoner's son, he found nothing but Dora, and he saw at once, in his far-sighted way, that she had been crying.

It was one of the A1est days we ever had, and the drive home was good, but Dora was horribly quiet, as though the victim of dark interior thoughts.

And the next day she was but little better.

We were all paddling on the sands, but Dora would not. And presently Alice left us and went back to Dora, and we all saw across the sandy waste that something was up.

And presently Alice came down and said –

'Dry your feet and legs and come to a council. Dora wants to tell you something.'

We dried our pink and sandy toes and we came to the council. Then Alice said: 'I don't think H.O. is wanted at the council, it isn't anything amusing; you go and enjoy yourself by the sea, and catch the nice little crabs, H.O. dear.'

H.O. said: 'You always want me to be out of everything. I can be councils as well as anybody else.'

'Oh, H.O.!' said Alice, in pleading tones, 'not if I give you a halfpenny to go and buy bulls-eyes with?'

So then he went, and Dora said –

'I can't think how I could do it when you'd all trusted me so. And yet I couldn't help it. I remember Dicky saying when you decided to give it me to take care of – about me being the most trustworthy of all of us. I'm not fit for any one to speak to. But it did seem the really right thing at the time, it really and truly did. And now it all looks different.'

'What has she done?' Dicky asked this, but Oswald almost knew.

'Tell them,' said Dora, turning over on her front and

hiding her face partly in her hands, and partly in the sand.

'She's given all Miss Sandal's money to that little boy that the father of was in prison,' said Alice.

'It was one pound thirteen and sevenpence halfpenny,' sobbed Dora.

'You ought to have consulted us, I do think, really,' said Dicky. 'Of course, I see you're sorry now, but I do think that.'

'How could I consult you?' said Dora; 'you were all playing Cat and Mouse, and he wanted to get home. I only wish you'd heard what he told me – that's all – about his mother being ill, and nobody letting her do any work because of where his father is, and his baby brother ill, poor little darling, and not enough to eat, and everything as awful as you can possibly think. I'll save up and pay it all back out of my own money. Only do forgive me, all of you, and say you don't despise me for a forger and embezzlementer. I couldn't help it.'

'I'm glad you couldn't,' said the sudden voice of H.O., who had sneaked up on his young stomach unobserved by the council. 'You shall have all my money too, Dora, and here's the bulls-eye halfpenny to begin with.' He crammed it into her hand. 'Listen? I should jolly well think I did listen,' H.O. went on. 'I've just as much right as anybody else to be in at a council, and I think Dora was quite right, and the rest of you are beasts not to say so, too, when you see how she's blubbing. Suppose it had been *your* darling baby-brother ill, and nobody hadn't given you nothing when they'd got pounds and pounds in their silly pockets?'

He now hugged Dora, who responded.

'It wasn't her own money,' said Dicky.

'If you think *you're* our darling baby-brother –' said Oswald.

But Alice and Noël began hugging Dora and H.O., and Dicky and I felt it was no go. Girls have no right and honourable feelings about business, and little boys are the same.

'All right,' said Oswald rather bitterly, 'if a majority of the council backs Dora up, we'll give in. But we must all save up and repay the money, that's all. We shall all be beastly short for ages.'

'Oh,' said Dora, and now her sobs were beginning to turn into sniffs, 'you don't know how I felt! And I've felt most awful ever since, but those poor, poor people –'

At this moment Mrs Bax came down on to the beach by the wooden steps that lead from the sea-wall where the grass grows between the stones.

'Hullo!' she said, 'hurt yourself, my Dora-dove?'

Dora was rather a favourite of hers.

'It's all right now,' said Dora.

'*That's* all right,' said Mrs Bax, who has learnt in anti-what's-its-name climes the great art of not asking too many questions. 'Mrs Red House has come to lunch. She went this morning to see the boy's mother – you know, the boy the others wouldn't play with?'

We said 'Yes.'

'Well, Mrs Red House has arranged to get the woman some work – like the dear she is – the woman told her that the little lady – and that's you, Dora – had given the little boy one pound thirteen and sevenpence.'

Mrs Bax looked straight out to sea through her gold-rimmed spectacles, and went on –

'That must have been about all you had among the lot of you. I don't want to jaw, but I think you're a set of little bricks, and I must say so or expire on the sandy spot.'

There was a painful silence.

H.O. looked, 'There, what did I tell you?' at the rest of us.

Then Alice said, 'We others had nothing to do with it. It was Dora's doing.' I suppose she said this because we did not mean to tell Mrs Bax anything about it, and if there was any brickiness in the act we wished Dora to have the consolement of getting the credit of it.

But of course Dora couldn't stand that. She said –

'Oh, Mrs Bax, it was very wrong of me. It wasn't my own money, and I'd no business to, but I was so sorry for the little boy and his mother and his darling baby-brother. The money belonged to some one else.'

'Who?' Mrs Bax asked ere she had time to remember the excellent Australian rule about not asking questions.

And H.O. blurted out, 'It was Miss Sandal's money – every penny,' before we could stop him.

Once again in our career concealment was at an end. The rule about questions was again unregarded, and the whole thing came out.

It was a long story, and Mrs Red House came out in the middle, but nobody could mind her hearing things.

When she knew all, from the plain living to the pedlar who hadn't a licence, Mrs Bax spoke up like a man, and said several kind things that I won't write down.

She then went on to say that her sister was not poor and needy at all, but that she lived plain and thought high just because she liked it!

We were very disappointed as soon as we had got over our hardly believing any one could – like it, I mean – and then Mrs Red House said –

'Sir James gave me five pounds for the poor woman, and she sent back thirty of your shillings. She had spent three and sevenpence, and they had a lovely supper of boiled pork and greens last night. So now you've only got that to make up, and you can buy a most splendid present for Miss Sandal.'

It is difficult to choose presents for people who live plain and think high because they like it. But at last we decided to get books. They were written by a person called Emerson, and of a dull character, but the backs were very beautiful, and Miss Sandal was most awfully pleased with them when she came down to her cottage with her partially repaired brother, who had fallen off the scaffold when treating a bricklayer to tracts.

This is the end of the things we did when we were at Lymchurch in Miss Sandal's house.

It is the last story that the present author means ever to be the author of. So goodbye, if you have got as far as this.

Your affectionate author,

OSWALD BASTABLE.

LITTLE WOMEN and GOOD WIVES
Louisa May Alcott

The most famous stories about the March girls together in one volume.

These enchanting stories about the good-natured March girls have delighted generations of readers.

Little Women tells the story of a year in the life of the March family, who all lead interesting lives despite the family's lack of money and their father's absence at the war. Whether they're making plans for putting on a play, or forming a secret society, their enthusiasm is infectious.

Good Wives picks up the story of the March girls three years on and chronicles their continuing triumphs and successes.

THE SECRET GARDEN and THE LITTLE PRINCESS
Frances Hodgson Burnett

Two of the world's most enjoyable stories together in one volume.

In *The Secret Garden*, Mary is brought back from India after the death of her parents and sent, as an unwanted child, to live at her uncle's house on the bleak Yorkshire moors. Mary is miserable until the wonderful day when she discovers a hidden door to a mysterious secret garden that has something magical about it.

In *The Little Princess* Sara Crewe appears to have everything. Not just wealth, but also a loving heart and a quick imagination. Find out how she copes when poverty strikes – especially when she is helped by a little bit of magic!

AROUND THE WORLD IN EIGHTY DAYS and TWENTY THOUSAND LEAGUES UNDER THE SEA
Jules Verne

Two of the world's most famous adventure stories together in one volume.

In *Around the World in Eighty Days*, Phileas Fogg and Passepartout set off on the most incredible and exciting adventure of their lives. From London to Paris, Bombay to Singapore and Hong Kong to New York, there are all sorts of thrills and surprises along the way.

In *Twenty Thousand Leagues Under the Sea* a hazardous mission to rid the seas of a monstrous creature leads to the most sensational underwater journey ever undertaken, from Atlantis to the South Pole.

THE CALL OF THE WILD and WHITE FANG
Jack London

Two of the most famous animal stories ever written, together in one volume.

The Call of the Wild tells the story of Buck, a dog who is born to luxury, but sold as a sledge dog. Buck then rises above all his enemies to become the leader of a wolf-pack and the most feared and admired dog in the north.

In *White Fang*, this half-wolf, half-dog is the only one in the litter to survive the extreme cold and desperate hunger. This is a remarkable story about a fiercely independent creature of the Wild, where each day becomes a fight to stay alive.

TREASURE ISLAND and KIDNAPPED
Robert Louis Stevenson

Two swashbuckling tales of kidnap and murder from the master storyteller.

In *Treasure Island* the discovery of a treasure map in Captain Flint's sea chest plunges Jim Hawkins into a series of adventures unrivalled for excitement and suspense.

Set in the Scottish Highlands after the Jacobite rebellion, *Kidnapped* tells of the flight of young David Balfour after he is treacherously cheated of his rightful estate and then wrongly suspected of murder.

OLD PETER'S RUSSIAN TALES
Arthur Ransome

Vanya and Maroosia lived with Old Peter, their grandfather, in a little hut in the middle of the forest. At night there was nothing they liked better than to sit snug and warm by the stove listening to his stories. And Old Peter's tales will enchant you too, with their firebirds and flying ships, stepmothers and stepdaughters, witches and princes. They are as fresh, joyful, bewitching and eerie as they were when Arthur Ransome first heard them in their native land of Russia many years ago.

Mr Midshipman Easy
Captain Marryat

Little does Jack Easy realize when he joins the Royal Navy that he is entering a service in which equality could never for a moment exist. Life on the high seas is not all swashbuckling adventure and the wild ideas of Jack's ardent youth are soon put to the test. This rollicking, comic yarn offers a lighthearted view of life in the Royal Navy, and, more seriously, a dig at Jack's egalitarian philosophizing.

The Great Adventures of Sherlock Holmes
Sir Arthur Conan Doyle

No case is too challenging, to mystery too mysterious, no crime too serious for the Victorian super-sleuth, Sherlock Holmes, with his redoubtable assistant Dr Watson. The world's most famous private detective uses his unique powers of deduction and reasoning to solve the unsolvable, from the bizarre case of The Red-Headed League to the strange tale of The Solitary Cyclist and the extraordinary saga of The Engineer's Thumb.

GREAT EXPECTATIONS
Charles Dickens

When young Pip is accosted in the graveyard by Magwitch, an escaped convict, and forced to help him, he little knows that their lives are destined to cross in future years. Pip's upbringing with his kindly uncle Joe, his involvement with the crazy world of the eccentric Miss Haversham and her beautiful young ward, the icy Estella, and then a new life in London, are all part of this classic story of a boy discovering the reality of 'great expectations'.

JANE EYRE
Charlotte Brontë

As an orphan, Jane Eyre's childhood is far from happy. She endures the hatred of her aunt and cousins, but finally begins to find some pleasure as a teacher. When she becomes a governess working for Mr Rochester, Jane hopes she might at last have found love and kindness, but are events to prove her wrong once more?

An enthralling story about love and betrayal, *Jane Eyre* is one of the most unforgettable of English novels.

HORNBLOWER GOES TO SEA
C. S. Forester

The dramatic sea-battles and adventures Hornblower faces take him from being a quiet yet strangely impressive young man, newly commissioned into Nelson's navy, to an intrepid commander on the high seas, making his mark as one of the most formidable officers ever to set sail.

THE ADVENTURES OF ROBIN HOOD
Roger Lancelyn Green

Permanently at war with the Sheriff of Nottingham and the Norman invaders who have ruled harshly since the Battle of Hastings, the legendary Robin Hood is the champion of the poor and oppressed in twelfth-century England. In this vigorous account of his life and times, Robin and his band of Merrie Men outwit their foes again and again in a series of adventures that are as exciting as they are daring. First published in 1956, this retelling of the Robin Hood legend is one that has become a classic to millions of readers.